Nathan D. Griffith

Kendall Hunt
publishing company

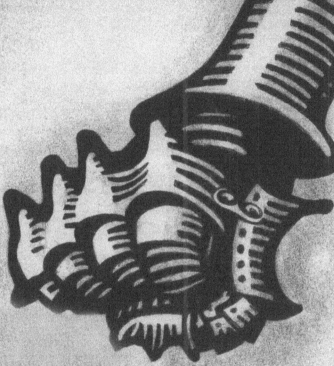

A Dangerous Servant and a Fearful Master

Cover and interior images: © Shutterstock, Inc.

www.kendallhunt.com
Send all inquiries to:
4050 Westmark Drive
Dubuque, IA 52004-1840

Table of Contents

Introduction

This book is different. You may have noticed already—the cover, the title—and you'll probably notice some more. It is meant to be a book first and a textbook second. So there's a lot you won't find here, and I want you to know it's intentional. No glossy photos, no fancy graphics, no call-out boxes, lists of terms, or slick pages. Their absence is intentional.

The goal of all those pointless decorations is to help you learn. Supposedly they engage your attention, help you anchor information with images, and help you check your understanding of what you have learned. In my experience, however—and in yours, if you're honest—they serve as distractions which rob you of the focus necessary to learning, and as crutches which keep you from learning to walk (or in this case, just plain learning). Take the ubiquitous "list of important terms" at the ends of each chapter. Used appropriately, they are meant to let you check your understanding from reading, and recalling these terms *after you've read* about them will help you actually learn what they are and how they relate to each other (and how the rest of the chapter relates to and through them).

These are sound pedagogical goals. Two things help you learn (as opposed to memorize): repeated recall and connecting ideas and information to each other and to their context. If you do that, you'll actually **understand** what you've read, and you'll find it easier to retain. However, most (if not all) students never use those lists that way. They misuse them, believing they are being more "efficient." That is, they approach them as a list of words whose definitions, if they look them up and memorize them, will tell them all they "need" to "know." The problem is that, being immature (in the sense of "unripe" or "unfinished," but yeah, also the other) students, they have very poor definitions of "efficient," "need," and "know." They define "efficient" as "best grade for least effort." They define "need" as "the answer to a question on a test." They define "know" as "remember long enough to regurgitate on a test."

So we're going to have a little conversation, you and I, about the appropriate definition of those terms in an educational context. It's going to cover a lot of things your teacher or professor would like to say to you, if they weren't so polite, or if years of dealing with students more committed to expending more effort on *not* learning than it would take to learn in the first place hadn't already ground their souls to a fine powder. It's going to get a little angry, and it's going to be a little blunt. One thing you'll find is true in life, though, is that only people who care can get angry, and the people who are honest and direct with you are the ones who care about you the most. And yes, I am aware of the irony, that the students still reading are the ones least in need of hearing this. Still, what they know implicitly they can know better explicitly, and maybe some of the inert will suffer a momentary fit of interest and learn something. Or maybe I just need to tell them this will be on the test.

Let's start with attitude. One thing the best students realize—consciously or subconsciously—is that the more they put into a class, the more they get out of it, and the more worthwhile they find it. That is, if they are at least interested in how a class could be interesting, they will find it more interesting. That spoonful of sugar makes the medicine go down much easier. Consider, too, the absurdity of the opposite: a student (by definition, one who does not yet know) deciding before they have learned something that they don't need it. There are at least two problems with that reasoning (confirming they know less than they think they do): they don't know it, so they can't know how useful or interesting it is. I have something in my pocket; would you like it?

You can't answer intelligently until you know two things: what I have in my pocket, and what your likes and dislikes are. You don't know the former, and you only partially know the latter.

The second hole in that statement is that none of us, the student especially, know what the future holds. Those of us who've gotten further into our future have some partial information, but a student usually lacks even that. For example, I teach our department's methods class. This entails learning some about statistics. The thing about statistics, however, is that you don't usually notice how often (and how badly) they are misused (and therefore, how helpful it is to understand them) until after you have learned about them. Students routinely complain about having to learn that material, and routinely contact me after they graduate to thank me for making it part of their education. Experiences they haven't yet had when they take the class change their perspective and their preferences, once those experiences happen.

So you can't know whether a class is worth the effort until you take it, and the more effort you put into it, the more worth it will have. "Not worth the effort" is a self-fulfilling prophecy, because your learning depends not upon the subject, but upon you and the professor. Education is a co-produced good; students and teachers must both contribute effort to produce it, and the better the effort they contribute, the better the product. So there are *professors* who aren't worth your time, but very few subjects. Those professors are easy to find, because students always know who the easy professors are. And there are plenty of professors willing to ask next to nothing of you, because it demands next to nothing from them. Sadly, these professors are quite popular, **because** they don't challenge you to do your best.

To which I can only ask, "really?" No, more than that—how *dare* you? Those classes are a waste of what little effort and increasingly substantial amount of money they cost, and they exist because students demand them. Students want lazy classes where they can feel like they learn without engaging in all the trouble and mental effort of stretching their minds to accommodate new information, so professors supply them, because it means the professor can be lazy and well-loved. They deserve the same indignant question—*how dare you?!*—but I'm talking to you right now.

How dare you sell yourself so cheaply? As one of my favorite movies points out, our integrity is the very last inch of us, and within that inch, we are free. You would sell your integrity, your freedom, your self for easy grades, for the lie of a pretend accomplishment? Let me ask again: *HOW DARE YOU?! You are fearfully and wonderfully made*; there are teachers around you who want nothing more than to make you better by adding their efforts to yours, who want to weed and prune until you fulfill the awesome potential you have as a member of the human race. You choose instead to prostitute yourself with charlatans who promise you the appearance of achievement without the substance, and in that choice you press those teachers to become charlatans themselves.

Do you choose a doctor who always tells you you're fine, even when you're not, because it's what you want to hear? Because it's easier than fixing whatever ailment you might have? How do you expect that to work out—do expect your condition will improve? Or do you go to doctors who give you the medication you want, whether or not you need it, whether or not it will heal you (rather than make you sick)? Again, are you expecting that to improve things? Not addressing a problem is easy, but it's dumb. Most problems get worse, not better, when you ignore them. Medication you don't need can induce illness, or at least the symptoms. Would you hire a personal trainer because they let you sit on the sofa all day and eat doughnuts?

Sadly, I fear some of you are wondering what that trainer's number is, and not just as a punchline. You don't need a trainer to encourage you to be a couch vegetable, you need one to help you learn to do better. Does that mean challenging you, does it mean hard work? Yes. Those who do it, however, almost always find it worth the sweat and tears. Your classes—especially your general education classes—are supposed to work the same way.

General education is meant to be cross-training, by the way, to develop a healthy mind as a whole, not just oversized biceps or calves. If you have problems with analogies or metaphors, let me be blunt: the point of general education is to keep you from being an ass.[1] You see, there are people in this world who can understand what goes on around them, who can grasp how things work, why some things are worth defending and others

---

1 Also, if you're not making the connections necessary to understand and learn from analogies, now you know one area you need to work on in the intellectual gym your classes are supposed to be.

worth immolating, why some things are funny, in short, people who are fully realized humans. Those jokes you don't get—the ones that aren't about farts or sex—yeah, we understand them. And we think it's cute when you pretend to get the reference to *Lysistrata*, or Luther, or *Leviathan*, or when you use words you obviously haven't mastered and think we're fooled by it. Just because we're too polite to point it out to you doesn't mean we aren't laughing at how unintentionally funny you're being.

General education classes help you understand the world and the people in it. I've mentioned the importance of context for understanding things, and general education provides the context for everything else in your life, as well as for whatever you learn and plan to use in your major. For example, let's say you study business. It's an important and valuable thing to study—how businesses work. But you also need to know why they work; that is, you need to understand people, in order to find new products they want, in order to manage their behavior as employees or predict it as consumers.

This context, however, and the understanding which results are consumption goods. We didn't use that word, but we've discussed this idea before—you don't know how much to value something until after you've bought and used it. That understanding helps you not be a braying donkey, stubbornly making loud and pointless noises and no progress. But you don't appreciate it without experience. Do dogs—as sweet, loyal, brave, and wonderful as they are—understand opposable thumbs? Can they appreciate them? If they could experience them, they might be able to appreciate what we take for granted. As it stands, however, they have no context for understanding. So if you settle for less than you can be, will you ever know what you could have been?

Sure it's a rhetorical question, but it has an answer: you won't. And you won't listen or understand when someone else tries to tell you. So let's get back to the bottom line, and let me give you another blunt analogy. Education is like pregnancy. With one exception,[2] it doesn't just happen to you. You have to be involved in the activity. Further, that participation must be voluntary. With pregnancy, it is possible but very, very wrong to coerce someone's involvement. With education it is less possible, but no less wrong.

So back to those words for a moment, just to make sure we put this all together. Anytime someone says "efficiency," you must immediately ask them to define their units. "Efficiency" only tells you about a change in a ratio: that you are getting more output relative to input. (So increased efficiency means you are either getting the same output for less input, or you are getting more output for the same input, or more output for less input.) What exactly the output and input are, one must define. Increasing the amount of excrement one produces for the same amount food intake is not usually a good thing, though it is an increase in efficiency. Studying "efficiently" is only efficient if it produces more learning, not better grades. Now, more learning should correlate with better grades, but skipping the learning part makes it terribly inefficient, because the product of studying is supposed to be learning.

"Need," as we've discussed, is something you really can't judge until you know. What most students mean is that they don't immediately see an interest, or have no desire to know something. Need, however, is something again which cannot be judged without relation to its purpose. "Need" means necessary, something without which a product cannot be produced. It should mean in this context the knowledge (and we've yet to clear that one up) which is necessary to produce increased understanding of self and world. Students generally view it as the minimum necessary for the desirable grade. Again, that should be the by-product, not the point.

So we are left with "know." We're going to drink deeply from the well on this one. The Greek word for "to know" is *episteme*. It's where we get the word "epistemology," which is the fancy academic way to say "the study of how we know things." The fun part is what the Greek components of that Greek word are. You might have a guess at *epi-* as a prefix, if you think about it. Some of you may be familiar with the top (outermost) layer of skin, the epidermis. *Dermis* means skin, and *epi-* means "above" or "upon" (or a few other variations). So the epidermis is the skin on top. An epidemic is something upon (or among—context matters) the *demos*, or people.

Steme, on the other hand, is less recognizable. It means "to stand." So when the Greeks said they knew something, what they were saying is that they were willing to stand on it. They had tested it, and were confident it would support weight. That is not what most students mean. They mean that they can retain it in their

---

2 A couple of thousand years ago in the Middle East.

memory just long enough to vomit it back out on a piece of paper at a convenient time. Their "need" and their "know" are both related to a test.

The problem is that the test is not a piece of paper; the test is life. You learn these things to have a better idea of what to expect, from other people or from the physical world. The test is not a piece of paper, but the rest of your life. The moments when you will need to know something that may make your life better are unannounced, and you cannot cram your way to passing them. As a result, the bulimic approach to education—stuff it in and regurgitate it almost immediately—is no healthier for the mind than it is for the body.

Maybe now you can understand not just how this book is different, but why. It doesn't have things that pretend to help you, but really only serve to harm you by encouraging bad habits. The fact that it aims to encourage good habits—focus, attention, linking ideas to each other in the abstract and to information in the concrete—means like most things that develop good habits, it is more challenging. It will ask more of you, but if you commit to it, it will become easier, and you will become better.

Now, if you have bothered to read all that, and if you nevertheless continue to read the rest, you'll notice a few things this book does have. Let's start with the bad jokes. If you like uncle jokes (not jokes about uncles—though we'll probably get around to some of those too—but lame jokes like your uncle always makes), you're in luck! Now, given what I've said about focus and attention, you may be—should be—wondering why those are there. And yes, they are there to be brief moments of mental relaxation. At least, that's what they are for me, and I mean them to provide the same service to you.

What service is that? Think of a runner. Or rather, think of runners. If you've ever been to a track meet (or watched the Olympics), you may (should) have noticed that runners don't run all the same distance. Those who run the 100 m sprint; those who run the 400 m or 800 m run, but they don't sprint until the last 100 m or so. The point? You can't go at a full sprint continuously. It works for a short while, but the body can't sustain that level of effort indefinitely. The same is true of motors: you can red line them for a little while, but if you try to keep them at that level, they'll explode (more or less figuratively). So all the corny little jokes (and yes, I realize it's an insult to jokes to call them that) are there to help break up the mental effort, to give you a chance to catch your mental breath, as it were.

They can do something else as well. They can help you create some connections between the subject in the book and things from the outside world, which you may already know. As I've mentioned before, this sort of cross-indexing helps you retain information. In fact, you'll find a lot of little digressions meant to do exactly that, to connect what we're talking about to something either already familiar or easier to remember. For that same reason, I will often include little details about the things we're talking about, or the story behind them. Those things help your brain know where to place the information, so that it can find it when you need it.

Other unusual features of this book include the fact that (as you may have noticed) it is written to you, often directly. Although books don't have three walls like a stage play (or movie), these are meant to make the challenge direct and personal. I'm not asking people to think; I'm asking **you** to think. As that would suggest, this book also has a perspective. That's not particularly unusual; what's unusual is the author admitting it up front. I want you to learn to analyze the world using what you learn here. It is impossible to analyze without a point-of-view, without at least a theoretical perspective (because it involves applying theory to reality). You can learn to use mine, though like any tool, you can pick it up and put it down as it is useful. It doesn't become part of you.

This desire (in most textbooks) to speak as the voice of God has several causes. First, covering everything means that everyone can find what they're looking for in your book. Covering it in a voice which pretends to be neutral means that no one will be offended because your thoughts, your perspective, aren't theirs. It means there is nothing against which to argue, nothing to which you should object. In other words, it is the peace of the grave, where an argument is not settled so much as silenced.

I have a problem with that. Now, don't get me wrong—I'm not in favor of what you probably think when I say "arguing." I mean debating, not yelling and throwing things. Science progresses when we take a position and defend it with facts and reason. Sometimes our position proves to be faulty, and we have to surrender. As with any game of King of the Mountain, though, the fun (and the learning) is in the attempt. Even when you surrender or fall back to a better position, you have learned. So books that speak so as to avoid that productive clash of ideas while claiming to teach you something are fooling themselves; their goal is to get someone to adopt their book, not to teach you. Don't get me wrong—I'd love for lots of people to buy this book, but because it provokes them to think, not because it provokes nothing at all.

So yes, if you want to know the bare minimum, you've picked up the wrong book. Or more likely, you've been required to purchase it for a class. I could spend a great deal of time reminding you that, while this may feel involuntary, it is in fact a result of choices you have made, and thus voluntary. That is, you want a particular degree from a particular school, and choosing that goal entails choosing this path. I could attempt to justify the inclusion of this course among your requirements, waxing eloquent on the centrality of political science in your life, its usefulness for a variety of career goals, the nobility of its pursuit as a profession. But none of that will change the fact that this is a book you don't want to read in a class you'd rather not take.

Life has just handed you a lemon—are you going to suck on it, coming to class each day in a sour, resentful mood? You can spend class time daydreaming, if you spend it in class at all. You can try to cram just enough information into your head for just long enough to jump through enough hoops on an exam to get the grade for which you're willing to settle. In the end, you'll find that the class was the waste of time you thought it was.

Remember, that's a self-fulfilling prophecy. So maybe it's time to cowgirl up and figure out what a good student would do—not so you can learn to fake it, but so that you can become one. Since you're reading this book, you've obviously got a good teacher.[3] So let's go Greek on this: get somebody to haze you, then charge you a lot of money to be your friend. Or even better, let's look at the Greek origins of *another* word!

Critical thinking is something of a buzzword in academia these days, but the fact that it is the object of a fad does not mean that it is without merit. Certainly, the objects of many fads are, but that does not mean that the object of every fad is. Like most buzzwords, however, it suffers from being widely used but narrowly understood—a lot of people use it, but each person means something different by it. I owe it to you, then, to define what I mean when I use that term.

So what does it mean to think critically? Let's begin with *thinking*. We know what thinking is not. Memorization and regurgitation require not a mind, but solely a memory. Computers have that, and they are a lot cheaper to employ than you are (nothing personal; the same is true of me). After all, they do not need food, a shelter separate from the office, transportation, or health care, and neither do their dependents (because they have none). A standard USB memory stick can remember and quickly access more than you or I. So if your schooling teaches you to be no more than a USB memory stick, well, you should ask for your money back.

Thinking is part of the human ability to adapt. Thinking is finding the patterns in a set of circumstances that explain not only that set, but others, because of their similarities or differences with the first. Thinking is approaching the world with the tools of logic in order to "get under its hood" and understand how that incredibly complex machine works. Thinking is a question in action, not an answer in repose.

What then shall we make of *critical*? We certainly have an idea of critical as meaning important or essential, as in receiving critical care at a hospital. We also have an idea of it related to criticism, by which we normally refer to negative evaluations. That does not mean, however, that the word means "essentially negative." The root of *critical* is the Greek word transliterated as *krites* (cry-tees), which mean "judge." So critical means judicial (and means important in the sense of decisive, negative evaluation in the sense of judgmental).

In other words, then, I want you to think like a judge. How does a judge think? A judge must decide between two or more claims on the basis of reason and evidence. A judge hears arguments and evidence from both sides, evaluates it fairly, and makes a decision as to which argument and evidence are more convincing. Thus, when I aim to promote critical thinking, I aim to encourage you to evaluate the reasoning and evidence of arguments, to approach the world with a careful, fair, and discerning eye.

Those of you who have watched enough *People's Court* reruns will know that one of the particular tools judges use to reach their decisions is questioning. Judges ask a lot of questions, probing the arguments the attorneys put forward. In fact, the justices on the Supreme Court are known for their merciless interrogation

---

3 And by "good," I mean susceptible to cheap flattery like that.

of the advocates before them. One habit you should develop, then, is asking questions of the material you read (and not just in this textbook). In particular, you should ask "how" and "why" questions, as these tend toward the heart of an argument. "How" questions get at the connections between the mechanical elements of a logical argument, for example, "How does this claim depend on the truth of that assumption?" "Why" questions get at the justifications for arguments, at the nature and validity of the assumptions upon which the argument is built, for example, "Why do you claim people behave in their own self-interest?" Between the two, they lay bare the foundation and structure of the argument, and once you have those, you can fill in the architectural details.

So one thing good students have in common is curiosity, the desire (more than willingness) to ask questions, to find out how and why things work. You probably had some of that when you were younger, and your educational experience thus far may have only beat it out of you. Curiosity may kill cats, but it makes learning possible and classes much more interesting.[4] It also makes class more challenging for the teacher, which is why it may sadly have been beaten out of you.

You will encounter these questions immediately, as I will introduce several different theoretical positions and their assumptions, arguments, and conclusions about government. Much about our government makes sense only when you see the purpose, the "why," behind it. Much of how you evaluate government also depends upon your theoretical perspective, on what you think the purpose of government is. In order to evaluate it fairly, it is important to understand the purpose which informs its design, as well as the purpose which informs your positions. If you and a classmate build upon different assumptions but do not see that difference, you will end up talking past each other, rather than to each other. The truth is, people often reach different conclusions, and do so for reasons other than the stupidity of one or the malice of another. When we are blind to our assumptions and those of another, we do not see the source of our disagreement and so cannot address it; nevertheless, the disagreement remains, and we believe it is due to the pig-headedness of the other, rather than the product of different assumptions (a difference which we can address).

I will also use examples from other forms of government as we cover different topics, as it is often only in seeing alternatives that we see the why and how of an answer. In fact, until we see that there is another answer, we may not even be aware that there is a question. Not every country elects their executive separately from their legislature; not every country has a federal structure. Knowing why our founders made these choices, and coming to a conclusion about which choice we would prefer, requires some knowledge of alternatives. After all, the scientific method is at its heart comparative, comparing what happens when a variable is in one position as opposed to in another position.

I will also use several Supreme Court cases (and some from other courts) to illustrate concepts. The law is an abstract thing, written in general terms to apply to a range of circumstances. In cases, the abstract rubber hits the concrete pavement of a particular set of circumstances. Often these concrete circumstances help us get a handle on the more abstract issues involved in the law. In the same way, particular cases or examples help to illustrate the abstract concepts we will study in this book.

Of course, I will also use examples other than Supreme Court cases, but those will be more noticeable as a group, and now you understand the purpose of all of them. Besides, I did not want you to fear you had wandered into a Constitutional Law text by mistake, anymore than that you had stumbled upon a Comparative Government text. Both of these subjects, however, help illuminate our subject, the former in depth, the latter in breadth. Thus you are forewarned.

---

4 This does not lead to the syllogism that killing cats makes class more interesting. Unless it's the metaphorical cat of apathy, in which case, don't bring your pets to class with you.

Chapter 1: Government

But what is government itself, but the greatest of all reflections on human nature? Stop and think about this question for a moment. Go ahead, I'll wait. Certainly it sounds like a rhetorical question: profound, esoteric, flowery, and grand. A young farmer's son from Virginia once posed this question, but not merely for effect. The answer, as he saw it, was a matter of life and death.

How is government a reflection on human nature? Well, what do you usually think of when you think of "the government"? For many people, this word connotes politics, and neither term has a pleasant association. You might associate these words with nepotism, with getting something on a basis other than merit, with greed and corruption, lying and backstabbing—the worst of the human condition. You would not be alone.

And yet, many people—including me and your professor—have dedicated their lives to the study of politics and government. If politics and government are the raw, stinking cesspool they seem to be, political scientists must be crazy. It would seem that we have dedicated several years of our lives to the study of sewage. Let's assume for a moment, though, that we're not crazy (no matter how far-fetched an assumption that may seem). If sane people devote time to studying it, it can't be as filthy as it appears. So aside from morbid fascination, what draws us to study it voluntarily?

It could be that we hope, like Hercules, to clean out these Augean stables by diverting the swift and clean-flowing waters of relentless logic. Yet the belief in one's ability to single-handedly shape the destiny of whole societies does not seem any more encouraging as a sign of mental health. So let me suggest that some of us see politics as something other than the pursuit of gain in spite of merit, rather than because of it. **Politics, instead, is the act of cooperating with other individuals to accomplish goals we could not otherwise**.

As a string of words, that sounds noble and idealistic—like the sort of thing you memorize, repeat on a test, and then store in your memory right next to other highly useful things, like the fact that Harry S Truman's middle name (not initial, but name—think about it for a second) was "S," or that Woodrow Wilson is the only political scientist to have been President of the United States.[1] Memorizing a definition does you no good if you don't know what it means. After all, circumstances don't walk up to you with a sign around their neck saying, "I'm the act of cooperating with other individuals to accomplish goals we could not otherwise." So what does that definition *mean*? How will you know it when you see it?

Let's begin with "accomplishing goals we otherwise could not." There are any number of things which each of us must or would like to accomplish. Obviously, if they are things we must do—necessities, things without which we cannot live—they are more important than desires, the things we would like to have. The key point is that there are some of each which we cannot accomplish without the cooperation of other humans. Perhaps this does not at first seem such a daunting task. After all, people just naturally cooperate with each other, don't they?

Well, let's think about that for a moment, using the example of two suspects under interrogation at a police station. What's the first thing the police on television shows do when they take two suspects into custody (after

---

1 Should this information help you win money on a game show, I would appreciate a small gratuity. I doubt there are many other uses for it, though.

they read them their Miranda rights, of course)? They put them in separate rooms, so they can't get their stories straight. So, let's assume these prisoners have had no chance to communicate about a strategy, and that they are not part of a larger organization—such as the mafia—that might provide such a strategy. We'll also assume that they are, in fact, guilty of the crime for which the police are detaining them. Other than that, let us make no assumptions (for example, that they are relatives or old friends) yet. Once we see how the basic example works, we can see how adding other assumptions would alter it.

So, just like on all those cop shows, the suspected accomplices are put in separate rooms. And, just like on all those cop shows, the district attorney goes to each of them separately and offers them a deal—the first one to rat on their accomplice gets off with probation, while the district attorney (DA) will use her testimony to throw the book at the other. As it turns out, DAs and police officers do this for a very good reason (not just because script writers lack imagination). The DA has just placed the two suspects in a game known as the Prisoner's Dilemma, a game political scientists represent with the square in Figure 1.1.

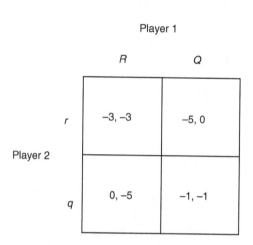

Figure 1.1 The Prisoner's Dilemma

Here are the circumstances this drawing describes. If both prisoners keep quiet, the DA has enough evidence to convict each of them on misdemeanors, resulting in a one-year prison sentence for each. If one testifies against the other while the other keeps quiet, the former receives probation (no years in prison) while the other is convicted of a felony with a five-year prison sentence. If both accept the DA's offer (and they must make their decisions simultaneously), the DA can't throw the book at them, but does have the leverage to get each of them to plead to a lesser offence with a shorter (three-year) sentence.

Put yourself in the shoes of one of these prisoners. What are your options? You can keep your mouth shut (the strategy labeled with an upper- or lower-case *q* for *quiet*) or turn stool pigeon and sing like a canary (labeled *r* for *rat*, to further mix metaphors). But the outcome you achieve depends not only on your decision, but on that of your accomplice as well. This is what makes the Prisoner's Dilemma a strategic game—no player determines the outcome for herself.

So let's evaluate your choices based on assumptions about the other player's choices. If the other player (Player 2) keeps quiet, you (Player 1) get a year in jail if you keep quiet or no years in jail if you rat them out. If she keeps quiet, you're better off ratting on your accomplice. But what if she rats you out? Then you have a choice between five years for keeping quiet or three years for ratting her out. If she rats you out, you still do better if you squeal.

This is what's known as a dominant strategy—a strategy which always produces the better outcome, given the other player's choice. And since the other player is thinking through the very same process in the next room, you can see why DAs like to put suspects in this position. They are likely to get two plea bargains and save the expense of a court case.

While this is an excellent outcome for the DA, it is less good for our small society of criminals. Had they cooperated with each other, they could have achieved a better individual result (only one year instead of three) and the best collective result (two total years between them). Instead, they achieve the next-to-worst individual outcome and the worst collective one (six total years, rather than five or two). If they could cooperate, they could achieve a better outcome, but their individual incentives lead them to abandon cooperation. This is the essence of the Prisoner's Dilemma—what is individually rational is collectively irrational.

Still, it's hard to get choked up over a couple of criminals getting most of the jail time they deserve, rather than less. In fact, assuming still that they're guilty, most would prefer to find ways to increase their sentences, rather than lessen them. But let's substitute the ant and the grasshopper from Aesop's fabled fable for our two suspects. Instead of choosing whether to keep quiet or rat on the other, each has to decide whether to work or play all summer. If both work, each will have food in the winter. If both play, neither has food and both starve through the winter, surviving on whatever each can scrape together. If one plays while the other works, there will be food enough for one come winter, but the one who grew it will be tired from the work. The one who is rested from playing all summer will steal the food from the worker, leaving him to starve through the winter.

This is essentially the same situation in which our prisoners found themselves. If both play during the summer, they are well-rested, but starve through the winter (−3).[2] If both work, they are tired from work, but at least each reaps the benefit of that work (−1). If one works while the other plays and the latter then steals the former's produce, the worker bears both the cost of working and of starving through the winter (−5), while the thief is rested and fed (0). Like the prisoners, each is better off choosing to goof off, regardless of the other player's decision. Yet this time the results for society are much worse—everyone is starving.

So let's go back to our original example and see if we can figure a way out of this dilemma. More specifically, let's re-examine two of our three assumptions. We assumed that the prisoners could not communicate beforehand, and that they were not members of an organization like the mafia which would enforce an agreement on what to do in that situation. Let's relax the first assumption and allow the prisoners to communicate once with each other. Assume that they sneak in a couple of sentences in the back of the patrol car while the officers nip into the doughnut shop for a quick energy boost. Even one chance to communicate increases their ability to cooperate and thus achieve the collectively best outcome. Moreover, if we give them repeated chances to communicate, they do even better, cooperating around a third of the time.[3]

While a third of the time is better, it still leaves a lot unexplained. Even if a third of a society chooses to be ants, working through the summer to make a better winter, that still leaves two-thirds of society choosing to be grasshoppers. The ants should have a short life expectancy, one which the grasshoppers will only slightly exceed. This is exactly the situation that concerned not only our farmer's son, but an English philosopher named Thomas Hobbes,[4] as well. Hobbes published his *Leviathan* in 1651. In 1649, Parliament had convicted Charles I of treason and beheaded him, bringing an end to seven years of civil war, but beginning a chaotic decade that did not end until the restoration of the monarchy in 1660.

Hobbes sought to explain why we need government and why, on the basis of that need, we should never rebel against government authority. Hobbes asked his readers to engage in a thought experiment, to imagine a world in which there was no government, no common authority to keep men to their agreements. We call this condition *anarchy*, a word which means "without ruler," and not, as we often use it, "chaos" or "disorder." In this state of nature, Hobbes wrote, the life of man became "solitary, poor, nasty, brutish, and short." Without a common authority, might made right, and individuals could not rely on the word of others—in short, no one could trust anyone else. As in the Prisoner's Dilemma, ants were subject to the predation of stronger grasshoppers. This removed any incentive to improve the land, whether in terms of growing crops or building shelter. Even if everyone agreed beforehand to leave each other alone so that each would enjoy the fruits of his own labor, the weak could not trust the strong to keep their end of the bargain, since the weak could not make them observe the restrictions to which they had agreed. As a result, the life of man became solitary (you couldn't trust anyone), poor (no one had any capital or the incentive to create any), nasty (no houses, remember?), brutish (a war of all against all), and short (no food, no shelter, constant fighting for what resources nature provided . . . not conditions which improve life expectancy).

Hobbes explained that this was why we formed government. The weak, when incorporated as a government, had the ability to make sure that everyone kept the agreements they made. Thus the monarchy was a Leviathan, the combination of many people into a larger legal personality, even if one man represented this

---

2 I keep the same numbers only to show the parallel with the earlier example. In this case, the numbers represent relative rather than absolute values. Don't worry about whether a winter of starvation is a −3 or a −4; focus on whether a winter of starvation is worse than a summer of work plus a winter of food.

3 For more on this, see Elinor Ostrom, James Walker, and Roy Gardner, "Covenants With and Without a Sword: Self-Governance is Possible," *American Political Science Review* 86, no. 2 (1992): 404.

4 You may be more familiar with his namesake, the tiger from Bill Watterson's *Calvin and Hobbes* comic strips.

personality. So for Hobbes, we form governments in order to survive, to avoid the ruinous state of nature in which we would otherwise find ourselves.

Notice that this brings us back to the second assumption we made about our prisoners. We assumed that they were not part of a mafia or other organization that would enforce an agreement between them. In relaxing the first assumption, we allowed them to make an agreement, and as Hobbes predicts, those agreements prove unreliable, or at least, not reliable enough to solve the problem on their own. In relaxing this second assumption, we allow them a means of enforcing agreements. If a member of a mafia violates their shared agreement not to divulge information that might tend to incriminate another member, they know that the rest of the group will levy a (substantial) penalty on them (if the *Godfather* movies have taught us anything). In other words, the mafia is to criminals as the government is to other citizens—it punishes the violation of agreements.

Here, too, we finally see the answer to our question about human nature. James Madison[5] posed his rhetorical question about government and human nature in Federalist No. 51, and immediately answered it: "If men were angels, no government would be necessary. If angels were to govern men, neither external nor internal controls on government would be necessary." So if we were perfect creatures, we would not need government. We would always keep our word and always cooperate where we need to cooperate. As fallible humans, though we may strive for perfection, we will on many occasions fail to reach it. As a result, we need government.

Madison, however, does not stop there. What is the importance of his next statement—what would be different if angels were to govern men? To answer this question, we must turn again to an English philosopher, but this time to John Locke rather than Hobbes. Locke, who was a medical doctor as well as a philosopher, was two generations removed from Hobbes. The English civil war which spurred the adult Hobbes to write *Leviathan* was part of Locke's formative years; he turned ten the year it began.

The restoration of the monarchy in 1660 did not heal the divisions in British society. Charles II was a Catholic, while his country was in large part Protestant. As a Catholic, he favored cooperation with the strongest protector of Catholicism at that time, the king of France. His brother, who succeeded him as James II, was even more of a Francophile and less tolerant of Protestantism. For example, he used the "Bloody Assizes," secret trials which violated many of the rights enshrined in British law and tradition, to punish Protestants with death or sale into slavery.

Locke wrote the *Second Treatise of Government* in 1681, shortly before going into self-imposed exile (in 1683) to avoid these witch-hunts. For the same reason, he did not publish his two treatises on government until 1689. In 1688, the Glorious Revolution occurred, in which Parliament invited the Dutch Protestant (and son-in-law of Charles II), William of Orange, to assume the throne after James II fled for his life to France. Locke (and other refugees) returned to England.

Locke begins with essentially the same circumstances as Hobbes—an anarchic state of nature in which the weak are prey to the strong. Whereas Hobbes, however, is concerned with the insecurity of life in this situation, Locke is concerned with the insecurity of life, liberty, and property (and if that sounds familiar, yes, Thomas Jefferson borrowed liberally[6] from Locke). What's the difference between these two?

To Hobbes, citizens contracted with each other to hire an agent (government) and, by all agreeing to submit to the authority of that agent, to escape from the war of all against all that would otherwise prevail. In other

---

5 Right. If you're reading this, I probably need to explain who he is. James Madison was the fourth president of the United States. Before that, he was Secretary of State (to President Thomas Jefferson—him you've probably heard of. Or at least seen—on $2 bills, on nickels, or on Mount Rushmore). Before that, he was a member of Congress, one who wrote and proposed the amendments that became the Bill of Rights. Before that, he and Alexander Hamilton (and occasionally John Jay), under the name of Publius, wrote op-eds (now known as *The Federalist Papers*) advocating the adoption of the Constitution. Before *that*, he was instrumental in shaping (or framing) the Constitution. He also pushed to call the convention in the first place. Not bad for a Princeton man. You can see why he was known as "the Father of the Constitution." He was also the greatest political scientist of his age, and perhaps of any other. All in 5' 4" and 90-odd pounds of Virginia gentleman.

6 No pun intended.

words, citizens delegated all of their sovereignty in exchange for protection; since government of any sort was better than the alternative (the state of nature), there was never any justification for rebellion. For Locke, though, the contract was more specific. Citizens delegated some of their sovereignty, including the right to enforce their rights, to government, in exchange for the protection of the rights they retained—including life, but also liberty and property.

This conception of the social contract leads to a different conclusion about the obligations of the parties to it. Since citizens have hired an agent to protect their life, liberty, and property, they may fire their employee and hire a new one if the old one breaches its contract—if it fails to protect the rights citizens hired it to protect. That is, there *is* a justification for rebellion: when government fails to protect or even itself endangers citizens' rights. Since Hobbes envisioned a complete surrender of sovereignty, government fulfilled its obligations so long as it kept citizens from killing one another. In changing the conception of the contract so that citizens kept some rights, Locke provided another criterion for judging the performance of government. Government had to prevent the violation of those retained rights, whether by other citizens or itself.

Of course, you can see why this theory proved more popular with the colonists. They felt that Parliament and King George were violating the rights government was supposed to protect. According to Locke, this meant the colonists had justification to rebel.

Of course, you can also see how this leads to Madison's second observation on human nature—"If angels were to govern men, neither external nor internal controls on government would be necessary." Since the goal of government is to preserve the rights of individuals (rather than the existence of a society), it must also protect those rights from itself. A government strong enough to protect rights is one strong enough to threaten them. If angels were to govern us, we would not have to worry about their succumbing to the temptation to abuse that authority. Unfortunately, the only beings we have available to govern us are humans as fallible as ourselves, and we must concern ourselves with an immortal conundrum: who watches the watchers?

Madison phrased this riddle more precisely. "In framing a government which is to be administered by men over men, the great difficulty lies in this: you must first enable the government to control the governed; and in the next place oblige it to control itself." Keep this in mind for the next few chapters as we discuss Madison's answer to this riddle. For now, though, you'll have to enjoy the dramatic tension as we consider other answers to the question of why we have government.

Thus far, our answers, loosely constructed, have been that we need government to ensure the survival of the human race (Hobbes) and to protect individual rights such as life, liberty, and property (Locke). Just as Locke built upon the foundation Hobbes had laid, so David Hume, an eighteenth-century Scottish philosopher, built upon Locke. In his *Treatise of Human Nature*, published in 1739, Hume contended that we need government not only in the negative sense of keeping others and itself from harming us, but also in a positive sense, forcing us to do our part to accomplish things we need to do together.

To see what Hume means by this, let us consider the concept of externalities. The production or consumption of a good or service can have an effect on someone not party to that exchange. For example, your production of entertainment services for your own consumption—playing German punk music at sound levels appropriate to the genre—may produce (as a by-product) consequences for your downstairs neighbor. Your neighbor is not party to the exchange—neither producer nor consumer—yet the exchange affects her. Perhaps it interferes with her favorite television show, perhaps it gives her a headache, perhaps she wishes to study in peace for finals, or perhaps she enjoys the thumping bass. No matter which is the case, the production (and consumption) of that entertainment has an effect external to the exchange which creates it.

The classic example of an externality is pollution. Let us imagine you live near an airport, and the noise of the airplanes landing and taking off keeps you up all night. You are not getting paid to fly people to or from exotic locales, nor are you the one enjoying those exotic locales. Nevertheless, that activity affects you. For most people, this is a negative externality, meaning that they incur a cost of some sort—loss of sleep, for example. For others, however, this might represent a positive externality, which means they gain a benefit without incurring the cost. For airport noise pollution, think of Wayne and Garth in *Wayne's World*, enjoying the take-offs and landings at the airport from the hood of Garth's Gremlin. In the music example, think of your neighbor if she did enjoy the music. She got to enjoy it without paying for the music, the equipment, or the electricity.

As you might imagine, the invisible hand of the market is not as talented when it comes to producing goods with positive externalities. As Adam Smith[7] observed, the heart of the free market is the proposition that, where I have something you want and you have something I want, we are each better off when we trade. This leads us ("as if by an invisible hand," in Smith's memorable phrase) to find ways to be useful to others—to produce things they want, so that we can get what we want. For all the good this institution creates, however, it breaks down when you can enjoy what I produce without giving me what I want, since it removes my incentive to produce it.

In other words, the market which usually coordinates our actions to promote our mutual benefit so successfully fails us. In fact, we have a name for the types of goods (and services) which tend to cause these market failures: public goods. Public goods are those goods and services which are non-rivalrous and non-excludable. One person's enjoyment does not diminish or prevent another's enjoyment (there is no rivalry in their use), and once produced, everyone enjoys the benefits, whether they contribute to its production or not (no one may exclude another from the benefits of the good). As a result, each individual wants to wait for someone else to pay for the good, and no one has an incentive to produce it, other than charity. As we've mentioned before, however, if men were angels, and we could rely on them to consider others, we wouldn't have these problems.

This situation is not only similar to our prisoner's dilemma rhetorically; it is a special case of the prisoner's dilemma known as free riding. Remember that in our original game, both players are better off if they can cooperate, but their individual incentives lead them away from that outcome to one which is worse for them both. This is the same dynamic as in free riding, except that we are talking about a more particular class of cooperation—producing a public good. Here, both players are better off if they contribute their share to production. They each have an incentive to take advantage of the other (or "sucker" them), letting them bear the full cost of production (since the other cannot exclude him from enjoying the benefits, once produced). Neither, then, is willing to commit their time, effort, or money until they can be sure the other will, as well.

The classic example of this is national defense. Imagine that one neighbor in a Minneapolis neighborhood purchases an M1A1 Abrams tank. Even if none of her neighbors contributes to the cost[8] of the tank, they still benefit from its presence. When the well-oiled Canadian war machine comes crashing across the border, they will avoid that neighborhood. Since few people have several million dollars, though, it's unlikely that one neighbor would be able to bear all of the cost, even for so important a cause as protection from Canadians. If there are 1,000 people in the neighborhood, though, each of them would only have to chip in $4,300.[9] So they pass the hat—some earnest and altruistic neighbor goes door to door asking for collections. Will she collect enough money to pay for the tank?

Would you put $4,300 in cash into the hat? Let's think this one through for a moment. Once you have contributed your money, they're only $4,295,700 short. What if they don't collect the rest? You're minus $4,300 and still having to eat round ham and call it bacon. If you could be sure everyone else would, you'd be more likely to contribute. Then again, if you could be sure *everyone* else would contribute, maybe you wouldn't need to contribute. If the community is only $4,300 short, and you happen to be out of town for the next two weeks, the other 999 neighbors only have to chip in an extra $4.31,[10] which they would surely do to avoid having to append "eh" to all of their sentences.

---

7 Adam Smith was another eighteenth-century Scottish philosopher (and friend of Hume's). His *An Inquiry Into the Nature and Causes of the Wealth of Nations*, published coincidentally in 1776, is the foundational work of modern economics.

8 M1A1 Abrams: $4.3 million.

9 Protection from Canadians: priceless.

10 Actually, it's only $4.3043, so they'd have a little extra to buy an antenna topper to make it easier to find the tank at the mall.

Sounds familiar, doesn't it? If no one else contributes, you're better off if you don't contribute. If everyone else contributes, you're better off not contributing, because you'll get the benefit without any cost. Even though you're all better off if you each contribute, each of you has an incentive to free ride—to let everyone else pay. Since everyone faces the same incentives, the public good is undersupplied. Of course, this depends on contributions being anonymous. If everyone knew which neighbors contributed and which didn't, they might not be able to exclude them from the tank's protection, but they would have other means of persuasion at their disposal, like ostracizing that neighbor or slashing her tires. If we think of a nation rather than a community, however, it becomes impossible to tell who contributed and who did not. In fact, we aren't even able to definitively count every citizen in the United States; the Census Bureau uses statistical sampling to improve its estimate of the population.

Now let's return for a moment to the example of neighbors and loud music. Loud music that your neighbor enjoys may produce positive externalities, but it is **not** a public good. Although her enjoyment does not diminish yours, you could exclude her from enjoying it (with a pair of headphones or good soundproofing). While there is a positive externality, it is one which you can internalize. You could reduce the volume or use headphones unless she chips in for the cost of the album and the electricity.[11] So, while a public good begins with a positive externality, it has to be one which is non-excludable and non-rivalrous.

So how do we internalize non-excludable externalities (and isn't that a fun mouthful to say)? As we briefly discussed above, smaller communities may be able to overcome this problem, since they can identify those who shirk and punish them with shame, ostracism, or mysterious appearances of excrement. Hume discusses two neighbors wishing to drain a swamp which straddles their property line. If one neighbor fails to appear at the agreed-upon time, the other will surely notice, and will abandon the project. Thus, the first neighbor knows that his contribution is necessary if he is to enjoy any benefit. Moreover, the first neighbor knows that the second neighbor would be less likely to trust him in the future—since there is no anonymity, he would damage his reputation. We can be confident that both will show up, as neither has anything to gain from reneging (there is no gain, only cost).

If the scope of the benefits extends to a larger group, though, we cannot be as sanguine about the prospects for success. The size of the group makes it much more difficult to identify and punish shirkers. Indeed, as Hume reminds us, it would be difficult for a large group to even decide what project to do and when to do it.

> But 'tis very difficult, and indeed impossible, that a thousand persons shou'd agree in any such action; it being difficult for them to concert so complicated a design, and still more difficult for them to execute it; while each seeks a pretext to free himself of the trouble and expence, and wou'd lay the whole burden on others.

Even if they do manage to decide on a plan, they will still face a hurdle in executing the plan: the free rider problem (or, as Hume describes it, each seeking to stick the others with all of the trouble and expense of carrying the plan into action). The solution which Hume proposes for this is government. If government (whether town, county, state, or nation) levies a tax on everyone and pays for the construction of the public good. This ensures (if at the appropriate level of government) that all beneficiaries contribute their share and solves the problem of free riding. As Hume says, "Thus bridges are built; harbors open'd; ramparts rais'd; canals form'd; fleets equip'd; and armies disciplin'd every where, by the care of government."[12]

Note that the solution to this problem is not the tax instrument itself, but the government coercion which collects it.[13] Government could use some less blunt instrument, such as requiring all cars to carry a transponder allowing the government to track their use of public roads and bridges, and then billing accordingly. It could also use a considerably blunter instrument, such as requiring citizens to spend one weekend a month

---

11 However, this would likely violate copyright law, so don't try this at home.

12 Evidently, Hume got paid by the apostrophe.

13 Think taxes aren't collected by force? Try not paying them for a while. You will have the exciting opportunity to meet several uniformed government employees carrying firearms.

on public works projects, like building bridges or doing military service. The key element is that government uses its monopoly on legitimate coercion to get people to do their part, just as it uses that authority to keep them from harming each other. The foundation is still the same conception of human nature—that men are neither angels nor devils, neither perfectly good nor perfectly evil. This fallibility prevents them from cooperating naturally and creates a need for institutions of governance.[14]

I use the term *institutions of governance* to make a distinction between "government" as we normally think of it and other institutions which we create to accomplish these same goals. To accomplish these goals, we form *a* government, not necessarily *the* government. While *the* government—what we normally associate with the District of Columbia, our state capitol, or the county courthouse—is *a* type of government, so too is a union, a church, a farmer's co-op, a parent–teacher association, a neighborhood or tenants' association, or the board of trustees at a university. What all of these have in common is that they facilitate individual cooperation to achieve some goal. What distinguishes *the* government from the rest is its authority to coerce. All of the others are voluntary associations and cannot force their members to do things (short of legal agreements which rely on *the* government for enforcement).

Why are we taking the time to make this distinction? These "voluntary governments," or associations, are sometimes another solution to collective action problems like the prisoner's dilemma. In fact, Alexis de Tocqueville credited these types of associations with much of the success of the American experiment with democracy.[15] To see how they can be so important, let us look at another variation on the general prisoner's dilemma game, a tragedy of the commons.

Commons are resources which no one (and thus everyone) or everyone (and thus no one) owns. Instead of positive externalities, the problem here is one of negative externalities. Individual actions create costs which others bear, as well, reducing the amount which the individual actor must bear directly. To translate that into English, the common resource is limited. When one person uses some of it, they reduce the amount left for others to use (including himself in the future). They get the entire benefit of using it, but the cost—the reduction of the resource—accrues to the entire group, so the individual bears only part of it.

Think of a refrigerator which four roommates (Doug, Harry, Jeff, and Larry) share. Each is equally entitled to place goods in the fridge, consuming some part of the available refrigerated space. If Larry places a two-liter bottle of diet soda in the fridge, there is less room for the others to use. Of course, there's also less room for Larry to add to his store of food, but he is benefiting from the use of the space, while the others have only less space. The loss is shared, but the benefit is not.

Think, too, of the incentives which this creates. When the roommates move in, and Larry places his bottle in the heretofore empty refrigerator, it consumes space—but there's still plenty left for the others. In fact, if none of them put more than a two-liter in it, they will never run short of space. Each, however, has the incentive to use as much of the space as possible as quickly as possible. If Harry thinks he may want to store his next shipment from the Cheese-of-the-Month Club in the fridge, he'll want to get either the cheese or something of an equivalent volume in there.

Why? Because the refrigerator space is "first come, first served." It's there for the taking, until you or someone else takes it, so you'd better grab it first. Once someone else does, it's gone.

This is what makes the tragedy of the commons a tragedy. Each individual benefits in direct correlation to the amount she consumes, but she bears only a part of the cost. Moreover, she bears that same part of the cost whether she consumes any, much, or none of the resource. Each individual, then, tries to maximize their consumption. Notice how this is the other side of the free-riding problem. There, each individual tries to minimize their cost while enjoying a fixed benefit. Here, each individual tries to maximize the benefit they receive from a fixed cost. In both cases, though, the problem is not that one person has these incentives, but that everyone does. With a public good, this means that no one produces it, waiting on someone else to do it.

---

14 For a Biblical reflection on this theme, see Romans 13:1–4.

15 We will discuss this at greater length in a later chapter—you'll know it by the frequency with which Tocqueville's name appears.

With a commons, this means that everyone uses as much of it as quickly as possible, since waiting only reduces your net benefit.

The classic example is of a public field in which all members of a community may graze their livestock.[16] To make the math simple, let's imagine a village of four farmers, each of whom has a herd of three cattle (one bull and two heifers). The field can support 15 cattle before the rate of grazing exceeds the rate at which the grass regenerates, turning the field into a mud pit. So far, we have no problems. The field will support 15 cattle, but only 12 are grazing it.

This spring, however, each of the farmers discovers that one of his heifers is in a family way.[17] Let's put ourselves in the place of one of those farmers. How do we decide whether to let our herd increase to four? To avoid more discussion of bovine procreation, let's assume the calf is female.[18] An additional cow means more milk and resulting dairy products, but also requires more feed. So if the benefit of the additional dairy products is greater than the cost of feeding the cow (and the steak dinner we will forego), we will keep it. So is the benefit greater than the cost?

I know what you're thinking—why am I asking you, when I'm the one writing the book? How would you know? Well, there is one thing we know already that should make that an easy question to answer. What is the cost to the farmer of feeding an additional cow? Since the farmer can place the cow on the commons, the additional cost is essentially zero. It would move the total number of cattle from 12 to 13, but the field is still able to provide plenty of grass for all at that number. (For the future lawyer or accountant in you, the cost is not exactly zero. The grass in the field will grow back a little more slowly, and the field will be slightly more congested. But everyone shares these costs, so they are small and even smaller when divided.) The cow's life-time production of dairy products followed by a hamburger dinner surely outweighs that cost, so we allow our herd to increase.

The problem is that everyone has the same incentives. Suddenly, there are 16 cattle grazing the commons, and none of us is to blame. After all, we each only added one more cow. The cattle overgraze the field, it becomes a mud pit, and none of us are able to feed our cattle. How can we prevent this tragedy from occurring? How can we internalize this negative externality?

There are several ways to solve this problem. The simplest one is to get some barbed wire, partition the commons into lots, and sell them. Then each farmer has his own field. If he overgrazes it, he bears the entire cost. As the poet[19] says, "Good fences make good neighbors." Private ownership removes the ability to force others to bear part of the cost.

Another solution is to create government regulations about herd size. A Bureau of Bovine Population could decide which farmers may have herd sizes of four and which may not. It could opt for a more market-oriented regulation, giving each farmer the right to a herd of 3.75 cattle and allowing them to sell part of their allotment to other farmers, bringing a whole new meaning to "cattle futures trading." But this is more costly—it requires hiring administrators to devise and oversee a program, and it requires obeying the administrator.

A third possibility is for the farmers to solve the problem themselves through voluntary cooperation. So long as they design a system they all agree to and can enforce themselves, they do not require an administrator. They would directly govern themselves. For example, they might decide on a rotation. Three farmers could have a herd size of four, and every five years, one of those three would rotate to the herd size of three and enjoy some steak. So each farmer would have 15 years of a herd size of four, with five years at three. To enforce it, they could agree that any cattle present on the commons in excess of the agreed-upon amount became the property (i.e., steak dinner) of the finder. This severely limits the incentive to cheat, as someone is likely to notice an extra cow, and the attempted cheater will not only fail to benefit from cheating , but will lose what benefit could have been had from slaughtering the cow themselves.

---

16 Such a field has been known historically as a "town commons." Coincidence? I think not.

17 For more information on this, consult your local biology professor (or ask your parents).

18 If it were male, the following still applies, though the nature of the benefit would be different.

19 Robert Frost.

This has a higher upfront cost, in that they must agree to a plan in all its details. Since they are literally governing themselves, however, they must surrender less freedom, and have less to fear from abuse of the system. Although privatization is probably the simplest and least costly solution in this situation, there are commons which it is not technically feasible to partition, such as schools of fish or the air. Where the number of people involved is small, such as with a local fishing ground, this voluntary cooperation can be a very good solution. For larger numbers of participants, such as the air, the costs of arranging and monitoring this sort of cooperation can be too much to overcome, leaving only the second solution as a possibility.

Here we must briefly pause for two purposes. First, we must remember that, while a tragedy of the commons involves negative externalities, the presence of negative externalities is not sufficient to create a tragedy of the commons. Recall once more the example of loud music heard in a neighboring apartment. Your consumption of loud German punk music may impose a cost on your neighbor, but this does not create an incentive for your neighbor to consume more of it. When this was a positive externality, it was not a public good because the consumption was excludable. As a negative externality, it is not a tragedy of the commons because the consumption is non-rivalrous—the fact that you are listening to the music neither increases nor decreases your neighbor's ability to hear. Your consumption does not leave less for your neighbor (however much the neighbor may wish it would).

Second, notice the criteria which we used to evaluate the different solutions we considered. In seeking to reduce the negative externality, we had three alternatives for arranging our cattle-grazing activity: individual, voluntary, and collective. We could create private property rights to leave each individual to his own devices, we could devise a cooperative scheme in which we governed ourselves directly, or we could form a collective entity—a government—and have it administer the land on our behalf.

None of these options is always best. We want the one that minimizes the most externality for the least cost. Where we have to deal with others we have the time and trouble of reaching decisions together. Where we form a government, we also have the cost of the liberty which we surrender in agreeing to abide by future decisions, even if we come up on the short end of them. We choose between alternatives for arranging our activities so as to minimize the sum of the externalities we expect to bear as a result of others' actions and the decision making and autonomy costs.

Take, for example, selecting socks in the morning. If you choose some particularly heinous brown, orange, and green argyles to go with your blue shorts and yellow shirt, others are likely to incur some negative externality costs when they encounter your fashion statement. Those costs, however, are not likely to be very large—no physical pain or discomfort, and no one's making them look. Instead of leaving the activity of selecting matching socks individually organized, we could attempt to organize it differently. Getting everyone to decide on a common standard for sock selection and monitoring compliance could reduce the negative externality involved, but the time and trouble would be greater than the gain. Burning down your house may reduce your dust bunny problems, but the cure is worse than the disease. The same is true of forming a government to formulate and enforce a sock policy. You have to decide on a policy (or a representative to decide on it) and submit to its enforcement, even if everyone else decides you can only wear black dress socks, whether you're wearing heels, tennis shoes, or sandals.

In other areas, though, one of the other alternatives could well be more attractive. If your neighbor might choose to use his backyard as a toxic waste dump, it's probably worth the time, effort, and loss of autonomy to eliminate that option through government. Likewise, your church congregation may want to find a way to cooperate with other like-minded congregations to support a mission or charity without surrendering their autonomy over their beliefs.

It is also important to note that decision making and autonomy costs are inversely related. Because voluntary organization's *de facto* decision-making rule is unanimity, it has high decision making costs. The higher the percentage of the group which must agree, and the larger the size of the group, the higher the decision-making costs. It takes a lot of time and effort to get everyone to agree on something—have you ever tried to order a pizza with friends? And since everyone's agreement is necessary, each individual has an incentive to be the last holdout, who can then hold the rest of the group hostage, as it were, to extract concessions. Of course, as a result, voluntary organization has low autonomy costs. You can effectively block anything which you find unacceptable, since your agreement is required. The difficulty is in finding something which is acceptable to everyone.

Lowering these decision making costs is one reason to use collective organization instead. With a means of public enforcement to ensure that those who don't agree with the decision keep their promise to abide by it nonetheless, it is possible to make decisions by less than unanimity. This lowers the costs of reaching a decision, but increases the chance that someone will have to bear the costs of complying with a policy that is not in their personal interest.

"Less than unanimity" offers a wide range of alternatives, however, from any one person making decisions for everyone to one short of unanimity. The lower the number required to agree, the lower the decision-making costs. Think about a situation in which any one person—and not a particular person—can authorize action on behalf of the entire group, binding the group to that decision. Three siblings (of driving age) have to share a car; one has promised to take a significant other on a date, while the second has promised to take grandmother to the airport, and the third is going to work (delivering pizzas). Sounds like something out of a bad sitcom, doesn't it? Yet what it shows is astronomical autonomy costs. If they each have to keep their promise, and the car can only be in one place at one time, someone has to hurt a date's feelings, deliver pizzas on a bike, or pay for a cab for grandma (and endure her displeasure at having to ride with some stranger who, after all, might have abducted her).[20]

As we've already seen, when we reach the other end of the spectrum (unanimity), we can lower these autonomy costs by raising the number who have to agree. The trade-off, though, is that we have to incur greater decision-making costs. The siblings could consult with each other before making plans and find a way to accomplish all of their ends, but it would take time and effort to reach that decision. If only two have to agree, the third can easily find herself the odd man out. It's easier for two to reach an accommodation, but whoever winds up as the third is likely to have a bad evening.

Given the wide range of alternatives, why do we then associate democratic decision-making with a simple majority? There are two different answers to this question. The first is tradition. There are certain ratios we have traditionally used, so when we need to make a decision, it is easier to agree on one of these focal points than to create and justify another ratio *de novo*. They are familiar, so we do not have to explain and reassure as much when we propose them, and none is more familiar than a simple majority.

The second answer is that there is, in fact, more than one of these ratios. We just don't think about the fact that we often use the others. The most commonly used percentages are a simple majority (50% + 1, which is in most cases different from 51%), supermajority (two-thirds and three-fourths being popular fractions), and unanimity (100%). While Congress passes most measures by a simple majority, it requires a two-thirds majority in each house to propose a constitutional amendment to the states (the same as to override a Presidential veto), and three-fourths of the states must ratify the amendment. Two-thirds of the Senate must consent to a treaty before it is ratified, the same as must vote in favor of an impeachment. Three-fifths of the Senate must vote to end a filibuster.

Why do we require greater numbers to agree at these times (and some others)? You know the answer. When we raise the quotient of the decision-making rule, we surrender time and effort to an increase in decision-making costs. What do we gain in return? Lower autonomy costs. These are areas where our founders felt it more likely to do greater damage to someone if the collective decision went against them. This is perhaps easiest to see in terms of constitutional amendment. If you can change the rules of the game, you can severely damage other players (or their interests). If a simple majority of Congress could amend the Constitution, one party could change the rules to damage the other—and perhaps make sure the other never got a majority.

Sounds great, as long as your party is the one in control, right? The problem is knowing whether yours will be that party. If yours is the party that will lose the election, you'd surely prefer that not mean the utter destruction of your party. Better to risk less, even if the prize is not as great. Besides, as Lord Acton reminds us, even

---

20 Of course, on the sitcom, it turns out to be a very unusual date delivering pizzas with grandma, in which the siblings learn valuable life lessons.

the winners of such a contest might come to rue their fortune. Power corrupts, and absolute power corrupts absolutely. Controlling the rules of the game is a little too close to absolute power. So we make it difficult to change the rules; the more people who have to consent to a change, the easier it is for people the change would hurt to block it. We have higher decision-making costs, but lower autonomy costs.

Notice, though, that in explaining the popularity of the simple majority, "fairness" has not appeared as an argument. The reason for this is simple: it's not one, or at least, not a good one. A simple majority does not make the most people happy—if we wished to make the greatest number happy, we would choose unanimity. It does not ensure the best decisions.[21] Why is it "fair" or "just" that fifty-one people should get to tell forty-nine others what to do? It's not. But it is convenient. A simple majority doesn't minimize the sum of externality, decision-making, and autonomy costs in all situations. But it's probably close enough in enough situations that it's not worth figuring out the precise percentage for every situation. And as long as we all have the same chance of being in the majority, it makes a pretty good approximation of the optimal rule.

Let's take a moment to review where we've been. So far, we have looked at three answers to our primary question, why we need government. Those answers are security (Hobbes), liberty (Locke), and public goods (Hume). We have discussed several concepts to help us understand how we arrive at those answers. We have looked at game theory, in the form of the prisoner's dilemma and two more specific versions of it, free riding and the tragedy of the commons. We have also employed the concepts of externalities, decision-making costs, and autonomy costs.

When we encountered the prisoner's dilemma, we used it to explain why we need government, but by the time we reached the tragedy of the commons, we were talking about choosing from not the binary government/no government pair, but from three alternatives: individual (private), voluntary, or government (collective). We have not switched horses in mid-stream; rather, these two sets of concepts complement each other. The examples from game theory help us understand when and why we have (or should expect to have) a problem. The concepts from economics (in this case, constitutional economics) help us understand how best to solve those problems. In other words, not every prisoner's dilemma involves externality costs large enough to warrant the involvement of government.

Take, for example, two roommates who agree to alternate weeks cleaning their apartment. Each has an incentive to skip her cleaning and let the other do all of the work. Certainly they find themselves in a prisoner's dilemma. Both are better off if both clean, as each will have only a week's worth of grime of which to dispose. Yet each individually does better to not clean at all and let the other suffer through two weeks' worth of accumulated dirt.[22] Yet this situation is hardly what one would call a federal case, or even a municipal one. Certainly, city government could pass an ordinance requiring roommates to perform weekly cleaning duties on an alternating basis, and they could have policemen perform spot inspections. The cure, however, is worse than the disease, both in terms of police time better spent in pursuit of more serious threats to public order and of the individual liberty lost.[23]

Better, instead, to rely on each group of roommates to come to their own understanding, to make their own voluntary arrangements for enforcement—like Hume's two farmers draining their marsh. This may not eliminate all externalities, but the costs of completely eliminating them are worse. Rather than police inspections and city ordinances, the one who does clean may withhold her part of the rent and utilities, or she may put the hair she removes from the shower drain in the other's bed or coffee filter. The point is, there are other, simpler solutions than having government take over the issue. This, incidentally, is what Ronald Reagan meant when he said that government was the problem, not the solution.

---

21 If you don't think the majority can be wrong, I refer you to When Brittany Spears Ruled the Earth. And although we don't have polling data to prove this, a majority of Roman citizens seems to have thought feeding people to lions was great sport. Perhaps, though, if we combine these examples and feed Brittany Spears to lions . . .

22 If these were guys, the time periods would have to be in months, rather than weeks, but the example still holds.

23 Don't think regular cleanliness inspections are an invasion of liberty? Have your mom drop by your dorm room or apartment on a regular basis.

Thus far, the answers we have considered to our question of why we need government have built on the same conception of human nature—that humans are inherently flawed, seeking to do the right thing but often failing. Let us now consider two answers based on a different conception of human nature. The French philosopher Jean-Jacques Rousseau believed that man in his natural state is inherently good. Inspired by reports of Native American life, Rousseau argued that man, in a state of nature, existed as a "noble savage." Because he did not depend on his fellow man or claim property for his own, relying instead on the bounty which nature provided, the noble savage lived in harmony with his fellow man.

The astute reader will have already noticed that this is a tragedy of the commons. As soon as the population outgrows the naturally available resources, competition begins. To increase yields, it is necessary to add labor to what nature provides, to plow and tend crops, to prune and maintain orchards, and so on. In fact, this is John Locke's justification for someone claiming private property—that he has added his labor to it. As you will remember from our earlier discussion of the tragedy of the commons, fencing off the commons is one way to solve this problem.

Rousseau, however, did not find private property an acceptable solution. In fact, he did not see a tragedy of the commons at all. Rousseau thought it better to remain in the state of nature; he lamented the first person to claim property as his sole possession and convince his fellows to recognize that claim. The need to enforce these claims led the rich and powerful to create society, an artificial set of rules that bound the more numerous and less fortunate to support their status.

Although this may sound somewhat strange to modern ears, remember that Rousseau lived in pre-revolutionary France, a feudal society stratified into classes with stringent rules governing the interactions between those classes. Nobility had power because they owned land, which they allowed peasants to live on in exchange for labor and money, which the nobility spent maintaining a lavish lifestyle at the court of the king in Paris. A peasant evicted from the land had little way to feed himself, since guilds strictly controlled entry into skilled professions, such as carpentry or weaving. Someone at the mercy of this arbitrary hierarchy might well think abuse to be the purpose of that system of government, rather than its by-product.

So, as Rousseau observed at the beginning of *The Social Contract*, "Man is born free; and everywhere he is in chains." Some being dependent on others created inequality in society. Once dependency had entered the world, the only way to solve this problem was a social contract. Rousseau used this term to mean something a little different from what either Hobbes or Locke had meant. The purpose of Rousseau's social contract was to eliminate inequality by making everyone equally dependent on everyone else. This, in turn, would leave everyone free.

The key to this transformation was the general will. This is not the same as the will of the majority, which could be wrong or mislead by the interests of the individuals comprising that majority. The general will is what every single person would want if they knew what they *should* want—even if they don't know they want it. Let's try to make sense of that.

Recall the expression, "Everybody owns it, therefore nobody owns it." I used this expression to describe public property when we discussed the tragedy of the commons. Because the property belonged to everyone, no one person was responsible for it. Thus, people were free to do as they wished with it. Rousseau had something similar in mind with his idea of the social contract. Because each person belonged to everyone, in common, no one person could tell another what to do. Only everyone could command a person, and this "everyone" existed in the form of the general will. The general will is not the sum of the interests of a majority of the citizens, or even all of the citizens. It is the common interest of all; moreover, it is the common interest of all *rightly understood*, which means it is what is in their interest, not what they might think is in their interest.

Think again of our prisoners in the prisoner's dilemma. Their common interest is to both keep quiet. Their individual interest is to talk, and the sum of their individual interests is that both talk. If that small society of criminals could force each other to follow the general will, then they would (literally and figuratively) force themselves to be free—or at least, more free than they would otherwise be. Rousseau, of course, meant this figuratively (the story of the prisoners is a more recent invention). In forcing ourselves to follow the rules we adopt for our own benefit, we force ourselves to be free, because we are doing what we really wish. Or, we are doing what we would wish, if we understood the world properly.

Of course, as fans of *Dr. Strangelove* can attest, this assumes that we understand the world properly when we adopt the rules we force ourselves to follow. One of the most common themes in world mythology is the promise to which someone binds himself without appreciating all of the potential ramifications. This is the difficulty Rousseau avoids with the general will. By definition, it has perfect foresight. It is the best of all possible wills.

Therein lies the great difficulty in Rousseau's theory: practice. In practice, it is difficult to know the general will, because people are flawed, and do not always see it correctly. The law, according to Rousseau (and some of the French constitutions), is the expression of the general will, and laws which are contrary to the general will are no laws at all. But if we produce them all in the same way—and the general will is notoriously difficult to interview—how do we know which ones to follow and which ones are void?

We know only that we do not see how it is in the common interest, but we do not know if the error lies in our perception or in the expression. We have no outside means of verifying the accuracy of the expression, so either we run a strong risk of forcing someone into chains (thinking we are forcing him to be free), or each individual follows the law according to their own editing (meaning each person follows their own law).[24] Expressions of the general will are non-falsifiable; there is no way to prove them false, so anything may be an expression of the general will. Or, to put it in more modern terms, the general will has no photo identification against which to check its identity.

So for Rousseau, the answer to why we need government is rather complicated. On the one hand, we don't need government. We'd be better off without it. So Rousseau would ask not why we *need* government, but why we *have* government. He would answer that we have it because the powerful use it to protect their interests. The important question for Rousseau, then, is what to do about government once we have it. Since we cannot escape it, the best alternative is to enter into the common dependency of the social contract, submitting ourselves to the general will. Thus, we have government to produce equality.

Just as Hume built on Locke, and Locke built on Hobbes, so another political philosopher built on the ideas of Rousseau. Like Rousseau, Karl Marx was concerned with equality and saw government as something the haves created to maintain their position relative to the have-nots—to maintain inequality, in other words. In fact, the last sentences of *The Communist Manifesto* echo Rousseau's opening from *The Social Contract*. Compare "Man is born free; and everywhere he is in chains" to "Workers of the world, unite! You have nothing to lose but your chains."

This comparison, however, also highlights some of the differences between the two. Notice that Marx appeals specifically to the working class, also known as the proletariat. Marx saw the world not primarily as many separate individuals, but as groups made of individuals. Marx classified these groups according to their relationship to the means of production, or capital. Capitalists owned the means of production, such as factories. The proletariat supplied the labor to cause the capital to produce.

Marx married these ideas to G. F. W.[25] Hegel's theory of the dialectic. Hegel argued that human understanding occurred through the dialectic process. This begins with an idea, called a thesis.[26] Each thesis, however, stimulates the creation of its opposite, the antithesis. The dialectic is the process of reconciling each thesis with its antithesis, and each such reconciliation produces a new thesis, one with fewer flaws than its predecessor and known as their synthesis.

While Hegel saw this as a never-ending process, moving constantly toward the unattainable goal of perfection without reaching it, Marx applied the dialectic to history and thought it would lead to utopia. History became a dialectic progression. Mankind formed societies and governments to solidify some set of relationships to the means of production. Each stage of history was a thesis, and each thesis contained the seeds of its own destruction in that it caused the creation of its antithesis. So, while feudal society had calcified a

---

24 Rousseau's adherents have tended to err toward the former.

25 Gottfried Friedreich Wilhelm—but since I'm not getting paid by the letter, let's stick to G. F. W., shall we?

26 So yes, when you write one, you are supposed to have an idea. Persistent overachiever Martin Luther had 95, but that's another story.

hierarchical relationship in which very few owned property and had a great deal of control over others, it also created the need for cities outside of that hierarchy and a merchant class (also known as the bourgeoisie). The growing power of this merchant class led them to destroy the feudal system and build upon its remains a system more favorable to them—capitalism.

Likewise, capitalism contained the seeds of its own destruction in the creation of the proletariat. Industrialization would bring large numbers of people together, people Marx thought would have a common interest. According to Marx, the value of a good consisted entirely of the labor that went into it.[27] Capitalists, then, were expropriating the proletariat's labor, because they kept some or all of the value which production added (otherwise known as profit). Marx thought that once the proletariat became aware of this theft and realized their superior numbers, this consciousness would allow them to destroy capitalism and build upon its ruins a more perfect system, socialism. Under socialism, labor would own the means of production, and there would no longer be a disjuncture between the value they contributed and the value they received. Eventually, we would progress beyond socialism even, to the point of complete equality, when the state would wither away.

Notice the similarity between Marx's class consciousness and Rousseau's general will. Class consciousness is the individual's identification with a group, and the individual's subordination of her own interests to those of the group, just as the general will is the common interest. And although Marx presents class consciousness as a voluntary individual act, it did not take long for others to advocate forcing their fellows to be free if they could not see what was really in their interest (because what Marx called a false consciousness was deluding them). In fact, this is Lenin's notion of the vanguard, that those who could see the common interest had a duty to force others to act in that interest, even if they could not see it themselves.[28]

Again, there are practical concerns with the application of this theory. In essence, socialism transforms every piece of capital into a commons, thrusting them into the dynamic of the tragedy of the commons. Think of two carpenters, each of whom wishes to use a commonly-owned hammer. Both attempting to use it at the same time causes damage to the hammer, if not to the carpenters as well. We could make it a private good, as when we fenced off the common field, but then we have re-introduced inequality (one carpenter has a hammer, the other does not). We could license the use of it, so that both take turns using the hammer, but this requires some administrator to set the terms and monitor compliance, which means the state will not wither away. Nor should we assume that the state will impartially administer. One carpenter could be the bureaucrat's brother-in-law.[29] If angels were to govern men . . . .

In fact, Madison's observation highlights the fundamental difficulty here. Socialism can work only if each individual *always* gives equal weight to the interests of others and subordinates both private interests to the public interest. While this is something to which all major religions (and any worth the name) encourage us, experience would not seem to recommend relying on it. Thankfully, people do often consider others first or set their own interests aside for the common good. But they do not always.

So, why do we need government? We have discussed five answers to that question, which we may group into two families, based on their assumptions of human nature. The first family assumes only that human nature is fallible, and its answers are security, security of liberty, and security of liberty and public goods. The second family assumes that human nature is good, and so its question is not why we *need* government, but why we have it (and what to do about it now that we do). Its answers are that we have government because of inequality, and we must change it to increase equality.

We also discussed several concepts which explain those answers. In the first family, we talked about the prisoner's dilemma, free-riding, and the tragedy of the commons. We also talked about positive and negative externalities, decision-making, and autonomy costs. Likewise, in the second family, we discussed the noble savage, the social contract, the general will, the dialectic, class consciousness (real and false), and the means of production.

---

27 Notice the similarity with Locke on this point, but the dissimilarity in the conclusion each reaches in regard to private property.

28 An argument often heard in environmental circles; witness the precautionary principle.

29 Although we may not know whether this would improve or impede his chances, it would likely alter them.

These ideas are some of the tools we will use to help you construct your understanding of the world around you, but more particularly, the world of government in the United States of America. As this suggests, these ideas are very important to your success in this course.[30] With that in mind, may I humbly suggest the following? First, make some charts or tables. These are great tools for showing how a set of concepts differ on important points. So make a table summarizing the five answers we explored in this chapter and how they relate to one another.

Second, watch some television. Yes, you read that correctly. Watch some television and see if you can apply some of these concepts to better understand what's happening in the show. Do the same in the real world, too. Is that person[31] who skips class all the time and wants to borrow your notes before the exam a free rider? Why, or why not? The best way to learn something is to use it, and the best way to check your understanding is to have to explain it to someone else. So once you've found an example, explain it to a friend and see if they buy it. Will you feel like a geek? Probably, at least at first. But then, geeks tend to get really good grades, don't they.

---

30 At least, if they aren't, your instructor has made an odd choice of textbook, for which I thank her.

31 Doug Omer.

Chapter 2: Constitutions

You undoubtedly know that we have a constitution.[1] You probably know that it was written in Philadelphia, and perhaps you remember that it was the summer of 1787. You may even know it was our second constitution. And you may know Dasher and Dancer and Donner and Blitzen. But have you ever wondered *why* we have a constitution?

Maybe it would help to try to imagine our country without a constitution of any sort.[2] If the President wanted to declare war on another country—we'll call it "Larry"—and Congress said he had to get their permission first, how would we know who was right? Some of you may be weighing options in your mind: the President has all the guns, but Congress has the money . . . . If so, I applaud you for your intrepidness—thanks for playing at home!—but you have missed an important point. That question is nonsense, and not just because we named a country "Larry."[3] Without a constitution, we don't know who the President is, or what he is supposed to do and forbidden from doing. We have neither the office nor the method for filling it.

Let's investigate this through an ever-popular sports metaphor. If you want to play a game of baseball, where do you look to find out what each position is supposed to do, who decides which player plays which position, or what a strike is? The rulebook. The rulebook defines the terms of the game and the powers and limitations of each position, governing their interaction on the field. A constitution does the same thing for government, defining the terms and actors and governing their interactions. So, just as the rules of baseball say that the manager fills out the roster, the Constitution of the United States (in conjunction with the state constitutions—more on that later) says that voters choose the President and Congress (the latter directly). And, in the same way the rules of baseball say that once a pitcher has begun moving toward the plate he must throw there, the Constitution says that Congress is not allowed to make things illegal retroactively.

Now, to make sure that we beat this metaphor well and truly into the ground, how many of you have played baseball (or another sport), but never read the official rulebook? Your parents, coaches, siblings, and friends probably taught many of you as you were playing. I, for example, love playing the card game Rook, but never read the rules until I had played it for many years. My father taught me, and his mother taught him, and I still play by those rules and have taught them to others. In other words, it is possible for people to know the rules by tradition or word-of-mouth, handed down from one generation to the next simply as "the way things are done."

Likewise, not every country has (or needs) a written constitution. Britain is perhaps the leading example of a country with an unwritten constitution. Its constitution exists not as a written rulebook, but as a collection of traditional rules. Although some of these exist in written form in various documents, their authority comes from tradition, not from the document. In fact, it is usually their authority as a traditional

---

1 Unless, of course, you have suffered from a very selective form of narcolepsy since elementary school.

2 After all, that's what Hobbes did when he wanted to understand why we have government, and we got a whole chapter out of that, didn't we?

3 Although that would be an improvement over obviously imaginary names like "Burkina Faso" or "Canada."

rule that leads to their description in written documents, and traditional rules matter more than the formal, written ones. Formally, the Queen still rules the United Kingdom. Customarily, however, the Queen does not. Despite this lack of a written constitution, Britain is among the oldest and most successful democracies in the world. Obviously, a written constitution is not a prerequisite for democracy, though one often finds the two together.

Let's apply some of what we learned in the first chapter to help understand this curiosity. Of the five ideas for explaining the origin and purpose of government which we have discussed, only one *requires* a written constitution. Which one? (Take a few moments, form a pool—your odds are a lot better at this than March Madness.[4]) We can rule out Hobbes. Hobbes envisions a complete delegation of authority in return for an end to anarchy. A deal that simple requires little more than a handshake. Similarly, we can eliminate Rousseau, because he also considers the transfer of authority as total and irreversible, thought it is surrendered to all in the form of the general will, rather than a single person. As with Marx, too, a constitution would only codify the exploitation of the weak by the strong. Once the evils of inequality have disappeared, there is no need to say what one may or may not do, since everyone will act in the common interest. What Hume adds to Locke, the provision of public goods, does not require written, detailed rules. All it requires is that someone makes sure everyone pays their share.

That leaves us with Locke.[5] According to Locke, the purpose of government is to secure some rights through the delegation of others. This requires, in the first place, a list of those rights retained and those delegated, to define the limits of the contract. In the second place, it recommends (if not requires) additional measures to help ensure the security of liberty from those who are supposed to secure it. Because the Lockean tradition is the only one to incorporate the idea of limitations of government, it is the only one in need of a specific, written contract. In this tradition, the law is king,[6] binding the governors as well as the governed. It is necessary, therefore, to describe the king in some detail.

This, of course, is not to suggest that every country with a written constitution is founded on Lockean principles. Countries, like people, often have many things they do not need or use.[7] China, for example, has a constitution, but it does not limit the authority of government; it represents that authority. To express it perhaps less cryptically, the constitution does not tell the people in power what to do; the people in power tell it what to say. If you are thinking that this describes Marx's and Rousseau's conception of government, you are correct (give yourself a gold star). If you are thinking that there is an irony in that, award yourself a red star, comrade.

Britain, on the other hand, does not have a written constitution. Britain is founded on more Hobbesian principles. The fundamental doctrine of British government is parliamentary sovereignty. Essentially, Parliament has taken the place of the monarch as (more or less) absolute ruler.[8] The only formal limitation on the power of a Parliament is that it cannot bind a future Parliament. This created an interesting[9] debate when Britain wished to pass a Bill of Rights similar to that of the United States. Parliament could pass the bill, but like any other bill, a future Parliament could pass a bill violating it (this is known as implied repeal; the passage of a conflicting measure implies that Parliament meant to repeal the existing law in so far as necessary to allow the new one, or they wouldn't have passed it). There is also no body to declare acts of Parliament *ultra vires* (beyond their powers) and therefore null and void. Since there are no explicit limitations on Parliament's authority, either from a written document or a previous Parliament, there is no limit for their actions to exceed.

---

4 And as an added bonus, it won't get you fired from your job as head coach at the University of Washington.

5 . . . in the billiard room, with the candlestick. Funny how it's always the last one in the list, isn't it?

6 One often hears this expressed in corrupted Latin as "Lex is rex."

7 And sometimes countries, like people, like to look like something they're not.

8 Technically, the ruler of Great Britain is the Queen-in-Parliament. Over the years, the emphasis has shifted from the former to the latter.

9 *Interesting*, of course, in a purely academic sense, which for normal people translates to somewhere between running a clock on a potato and knowing the difference between a sweet potato and a yam.

The only check on Parliament's power is indirect, namely the ballot box. Theoretically, the monarch could also interfere and reassert powers long abandoned, but this would happen only in extreme circumstances (and is itself subject to the willingness of the population to go along with it). Of course, the ballot box itself exists only because Parliament wills it, but like the monarch, the willingness of the populace to accept the removal of the ballot box without rioting limits Parliament's discretion in removing voting privileges. Notice the difference between this and the situation in the United States, where a government actor who pushes the bounds of her authority runs the risk that the other branches and the citizens will ignore it as something beyond her authority. In the United Kingdom, the risk is that people *won't* ignore it, and will punish Parliament (electorally or physically[10]) for using its authority that way. Parliament is free to do as it wishes, according to the rules, but the citizens judge it on the manner in which it uses that authority.

So long as a majority (or a sizable enough minority) does not object too strenuously, then, Parliament may do as it wishes with an individual. In the United States, however, that individual may sue to have the courts invalidate the act, even if the majority is in favor of it. The former comports much better with the Hobbesian and the latter with the Lockean tradition.[11] The individual retains nothing in the Hobbesian conception of the state. The people surrender all of their sovereignty to the ruler, checked only by the idea that the ruler cannot threaten the people as a whole. Parliament uses the ballot box not because the rules say it must, but because of its interest in self-preservation. It is a tradition, and violating it is beyond the pale.

The difference between the Hobbesian and Lockean foundations of the United Kingdom and United States, respectively, shows in another way, too. Britain has a fusion-of-powers system. The executive, the prime minister, comes from and answers to the legislature. His position as prime minister depends on the support of his fellow party members in Parliament. Not only is the executive part of the legislature, but the upper house of Parliament, the House of Lords, is the court of last resort in the United Kingdom, as well. So Parliament combines all three governmental functions: executive, legislative, and judicial. It writes the laws, it enforces the laws, and it has the final say in interpreting the laws.

In the United States, on the other hand, these three functions are separate, each entrusted to a separate body. The idea for a separation-of-powers system came from the French political philosopher, Charles Secondat, Baron de Montesquieu, generally referred to simply as Montesquieu.[12] In *The Spirit of Laws*, Montesquieu separated governmental functions into three categories: legislative, executive, and judicial. He noticed that the most despotic nations tended to be those where one person or body exercised all three of these functions. Likewise, across time in the same nation, liberty suffered as rulers concentrated more of these powers in the same hands. "Political liberty . . . is there only when there is no abuse of power. But constant experience shows us that every man invested with power is apt to abuse it . . . To prevent this abuse, it is necessary from the very nature of things that power should be a check to power." Lord Acton[13] summarized this more pithily in his famous observation, "Power tends to corrupt, and absolute power corrupts absolutely."

What Montesquieu and Acton describe is something we call a *moral hazard*. A moral hazard is a set of circumstances that give you an incentive to do the wrong thing—to lie, cheat, steal, or defraud another. My favorite example comes from a friend of mine in high school. The insured value of his car was greater than its actual value. As we got out one day, I alerted him that he had forgotten to lock his door. He said, "Thanks for reminding me," but instead of locking his door, he rolled down the window, as well. In response to my puzzled look, he explained about the difference between the two values of his car. He added that he wished he could leave the keys in the ignition, but that would invalidate his insurance.[14] A car insured for more than its value is a moral hazard; it gives the owner an incentive to be a lot less careful than he has told his insurance company

---

10 . . . even if some members of Parliament enjoy that sort of thing. Yeah, better not Google that one.

11 Does anyone else keep hearing Tevye from the score of *Fiddler on the Roof*?

12 But never Monty; he hated that.

13 John Emerich Edward Dalberg Acton, renowned historian.

14 Insurers call this "contributory negligence," and it is cause for them to refuse a claim (don't try this at home). Authors, on the other hand, call this "foreshadowing."

he will be. In fact, many of the best examples of moral hazards come from insurance. Since its purpose is to transfer risk to another, situations in which the insured also influences the probability of and benefits from the realization of that risk abound. This is why auto insurance excludes contributory negligence, fire insurance excludes arson committed or commissioned by the policyholder, and life insurance excludes suicide.

Note that the hazard exists whether or not a person succumbs to it, just as road hazards exist whether or not you actually puncture your tire or detach your muffler, or for golfers, just as water hazards exist whether you sink your shot or not.[15] And while every moral hazard presents a temptation, not every temptation is a moral hazard. Like nails in the road, a moral hazard makes you go out of your way to not cheat. Whereas catching sight of an opponent's card is a temptation to cheat at poker, playing in a mirrored room is a moral hazard—the situation presents a constant temptation to anyone who walks into it. In other words, a moral hazard is temptation made structural and systematic. So copying answers from a friend is cheating; a professor allowing you to grade your own exam presents a moral hazard. You may not cheat, but the situation encourages you (and everyone else) to do so.

Of course, the solution to a moral hazard is to remove those incentives. Thus, insurance companies won't pay if you suborn the theft of your car or take your own life. If they did pay, they would give people incentives to do those things. Similarly, professors do not generally allow you to grade your own work, at least not without altering your incentives so that they encourage you to do the right thing.

Montesquieu's moral hazard is the combination of all three governmental functions in one person or group. If you could write the law, interpret the law, and apply the law, you would have incentives to serve your own interests, rather than the public good or that of your constituents. We all know the person in the pick-up basketball game who calls a foul every time he misses a shot. Were our ruler perfect, we could trust her with all of that power, knowing she would never abuse it.[16] In fact, this is what Plato recommends in *The Republic*, one of the earliest works of political science. Plato argues that we should entrust absolute power to a philosopher king who, by virtue of being a philosopher, would not abuse that power. The fusion of governmental powers into the hands of a single person is then attractive because it allows for quicker decision-making.

In the absence of a philosopher king, however, there are different ways to address this. One—the one which the United Kingdom uses—is to reduce the incentive to abuse power with the threat of retribution, whether at the ballot box or in the streets. The other—Montesquieu's solution, which the United States adopted—is to split up the power among several persons or bodies. This weakens the ability of each to abuse power, not only because each has less to abuse, but because the others have some with which to resist any attempts to overstep authority. Of course, this also tends to slow down decision-making.

Naturally, the second also has more need of a written constitution, to spell out the details of its finely balanced division of power. What is important in this context is that this separation of powers only makes sense if one is placing limitations on government, seeking to prevent it from overstepping the boundaries of the authority delegated to it. If, as according to the Hobbesian principle, the delegation of authority is complete, then this would only serve to hamstring the government in its efforts to do its job. If, on the other hand, that delegation is partial, then separating the powers of government makes sense, in order to keep it from encroaching on the sovereignty the people retain.

So, now that we have investigated (beyond your wildest dreams) the question of why we have *a* constitution, let's look at why we have *the* Constitution. When the Continental Congress declared the independence of the thirteen colonies, there was no written constitution governing the relations between the colonies. They had merely sent representatives to discuss their common problems. The name "Continental Congress" was not a formal one, at least not at that point, but simply a description. Although we associate the word *congress* with a legislative body, all it means is "to come together."[17] The Congress of Europe, for example, was not an

---

15 The Dukes of Hazzard, however, are entirely imaginary.

16 Or, to put it in more familiar terms, "If angels were to govern men . . ."

17 To see this, it may help to consider it in relation to its etymological cousins, *ingress* (to come in toward), *egress* (to come out from), and *aggress* (to go against). And quit singing that *#@! Beatles song!

early attempt at European integration, but the idea that European heads of government (in the early 1800s) should meet together to discuss matters of common concern (and hopefully avoid fighting over them).

Similarly, the Continental Congress was a meeting of representatives from colonies across the continent. In fact, it was the Second Continental Congress which declared independence from Great Britain. And once they decided to go to war together, they decided they should have some formal rules to govern their interactions. They assigned the task of writing these to a committee headed by John Dickinson. The Congress approved the resulting Articles of Confederation on November 15, 1777 and sent them to the states for ratification, although ratification was not complete until March 1, 1781 (General Cornwallis would surrender at Yorktown on October 19 of that year).

The Articles created a U.S. Congress, consisting of delegations from each state. Although each state could send between two and seven delegates, each state had only one vote. The second article declares that the states retain all powers not expressly delegated to the U.S. Congress. To exercise what few powers the Articles did delegate to Congress, nine of the thirteen states had to agree. On other questions, the Congress could decide by simple majority, except for amendment. To amend the Articles of Confederation required the unanimous agreement of all thirteen states. Although Congress had the power to draft a budget, it could only request the money to fund it. It could not raise its own revenue, nor could it force the states to pay their part.

As you may imagine, this created a great deal of difficulty. You may remember stories of the deprivation George Washington and the Continental Army suffered through, at Valley Forge, for example. Soldiers lacked shoes, food, and ammunition. Washington wrote many impassioned pleas to the Congress asking them to provide the supplies they had repeatedly promised. Even as the army waited in camp for the negotiation of a peace treaty, Washington had to intervene to prevent armed rebellion by officers who saw little other prospect of getting their pay, since Congress was so badly in arrears.

Why didn't Congress have the money to pay them? The states failed to make the contributions the budgets required of them. But if all the states wanted independence, why wouldn't they pay the part they agreed to pay? Very simply, they were caught in a prisoner's dilemma, more specifically, a free riding problem. If they won independence, they all won it; the others could not "throw one back" to the British without endangering their own independence. So each state wanted to let the other states pay for the war. What was amazing was not that Congress did not have enough money for the war, but that they received anything at all.

Likewise, the states would have been better off if they all traded freely with each other. Here again they found themselves in a prisoner's dilemma. If all of the states traded freely, the maximum amount of commerce could occur. Everyone would be better off—producers would sell more, consumers would have more from which to choose. Each state individually, however, would like to have everyone else trade freely while they imposed a few taxes on imports. That state's proportion of the total goods sold would increase slightly, and it would also gain some tax revenue. The problem (stop me if you've heard this one) is that every state has the same incentive. So everyone has taxes, barriers to trade that reduce the common weal, and everyone is worse off than if they could keep their agreement.

Unfortunately, the Articles of Confederation did not provide a solution to these problems. The confederal government could print money, but the ability to lay and collect taxes was not one of the powers which the states had delegated. Without its own resources for revenue, its money had little or no value. In essence, it had a checkbook but no income. The states had promised to provide that income, to put money in the account, but each of them seemed to be waiting for the others to do it first (so that the one which waited wouldn't have to contribute). So the Congress had no way to purchase the supplies Washington needed.

Neither did the Articles include the power to regulate commerce between the states among those the states delegated to the central government. The Articles prohibited states from taking actions which violated treaties the United States had signed with other countries, but it said nothing about violating promises the states made to each other. Conceivably, the Continental Congress could have negotiated a treaty in which the United States promised to trade freely within its borders. Aside from being a rather convoluted solution, though, this would have run up against another problem—the Congress had no troops with which to enforce those terms. The states had militias, which they had seconded to (placed under the command of) the United States during the Revolutionary War, but the confederal government had no troops of its own.

To solve these problems, the Congress called for a convention to discuss amendments to the Articles of Confederation which would address these problems. The convention was to meet in Annapolis, Maryland on September 11, 1786. Only five states sent delegations: New York, Virginia, Pennsylvania, Delaware, and New Jersey. Notice that Maryland did not bother to send delegates to a convention held in Maryland. In the words of the delegates, "Your Commissioners did not conceive it advisable to proceed on the business of their mission, under the Circumstance of so partial and defective a representation."

By the time the delegates went home (after waiting three days to see if other delegates would arrive), events were already underway in Massachusetts that would lend more urgency to their enterprise. In their report, the delegates recommended calling another convention for the following May, in Philadelphia. In late August, a former captain in the Continental Army began an armed revolt in Massachusetts. The soldiers in the Continental Army had returned to their farms, farms which were laden with debt in the form of unpaid taxes after their long absence. Since they had not received their pay from Congress, they could not pay these debts, which meant that many of them were literally losing the farm. Daniel Shays and around 2,000 former soldiers took up arms to prevent courts from evicting bankrupt farmers and repossessing their farms for failure to pay taxes. Massachusetts called up a militia of 4,400 to quell the rebellion. For six months, Massachusetts slipped into anarchy.

Haunted by the specter of armed rebellion, the states were much more eager to attend the Philadelphia Convention to discuss freeing commerce to ameliorate poverty and enable the central government to settle its debts (and ameliorate poverty). The states and their citizens found themselves in a Catch-22. The states did not have the money to send to Congress because they could not collect taxes. The citizens could not pay the taxes because they needed the money Congress owed them. Congress could not settle its debts because the states did not pay the money they had promised.[18] Of course, this is something of an oversimplification, but you can see the frustration, poverty, and potential for violence that improper governance brings.

In this heated atmosphere, the delegates chose to conduct their business with the windows and shutters in Independence Hall closed, despite the literally heated atmosphere of a Philadelphia summer. They did not want reporters listening under the windows, catching parts of conversations, starting rumors in the headlines and spreading unrest. They wanted to consider the problems they faced with as much dispassion and reason as possible.

As the convention opened debate, a young delegate from Virginia rose to speak. James Madison, Jr. had been to the failed Annapolis convention, and the young Princeton graduate had pushed for this new convention. He did not intend to let this opportunity to fix these grave societal ills pass. Madison came prepared, having researched and drafted beforehand a plan for a whole new system of government. The plan which Madison had prepared (but had a colleague introduce to the floor) called for a national legislature with the broad, traditional powers of a parliament, rather than the limited, enumerated powers of the national government under the Articles of Confederation. The Virginia Plan, as the delegates came to call it, called for the apportionment of seats in this bicameral legislature according to population. The people would elect the lower house directly and the upper house indirectly, as the members of the lower house would elect the upper. The legislature would use a simple majority decision-making rule, rather than the 9/13 the Articles required.

The Virginia Plan also included a national executive, or more precisely, executives, since the plan called for an executive council rather than a single president. The lower house elected these officers, as well as the national judiciary. Together, the executive and judiciary would form the Council of Revision, which would review state laws for compatibility with national laws. Where state laws conflicted with national laws, the Council of Revision could declare those laws unconstitutional.

Put yourself in the shoes of the other delegates, who had come for the purpose of considering revision to the Articles of Confederation. Instead you find yourself listening to a proposal which radically departs from

---

18 There's a particularly twisted irony to one government punishing you for failure to pay a debt you owe it, when you can't pay because of a debt a related government won't pay you, in part because the first government won't pony up the money it promised. Someone's having their cake and eating it, too.

the principles of that government—state sovereignty and very limited central authority. In fact, Madison's proposal would wipe away the current government and replace it with what seems to you a dangerous, powerful behemoth that will be under the control of the large, populous states, or worse, the mobs in those large, populous states.

What Madison had done, however, was to set the terms of the debate with a brilliant strategic move. In response to this shocking proposal, delegates from the smaller states met and quickly drafted what William Paterson presented as the New Jersey Plan. The New Jersey plan featured a unicameral legislature in which states had equal representation, which representation the states also chose (indirect rather than direct election). This legislature would use a simple majority decision-making rule, but would exercise only explicitly delegated (enumerated) powers. Those powers, however, would include the ability to lay and collect taxes, as well as regulate commerce between the states. In other words, it would largely retain the Articles of Confederation, but would relax the decision-making rule and add to the enumerated powers those which experience had shown were lacking.

The strategic brilliance here is that the states most reluctant to cede power countered with a proposal that already made the most necessary changes. Instead of having to argue and bargain for each of those three elements, Madison took the initiative and set the agenda[19] for the convention. Without the Virginia Plan, the alternative was the status quo, which Madison's experience at Annapolis told him the states did not find objectionable enough. In effect, Madison changed the default position from the status quo, which states found only mildly uncomfortable, to an option which most found quite distasteful. As a result, the first counter offer was much closer to what Madison considered necessary for a successful national government.

The locus of power in a democracy is arguably the legislature, the branch which writes the laws. Certainly the founders thought so, and the structure of the legislature dominated the debate, both in time and heatedness. If you look at the Constitution, the first article, which deals with the legislative branch, is by far the longest. The second article, concerning the executive branch is much shorter. Although the former colonists were suspicious of executive authority—Madison proposed a plural executive as a way of restraining the power of the executive—they did not spend much time detailing the powers and responsibilities of the Presidency. This was because the man they all knew would be the first President was in the room, and they respected and trusted him implicitly to set the appropriate example. In fact, they had already elected him president of the convention: George Washington. The third article, describing the judicial branch, is even shorter, delegating much of the decisions about it to Congress. But we will discuss these in more detail in turn.

The convention referred the thorny issues of the number of houses and their manner of election to committee more than once in an attempt to resolve the issue. Each time, the committees recommended a bicameral structure with the lower house apportioned by population and directly elected, and the upper house apportioned equally and elected indirectly, only to have this compromise fail on the floor. Finally, a committee chaired by Roger Sherman of Connecticut produced the Great Compromise. Sherman's committee took the previous proposal, which seemed close to passing, and added one crucial element to sway those who had been too reluctant to approve it before.

The addition was to require that all revenue bills originate in the House of Representatives, the lower house. Revenue bills are those that raise money for the government; appropriations bills are those which allocate government money for spending. Revenue bills, in other words, are the ones which impose taxes. Larger, more populous states feared that the smaller states might use their equal weight in the Senate to pass taxes that would disproportionately benefit smaller states. Also, as you may remember, the connection between taxation and representation was an important issue to them, so having the house closest to those who would bear the burden of taxes be the only one which could propose them answered some reservations. And, since the Senate still had to approve revenue bills, the smaller states could protect their interests there.

The Great Compromise, however, was not the only compromise that occurred at the convention. Having decided to apportion one chamber of the legislature according to population, how to count the population

---

19 "Magic 8-Ball, will we hear this term again?" "Signs point to yes."

quickly became an important issue for the convention. The states in which slavery was legal—Maryland, Virginia, North Carolina, South Carolina, and Georgia—wanted to count slaves as part of their population when determining how much representation they should have, but not when it came time to determine who those representatives would be. This was especially important to South Carolina and Georgia, whose smaller populations were even smaller if they excluded slaves from the number. The northern states saw this as a cheap trick to increase southern representation at their relative expense. After all, they had agreed to a chamber where each state had equal representation, and here some of the smaller southern states were trying to inflate their population numbers to reduce the advantage of larger states in the lower house.

The solution to this dispute was the 3/5 Compromise. For purposes of apportioning seats in the legislature and direct taxes, 3/5 of the enslaved population would count toward the total population. Let's look at the exact wording in Article I, Section 2, though. "Representatives and direct taxes shall be apportioned among the several states which may be included within this union, according to their respective numbers, which shall be determined by adding to the whole number of free persons, including those bound to service for a term of years, and excluding Indians not taxed, three fifths of all other Persons."

This clause contains four categories of people. The first is free people. The second category is people who have contracted their labor for a set number of years—indentured servants, in other words. Many people paid for their passage to the colonies by contracting with an employer to work some number of years as a household servant. The third category consists of Indians (or more precisely, Native Americans). The clause instructs apportioners to add all of the first two together. To this sum the apportioner is to add 3/5 of the total number of people in the fourth category: all other people. Who exactly is left over after we account for free people, indentured servants, and Native Americans?

Tourists. But there weren't really such things as tourists back then. After all, people spent years laboring to repay the cost of passage. It took weeks, if not months, to cross the Atlantic. Although there were exceptions, it was a one-way trip for almost all. Industrialization had not yet occurred, let alone created the forty-hour work week and two weeks' paid vacation. Not only had tourism not been invented, but what exceptions there were would not have met residency requirements in order for the census to count them.

So, if we have accounted for free persons, indentured servants, Native Americans, and tourists, what other groups fall into the "all other Persons" category? Only one: slaves. So if they meant only one group—and if the process of elimination has not convinced us, the records of the debates in the convention make it clear—why the circumlocution[20]? Our constitution is in most respects the epitome of brevity. The operating instructions for your computer are probably longer than these operating instructions for a country of now 300 million. So why, suddenly, are they using more words than necessary, three instead of one?

We shouldn't decide on the basis of a single example. Perhaps the person who drafted this clause simply got poetic fever. So let's look at some other examples, such as Article I, Section 9. "The migration or importation of such persons as any of the states now existing shall think proper to admit, shall not be prohibited by the Congress prior to the year one thousand eight hundred and eight, but a tax or duty may be imposed on such importation, not exceeding ten dollars for each person." Who were "such persons as . . . states . . . shall think proper to admit"? The word *importation* is instructive. What do we normally import? Goods. Things. So, when the Constitution discusses the importation of persons, it means slaves, people who were property. Think about that for a second; there was a title to a slave just like there is a title to your car, a title to be bought, sold, and bartered.

Such persons as states may think proper to admit, then, were slaves, slaves imported from Africa. Congress could not stop the importation of new slaves for twenty years; even then, it could ban only the importation of new slaves. This would do nothing for those already enslaved and their children. In those twenty years, Congress could tax the importation of slaves, but only up to $10 per slave. Why did they put a maximum on the tax? Well, what might have happened if they didn't? It might help to know that Congress did ban the importation of new slaves as soon as it could (1808). It might also help to know that John Marshall (perhaps

---

20 It means, literally, to talk in circles—to talk all the way around something rather than address it directly.

the most prominent Chief Justice of the Supreme Court) once said that the power to tax is the power to destroy. How could Congress destroy the slave trade through taxation? By setting the tax rate at 2,000%. It would not have prohibited importation, but it would have made it prohibitively expensive.

Notice the circumlocution (back to our original question). Instead of *slave*, Section 9 uses a fairly complex phrase: *such persons as states shall think proper to admit*. Nine words where one would do (and would be much clearer). Well, once is an accident, twice is coincidence; three times is a pattern.

So let's look at Article IV, Section 2. "No person held to service or labor in one state, under the laws thereof, escaping into another, shall, in consequence of any law or regulation therein, be discharged from such service or labor, but shall be delivered up on claim of the party to whom such service or labor may be due." Who, exactly, is a "person held to service or labor"? It could be indentured servants, held by their contracts to a term of labor. But since they signed a contract, the Contract Clause (Article I, Section 10: "No state shall . . . pass any . . . law impairing the obligation of contracts . . . .") would suffice to prevent a state from becoming a haven for runaway butlers and nannies. No, this is the Fugitive Slave Clause, people who (under the laws of some states) could not enter into a contract.

Let's review, then. Instead of *slave*, the Constitution uses the terms *all other persons*, *such persons as states shall think proper to admit*, and *person held to service or labor*. They couldn't bring themselves to use the word *slave*, to stain the beautiful document they were creating. What does that tell us? They knew it was wrong. They were ashamed of it, because they knew it was wrong.

All of which brings us to this question: why is it in there? If the men drafting the Constitution knew slavery was wrong, why did they not eliminate it in their quest to form a more perfect union? There are narrow and broad answers to that question, but both teach the same lesson. The narrow answers are that the slavery provisions were compromises, or more precisely, logrolls. The Fugitive Slave Clause, for example, was an exchange for commercial policy provisions. The broader answer, on the other hand, has to do with geography. Florida at the time was a possession of the Spanish Empire. The French territory of Louisiana bordered the new nation to the west. To the north, the British Empire lurked in Canada. Care to guess the identities of the three greatest military powers of that age? Britain, France, and Spain (probably in that order).

As Benjamin Franklin expressed at the signing of the Declaration of Independence, "Gentlemen, we must all hang together, or we shall surely hang separately." What Franklin meant was that the signers had to work together, or they would fail, and failure meant each swinging from the gallows for the crime of treason. Likewise, the states felt that they could not spare a single member. If Georgia and South Carolina, for example, remained outside the union, it would present any of those three powers the opportunity to divide and conquer, taking advantage of the former colonies' weakness to get a leg up on each other. So, when southern states insisted they would walk out if the new constitution abolished slavery, the other states did not feel they could ignore that threat.

This is meant not to justify, but to explain what the founders were thinking. Understanding why someone does something is a long way from agreeing that they should do that thing. And it teaches us an important lesson about the political process. Why could delegates trade away provisions establishing slavery in the national government for other institutional features they wanted? Well, have you ever noticed a difference in your incentive to spend money when it was someone else's money you were spending? It's a lot easier to write a check when someone else's account gets charged instead of yours. It's also easier to surrender interests when they belong to someone else.

Although Madison designed our political system to protect minorities from the majorities, it failed early and often in regard to slaves. It was not that the system failed to function, but that slaves were left out of the system. On the one hand, they could not use it to protect themselves. On the other, those who did have access to it could use it to harm them. Had slaves had access to the political process, perhaps they could have used it to protect themselves. Had slaves been part of the delegations sent to Philadelphia, perhaps the convention would have been less willing or able to sacrifice their interests. Instead, the counter-majoritarian features of our government allowed the slave-holding minority to protect their "peculiar institution" from the majority.

This demonstrates a very important lesson, namely the importance of access to the political system. As we will see later, the Supreme Court considers rights relating to political participation fundamental, and offers them a much greater level of protection than other rights. Now you know why those rights are so important.

As you can imagine, working out all of these compromises took a great deal of time and effort. In other words, they are the evidence of some high decision-making costs. One of the things people do to reduce decision-making costs is to delegate. Delegation creates a principal–agent relationship; the principle delegates to an agent the authority to act (or make decisions) on her behalf.

How does this help with decision-making costs? Well, consider for a moment the delegates to the convention themselves. They were there acting on behalf of a large number of other people. The state legislatures which sent them could have traveled themselves and met to consider amendments to the Articles of Confederation. Why didn't they? It would have taken a great deal of time and effort to get a group that large together in the same room, let alone gotten them to make decisions. Instead, those groups sent people to represent them, reducing the time and effort it would take (both total and to them), lowering the decision-making costs. Likewise, as we have seen, the convention itself often delegated discussion of issues to committees to save themselves some time and effort in debate.

Perhaps it becomes clearer if we look at decision-making costs (and autonomy costs) in a more generic sense. Both decision-making and autonomy costs are types of opportunity costs. Now, I know what you're thinking: what's an opportunity cost? About a buck-fifty. (Sorry, it's hard to resist a straight line.) An opportunity cost is the next best alternative use for the resource in question. For example, if you have $15, you can spend it on an album from your favorite band. You can spend it on a nice dinner with friends. But you can't spend the same $15 twice, so you have to choose one or the other. The one you give up is the opportunity cost for that $15. You can have your cake, or you can eat it, but not both—the other, foregone alternative is an opportunity cost.

The same is true of your time and effort. You can spend an hour of your time on the treadmill or in the swimming pool, but you can't spend the same hour doing both (without serious risk of electrocution). Similarly, you can spend time making a decision, but you can't spend that time doing something else. So decision-making costs (the time and effort that go into making a decision with others) are opportunity costs (you could have spent that time doing something else). Delegation allows us to transfer these costs to someone else, so that they can spend their time making decisions for us, while we can spend our time on more attractive alternatives.

Of course, when we hire an agent, we may reduce our decision-making costs, but we also increase our autonomy costs. We bind ourselves to the actions of our agent, even if those actions are not what we would ourselves have wanted. Let's say you're sick and can't get out of bed. You give your roommate some money and ask him to get you some chicken noodle soup. He comes back with chicken gumbo soup instead. The difference between what you wanted done and what your agent did is an autonomy cost. If it's negative, we call it *agency loss*. The agency loss might be small (you like chicken gumbo, just not as much as chicken noodle) or large (you are allergic to okra). If it is positive (the spices in the gumbo help clear your sinuses better than chicken noodle), we would call it *agency gain*, if we worried about it at all.

Take, for example, Louisiana. Congress authorized Robert Livingston and (future president) James Monroe to offer Napoleon up to $2 million for the eastern bank of the Mississippi. President Jefferson authorized them to offer up to $10 million for the territory from Florida to New Orleans. During the negotiation, however, the French offered the whole of the Louisiana, and Livingston and Monroe negotiated a price of $15 million (approximately $11.25 million for the territory and $3.75 million to settle French obligations) and agreed to the purchase. They exceeded the instructions they had from their principal, President Jefferson, though Jefferson was glad they did.

Not all such situations turn out as happily. Had their actions cost Jefferson re-election, he might have been less pleased with their efforts. Certainly, the voters who sent George H.W. Bush to act on their behalf in preventing Congress from passing new taxes did not appreciate his failure to follow instruction, though he acted in what he thought was in their interest, as well. The Philadelphia Convention also delegated some decisions to others, saving themselves some long and difficult debate at the risk of suffering some agency loss.

Article II, which describes the office of President, is relatively short, a little less than half the length of Article I (both in terms of space on a page and in number of sections). Almost half of what length Article II does have is devoted to the process for selecting the President through the Electoral College. The delegates were so concerned about the potential for tyranny from having a demagogue elected that they concocted the complex Electoral College system to weaken the Presidency, insulating it from the mob and claims to a popular mandate. They considered making the executive plural to further weaken it. Yet in the end, they spent very little time enumerating the powers of the President. Article I, Section 8 has eighteen clauses; the first seventeen list in detail the powers of Congress, and the eighteenth specifically states that Congress has other powers not listed. Article II, Section 2, which lists the powers of the President, has three clauses and less detail. Having recently escaped monarchy and wary of the threat of authoritarianism, why did the convention delegate the definition of the President's power to future Presidents?

The delegates knew who their first agent in that regard would be, and they trusted him implicitly. They knew they had little to worry about in the form of agency loss from him. He was an historical oddity, a general who had led armies to victory and then gone back to his farm. The respect and awe in which his men held him allowed him to quell a coup d'etat with only a few words. The delegates themselves, in fact, had elected him President of the convention: George Washington.

To give you an idea of how well-placed their confidence was, consider the fact that Washington declined to run for a third term, despite having won the first two terms by unanimous ballot and unopposed. From that time, 1796, until Franklin Roosevelt in 1940, no President stood for re-election after having served two terms.[21] None of them were willing to claim that they were greater than George Washington—if two terms had been good enough for him, it was good enough for them. Not only did Washington set a good example in regard to the powers of the Presidency, but the force of his example lasted for nearly 150 years.

The convention made another delegation to the future. Article III of the Constitution, which defines the judicial branch, is not very definite. It has three sections with a total of six clauses, fewer than even the first section of Article II. It says there will be a Supreme Court, but leaves to Congress the establishment of lower federal courts (explicitly) and the number of Supreme Court justices (implicitly). It defines the Court's jurisdiction and separates it into original and appellate, but allows Congress to modify the appellate.

Why this delegation? The decision-making costs regarding the judicial branch were not likely all that much in and of themselves. After spending so much time and energy debating the legislative and executive branches and the provisions in the other articles, it was not the length and intensity of debate on the judiciary that posed a problem, but simply that there would be some debate, and the summer was almost over. Having set the basic parameters, leaving the details to Congress did not seem to promise much agency loss. After all, most of them were likely candidates to be in the first Congress.

In the next chapter, we will discuss the central feature (and greatest innovation) of the Philadelphia Convention, before moving on to look at the institutions the Constitution creates. First, though, let's take a moment to look back at where we've been. We need a written constitution to define the players and the rules of the game in government. Although this is a useful thing in a lot of theoretical traditions, it is necessary in the Lockean tradition, where the law is the highest authority.

A constitution is also necessary in that tradition because of the emphasis the Lockean tradition puts on the preservation of liberty. That emphasis encourages more complex governmental relationships, like the separation of powers. The separation of powers is useful in securing liberty since it reduces the moral hazard of holding power. When power is separated, there is less in any one party's hands to tempt them to malfeasance. It also creates alternative loci of power which may prevent that abuse should one officer or branch succumb to the moral hazard. Specifying who gets what power makes a written constitution very useful, if not an outright necessity.

---

21 And, despite the occasional flaunting of the powers of the President, not until Theodore Roosevelt in the early 1900s did a President argue that Article II contained an "elastic clause" that gave broad power to the President. In other words, not for 110 years did a President use the vagueness of Article II to claim additional powers under the Constitution.

The Articles of Confederation were the first constitution of the young United States, but as a confederation, it failed to solve some of the collective action problems the nation needed it to solve. In forming a confederation, the states had been too jealous of their newly-won sovereignty and had not delegated enough power to the central government for it to be effective. As a result, the situation in many of the states began to deteriorate, until an armed rebellion in Massachusetts provided the impetus states needed to initiate reform. They called a second convention in Philadelphia, where James Madison set the terms of debate early with a radical proposal for a truly national government.

Smaller states responded with a more modest proposal, one which kept the basic structure of the Articles but included changes to address the most pressing problems. Debate quickly focused on the composition and powers of the legislature, finally producing a compromise in which one chamber of a bicameral legislature would each have the selection and apportionment method of one of the proposals, and the lower chamber would have the sole authority to introduce revenue bills. The convention delegated the ability to define some executive powers to the first President, and delegated some decision-making about the judiciary to the first Congress. Delegation is attractive because it reduces decision making costs, but it also introduces the possibility of agency loss.

Delegation is also part of the definition of a republic. A republic is a representative democracy with constrained majority rule. Representative democracy is the alternative to direct democracy, in which the citizens themselves comprise the legislature. Some small towns in New England and Switzerland still practice this. The entire town comes together to discuss and vote on public matters. As you can imagine, though, this is difficult to do once one moves much beyond the size of a very small town.

Decision making costs are what make it so difficult. It's hard to get that many people in the same place, let alone get them to make a decision together. Think of you and your friends trying to order a pizza together; now think of your state trying to order a pizza together. To reduce these costs, we select people to represent us and send them to make decisions together for us. Thus, we have a representative democracy.

The separation of powers is one constraint on the power of the majority. If all of the power is in the hands of a majority, they can get whatever they want. The difficulty is that what a majority wants is not necessarily the right thing, either for the majority or for others. Remember, the prisoners in the prisoner's dilemma choose what they want, as well, but would rather have something which prevents choices that lead to suboptimal outcomes. The separation of power can help do that, in that it often requires the cooperation of other groups, increasing deliberation.

Madison, however, did not rely solely on the separation of powers into three branches to protect individual liberty. Another part of his design was federalism. We turn to that fundamental element of the Constitution in the next chapter.

Chapter 3: Federalism

It's easy to forget that federalism was one of the innovations of the Philadelphia Convention. Certainly, as Ecclesiastes[1] tells us and Shakespeare[2] reminds us, there is nothing new under the sun, but the compound republic was something the world had not seen before, even if it had seen some relatives. So before we get into the reasons for that innovation, let's look at what a federal structure looks like.

There have been many variations in the design of federal institutions since their inception in that warm Philadelphia summer. The United States' structure has changed over time, and other countries have made their own adaptations in adopting federalism. The defining feature of a federal system, however, is divided (or concurrent) sovereignty. Sovereignty is essentially the right to rule someone or something. As you may remember from Hobbes and Locke, individuals are originally sovereign over themselves, but delegate some of this sovereignty in order to make better use of the rest (according to Rousseau, they are duped into surrendering it).[3]

To see what we mean by divided sovereignty, let's look at some of the alternative structures. In a unitary government, people delegate sovereignty (in whole or in part) to a single, central (presumably national) government. That government may in turn create subnational administrative units in order to more easily carry out its duties.[4] These administrative units exist only due to the national authority and have only the authority the national government extends to them. France, for example, has a unitary form of government. The national government divides the country into *départements* (departments) for its own administrative convenience, and may redraw or eliminate those boundaries as it wishes. The same relationship exists between states and their counties in the United States. The flow of sovereignty is from the national government to the subunits (see Figure 3.1).

In a confederal government, on the other hand, people first create the more local level of government. Here terminology begins to fail us, as these more local forms of government may well begin their existence as nations, or at least with pretensions to be such. They have historically tended to be smaller, weaker nations, though that is not necessary to the definition. These nations then find that they have problems—collective action problems—that they could solve through the creation of a government between them. They create and delegate limited authority to a central, supranational government. The Articles of Confederation, for example, were such an attempt by the colonies to solve collective action problems, an attempt which succeeded imperfectly. Switzerland began its existence as a confederation of cantons for the purpose of self-defense (trying to make sure they were left out of the Holy Roman Empire). The flow of sovereignty in a confederation is again a straight line, only this time the central government is the creation of the local governments. People delegate sovereignty to a state (in the generic sense, whether called state, canton, or land), which then creates a central government between it and other states (see Figure 3.1). The central government is the creature of the state governments; its authority depends on theirs, both its existence and its extent.

---

1 Ecclesiastes 1:9.

2 Sonnet 59.

3 To quote the great existential philosopher Nelson Munz, "HA-HA!"

4 They are, in essence, a delegatory response to high transaction costs.

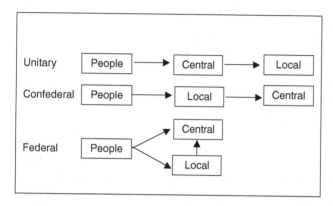

Figure 3.1 Delegations of Sovereignty

A federation, then, is different in that it has divided sovereignty. In the other sets of arrangements, the sovereignty which people delegate stays within a single chain-of-command, as it were. One government is, in terms of authority, a subset of another. In a federal system, however, the people divide the sovereignty they delegate into two parts, and entrust each one to a different level of government (see—you guessed it—Figure 3.1). Each one is independent of the other in regard to the source of its authority, so neither may (in theory) tell the other what to do in that other's bailiwick. At the same time, they often need to work together. Because neither can impose its will on the other (again, at least in theory[5]), there are no conformity costs, which should tell us that transaction costs on decisions between levels are high.

Why adopt such a high-friction structure for government? To answer that, let's begin with a puzzle from our old friend Montesquieu. Montesquieu once observed that the republican form of government was doomed to failure, for a republic would be either large or small. If it were the former, the republic would disintegrate from internal dissention, as it encompassed too diverse a set of interests to allow it to function. If the latter, the republic might function on its own terms, but, as a small state, would be vulnerable to the predation of larger neighbors.

James Madison, however, saw a solution to this problem: the compound republic. Madison's argument begins in Federalist 10 with the mischief of factions. Madison defines a faction as "a number of citizens, whether amounting to a majority or a minority of the whole, who are united and actuated by some common impulse of passion, or of interest, adverse to the rights of other citizens, or to the permanent and aggregate interests of the community." According to Madison, the mischief of faction is "that the public good is disregarded in the conflicts of rival parties."

There are, then, two ways to deal with this mischief: to remove the causes of faction, and to control the effects of faction. In medicine, they would pose this choice as treating the disease or treating the symptoms. There are again two means to accomplishing the first: to remove liberty, or to remove all differences between individuals. Madison explains the futility of the former using a wonderful simile. Liberty is to faction as air is to fire. Just as we could prevent a lot of destructive fires by eliminating all air, we could prevent destructive faction by eliminating liberty. Unfortunately, in both cases, the cure is worse than the disease. While air is necessary to fire, it is also necessary to life, just as liberty is necessary to both faction and political life. Certainly, a doctor may likewise prevent a patient of dying from cancer by killing her. We would hardly consider that an appropriate treatment, however; the point is to preserve the patient while eliminating the disease.

Let us then rule out the option of removing liberty as being counterproductive. We might still remove the cause of faction by removing the differences between individuals. If we could transform people so that they all had the same interests, then there could be no factions with interests opposed to those of others, and individual interests would be the same as the public interest. We could then safely leave individuals at perfect liberty. Think, though, about the level of conformity this requires. To keep from having different interests, we would all have to be of the same height, weight, gender, athletic ability, intelligence, disposition—even hair color and length. For that matter, we would all have to be the same age.[6] This is physically impossible.

Attempts to produce this level of conformity in the past have therefore usually involved removing liberty. The Communist Party of the Soviet Union, for example, tried to reshape humanity into "Soviet man" by

---

5 A friend of mine who teaches math and computer science has a saying: "If theory and reality don't coincide, the mathematician says, 'Screw reality.'" (His name is Dietmar Link.)

6 Remember Dr. Seuss' Sneetches and those without stars upon thars?

ensuring that every citizen had the same set of interests (coincidentally, the party's set of interests). They had to resort to coercion, to removing liberty, in order to create the effect of what they could not actually create.

Even if it were physically possible to re-engineer humanity to that degree, who would want to live in that world? The conformity costs are astronomical. We are talking about a world without the opposite gender. Not only does that remove future generations, but it also removes a great deal of joy (and pain) from life. Since we would all have to be the same age, presumably we would all mature in tanks. Think of all the joys of childhood you would have to miss. Let us reject this option as impossible, and unattractive even if it were so.

This leaves us with the second way to combat the mischief of faction. If we cannot keep factions from forming, then we must keep factions from being able to cause mischief. How are we to do this? Madison again outlines two cases for us. The faction whose mischief we wish to prevent may be a minority or a majority of the population. If the faction is a minority of the whole, Madison tells us, we have nothing to worry about from them. The use of a majority decision-making rule will prevent them from passing laws which favor themselves at the expense of others.

On this point, practice has regrettably proved Madison's expectations wrong. Certainly, no single minority can pass a law by itself. The difficulty is that several minorities can combine to form a majority on a given bill, or a given set of bills. Minorities are able to logroll, to trade votes across bills (thus the reference to a set of bills). The term comes from lumberjacking,[7] where lumberjacks used to float trees down rivers to mills. If they sent them down end-first, one of the logs was likely to catch that flat surface on some obstruction in the river and then catch other logs, until the logs jammed the river (a logjam). If they sent the logs down sideways, they could roll over obstructions. In fact, lumberjacks could "walk" logs down the river, making sure the logs kept rolling by spinning them with their feet.

In the same way, minorities can agree to roll their bills through a legislature. By combining their votes, they may be able to keep all of their bills moving through the legislature. The only caveats are that there must be enough of them to constitute a majority (or at least, a majority of those voting[8]), and they must find bills that do not threaten each other. Usually this is a redistributive bill, taking money from everyone and giving chunks of it to smaller groups. So long as you get your cut from the take, you're happy to let others get theirs.[9] In fairness to Madison, though, he did not design a government capable of much redistribution, so perhaps we may forgive him for failing to anticipate this.

What he did anticipate were the problems a faction could cause under majority rule if that faction constituted a majority of the population. In this case, a majority could use its authority to oppress minorities. Madison suggested a two-pronged solution to this problem. The first part of the solution was to increase the size of the republic, thereby increasing the diversity of the interests which the republic encompassed. The greater the number of interests, the less likely it is that any one interest could command the support of a majority of the population.[10]

This, of course, brings us back to Montesquieu's observation on the fate of large republics. This very diversity of interest would cause the republic to disintegrate into warring factions. Madison answered this quandary with the compound republic, a large republic made of smaller republics. Forging a larger republic above and between smaller republics, maintaining two sovereignties, combines the benefits of a large republic (strength against outside threats, diversity of interest against tyranny of the majority) with the cohesion of a small republic. At the same time, the benefits of each address the shortcomings of either separately.

A compound republic provides another security against democratic tyranny, as well. The separation of powers, remember, is a feature of a republic designed to guard against the abuse of power, by individuals or combinations thereof. The compound republic offers another level across which to divide that power. Think of

---

7 . . . and I'm okay.

8 This may come as a shock, but not every representative participates in every vote; this would make it easier for minorities to pass their bills.

9 Of course, the problem is that you are also among those being taken.

10 On the other hand, this increases the likelihood that minorities are able to form a majority for logrolling.

Mao Tse-tung's famous aphorism that power flows from the barrel of a gun. If we disassemble that gun, we can be more confident that no one will abuse (through intent or accident) that power. Federalism, the compound republic, allows us to separate that gun into more pieces, making it that much more difficult (and therefore less likely) for any one person or group to get their hands on enough of it to cause harm.

Of course, the drawback to this is that it can make it much more difficult to get things done. This tells us something about the values of our founding fathers, namely, that they preferred the risk of foregoing a useful bill to the risk of allowing a harmful bill. Our system is designed to allow groups to prevent things which harm them, rather than to achieve their desires at the expense of others.

So there's the purpose of this complex compound republic: to protect individual liberty. That this (admittedly complex) division of power serves such an important purpose raises a very difficult question. If the preservation of liberty depends upon the maintenance of this complex system, who's the superintendent? Who watches to make sure that this sovereignty stays divided?

One immediate and perhaps obvious answer to this is the U.S. Supreme Court. After all, they are the institution charged with ensuring the integrity of the Constitution. Surely part of that job is, or should be, to oversee the boundaries between state and national which the Constitution establishes as part of its system.

Yet the question we must ask is, can we rely on the Supreme Court to fulfill that duty?[11] Let us consider the question theoretically before we look at it practically. The role of the judge is to apply abstract law to particular circumstances. Although it may not at first appear so, there is a good deal of discretion in this. The judge must first decide which law is the appropriate one to apply, and then decide whether the circumstances of the case meet the criteria of that law.

For this reason, it is an oft-quoted principle of law that no man[12] should be judge in his own cause. It presents a moral hazard, and one that does not necessarily present a conscious decision. Certainly, a judge with an interest in the outcome of a case may consciously select and apply the law so as to produce an outcome more favorable to that interest. For this reason, judges with direct, personal interest in the outcome of a case recuse themselves from considering it. In fact, judges with an identifiable indirect interest often do as well, simply to avoid the mere appearance of impropriety.

More difficult, however, is a case in which a judge has an interest of which the judge herself[13] is unaware. Take, for example, your parents. Have you ever heard them remark that they just did something their parents did to them, and that they had sworn never to do to their children? When they were on the child end of it, they could not understand what made their parents behave that way. Once they *became* parents, however, their perspective changed, even though they were not aware of it—until they caught themselves repeating their parents' behavior.[14] Their perspective as parents colored their decision-making without their being aware of it. Or, to quote another famous aphorism, where you stand depends upon where you sit.

Likewise, Supreme Court justices probably do not feel they have any direct interest in increasing the scope of federal authority at the expense of state sovereignty. Nevertheless, they are officials in the national government, and this may affect their perspective without their knowing it. For example, they might be more inclined to believe arguments that state officers are less reliable than national officers. After all, as national officers, they know that they are reliable. And while they may not consciously identify with one side or another, they may do so subconsciously. This is not to cast blame on those judges, because the same would be true of me or you in that situation (unless, as Madison points out, we were angels). What it does tell us, however, is that we have some theoretical reason to believe that the Supreme Court might not be the safest guardian of the balance between state and federal sovereignty.

Do we have any practical reasons for thinking so? That is, do we have any evidence that the Supreme Court favors the national side over the state? Unfortunately, the answer is yes and no. We have some evidence, which

---

11 And don't call me Shirley.

12 Nor woman, gender making a person no less fallible.

13 Kalyn Burns.

14 Want to know the sad truth? One day this will happen to you.

we shall discuss shortly, but we do not have what we might call conclusive evidence. Nor can we. We shall look at a selection of the Court's decisions below, but we must keep in mind the limitations of that evidence, and what conclusions we may or may not properly draw from it.

First, if the Court decides a case in favor of the national government, it may well be that such was indeed the fair, appropriate, and unbiased disposition of the case. After all, the framers designed the Constitution to give some powers to the federal government at the expense of state authority. That was in fact the point of the Constitution. The question is whether the power in question belongs rightly, according to the Constitution, to the federal or state government. The mere fact that the Court decided in favor of one or the other does not answer that question.

Second, we must keep in mind that this evidence, while representing some of the most important and most relevant cases, does not represent a complete picture. In order to get a complete picture, we would have to look at every Supreme Court case, and know what the "true" disposition of that case was, in order to see if the Supreme Court deviated from those dispositions in some systematic fashion. So we must evaluate the evidence knowing that the selection is partial. Moreover, it is partial in two senses: it is incomplete, and I (no less fallible than others) have likely selected them with an eye toward making my point.

Finally, even if we could be absolutely sure of our interpretation of the Constitution, and if we could be sure we had looked at every Supreme Court case, we would still have one last methodological flaw: dogs that don't bark. Imagine that you want to count the number of dogs in a neighborhood, but you have to go at night. You can't walk around other people's property (without getting a seat full of buckshot), so you plan to listen for dogs to bark as you slowly drive past. Is this likely to be an accurate count of the dogs in that neighborhood? It's okay—stop reading for a moment and think about it. I'll be here when you get back.

So what do you think? Is this an accurate measure? In order for that to happen, we have to make an assumption, namely, that every dog barks at cars. Certainly most dogs do. But can we safely assume that, on this night, every dog will bark?

Probably not. Some dogs don't bark.[15] Some owners may have muzzles on their dogs. Some dogs are hard of hearing, and may not hear the car. Some dogs may be asleep, or inside a house where we cannot hear their bark. So simply counting the number of different barks, bays, and howls we hear is not sufficient to accurately measure the number of dogs in the neighborhood.[16]

In the same way, not every challenge of federalism creates a court case. Not all of the ones that do so reach the Supreme Court. So, in order to be sure, we would have to look at not only every Supreme Court case, or even every court case in the United States, and discern each one's impact (or lack thereof) on federalism, but we would also have to look at the court cases that *didn't* happen. This, of course, is physically impossible.

So what can we do with this evidence? If we wish to accuse the Supreme Court of bias, we can have circumstantial evidence, at best. We can look at the reasoning which the Court provides, and evaluate that reasoning for soundness and consistency. That is, if the Court suddenly changes the way it reads words, or makes logical leaps without foundations, we might have reason to suspect that they have something to hide—that they are trying to stretch the case to the outcome they want, rather than fitting the outcome to the case. But we must remember that we cannot claim to have proved our case. We must learn to live with probability, rather than certainty.

Some of you may need a moment to catch your breath at the notion of abandoning certainty that way. Certainty is a luxury we rarely have in life, though (for our own mental health) we often pretend otherwise. But remember that even in murder trials, the standard of proof is "beyond a reasonable doubt," not "beyond the shadow of a doubt." We cannot remove all doubt. It is always *possible* that the evidence in a court case speaks so firmly of the defendant's guilt because someone has done a really good job framing her. In most cases, however, it is very *unlikely*. That is the function of reason—to evaluate the quality of the doubt that remains.

---

15 The basenji, for example, is an entire breed of dogs that do not bark.

16 It's a beautiful night in the neighborhood, though. Won't you be my neighbor?

Let us, then, proceed to the evidence. The Court has interpreted many parts of the Constitution, in relation to a large number of issues. Three of these, however, are of particular importance: the appellate jurisdiction of the Supreme Court over state supreme courts, the necessary and proper clause, and the commerce clause. Each of these touches directly on the distribution of power between the state and federal governments. Of course, other issues have touched upon that relationship, as well—substantive due process, incorporation, the taxing and spending clause—but none have been quite so central to the question as these three.

One of the earliest and most important cases dealing with the division of sovereignty in the federal system is *Martin v. Hunter's Lessee*. This decision was the second time the Supreme Court had seen this case, and the case has a somewhat complicated backstory. I will attempt to present a simplified account; if you wish to know more, please consult the record of the case.[17] The story begins with Lord Fairfax, a subject of the British crown who owned land in Virginia before the Revolution.

Lord Fairfax returned to England when the Revolution began, and upon his death left his holdings in Virginia to his nephew, Denny Martin, also a subject of the British crown. A Virginia law passed after the Revolution (and before Fairfax's death) prohibited foreign subjects from inheriting land in Virginia. Upon Fairfax's death, the Commonwealth of Virginia seized his property and sold it to some investors, David Hunter among them. The Treaty of Paris (1783) and subsequent Jay Treaty (1794), however, implicitly and explicitly provided for the protection of British subjects' property rights. The Martin family tried to sell the land (to their family lawyer, John Marshall, and his brother, James, among others), and Hunter tried to lease it to someone else. Each party then sued to eject the other from the land, Hunter (and then his lessee) claiming title to it based on the act of Virginia, the Martin family on the basis of the acts of the United States.

This case took several years to work its way through the court system; in fact, by the time it reached the Supreme Court the first time, the Martins' lawyer had become Chief Justice John Marshall. In *Fairfax's Devisee v. Hunter's Lessee*,[18] Justice Story's[19] opinion for the Court found that the federal treaty took precedence over state law and instructed the Virginia Court of Appeals (the name of the Commonwealth's highest court at the time) to enter the Supreme Court's reversal of its judgment.

The Virginia court then heard arguments on whether it should enter the judgment or not. In *Hunter v. Martin, Devisee of Fairfax*, the Court of Appeals ruled that it had forwarded the record of the case "improvidently," because the Supreme Court of the United States did not have appellate jurisdiction over it (or other state courts). As Justice Cabell of the Court of Appeals explained, the Constitution created a system of dual sovereignty. The federal and state governments are each the sole authority within their own sphere of authority. Thus, the federal courts might *also* have jurisdiction over the case (concurrent jurisdiction), but they could not have appellate jurisdiction over state courts.

Article III, Section 2 of the Constitution defines the scope of the judicial power of the federal government in terms of cases. The judicial power, or jurisdiction, of the federal government extends to all cases involving the Constitution, federal law and treaties, ambassadors and other public ministers, maritime laws, cases to which the United States is a party, and those involving disputes between states, citizens of different states, combinations thereof, and between one of those and a foreign state or citizen. The second clause of this section divides this jurisdiction into two categories, original and extra crispy—err, appellate.

Original jurisdiction means that the court is the court of first instance, the first court to hear the case, also known as the trial court. The case begins, or originates, in that court (hence the name of this type of jurisdiction). The court hears evidence from both sides and reaches a verdict. In some cases a jury of citizens renders the verdict, with the judge refereeing the contest between opposing attorneys. Certainly these are the cases most prominent in television and movies, but they are not the only sort. In other cases, a judge (or panel of judges) hears the evidence and reaches a decision on guilt or innocence. The important distinction in this

---

17 14 US 304 (1816).

18 A *devisee* is someone who inherits through a will or other legal instrument.

19 Marshall recused himself from this case and the subsequent one.

context, however, is that courts in original jurisdiction hear evidence, decide which evidence is reliable and therefore factual, and apply the law to those facts, thereby determining the outcome.

Appellate courts, on the other hand, tend to hear arguments, rather than evidence. This is something of an oversimplification, because there are always exceptions. But the distinction helps clarify the difference between these two types of jurisdiction. Appellate courts review the decisions of lower courts (and at the first level of appeal, that's the trial court) for errors in the interpretation or application of the law. One party may claim that the trial court improperly admitted evidence—that the court did not correctly apply the law regarding the admissibility of evidence, and that this error harmed them. They appeal to the higher court to redress their grievance—to heal their injury.

Notice the difference in terminology we've already encountered—"lower" and "higher" courts. The exercise of appellate jurisdiction by one court over another implies a particular relationship between the two courts, namely, that one is subject to the other. This is the heart of Justice Cabell's argument. Since the two courts (the Virginia Court of Appeals and the United States Supreme Court) were each the highest courts of separate sovereigns, there could not be such a relationship between them.

The second clause of Article III, Section 2, however, defines the appellate jurisdiction of the Supreme Court in terms of cases, the same terms the first clause uses to define federal jurisdiction generally. Of those types of cases listed, it says, those having to do with ambassadors and other public ministers, as well as those to which a state is a party, are in the Court's original jurisdiction. All others fall in its appellate jurisdiction.

This is the heart of Justice Storey's argument. Clearly, this case involved the interpretation and application of a treaty of the United States. Clearly, Article III, Section 2 grants appellate jurisdiction over such cases to the U.S. Supreme Court. It makes no reference to the court of origin, but only to the nature of the case. Thus, it is the case, not the court, which determines jurisdiction. End of Storey.[20]

Or is it?[21] Let's examine Justice Storey's nice, clear logic a little more closely. Where does the appellate jurisdiction of the Court stop, if his reasoning is true? Let's imagine for a moment the circumstances in this case are reversed. Assume Britain had promised in a treaty to respect the property rights of U.S. citizens, and had dispossessed an American of his inheritance in Britain. That case, in a British court, would still involve a treaty made under the authority of the United States, and would still involve a conflict between a U.S. citizen and a foreign state (or one of its citizens). Thus, according to Justice Storey's argument, this case falls within the appellate jurisdiction of the U.S. Supreme Court. Think about that for a second—we've just declared that the U.S. Supreme Court has appellate jurisdiction over foreign courts! And it's not a close call—it very clearly conforms to not one, but two of the categories. Quick show of hands—who wants to be the one to tell the other countries?[22]

Suddenly, we are back at Justice Cabell's argument. As Cabell points out, Storey's reading of these clauses in the Constitution produces results which can't possibly be true—therefore, neither can that interpretation. If, instead, we read the distinction between original and appellate jurisdiction as a description of the division of labor between the Supreme Court and lower federal courts, we have no such problem. Then, since the case does not provide the jurisdiction, it also does not provide it over foreign courts.

Problem solved! We have a neat, clean answer, we've tidied up the kitchen and put the leftovers away. Time to punch out, go home and relax. Oh, wait a minute—what's that over there? Another problem. If the Supreme Court does not have appellate jurisdiction over state courts when it comes to interpreting treaties or the Constitution . . . then we might end up with fifty-one different versions of the law. We won't have one single, authoritative voice to tell us our rights and obligations. There will be instead a great deal of uncertainty, and the amount of freedom one enjoys might vary from state to state. People could rig cases by selecting venues more favorable to their case! (The petitioner, the person alleging an injury, picks the court with which to lodge the complaint.) Whatever shall we do? Wherever shall we go?

---

20 C'mon, you didn't seriously expect me to forego that pun, did you?

21 Of course it isn't. And you knew it wasn't. That's a leading question (I object, your Honor! He's leading the witness!).

22 Did I forget to mention that the highest court in Britain is the upper house of their legislature? Surely they won't notice.

Turn the panic alarm off, Judy.[23] First, lawyers do (or try to do) this anyway, based on the judge or jury pool in a particular area. More importantly, though, and as Justice Cabell reminds us, so long as there is a provision allowing the respondent (the person accused of harming the petitioner) to remove the case to federal jurisdiction—as there was then and is now—then no one may be disadvantaged by differences in state constructions of the law. Federal constructions would always prevail precisely there where they are most needed. Either the petitioner would file it in federal court because it advantaged his case, or the respondent would remove it there to avoid disadvantaging her case. Where there is no need, however, to make a federal case out of it, this still allows for states to introduce better interpretation (which the Supreme Court might want to adopt), or at least interpretation better suited to that state's circumstances. In fact, Section 9 of the Judiciary Act of 1789 expressly grants this kind of jurisdiction—concurrent jurisdiction—to the state courts in cases involving a foreigner suing under a treaty of the United States.

To Justice Storey, however, the unity of the law is more important—even though the law in question is that of a compound republic, with multiple sources of authority by definition. So Storey's logic doesn't fit with the nature of the law he's interpreting, and its logic is not compelling beyond its face.[24] So those qualities could not recommend it to him. This reasoning, however, does increase the scope of federal power (in fact, it increases it beyond belief, as we saw), and with it, the scope of the Supreme Court's power. This is not to say that Justice Storey was corrupt or conniving, but that his position may have influenced which purpose he found more compelling.[25]

Let's look at another case from the early years of the court, *McCulloch v. Maryland*. James W. McCulloch was the cashier of the Baltimore branch of the Second Bank of the United States. Perhaps we should take a moment to explain a little more about the Second Bank of the United States. We often see banks today giving a rank and region in their names, like "Third National Bank" or "First Tennessee Bank." These banks are all private, however—the regional part of their title may refer to the area of the country they serve, or they may have chosen it because it sounded impressive. They did not, however, choose it because of who owns or charters them. That is, the State of Tennessee does not own or operate a bank, and the national government only owns and operates one: the Federal Reserve Bank.

Well, that's not entirely accurate. What the federal government operates is the Federal Reserve System, which consists of twelve regional Federal Reserve Banks.[26] Yes, that's how committed we are to federalism in the United States; even our central bank is decentralized. The Federal Reserve System plays a vital role in the government's management of the economy, one which we may discuss in greater detail later.[27] For now, though, suffice it to say that the Fed regulates the economy by influencing the amount of money in circulation, and therefore the level of inflation. The Second Bank of the United States played a similar role in its day (as did the First Bank before it), allowing the government to regulate the money supply, and thereby the economy.

In fact, this may have been even more vital in the Second Bank's day, since the federal government was not the only entity which issued money. Any bank, including private banks, could issue currency, making it more difficult for the federal government to control the amount of money in circulation. Indeed, the mere existence of the Second Bank is testament to its importance in regulating the economy. The President who supported chartering it has strongly opposed the chartering of the First Bank, and allowed its charter to expire. Life without the Bank, however, convinced James Madison of its utility.

Others, however, were still not as fond of the idea. Many states, including the State of Maryland, took action to limit the ability of the Bank to regulate their economies. Maryland passed a tax on the banknotes the Bank issued, and James McCulloch refused to pay that tax. Now, McCulloch was hardly an upstanding

---

23 Or whatever you call the panicky little girl in your head (Scarlett, for example).

24 And logic, like beauty, is more than skin deep.

25 That position being "within arm's reach of John Marshall," who with his brother James had purchased some of the land in question from his erstwhile clients, the Martins.

26 On old currency, the Federal Reserve's seal featured a letter indicating which Federal Reserve Bank had issued it, and the Bank's name appeared in the circle of the seal. These letters are still on coins, usually under the date.

27 If there's a chapter about economic policy, we will. If there's not . . . you never know what might come up.

defender of constitutional principles. It was his embezzlement[28] of bank funds through fraudulent loans to himself and friends, as well as other means, which stoked the fires of opposition in Maryland. The total losses from his. . . mismanagement totaled about $1.7 million, and that's in early-1800s dollars. To give you an idea, the *U.S.S. Constitution*, the famous battleship commissioned about twenty years earlier, cost a mere $302,700. Think of someone making off with enough money to buy five battleships. So when McCulloch refused to pay the tax, arguing that Maryland did not have the authority to tax a federal entity, principles of federalism may have been less his concern than Maryland's cutting into his action.

Nevertheless, when Maryland prosecuted McCulloch for his failure to pay the tax, he appealed his conviction, and the case came eventually to the U.S. Supreme Court. According to Marshall's opinion for the Court, this case presented the Court with two questions. First, did Congress have the authority to charter a bank? Maryland contended that it did not, and that this prevented McCulloch from hiding behind federal authority. Second, if Congress *could* charter a bank, could Maryland (or any other state) tax it? McCulloch maintained that Maryland had no authority to tax a federal agency, and therefore he had not violated any valid law in refusing to pay.

Let's look at the questions in that order ourselves (since it may spare us from having to answer the second one at all). Look at Article I, Section 8 in the Constitution. These are the enumerated powers of Congress. Do you see the words *charter* or *bank*? Go ahead, see for yourself—it doesn't take long to read. Did you see anything there that directly gives Congress the authority to charter a bank? Remember, the principle of enumerated powers says[29] that if it ain't on the list, it doesn't exist.

Back so soon? Are you sure you want to take my word for it? I mean, I'm a decent fellow, but you don't know me, so you'd have to take my word for that, too. And being a decent fellow, I have to point out to you that you're still taking a stranger's[30] word, with no idea how reliable that word is. After all, people who want to defraud and deceive you will also tell you that you can take their word for it. If I told you to invest $500 in a stock because I knew it was about to double, would you?[31] Maybe you should go look for yourself.

In fact, neither the word *charter* nor the word *bank* occurs in the enumeration of Congress' power. There's something about coining money and regulating its value, but that doesn't require a bank. And that question becomes precisely **the** question because of the final clause in Article I, Section 8: the necessary and proper clause.

Have you ever made a shopping list and realized, when you got to the store or when you got back home, that you had left something off the list? Maybe it would be easier to ask if there's been a time when that hasn't happened. The Founders had had that experience, except that it wasn't with a shopping list. It was with our first constitution. After enumerating the powers of that U.S. Congress (under the Articles of Confederation), they wrote that it did not have any powers which weren't *explicitly* delegated. Literally, if it wasn't on the list, it didn't exist. In practice, however, they found their new confederal government hamstrung, because it did not have powers it needed in order to do the things they had formed it to do. And while they added the two powers (taxing and commerce) experience had shown were most lacking, they were wise enough to realize that they might have made the same mistake of omission this time, too. Thus the necessary and proper clause, which creates the implied powers of Congress.

What do we mean when we say "implied"? The logic of implied powers is tied to the enumerated ones. Essentially, if the framers gave a power to the federal government, they obviously intended for the government to use that power. Therefore, they also gave it any powers it would need in order to use the ones they gave it. Of course, allowing the implication of unwritten powers can lead to piling implication upon implication until limitations on government power are buried and disappear. To prevent this process of reasoning from becoming a "Six Degrees of Kevin Bacon"-like hop, skip, and jump to tyranny, the framers provided explicit limitations on what one may infer in this manner.

---

28 The fancy Latin word for this is "defalcation," from the verb "to defalcate," which literally refers to skimming off the top. Do, however, be sure to pronounce the *l* when speaking!

29 or, more accurately, "sez."

30 and let's face it, they don't come much stranger, do they?

31 If so, please send a check made payable to Nathan Griffith . . .

First, the requirement that the implied power relate to an enumerated one limits the scope for interpretation. "Six Degrees of Kevin Bacon" is a little harder than "Six Degrees of Anyone."[32] Second, and more importantly, the language of the clause provides two qualifications on that relationship—that the claimed power must be both necessary and proper to the enumerated power.

This, of course, begs the question of how to tell if the government needs a power it is claiming as implied, or whether it just wants it. What does it mean to say that something is necessary or proper? Let's begin with *proper*. What do we mean when we say that it is proper, or appropriate? Well, if your professor showed up for class wearing only a skimpy bathing suit, would that be appropriate? Some of you are probably struggling to keep your last meal down at this point, and some of you are probably hearing "Dreamweaver" over some Baywatch-esque mental imagery.[33] The smart alecks among you, however, are already thinking that it depends on what class you're talking about. And you're exactly right—for most classes for which you'd be reading this text, it would be highly inappropriate (leaving aside the question of undesirable).

For a swimming class, however, or one on lifeguarding skills, a swimsuit would be entirely appropriate—and standard classroom attire inappropriate. So *proper* means that it fits into the context, that the means relate to the particular end. In other words, a proper implied power is one which is related to one of the enumerated powers. It is a means which would reasonably promote the end for which it was selected. So if the enumerated power were eating soup, a fork would not be a very appropriate means.

That leaves us with *necessary*. What does it mean to say that something is necessary? This was the question at the heart of Marshall's answer to the first question in our case (*McCulloch v. Maryland*, remember?). Perhaps you're familiar with the ideas of necessary and sufficient causes. A sufficient cause is one whose presence—regardless of the presence or absence of other causes—produces the effect. A necessary cause, however, doesn't guarantee the effect by its presence, but guarantees the absence of the effect if it is absent. The effect can't happen without it.

The fancy Latin way to express this is *sine qua non*, or "not without this." And this is the standard legal interpretation of the word, as well. In international law as well as elsewhere in the Supreme Court's case law,[34] and for that matter in the dictionary, the word *necessary* means "not without this." Everywhere but in John Marshall's opinion in *McCulloch v. Maryland*.

Here, Marshall explicitly rejects that definition of the word necessary, saying that it is only the definition when one says "*absolutely* necessary." Marshall's reasoning for this is that to read it that way would deprive the legislature of the ability to adopt the best legislation, according to its wisdom. And this, Marshall maintains, is more than the Framers could have intended.

Except, of course, for the fact that this is exactly the point of a constitution, and especially of one based on enumerated (or limited) powers. The Bill of Rights exists specifically to tell Congress things it can't do, even if they are, in Congress' judgment, the best way to do things. Marshall instead reads the word *necessary* to mean *convenient*. That is, so long as Congress claims to be pursuing a goal the Constitution allows it to pursue, any measure which might accomplish that goal, and which the Constitution does not specifically forbid, is constitutional.

Note that this turns the logic of the necessary and proper clause on its head. The burden of proof was on Congress, to show how the measure was necessary to one of the enumerated powers. Marshall changes this, so that the burden falls on those who would challenge Congress' action, who must show that some part of the Constitution forbids it. This, of course, undermines the entire purpose of a constitution of enumerated powers. In fact, it comes closer to assuming the federal government has every power *except* for those listed as forbidden—enumerated lacunae,[35] as it were, rather than powers.

---

32 By the way, I can connect myself to Kevin Bacon is less than six steps. I was in home movies with my brother, who was in training films with a basketball coach, who is in a video with Vince Gill, who has been in videos with Reba McIntire, who was in *Tremors* with . . .

33 If the latter, you are likely a student of Joachim Rennstich or Susan Jellissen. My students have long since gone into convulsions at the thought.

34 in particular in the concept of strict scrutiny, about which we will later talk more (a threat, not a promise).

35 A lacuna is an empty space or cavity, from the Latin word for hole or pit (same root word as *lake*, incidentally).

Even if this decision is not consistent with the Constitution, it is consistent with some other things. First and foremost, it is consistent with political expediency. While chartering a bank might not be *necessary* for carrying into execution any of the enumerated powers, as we discussed above, events had made clear that such a bank was certainly useful and effective. A decision which would have required a constitutional amendment (and thus, the agreement of a lot more people) to allow Congress to charter a bank would have been most unwelcome. Interestingly enough, that seems to indicate that the decision meets the spirit, if not the letter, of the necessary and proper clause (as separate from the rest of the Constitution).

Second, this interpretation of the necessary and proper clause is consistent with John Marshall's personal political beliefs. Marshall was a Federalist, a party that believed in a strong and active central government. This reading of the word *necessary* certainly increased the scope of federal authority.

Third, and finally, the interpretation is also consistent with our suspicion that federal officers may not make the best judges of the limits of federal authority. Of course, evidence that is consistent with at least three different theories does not argue for any one of them above the other. Indeed, the three are not mutually exclusive, as all three could have helped shape Marshall's judgment to some degree.

On the other hand, it is very *difficult* to reconcile this decision with our usual ideal of judges, or for that matter, many people's conceptions of those who hold public office. Whatever the cause that motivated this decision, it seems very unlikely that the principles of the Constitution had much to do with it. At best, it is consistent with one part of the spirit of the necessary and proper clause, the part that prompted the inclusion of implied powers. It completely ignores, however, the other part of the spirit of the clause, the one that prompted written limitations on the implication of powers.

So men are not angels; if they were, they wouldn't be tempted to follow their interests when placed in government positions.[36] We would like to think that people's better or higher natures will take over when they hold a part of the public trust.[37] But reality is rarely so idyllic. Instead, we find that people are people. They try to do what is right, but often fail, whether by succumbing to venality or because it is difficult for us to evaluate circumstances with complete disregard for our own interests. The trick that Madison tried to perform is to get our individual interests to line up with what is right. And, as Madison said, we can do that by trying to change people, or by changing the rules of the game. Since people are notoriously difficult to change, Madison tried to change the rules to get people's self-interest to lead them to do what was right.

One example of this succeeding is the second part of the *McCulloch* decision. Having answered the question of whether Congress had the authority to charter a bank, Marshall set about answering the second question: whether Maryland could tax that bank. The answer is no.

Marshall begins with the power to create. The power to create, he reasons, implies the power to preserve. In effect, then, it implies the power to destroy—the power to decide that the created should not continue to exist (to decide *not* to preserve it). When the power to destroy rests with another, however, the two powers may come into conflict; where that happens, the power of the superior authority must prevail.

Well, Marshall had just settled the question of whether Congress had the authority to create a bank. It did (and does). States unquestionably possess a general power to tax. But as Marshall quite correctly observes, the power to tax is the power to destroy. Marshall considers this "too obvious to be denied," and in fact, we need look no further than the Constitution itself for confirmation. Article I, Section 9, Clause 1 restricts Congress' authority under the commerce and tax clauses, forbidding two things. First, Congress could not prohibit the *importation* of slaves before 1808.[38] Second, until that time, Congress could not tax that importation by more than $10 per head.

The Southern states, of course, insisted on having this language in the Constitution, to protect the "peculiar institution" of slavery. They were afraid that Congress would use its powers to destroy slavery—and notice that

---

36 Sounds familiar, doesn't it?

37 Certainly, civics education based in the ideals of the Progressive movement has taught us nothing less.

38 To Congress' credit, this is exactly when Congress prohibited it. Notice, though, that this involves only the end of the importation of slaves; freeing those already enslaved here (and their children) was sadly a different question.

the power to tax was one of the two powers they feared. Essentially, Congress could have ended the importation of slaves by imposing a tax so great that it would be too costly to import slaves, without making it illegal to do so.

Likewise, if states had the power to tax the exercise of federal powers, they could do so at a rate high enough to prevent the federal government from exercising its powers. And as Marshall correctly points out, that fundamentally contradicts the reason we form governments in the first place. That's right; it's our old friend, the Prisoner's Dilemma.[39] To allow individual states to defect from collective decisions undermines the entire purpose of forming the federal government—to solve collective action problems among the states.

Although Marshall is on much firmer footing with this reasoning, note that it still correlates well with this own political views. In fact, that is the only consistency between his answers to these questions: the desire for a stronger central government. So, when I say "political views," I do not mean that he favors a particular party, but what he conceives the proper role of government (and the proper relationship of the states and the federal government) to be. Again, then, we see that we can rely on federal courts to guard the division of power between the states and federal government only if they are not predisposed to favor one or the other. Given that they are agents of the federal government, however, we have reason to believe that they will in fact be more sympathetic to the expansion of federal power. Although to a lesser degree than the political branches, they still have a dog in this hunt.[40]

Let's look at one final case, this time a more recent one. After all, perhaps these issues about federalism just came up in the early years of the republic. Let me take you instead to 1942 and the case of *Wickard v. Filburn*. Roscoe C. Filburn[41] had a farm in Montgomery Co., Ohio, one which had been in his family for at least three generations.[42] And on this farm he had some dairy cows[43] as well as some chickens.[44] He also grew wheat on this farm, part of which he sold, the rest of which he used to feed his livestock, to make flour for his family's bread, and as seed stock for the next year's planting (obviously, he used different parts of the remainder for each of these).

Under the Agricultural Adjustment Act (AAA) of 1938, Mr. Filburn had permission to plant slightly more than eleven acres of wheat.[45] Congress claimed authority to pass the AAA under the commerce clause, which allows Congress to regulate commerce "among the several states." In order to reduce the supply of wheat and thereby increase the price of it (and hence, it was hoped, the income of farmers), Congress allowed the Secretary of Agriculture to set marketing quotas[46] for each farmer. They then required the farmer to obtain a marketing license in order to sell wheat, and would only issue a marketing card if a farmer observed the limit of his quota. Furthermore, the Secretary of Agriculture could levy fines on amounts of wheat harvested beyond the allowed quota.

So far, so good—except that Filburn planted twenty-three acres. Now, he only tried to market slightly more than eleven acres' worth of it,[47] keeping the rest for his own consumption on his own farm. When the local agents of the Department of Agriculture refused his marketing card application and fined him for his excess

---

39 Marshall even points out that confidence (that states would not so abuse the power) is not the issue—one state simply could not trust another to forego the opportunity.

40 To translate for Yankees and other foreigners, they have an interest in the outcome.

41 Yes, you may say it like the sheriff in *The Dukes of Hazard* says his name.

42 Apparently, much of the farm is now the location of the Salem Mall in Dayton.

43 E-I-E-I.

44 O.

45 A total of 11.1 acres, if you must know.

46 Note that these are *marketing*, not *production* quotas: the name (at least) indicates it is about how much you sell, not how much you produce.

47 In fact, 11.1 acres.

production, Filburn filed suit against the Secretary of Agriculture, Claude Wickard.[48] Filburn claimed that Congress did not possess the authority under the commerce clause to regulate wheat not in commerce of any sort—such as the wheat he had grown for his own use. It wasn't leaving his farm, let alone the state, and he wasn't buying or selling it, so it was in no way either "commerce" or "among the several states," let alone both.

Naturally, the Supreme Court said it was. In a unanimous decision, Justice Robert Jackson explained that if Mr. Filburn had not grown his own wheat, he would have had to purchase it. His not purchasing the wheat left more wheat available in interstate commerce. And while his own lack of consumption would have no noticeable effect, Congress could still regulate it because it would have an effect if everyone grew their own wheat.

Notice the two big "ifs" in this reasoning: *if* Filburn didn't grow his own wheat, he would have bought it; and *if* everyone else did it, it would have an effect, even if his own actions did not. We could spend a great deal of time examining the reasonableness of these two assumption—for example, that holding own production, the very point of which is to abstain from commerce, to be an act of commerce is at best asinine, or that a fundamental tenet of our legal system (and any just one, for that matter) is that the law can only hold you responsible for your acts, not the acts others might have done or might do—but the easiest way to point out the absurdity of this reasoning is to examine its consequences. Can you think of anything this reasoning leaves beyond the scope of federal commerce power?

Sadly, I can't hear your response, and cannot therefore show how it is subject to the commerce power under *Wickard*. Instead, I'll just have to let the voices in my head make suggestions, and hope they are at least as outlandish as yours (the suggestions, not the voices—though if the shoe fits . . .). How about . . . deciding whether to wear shoes or go barefoot? Maybe that's too obvious—if everyone went barefoot, no one would buy shoes,[49] and the interstate market in shoes would cease to exist. That's a fairly substantial effect. So Congress can order you to wear shoes, or limit the number you can buy, or set a minimum number you must own. Let's go for something a little more complicated: deciding whether to wear flip-flops or tennis shoes. If everyone decided to wear tennis shoes, the market for flip-flops would dry up. And then no one would understand that Jimmy Buffet song,[50] and that would affect the interstate market in Jimmy Buffet albums as well as flip-flops.

How about giving a mouse a cookie? Sadly, if you didn't give it to him, he might have to buy it (or you wouldn't have bought it, or wouldn't have baked it, which is of course the same as buying it), and if everyone did it, it would affect the interstate market in baked goods. Notice that Congress can, according to this logic, order people to give Christmas presents[51]—many retailers depend on the holiday shopping season, so not buying them would cause an economic disaster. People out of work leads to mortgages defaulted leads to bank defaults leads to . . . well, let's just say the mouse is probably going to want another cookie.

The point is, if you string enough conditional statements together, you can literally get from here to anywhere.[52] Imagine the Six Degrees of Kevin Bacon, and then imagine that you get to use conditional statements. Connect Kevin Bacon to Margaret Thatcher[53]—go! If Margaret Thatcher had been in *Apollo 13* with Kevin Bacon, then she was in *Apollo 13* with Kevin Bacon! Even the Staples Easy Button isn't that easy.[54]

But being able to rationalize anything into the commerce power removes completely the idea of a limited government. Whereas previously the federal government was one of enumerated powers, with the states holding all the rest, suddenly it becomes a generally enabled government, with the state holding only whatever

---

48 Does this case have the best names, or what? Mr. Wickard was an alumnus of Purdue University, but we should not make assumptions about his intelligence or character on that basis.

49 Except Imelda Marcos—it's a dated reference, so ask your parents (or Google).

50 "Margaritaville."

51 Though not necessarily in celebration of Christmas, because that would violate the First Amendment, as we'll discuss later. Instead, we'll call them "lovely parting gifts" (thanks to the lovely Sarah Shepherd for suggesting the name).

52 Which, coincidentally, was until recently the motto of the university where I work.

53 Again, Google.

54 For an easy cheap shot, replace "Staples Easy Button" with "yo momma" while reading to a classmate; be warned, however, that the First Amendment won't protect that speech (again, later).

scraps it leaves them. Certainly this decision expands federal power at the expense of the states, undermining the division of sovereignty in a federalist system. Does this provide any evidence that federal judges won't protect federalism (as opposed to merely that they didn't)? Is it part of a rule, or just a random exception?

Since the decision has next to nothing to do with the letter or spirit of the Constitution, we are left with two potential explanations:[55] the decision represents the influence either of the judge's personal ideology or of outside political pressure. Justice Jackson generally paid close attention to the letter and spirit of the Constitution, and took it as a point of pride that he separated his personal opinions from his reading of the Constitution (and reading his opinions supports his reputation for success in doing so).

Take, for example, Jackson's famous dissent in *Korematsu v. U.S.* Hugo Black's majority opinion rationalized that the crisis of national security in California after Pearl Harbor justified the forced removal of U.S. citizens of Japanese descent from that state, in violation of those citizens' constitutional rights (for example, the right not to be deprived of their liberty without having been properly convicted in a court of law). According to Black, the immediacy of the threat and the dire consequences of not meeting it (the invasion and occupation of California by the Japanese Empire) allowed the government to burden those citizens' liberties. Jackson, writing movingly in dissent, said that although the Court was powerless to help Mr. Korematsu (because the military would have ignored any contrary decision), they should rather admit their impotence and still declare truthfully that what was done to him violated both the plain letter and the unquestioned spirit of the Constitution. The Constitution, he argued, is not elastic[56]—once stretched to cover a particular set of political exigencies,[57] it would not return to its former bounds. Worse, it would become easier and easier to pull it into distortion as new exigencies arose, until finally the document (and its protection of liberty) would rip apart.[58]

We see Jackson's desire to adhere to the text of the Constitution. We don't see any evidence of his personal opinion. But we do see a consideration of external political influences, of the context in which the decision would have to operate. In this case, Jackson decided that the damage to the Constitution outweighed accommodating external political realities. Note that this equation has two parts, the damage to the Constitution and the need to adjust to the political reality in which the decision had to operate. For this dissent, the damage was large, and the need to adjust small—the decision in *Korematsu* came several years after the end of the war and the internment camps.

Of course, one could hardly find a better description of the history of commerce clause jurisprudence after *Wickard* than the warning the very same Justice Jackson give in his *Korematsu* dissent. So what explains the discrepancy? I suggest that the difference was not in the method—Jackson used exactly the same framework to reach his decision in *Wickard* and *Korematsu*. The difference lies in his evaluation of the potential harm to the Constitution and the importance of external political factors.

Let us begin with the latter. Before his appointment to the court, Jackson served as Solicitor General (1938–40)[59] and Attorney General (1940–41), having worked his way up through the Justice Department. In other words, he was very much involved in Franklin Roosevelt's defense before the courts of New Deal programs, such as the Agricultural Adjustment Act. Unquestionably, Justice Jackson understood the political reality that FDR[60] would brook no decisions overturning these programs (though other justices could have had few illusions on this score, either, after Roosevelt's court-packing threat).[61]

---

55 At least, two that I can think of.

56 With the exception of one clause.

57 A fancy word for an urgent or pressing need (like when you drink a Big Gulp on a road trip and can't make it to the next exit or rest stop).

58 Lest you think Justice Jackson unduly alarmist, after the terrorist attacks on September 11, 2001, some commentators suggested internment camps for U.S. citizens of Arab descent, citing the *Korematsu* decision.

59 I realize this sounds like the guy in charge of arranging the entertainment for bachelor parties, but it is in fact the title of the lawyer who represents the United States in court (*solicitor* is a British term for a lawyer).

60 The short way of saying "Franklin Delano Roosevelt." Just in case you didn't get that from the earlier "Franklin Roosevelt."

61 Yep, more on this later.

So the political cost was high. What about the damage done to the Constitution? This is a little harder to gauge, of course. But one can well imagine Jackson having to weigh whatever damage this might do against the damage a showdown with one of our most politically powerful presidents might do to another Constitutional principle, the separation of powers. Between the two, the likely damage from eroding limits on the commerce power particularly had to be less than eroding the separation of powers, which limits the scope for abuse of federal powers generally. He may well have seen it as a choice between damaging the Constitution a little or a lot.

On the other hand, he may have simply considered the damage as insignificant in its own right. Not all generations have understood the connection between property rights and liberty as clearly as our founding generation did. He may simply have underestimated the damage, so that any political opposition was likely to make reading the clause as written too costly. The tone of the opinion conveys an exasperation with having to consider antiquated notions of rights, which makes this sound plausible, too.

Either way, this once again confirms our charge against the Supreme Court. Whether because appointed by a President who wanted justices to ignore state sovereignty, or because his service in the federal government convinced him that only the federal government could address these issues, there seems to be an institutional incentive to prefer federal sovereignty over state. So, if we can't rely on the federal judicial process to protect federalism, where do we turn?

Remember that the graph showing the distribution of sovereignty in a federal system (waaaay back at the beginning of the chapter) also had a line showing a delegation of power from the states to the federal government. Our founders were not men[62] who delegated sovereignty without some accompanying form of representation.[63] Though it is easy for us to forget this, the state legislatures elected senators until the Seventeenth Amendment went into effect in the first quarter of the twentieth century.[64] Although the states could not recall their senators like a diplomatic mission, and the length of the senatorial term (six years) created a measure of independence for senators, they functioned as the representatives of the state *governments* to the federal governments. (This also helps make sense of their distribution—two to each state—because states are all equally possessed of statehood, as well as their Constitutional role in foreign affairs—especially treaty negotiation—because this was a power only the states could have surrendered.)

In this way, one could expect the states to protect their portion of sovereignty through the political process. Although the House might pass legislation expanding federal authority at the expense of the states, the states' representatives had to agree that it was in the states' interests, as well. Incidentally, all of the landmark expansions of federal authority at the expense of the states have occurred either since the Seventeenth Amendment changed the election of senators to popular vote (and the Sixteenth increased exponentially the resources of the federal government), or in consequence of the Civil War. After the Civil War, the Thirteenth, Fourteenth, and Fifteenth Amendments all altered the distribution of sovereignty appropriately, by amending the Constitution—which requires broad consent, including that of the states. Since the Seventeenth Amendment, expansions have come in the form of legislation (the New Deal and federal grants requiring states to follow federal directions, to give two examples), legislation which no longer requires the states' consent.

Which makes it all the more difficult to believe that the argument that states could protect themselves through the political process first originated well after the Seventeenth Amendment had changed the manner of electing senators. Of course, before the Seventeenth Amendment, the statement didn't require an argument to support it. But in 1954, forty years after the popular election of senators began, Herbert Wechsler argued that states could still protect themselves through the political process, due to their influence on elections and the structure of political parties. According to Wechsler, the fact that the states played a role in determining the composition and selection of the national government (Congress and the President) provided them with

---

62 John Adams, for example, appears to have simply been a singularly unattractive woman (though in his—I mean, *her* defense, she was from Boston).

63 Perhaps you remember their motto, "No taxation without insanely low prices!"

64 At halftime, Congress formed themselves into the letters "USA" on the Mall.

"safeguards" through the political process. Wechsler, a law professor at Columbia University, cited the fact that states control electoral laws for national elections (for example, who gets on the ballot, the format of the ballot, and times and places for polling places) and that political parties exist nationally largely as coalitions of state parties as evidence for the continued ability of states to fend for the themselves in the federal political process, specifically despite the popular election of senators.

Now, one could point out that the federal government has been taking a larger role in determining the rules for elections since 1954. But the bigger problem with Prof. Wechsler's argument is that, after the Seventeenth Amendment, it makes no sense. Or rather, the sense it makes answers a different question. Do these things allow states to influence elections? Certainly, if decreasingly, they do. But they are very indirect—that is, the existence of states makes a difference, but the interests of states do not. The fact that parties are organized primarily at the state level does not give the state *governments*, but their *populations*, an influence over elected officials.

Perhaps it is easier to think of this way: weather and the state of the economy also affect elections. But when is the last time a candidate worried about whether the weather[65] or economy would like his vote? Affecting an election is not the same as electing a candidate. Candidates worry about the state of the economy only because it matters to those who vote for them, not because they care about the state of the economy itself.[66] So is there any reason to expect voters to care about federalism, and therefore induce candidates to care about it?

Well, let's take you for an example. Would you still be reading this if it hadn't been assigned?[67] The balance between state and federal sovereignty is a rather arcane[68] topic for most people. It's abstract, and so although it affects their rights, it's hard to see how. Add to that the fact that the phrase "states' rights" has largely been abused in attempts to justify first slavery and then segregation—two unjust and unjustifiable things—and it's hard to get people to rally around that flag. Or to perhaps state it more clearly, are people known for insisting on the rights of others (or voting for them)? Some people do, but only on rare (and beautiful) occasions does "some" turn into the "many" necessary to have an electoral effect. Certainly the Civil Rights Acts confirm this—it says something that they passed, but also that we still needed them hundred years after the end of slavery.

Now, let us add to this that those whose rights are suffering here are abstract legal entities: state governments. This makes it all the more difficult to humanize the damage, to get people to put themselves in the other's shoes and want to protect them. At best, people might associate it with state politicians, but we tend to have little sympathy for them, as well. So although it's possible, it seems hardly likely that this arrangement will protect the rights of states, let alone allow states to protect them for themselves.

If we can neither turn to the federal courts nor rely on the federal political process to protect the division of sovereignty in federalism, where should we look next? There are at least two alternatives, one of which we have encountered already. Both have the advantage of claiming some measure of support among the founding generation. Not that we owe them any particular sort of reverence because they were better or smarter than us, but it does make sense, when examining the design of a machine, to consult the engineers who designed it.

If federalism is a peculiarly American invention, then so too is the concept of interposition (or nullification). Just as federalism was an innovative response to the challenges of our political conditions, interposition was an innovative response to the challenges the political conditions which federalism created—and specifically our question of who watches the watchers. The question of who should monitor the boundaries of federal power came up quite quickly in our new compound republic. During the administration of John Adams, Congress (controlled by Adams' Federalist Party) passed two laws which many felt exceeded the authority of the federal government.

---

65 It's time for Phun with Homophones!

66 As evidence, I submit the federal budget deficit and our national debt.

67 It's okay, you can be honest—I've got thick skin (also dry), and I can't hear you anyway.

68 As opposed to an arcade topic, which is one full of quarters and sore thumbs—ask your parents.

The first, the Alien Act, authorized the President to authorize the removal of citizens or nationals of another country if the United States were at war with that country (whether officially declared, or if the country had invaded U.S. territory). The second, the Sedition[69] Act, made it a crime to "combine or conspire together, with intent to oppose any measure or measures of the government of the United States," as well as to speak or write anything "false, scandalous, and malicious" with "intent to defame" the government, Congress, or the President. Punishment for this crime was a fine of not more than $5,000[70] **and** imprisonment for six months to five years, with permission for the court to require the deposit of a bond against the convict's future good behavior (for as long a time as the court felt prudent).

Opponents of the acts pointed out that they (quite clearly) exceed limitations of Congress' power in the Bill of Rights.[71] The First Amendment says that "Congress shall make no law . . . abridging the freedom of speech, or of the press; or the right of the people peaceably to assemble, and to petition the government for a redress of grievances." The Sedition Act did all four. And the Fifth Amendment declares that "No person shall be . . . deprived of life, liberty, or property, without due process of law," which is exactly what the Alien Act did. Note that the amendment says *person*, which in legal terms means it is specifically **not** restricted to citizens only. Forcibly deporting someone who has not been duly convicted of a crime deprives them of liberty without due process of law (and implicitly declares them by legislative act to be guilty of a crime, which is something the Constitution also explicitly forbids, too).[72]

Moreover, there is no clear delegation of authority to Congress which would authorize it to pass these bills (and Congress cited none). That is, our old friend Article I, Section 8 contains no clause which allows Congress to legislate either on political speech generally or sedition particularly, or on the removal of foreign citizens (though there is one allowing Congress to determine the method and conditions of their naturalization). They lack a positive grant of power, and have an explicit negative.

Note that all of this occurred in 1798, several years before the federal Supreme Court declared itself the final arbiter of Constitutional questions (in some case you may have heard of, but of which you will certainly hear when we discuss the judiciary). But when federal courts began applying these acts without questioning their constitutionality,[73] opponents turned to the states, as parties to the compact establishing the federal government, to enforce the limitations on its power. Virginia and Kentucky passed resolutions (written by James Madison and Thomas Jefferson, respectively—you may have heard of them) declaring that it was their duty as parties to the contract to interpose[74] their sovereignty between the federal government and their citizens, where the federal government acted outside the boundaries of its power.

In and of itself, this idea makes sense. But when we start to consider the implications of it, it may again serve only to push our question back a step. Because if we consider that federal entities might favor federal interests, we must in fairness consider the likelihood that state entities will favor state interests. As at least a partial remedy

---

69 *Sedition* is a common law offence in Great Britain, consisting of incitement to riot or violence against public authority; here it was used in somewhat looser terms.

70 To give you an idea of how much this was, in 1798, the median value of a home in the United States was $96 ($614 in cities).

71 In fancy legal Latin, the claim is that Congress acted *ultra vires*, beyond its powers. No extra charge for the fancy Latin—just our way of saying thank you for learning with us!

72 Article I, Section 9 contains a list of things outside the scope of Congress power, one of which is passing bills of attainder, which is the name for legislation that declares someone guilty of a crime.

73 Consider, for example, the case of Thomas Cooper. Mr. Cooper received a $400 fine, six months in prison, and the requirement of posting $1,000 himself, and two others $500 each, as security against his future good behavior. His crime was to have written that even those who doubted President Adams' capacity thought he had good intentions, and to assert that Adams' favored establishing a navy, had created a standing army, had damaged the credit of the United States, might have justly provoked a war with the bluntness of his expression, and had advised authorities to surrender an American to the British (who had charged the American with murder). In fact, the justice presenting the case to the jury emphasized as an aggravating factor that Cooper had done this (gasp!) to influence people's votes in the upcoming election. If it takes you longer than fifteen minutes to find people saying worse than this about whoever the current President is, then you obviously don't know how to Google.

74 To interpose is to place between.

for this, one of nullification's strongest proponents[75] argued that state conventions, rather than state legislatures, should have this power.[76] John C. Calhoun[77] thought this would put a sufficient brake on the ability of the state to use this power as to minimize its abuse. That is, it would have to be worth the trouble of calling and convening a convention of citizens, and the legislature would have to persuade the convention of its case.

Calhoun also proposed the idea of a concurrent majority. A simple majority requires only that one more than half of those voting in favor. A concurrent majority would also require that the simple majority represent a majority of the groups in society, as well. This increases the ability of groups not large enough to be a majority to block legislation which would harm them.

So, for example, if there were three groups in a society of hundred individuals, and the first group had fifty-one members, it would always be able to get the legislation it wanted under simple majority (*ceteris paribus*). It could take advantage of the other two groups (of, let's say, twenty-five and twenty-four members, respectively). Even if they banded together, they could do little about it. If, however, legislation also required the approval of a majority of the groups, the first group would have to get at least one of the others to agree, allowing them to protect themselves.

Of course, how exactly to do this remains the question. Perhaps the simplest way would be to require a majority of state legislatures to also agree to legislation. The difficulty with this is that the Constitution already required something in this vein. Since Calhoun wrote before the Seventeenth Amendment, the Senate still presumably (though certainly with some degree of variance, as part of the point of their six-year term was to separate them from purely regional concerns) represented the interests of their state legislatures. And really, in that sense, we can see that what Calhoun proposed was an extension or refinement of federalism.

But if not the state legislatures, which might be redundant, then the idea becomes even more problematic. In order to know how many groups we have—to define who votes and how many it takes to win—we first have to define groups. How would we do that? Presumably, we want people with similar interests, so we could use political parties. But anyone can claim an interest, and can claim that their interest is separate from some other group's, even if it isn't. Besides, could we trust government—people belonging to already existing and successful parties—to fairly define rules about who else gets counted as a party? Before you answer, remember that deciding who counts and who doesn't will have a significant effect on the outcome.

Right. So we need to define groups based on some immutable, readily observable characteristic. What can we know about people that they can't readily change? Even eye color and hair color are mutable. Even if they weren't, these aren't good alternatives, as the history of skin color shows beyond a shadow of a doubt. People who share immutable characteristics don't necessarily—in fact, don't generally—share the same interests.

Really, the basic idea—and one to which we shall return later—behind Calhoun's proposition is that how you count votes makes a difference in the outcome. And if the number and nature of those required to agree makes a difference in who can protect themselves (and thus, the division of sovereignty in a federal system), then the changes in outcome it produces give people an incentive to choose one venue over another. That is to say, if the Seventeenth Amendment and Supreme Court interpretations of the necessary and proper, commerce, and Fourteenth Amendment due process[78] clauses have altered that distribution, it may be because people have an interest in getting them to do so.

Let me explain using the example of some subdivisions in a suburb.[79] Imagine four subdivisions in a 2 × 2 square pattern (such as in Figure 3.2), with four houses in each neighborhood, arranged in the same pattern

---

75 And the Vice President of the United States at the time.

76 He also argued for another principle, that of the concurrent majority, that would have required a majority of state legislatures to also agree to bills before they become law.

77 I know what you're wondering, and yes, the "C" stands for "Caldwell."

78 As we will discuss later (and by later, I mean Chapter 12, this is how the Supreme Court applies the guarantees in the Bill of Rights against the states—but if you remember that now, it'll spoil all the fun later!

79 Economists call this the Road-Building Game. Economists do a lot of their thinking in terms of games, which takes all of the fun out of them. Must be why it's called "the dismal science."

(oh, say, like the ones in Figure 3.2). Let's say that the shaded houses like asphalt. When it comes to a question of more or less asphalt, they prefer the paving: less wear and dirt on their cars. Let's also assume that the un-shaded houses are of the mindset that every inch of pavement is one less of paradise; they always oppose it. And we'll refer to each block of four houses as Neighborhood A, B, C, and George, respectively.[80]

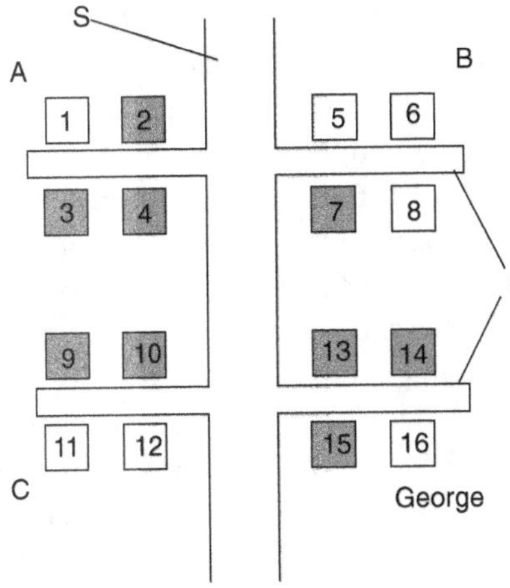

Now, each neighborhood has to decide if it will pave the road that runs into its neighborhood (such as those labeled *r* in Figure 3.2). How will each of the neighborhoods vote? Which roads will get paved? Tune in next time for the exciting . . . all right, so it's not that interesting. But, using a simple majority rule, neighborhoods A and George will vote to pave their roads, while the measure will fail miserably in neighborhood B and narrowly in neighborhood C.[81] Moreover, this makes eleven people happy and four unhappy.[82]

Next the neighbors have to vote on whether to pave the street (labeled *s*) that connects their roads to the major traffic arteries. Tune in next . . . still not buying it, huh? Can't blame a guy for trying.[83] Again, using simple majority, the street gets paved, 9-7. Now, let's say you're in house no. 10.[84] What thought, what possibility do these results suggest to you? That's right, it's time to play America's favorite new game show,[85] "How Devious Are You?"[86] Do these results suggest a way to alter previous decisions in your favor? If not we have some lovely parting gifts for you.[87] Remember the idea we started with—the way you count can affect the outcome. In this case, if we have the decision to pave neighborhood roads made at the neighborhood level, then only two are paved. But if the decision were made all for one and one for all at the suburb level . . . well, then they would all get paved (by vote of 9-7)!

By changing the level at which we aggregate, house no. 10 can change the outcome in its favor. House no. 7 goes from being a minority at the local level to part of a majority at the national level. Note, however, that while this makes house nos. 7, 9, and 10 happier, it results in a net loss of happiness among voters. Now only nine people are happy with their paving (or lack thereof), whereas before eleven were (and therefore, seven are unhappy, instead of five).

Thus we see that some groups in a federal system have an interest in shifting policy from the local to the national level. And we also see one of the arguments in favor of federalism. The first, Madison's, we have already encountered. Madison advocates federalism in order to protect individual liberty, because a compound republic allows for the taming of factions. Here we see a second—that federalism promotes better policy, in that it allows government to make better use of what F. A. Hayek called the "knowledge of local time and place."

Now, Hayek didn't have federalism in mind when he spoke of this. He was explaining why socialism—defined as centralized economic planning—is bad in theory as well as practice. Communism fails not because

Figure 3.2 The Road Building Game

---

80 Whereas we know their names would, in real life, involve woodland creatures, water features, and nostalgic pre-industrial machinery (like Pheasant's Creek or Otter's Mill).

81 Note the distorting effect of small numbers. A simple majority is also a ¾ supermajority!

82 I know what you're thinking, and yes, that's not correct. It is of course five people who are unhappy. I just wanted to see if you had switched your brain to autopilot yet.

83 Well, not for trying *this*. But bank robbery or copping a feel, on the other hand—those you can blame a guy for trying.

84 In the United Kingdom, of course, this would make you prime minister. Here, it just makes you mental.

85 Among those created in the last 5 seconds.

86 It helps if you shout the words, with pauses after "how" and "devious." No, really, it does.

87 Or parting gits; it's your choice.

it's always bad people who try it, but because central planners can't aggregate dispersed local information fast enough to react to it (whereas the market doesn't have to aggregate it, but allows dispersed processing). And, incidentally, when you concentrate enough power to run an economy that way, it tends to attract power-hungry sorts of people. You chum[88] the waters, you get sharks.

But his point is equally valid in regard to government policy. There are many policies where "one size fits all" doesn't fit anyone. Think of a road with a pothole in it. If a central government is in charge of fixing it, citizens (or local administrators) will have to fill out paperwork, submit it to the central administration, and wait for the central administration to authorize repair. When they repair it, they will have to do so according to a single central standard. So, even if they know that a different blend of materials will produce a better patch because of the particular weather or drainage in that area, or that the problem is caused by an inattentive driver on his tractor who forgets to raise his plow, they aren't able to make use of that knowledge (or even their knowledge that the hole is there). When these local officials have their own authority, however, they are better able to make use of this information they possess, but cannot easily (or sometimes possibly) transmit.

But the benefits of federalism don't stop there. The division of sovereignty between national and local levels not only allows for better policy, but also prevents local policy from exploiting local citizens. As Charles Tiebout[89] and James Buchanan have separately observed, having multiple independent jurisdictions (like, say, states) creates a competition among them for citizens. If one state passes laws that injure its citizens, that take too much of their freedom, citizens can "vote with their feet" and move to another state.

You may have noticed, for example, that states often compete with each other to attract large businesses. Because states have to compete, businesses can play one against the other to get a more favorable regulatory or tax environment. Delaware, for example, is home to many incorporated businesses because of its laws regarding shareholders (the laws favor the company). Many credit card companies locate there because Delaware's laws favor them. Some states have laws that favor insurance companies. In fact, google major credit card companies (not the type of card, but the issuer) or insurance companies and see if you find a pattern in the location of their home offices—they tend to cluster in a few states.

Well, the same is true for individuals, too (though since they are not as organized,[90] they cannot realize as much of their bargaining strength). A state with much higher taxes than its neighbors will see its citizens move the taxed activity to neighboring states (whether buying goods and services or selling them). If you've never lived near a state line, ask a classmate who has. There's always something you go to the other state to purchase because the tax is lower. Again, you can often tell if you see one sort of business (gas stations, let's say) clustered on one side of the state line. In Bristol, which straddles the state line between Virginia and Tennessee, many of the restaurants (and the mall) are on the Virginia side of the line, because it has a lower sales tax. But people prefer to live and work on the Tennessee side, because Tennessee does not have an income tax.[91]

Folks close to state lines take advantage of these things because it's relatively costless for them to do so. The rest of us would have to be planning one heck of a meal to drive all the way across a state line just to save a few percentage points on the sales tax. We'd spend more getting there than we would save. But if our state raised its tax on gasoline high enough, we'd be on our way with every gas can we could lay hand to.[92] Entrepreneurs certainly would, and they'd start reselling it on the side. And this would force the government to scale its tax back, because they would be receiving no revenue, and local gas stations would be going out of business. Thus the presence of another jurisdiction (between which there is a free movement of people, which is why it doesn't

---

88 Chum is a less repulsive word for rotting fish guts. Hey, is it lunch time yet?

89 Pronounced "tee-boo," and quite a lot of fun to pronounce, I might add. Go ahead—give it a try. Say it like you're poking the Pillsbury Doughboy in the stomach. And the next time you read it, you will cluck like a chicken.

90 Remember Mancur Olson?

91 Tennessee is also simply a better state, but we're too classy to point that out.

92 In Tennessee, this would undoubtedly involve mayonnaise jars. We're not too classy for that.

always work between countries) limits the ability of the one we're in to encroach on our liberties.[93] The state can only burden our freedom until the cost (to us) of the burden is greater than that of moving out of state.[94]

Last but not least, we have one more benefit of federalism. In *New State Ice Co. v. Liebmann*, Justice Louis Brandeis referred to the states as "laboratories of democracy."[95] What did he mean by this? Really? No one else had the whole "mad scientist and hunch-backed assistant in a voting booth" image? Huh. Well, what are laboratories? (Hint: if you don't know, ask a natural science major near you.) (Extra Double-Secret Hint: if you're a natural science major and don't know, perhaps you should consider a different major.[96]) That's right! The lab is where you go to try things out, to experiment. And Brandeis' point is that having multiple independent jurisdictions allows us to try things out, to experiment with new policies to improve our current ones.

For example, if we want to find a new policy for funding education, we might let Michigan try it first. If it doesn't work and causes all of the schools to shift into a neighboring dimension,[97] leaving an entire generation of Michiganders[98] uneducated and ignorant . . . okay, so maybe no one would notice. Bad example.[99] But let's say it happens to Wisconsin. Nice people, good cheese.[100] But we'd still have forty-nine other states (even if one of them is Michigan).[101] And if it works, the forty-nine other states will be able to adopt the new policy (and maybe learn from Wisconsin's experience to do it better).

If, on the other hand, we had to try the new policy out on the whole nation at the same time . . . well, that'd be putting all of our eggs in one basket, wouldn't it? Betting the farm. Going all-in. All those things your grandparents warned you not to do. What those fun aphorisms are really saying is that you shouldn't take unnecessary (or unnecessarily large) risks. And if we had to risk damage to the entire country, we'd be a lot less likely to try new things. So the ability to experiment on a smaller scale—only betting the milk money, instead of the mortgage payment—allows us to try more new ideas. The benefit (weighted by the probability of success) is more likely to be greater than the cost (weighted by the probability of failure) if the cost is smaller.

So there you have it. Federalism allows us to keep other people from using government to hurt us (Madison), limits government's ability to take advantage of us (Tiebout, Buchanan), allows us to tailor policy to local conditions (Hayek), and gives us greater incentive to try new policies (Brandeis). It slices! It dices! It even juliennes!

Oh, but there is a dark side to federalism.[102] Let's go back to the competition for citizens for a mo.[103] Remember how businesses could play states off against each other? Well, what if a business threatened to leave if a state didn't change its regulation of workplace safety or sexual harassment. And by change, of course, I mean to reduce the standards, on the assumption that meeting them costs the business money (in safer equipment or lawsuit settlements).[104] Surely there is a town somewhere in another state whose people need jobs more than high standards. And that town has probably let the company know that it's welcome to a vacant

---

93 If you don't considering buying and selling freely an important liberty, feel free to substitute a ban on your religion (or lack thereof) for the gas tax. Also, feel free to move to Cuba and experience the importance of the former for yourself.

94 Well, there's more to it than that, such as discounting for risk and for expected future value, and doing so for benefits as well as costs, across more than one issue—but that gives you the idea, and I have to leave you some fun for your first public policy class!

95 Not to be confused with "lavatories of democracy," which would probably be public restrooms—eeww.

96 Like criminal justice, 'cause you need to get a clue.

97 Known as "Ka'a-n'da," a strange dimension where moose are the highest form of life.

98 Yes, that's the word for someone from Michigan. Does that make the women Michigeese?

99 Just kidding, of course.

100 In fact, I think that's on their license plate, isn't it? It should be, anyway, or at least a t-shirt.

101 Sorry! I thought Michiganders could take a joke. At least, the ones we used for lab animals during testing could . . .

102 Krr-tsch. Krr-tsch. (Or however else you spell the sound of mechanically ventilated breathing.)

103 British slang for "moment"—or don't you watch Wallace and Gromit? All the cool kids do. *They* knew what it meant . . . Yes, give in to your hate . . . (I told you it's the dark side of federalism)

104 Though it might gain them other things, such as happier and more productive employees, a better reputation, a soul . . .

building in the nice part of town, so the threat to leave is credible. Suddenly, the state's decision is no longer between employment on their terms and employment on the company's terms, but between employment on the company's terms and no employment.[105]

Now, there are at least two solutions to this problem, and people tend to overlook the first (and so, therefore, do governments made up of people). One alternative is to let the company go. If the violations of local principles and values are worth much, this will outweigh the benefit of keeping those jobs on those terms.

It does not seem, however, that states place much worth on their values (and admittedly, it is hard to eat one's principles, but it is also hard to keep a good man down). The more common solution is to use the law to get what you want without paying for it. And if those other states with their other priorities and interests didn't exist, you could do it. If you could just make them have the same values and interests that you do, then the company's threat to leave is no longer credible. It will face the same circumstances and costs there, plus the cost of moving. If only there were some way to make the other states share your values and interests . . .

Oh, wait! You can! Your governor calls up all the other governors, they sit down together and agree to pass the same labor standards. Whew! Crisis averted. See, you're all better off if you agree to cooperate with each other. No one loses businesses to another state! But then, no one gains businesses from another state, either. Each state, then, would like the others to keep the bargain they've made, so that they don't lose any of their businesses. But each would also like to not keep it themselves, so that they can gain employers.[106]

Hmm . . . that starts to sound familiar, doesn't it? What do you call that thing? You know, that thing where they're better off together keeping their agreement, but each one does better if they cheat, so they all do, and they're worse off? Seems like it starts with a "p" —and ends with "risoner's dilemma." Just as competition in the market drives prices to their lowest point (unless companies collude), so too competition between states can drive regulation to its lowest point (unless states collude)—and we do need some regulation, if not quite so much as we have. Our recent acquaintance Justice Brandeis referred to this as a "race of laxity"[107] in *Liggett v. Lee*, and Senator Daniel Patrick Moynihan once referred to it as the "race to the bottom."[108]

States, then, sometimes have an incentive to transfer sovereignty to the federal government to solve this problem and keep companies from playing them off against each other. Setting one federal law means that moving to another state no longer produces an advantage, because the rule will be the same in that state. But this means increasing the scope of federal authority at the expense of that of the states.

Which means, as you might have guessed, that the federal government also has an incentive to increase that transfer, and can itself play states off against each other to that end. Although the states have a common interest in defending state sovereignty, the federal government can use the vast amount of money[109] in the federal budget[110] to give them individual incentives to abandon their common interest. This is the time honored divide-and-conquer strategy; surely you've seen *Braveheart* and remember Longshanks' bribing Mornay and Lochlan to defect from Wallace's alliance.

---

105 At least, not from *that* employer.

106 Of course, jobs are not physical things that get crated up and shipped somewhere else, even though we often talk as if they were for the sake of convenience. Employment is a status, and there are a lot of people capable of granting that status to others.

107 Be careful to distinguish this from a race of laxatives, which is just totally gross.

108 Also nothing to do with laxatives.

109 Seriously, have you seen the numbers? They've got more zeroes behind them than the Japanese did at Pearl Harbor. Check it out at origin.www.gpoaccess.gov/usbudget/.

110 And I use the term loosely, as Congress manages to spend an even larger amount than they take in. Have a look at the National Debt Awareness Campaign at www.federalbudget.com.

But let's use an example nearer and dearer to the collegiate heart,[111] the drinking age. The Constitution leaves the regulation of things like the drinking age to the states.[112] What state are you in? What's the drinking age? Wait! Don't tell me. Just to prove that I'm psychic, I will now tell you the drinking age of the state you're in.[113] Let's see . . . I'm getting images . . . bright lights, a lot of sand . . . a three-leaf clover stained black . . . red hearts . . . stars and horseshoes, clovers and blue moons—no, wait, that's what you had for breakfast. Bear with me, I'm close . . . there's a table with green fuzz on it. It's your bathroom sink! No, there are cards on it . . . I hear someone yelling . . . twenty-one! The drinking age in your state is twenty-one! Now, think of a number between . . .

All right, so I'm not psychic (or this book would cost a lot more). In 1984, Congress conditioned the receipt of five percent of federal highway funds on having a drinking age of at least twenty-one. As a result, all states "voluntarily" adopted Congress' standard. All states had an interest in holding the line against federal encroachment of state sovereignty, but each one individually was better off letting the other defend principles while they got potholes fixed (and thus re-elected). Some states resisted, but so few that they quickly identified the cause as lost. And since the battle for states' rights was lost, they could at least mitigate their losses with some highway funds.

South Dakota, on the other hand, filed a lawsuit challenging the federal government's authority to put states in that situation. South Dakota claimed that the condition was an attempt to regulate a matter left to the states. In *South Dakota v. Dole*, the Supreme Court said it wasn't. Congress wasn't ordering the states (which *New York v. U.S.* had already settled they couldn't do), but simply providing them with a choice they were free to decline.

What the Court too readily dismissed was that states weren't entirely free to decline. Declining the funds was a valuable strategy only if the other states declined, too. Allowing one side to dictate the terms of the choices allows them to determine the outcome. That is, the amount of money the federal government has, coupled with the fact that states have to coordinate their response for it to be effective, means that the federal government can make them an offer they can't refuse.

Other courts, however, are more knowledgeable when it comes to game theory. South Dakota would have gotten a very different answer if it were a German *Land*. Germany is also a federal system, in some ways more federal than ours (the upper house of the legislature still consists of the representatives of state governments, for example). The federation is the *Bund*, and its states are *Länder*. In the *First Television Case*, the Federal Constitutional Court[114] explained a central precept of its federal system, *Bundestreue*.

Bundestreue,[115] or federal comity, means that the federal government cannot set the states against each other. It has an obligation not to undermine the common interests of the states, but rather to protect them. Likewise, the states have an obligation to each other to consider the effects their actions will have on other states. Laws which fail to do these things, which are (in other words) part of a race of laxity or of dividing and conquering, are unconstitutional. Thus, the German court solves these prisoner's dilemmas of federalism. South Dakota would have gotten the answer that the federal government could not use its funds that way.

---

111 Or more accurately, esophagus.

112 At least, as originally written. There is no such power among those enumerated in Article I, Section 8, and the Tenth Amendment reserves all others to the states individually or the people, so it is therefore long settled that the states have police power (the ability to regulate for the health, safety, and welfare of citizens) and the federal government does not. This has certainly failed to stop the federal government before, though. (Cough.) Wickard! (Cough.) It does not take much to imagine a ruling that regulating the drinking age is necessary and proper to the power to create post roads. In fact, the Court has already said in *South Dakota v. Dole* that drinking age is reasonably related to the building of highways when it comes to federal grants.

113 If you're not singing an Eric Clapton song, shame on you! Know the classics, man.

114 Or *Bundesverfassungsgericht*—ain't that a cool word?

115 Pronounced roughly "boon-dess-troy-eh," which literally means "federal loyalty."

We've come at last to the end of the wonderful ride that is the federalism chapter. Whew! Take a moment to look back at all you've learned. Go on, I'll be here when you get back—we've discussed this before. What is a federal form of government? Why do we have one? What developments have altered it, and why and how have they altered it? Are there other ways we might want to change it? You should be able to answer each of those questions with impressive fullness and depth. If those answers aren't springing to mind, I humbly suggest reading the chapter again, keeping a weather eye out for the answers. Otherwise, take a deep breath as we head into Chapter 4!

Chapter 4: Civil Society

In the last chapter, we looked at an institution—a set of rules—that helps us create a functioning democracy. But that institution alone is not sufficient to the task of creating a functioning and durable democracy. As it turns out, democracy is a lot like education. Education doesn't just happen to you because you're in a class-room, and a stable democracy doesn't just happen to you because you (or people near you) vote. In both cases, you've got to be an active participant (not to be confused with activist). Your car doesn't drive just because you sit in it; you've got to learn how to operate it, make yourself into a driver. Or as Karl Popper puts it, "Institutions are like fortresses. They must be well designed *and* manned."[1] Yeah, I know, it sounds more than a little corny. But that doesn't mean it isn't true. And yes, I'm going to spend this chapter explaining that.[2]

Let's start with this question: what is a democracy? Yeah, I know—it's kind of hard to put it into words, but you know it when you see it.[3] But let's try to be a little more specific, just to make sure we're all seeing the same thing. The original Greek word means something like "the rule of the masses," though we often substitute "the people" for the "the masses" to make it seem a little less scary.[4] After all, we're people, and we work with people and have dinner with people, whereas masses trample us in riots or rush off cliffs together.

And really, this distinction starts to clarify some of our ambiguity about the word *democracy*. Everyone can't be in charge of government—the apparatus would simply be too clumsy (the costs of reaching a decision would be high). Nor can everyone attend to the business of government every day—someone needs to be doing some-thing productive, like raising crops, baking bread, or machining tools (the opportunity costs are too high). So the job gets delegated, and a smaller group of people end up ruling the others on their own behalf.

This brings us to the concept most of us associate with a democracy: voting. We have to have some way of selecting those who will exercise the authority of the masses on behalf of the masses over the masses.[5] Voting (presumably) allows the masses to register their preferences about who those people in charge should be and what they should do, and the need to win those votes again keeps office holders responsive to the masses.[6] Thus the masses select their rulers, and do so temporarily, so that the rulers need to seek their continuing approval.

---

1 Popper, Karl. *The Open Society and its Enemies*. New York, Harper and Row, (1962), 126.

2 Yes, that's a threat, not a promise. And I know what you're thinking: "What's the chance this will be on the test?" To which I reply: You're asking the wrong question, grasshopper. And if your professor's making you read this, probably pretty good.

3 Incidentally, this is also the conclusion Justice Potter Stewart reached when trying to define pornography.

4 Demographics, of course, is drawing a picture of the masses. Sounds like something you'd do for a physics dissertation. (Pun most definitely intended.)

5 You could say, "of the people, by the people, and for the people," but it's been done—and it involves a little sleight-of-hand.

6 If it sounds like we're talking about a principle-agent problem, we are. Very good, grasshopper. But it only looks solved. And as we'll see, we shouldn't be too sure about measuring those preferences, either.

This much the Greeks figured out. But somehow, their democracies tended to be short-lived. In some cases, it lasted only so long (to paraphrase the Scottish historian Alexander Tytler) as it took for the majority to figure out they could spend everyone's money on just themselves (or write the laws, including those about spending public money, to benefit themselves at the expense of others). In other, more prominent cases, the masses fell under the control of one person.[7] Either way, the rule of the masses ended, whether it changed from "all of the people" to "some of the people" or "one of the people."

Preventing this was exactly why our founders created a republic, and a compound one at that. They might have defined *democracy* differently, as "self-rule." In this sense, each citizen should govern herself so that as little government as possible is necessary. That is, the more each guards himself against misusing his liberty to harm others, the less we need others to guard us. Which is true, and makes us feel all warm and fuzzy inside, until we ask how we are to create this state of affairs. In essence, we are saying that if people were more angelic, we would have less need of government. But how do we design institutions to encourage and equip people to regulate themselves?

And trying to answer that question is why, if they had been selling shares in the American republic at its founding, everyone would have been selling it short.[8] So imagine everyone's surprise when, fifty years later, the American experiment in republican government was still running. Especially since the cultured and educated French had in the meantime experimented with democracy, only to fail spectacularly. In fact, France's failure realized our founders' worst fears about democracy, devolving into a Reign of Terror[9] in which the Orwellianly named Committee for Public Safety decided that many of the public were safest under six feet of dirt, and culminating about ten years after its beginning in the rise to power of a dictator, Napoleon Bonaparte.

Had the Americans done something clever, or had they just gotten lucky? The future of democracy as a form of government hung in the balance of the answer.[10] If it was a question of designing institutions correctly, other nations could have stable democracy without the pesky reigns of terror. If the colonists had just gotten lucky, then old-fashioned, moderately repressive monarchy was the best for which humanity could hope. To find out which it was, a young French aristocrat travelled to the United States. Alexis de Tocqueville[11] travelled all across the young republic, speaking with average citizens in their frontier cabins, wealthy socialites in cities, and even President Andrew Jackson (the first President from a frontier state—Tennessee).[12] The ostensible purpose of his trip was to study the American penitentiary system at the request of the French government. But he took the opportunity to investigate the question he thought much more important: how can these backwoodsmen[13] be succeeding where the French failed?[14]

---

7 For whom we have the term *demagogue*, from *demos* (people) and *aggos* (leader); even though not etymologically related to the word "agog" (meaning astounded or bewildered), this does refer to an orator who holds the masses under his spell—sort of like a pied piper of politics (say that five times fast).

8 When you sell something short, you sell a promise to sell something at a lower price in the future. If the price goes even lower, you make a profit. If it goes higher, you have to buy it at the higher price and sell it at the one you promised. Essentially you take on the risk of the price changing for the person who buys your promise. But, unless you enjoy pain, you'll only do that if you expect the price to be lower in the future rather than higher (or enjoy gambling, but that's a different discussion).

9 It's never a good sign if your government goes by the nickname "Reign of Terror." Government nicknames don't work like "Little John" in Robin Hood, where they actually mean the opposite.

10 If you'll pardon the melodrama (and the fact that it sounds like an episode of *Behind the Music*).

11 No word on whether his classmates in elementary school teased him about "Tocque-ing up," but probably not.

12 For that matter, the first President from a state not named "Virginia" or "Massachusetts." (Virginia won the best-of-seven series, 4-2, though the election of John Q. Adams went into extra innings.)

13 In fairness, Andrew Jackson was President, and he was not the most sophisticated of men. His inauguration ended with what can best be described as a frat-house kegger at the White House.

14 And he did do the research the government had sent him to do, so there was no agency loss, if that's what you're thinking. Sure you were.

The book he wrote, *Democracy in America*, is renowned for the beauty of its prose and the clarity of its insight. Tocqueville not only wrote perceptively about the democratic republic he saw, but clairvoyantly about the challenges the young republic would face. In fact, his writing is so eloquent, clear, and still relevant that Tocqueville remains among the most quoted authors in the United States. An editor of *The Washington Post* once forbade his writers to quote Tocqueville anymore, because it had become so commonplace to do so. So although I am going to give you the short version of Tocqueville's answer, I encourage you to read the book for yourself.

Tocqueville found three factors responsible for the success of democracy in America. The least important of these was providence, or the lucky happenstance of history. The American republic had vast oceans separating it from the great military powers of the age. Moreover, they had an immense continent full of resources, relatively sparsely populated. This provided insulation from outside pressure, and a pressure valve to release domestic pressure. Forming a democracy in the midst of powerful enemies, with a densely packed population where scarcity of resources made difference in distribution of wealth more noticeable (and more difficult to redress), would be a greater challenge.

Although being lucky helped some, it was not the most important factor. More important than its lucky geography were the laws under which the American republic operated. Tocqueville pointed to the beneficial effect of several of these, most particularly the federal system and the jury system. In terms of the federal system, Tocqueville pointed both to the role of local (or municipal) institutions in administering federal regulations and to their role in cultivating democratic virtues in citizens. In the first sense, local institutions provide what Tocqueville called "hidden reefs," breaking the tide of central power. That is, even if the federal government, despite its internal checks and balances, passed an improvident piece of legislation, the fact that they had to rely on local governments to implement them restrained the bad effects they might have. Like a reef surrounding a harbor, it smoothed out rough seas.[15]

Municipal institutions also provided an opportunity for individuals to participate in governing themselves and their fellows. Administering laws is, of course, valuable instruction in what government is and how it works. But administering them over friends and neighbors—people you know, rather than anonymous strangers—teaches restraint and moderation. Suddenly you feel the excesses of the law, even if it doesn't bear on you directly. It teaches you to compromise, that is, to consider the interests of others in order to discover ways of reconciling them with your interests. Because you have to have the support of others to accomplish anything, your proposals have to serve their interests too, or at least not oppose them. As Tocqueville says,

> It is difficult to drag a man away from his own affairs to involve him in the destiny of the whole state because he fails to grasp what influence the destiny of the state might have on his own fate. But if it becomes necessary to make a road across the end of his own estate, he sees at once the connection between this minor public affair and his greater private interests and will discover, without being shown, the close link between individual and general interests.

> It is therefore by entrusting citizens with the management of minor affairs, much more than handing over the control of great matters, that their involvement in the public welfare is aroused and their constant need of each other to provide for it is brought to their attention.

> The favor of the people may be won by some brilliant action but the love and respect of your neighbors must be gained by a long series of small services, hidden deeds of goodness, a persistent habit of kindness, and an established reputation of selflessness.[16]

In a similar vein, the jury system both puts power in the hands of those who are ruled and teaches those hands the virtues important to the survival of democracy. As Tocqueville says, jury service not only teaches citizens what their laws are (helping them keep an eye on the legislature and allowing them to resist excesses), but it teaches them the mental habits of judges.[17] That is, people learn to withhold judgment, to weigh evidence,

---

15 Of course, the growth of the federal bureaucracy undermines this. Thanks, FDR.

16 Alexis de Tocqueville, *Democracy in America* (New York: Penguin Classics, 2003), 593.

17 Sound familiar?

to ask questions about information presented to them. They learn how to weigh consequences and evaluate arguments, to apply abstract concepts to concrete circumstances. Plus, they bring you food, and if you're sequestered, it's miniature bottles of shampoo for everyone![18]

Most important, however, was the last element: customs and mores, or as Tocqueville puts it, "habits of heart and mind." Tocqueville pointed to several customs that influenced the success of democracy in America, but two he highlighted most of all: religion and associations. Religion, Tocqueville says, refocuses people's attention from their short-term interests to their long-term interests, and from their own interests to the interests of others.[19] It promotes freedom, because it gets people to limit themselves, that is, to govern themselves. Thus laws may allow for much greater freedom, because religion prevents people from abusing it.

Associations, too, displace government. Many people misread Tocqueville on this point, thinking he was talking about what we call interest groups, or lobbies. Those are indeed associations of individuals, but Tocqueville distinguishes between those political associations—ones formed to extract some favor or benefit from government—and civil associations—those formed to enable a group of individuals to accomplish something together that they could not do alone.[20] Tocqueville had in mind everything from lyceums—groups of citizens who organized to bring lecturers to their town for their edification, which they could not have afforded alone—to barn raisings to bowling leagues (sure, you can bowl alone, but it's hard to enjoy it as much without some friends and some friendly competition).

You can see immediately that these civil associations displace government too, but in a different way. Religion involves self-imposed restraints, whereas this involves self-provision of goods and services, specifically goods and services the market might not otherwise provide.[21] Since this reduces the demand for government to provide these things, it also allows government to be smaller and more limited, restraining one strong impetus for its growth.

What theme runs through all of these causes? They all promote decentralization of power. The gifts of Providence[22]—no powerful neighbors, readily available resources—remove two powerful motivations for the centralization of power. To fight a powerful enemy requires a unity of command; the time and effort it takes to coordinate action among disjointed actors can often be costly. That is, the centralization of power eliminates some coordination problems. Similarly, the "pressure valve" of the western frontier reduced the need to respond to domestic threats, which is often another justification for centralizing power (certainly these were true in France after its revolution). Associations and religion, too, reduced the demand for a government centralized (or unitary) enough to supply that much order or goods and services. And the jury system and decentralized administration of central powers both functioned to check the ability of central government to draw more power to itself.

Balancing the power between the federal government and the states was the primary concern of the founders; whether they had done so was the subject of the debate between the Federalists and Anti-Federalists. But the debate continued long after ratification, as witnessed in the Virginia and Kentucky Resolutions, or the South Carolina Exposition and Protest, for example.[23] Tocqueville reached the same conclusion about the importance of balancing centralization and decentralization from a broader, more abstract view. He begins with the observation that everywhere, equality is increasing. The difference between classes—between nobles

---

18 But don't touch the mini-bar or the pay-per-view.

19 That is, it makes them more angelic—it makes them more likely to defeat the prisoner's dilemma.

20 Sound familiar? What is politics, again?

21 If you haven't caught the connections with Chapter 1 yet, I may have just lost all hope in humanity. But I'll pause for a moment while you refresh your memory of all the fun we had thinking about why we have government. Ah, good times. Good times.

22 Also a great name for a souvenir shop carrying Rhode-Island-themed merchandise; but then, who would buy it?

23 Or for that matter, in the War Between the States (the Civil War, for any Yankees who might be reading this).

and commoners—was disappearing. This is what spurred his interest in democracy in the first place. As equality increased, so would demand for government that reflected that equality among individuals: democracy.

Increasing equality would also, however, increase what Tocqueville termed *individualism*. To the American ear, the word has positive associations with self-reliance, but Tocqueville defined it differently. He defined it as a withdrawal from society into the company of one's close friends and relatives. In other words, equality creates a large mass of undifferentiated individuals of equal status. In the face of this sea of faces, the individual draws back and insulates himself in a small group; in a sense, his reaction is to make humanity once again tractable, by reducing the scale on which he engages with it. No one has deep and abiding common interests with others, as the various classes—aristocrat, merchant, peasant—once did among themselves. Even worse, no one has any reason to expect allegiance or aid from any other; the individual is at once free, but faced with a million equal competitors, with no one on whom he can rely.

One potential response to this vulnerability is to centralize power, so that the central government can provide security from the vicissitudes of life. In fact, Tocqueville says this leads to a new kind of despotism, unique to the democratic age. The sort of despotism which democracies have to fear is not the hobnailed boot of a brutal dictator, but the velvet, insistent nag of the overbearing parent.[24] Rather than turning to your fellow man corporately, however, you could turn to him individually—which associations represent, religion nurtures, and participation in government teaches. Thus these factors—especially the customs or habits of association and religion, and laws that rely on participation—restrain (through decentralization) the tendency of democracy toward tyranny (of the majority, then in the name of the majority).

Perhaps I have not fully explained that last (parenthetical) thought. If we centralize power in the hands of the majority, we might hope that the large number of the majority would make it difficult for them to organize sufficiently to make much use of it. As a practical matter, that is not much of a hope; a child playing with scissors is also unlikely to be able to make good use of them, but very likely to be able to make such use of them as to harm himself or others. That is, he may be incapable of achieving what he set out to accomplish (giving his sister's Barbie a trim), but quite capable of achieving what he did not intend (cutting his finger). Regardless, though, we know that the majority is unlikely to directly exercise its power. We may believe it is just that the majority should exercise such exercise such authority, but we know that the collective action problems involved will dictate another outcome—the delegation of that authority into the hands of those who govern on behalf of the majority. As Tocqueville describes it,

> They conceive a single, protective, and all-powerful government but one elected by the citizens. They combine centralization with the sovereignty of the people. That gives them some respite. They derive consolation from being supervised by thinking that they have chosen their supervisors. Every individual tolerates being tied down because he sees that it is not another man nor a class of people holding the end of the chain but society itself.
>
> Under this system citizens leave their state of dependence just long enough to choose their masters and then they return to it.
>
> At the present time, many people very easily fall in with this type of compromise between a despotic administration and the sovereignty of the people and they think they have sufficiently safeguarded individual freedom when they surrendered it to a national authority. That is not good enough for me. The character of the master is much less important to me than the fact of obedience.[25]

Which raises a very important question: have we reached the point of which Tocqueville warns us? More importantly, can we answer that question without sounding like Lyndon Larouche, Oliver Stone, L. Ron Hubbard,

---

24 At least, he says, you could call it parental, if its goal were to help you mature, rather than keep you in a perpetual need of its care (see Kathy Bates' character in *Misery*). But then, this does seem to be a recent trend in parenting.

25 Alexis de Tocqueville, Democracy in America (New York: Penguin Classics, 2003), 806–807.

or some other crank conspiracy theorist?[26] Robert Putnam[27] argues in his book *Bowling Alone*[28] that Americans, since the 1960s, have been disengaging from public life, failing to build the connections with neighbors and fellow citizens that we call *social capital*. Capital goods are goods used to produce other goods, rather than being consumed. So, for example, your car is a capital good. You use it to produce transportation services which you consume. Likewise, social capital is the stock of human relationships that produce other goods. The trust and affection between individuals that produces rides when your car is in the shop are social capital. According to Putnam, we aren't voting, we aren't joining clubs, we aren't even forming bowling leagues anymore. Instead, we bowl by ourselves, and fail to produce social capital that would allow us to produce political goods.

As proof of this, Putnam looks at membership rolls of clubs like Kiwanis and the Rotary Club; at church membership rolls; at surveys that asked individuals to report how they spent their time; and he looks at changing patterns in both employment (the entrance of women into the (official) workforce) and residence (the move from physically close city neighborhoods to "sprawling" suburbs), among a great many other things. What Putnam particularly looks for is correlation—the degree to which potential causes vary with the effect (the drop in "joining"). He finds that the most important correlations with the decline in association are generational change, the increase in television watching, and the increase in the number of people living in suburbs.

Of course, the problem with correlation is that it does not establish causation. Correlation is a necessary condition for causation, but it is not sufficient by itself. That is, one thing is extremely unlikely to be causing another to happen if there is no pattern to their appearances—whether one is always there when the other is (Superman appearing and Lois Lane being in jeopardy) or they are never present together (Clark Kent and Superman). But even if there is correlation, it does not mean that one causes the other. It means it is possible rather than impossible, but possible is still a long way from actual (ask anyone who's bought a lottery ticket).

To begin with, we can't tell which one is causing the other. It could be that Lois Lane being in danger causes Superman to appear; it could be that Superman's presence causes Ms. Lane to get into danger. Perhaps she takes greater risks knowing that he will save her, or his presence entails the presence of a supervillain who is placing the public (including Ms. Lane) in danger. In fact, this last possibility points to a more serious flaw. There could be another variable (threatening supervillain) that cause both the danger and Superman's presence.

For example, ice cream sales and violent crime are highly correlated.[29] It could be that sugar rushes from ice cream cause violent rampages, or it could be that violent criminals like to celebrate with a more innocent version of "a cold one." Or it could be that hotter weather causes increases in both. And since we can see that those committing violent crimes don't have ice cream dribble on their chins, we're pretty sure the weather causes both.

Last but not least, the correlation could be entirely coincidental (or *spurious*—it looks like there's a relationship, but there's not). For example, you may have had the experience of encountering the same person at about the same time and place every day (or every Monday). Neither of you knows the other, so it's certainly not that the presence of one prompts that of the other. You're not going to the same class, or to the caf,[30] so it's not that the same cause is prompting both to appear. Your schedules just happen to lead you to cross paths, for wholly independent reasons, on a regular basis. But you can't help but wonder if you're being stalked (or if

---

26 H. L. Menken defined the proud American tradition of crank conspiracy theorizing as "the central belief of every moron is that he is the victim of a mysterious conspiracy against his common rights and true deserts. He ascribes all his failure to get on in the world, all of his congenital incapacity and damfoolishness, to the machinations of werewolves assembled in Wall Street, or some other such den of infamy." Word.

27 He's a Harvard professor, so he *must* be right.

28 And argues more briefly in the scholarly article by the same name in the *American Political Science Review*.

29 You heard me. (Or, well, read me.) And I'm not making this up.

30 For the college-lingo-impaired, "caf" is short for "cafeteria."

they are perhaps preparing a restraining order themselves).[31] For some reason, we very much want to ascribe causation to regular patterns of interaction.[32]

So back to Dr. Putnam. Even if we accept that generational change, television, and suburbia are correlated with a decline in social capital, we don't know that they actually caused it. It could be that those things have occurred because of the drop in social capital. Or it could be that they only seem related. Especially disturbing in that context is the fact that we do not have *a priori*[33] a clear theoretical expectation. The increased physical space between people in suburbia might cause them to separate metaphysically, as well; or the press and jostle of urban living might cause people to withdraw from relationships as a way preserving some privacy. Since the elbow room of suburbia allows room for privacy, it may also enable people to associate more. Notice that no matter which correlation we find, we can always rationalize a causal connection. We just have no way of knowing if we have explained it correctly.

There is an even greater problem with the explanation of "generational change." This explanation is really just saying that there is something different about younger generations compared to older generations. I know what you're thinking,[34] and you're exactly right. That's obvious. The problem is that it is so obvious, it is the explanation for itself. It's a truism. It's like saying the sky is blue because it's not red. We still don't know why it's blue, just that it is. And the same is true with "generational change" as an explanation. We need to know what difference in the generations produces the effect. Greater or lesser ingestion of paint chips? Wearing iPod earbuds? Tighter undergarments? Hair pomade?[35]

But the heart of the problem is that Putnam misses Tocqueville's point.[36] Putnam thinks that we, the people, are here to provide government with legitimacy. If we all vote and write our Congresspersons, the outcome of the democratic process will be what the majority wants—and that will be a true and just outcome. Putnam wants you to participate in the system, making its work legitimate. Tocqueville, however, praises associations for making the system unnecessary, not for making use of it. In fact, what Putnam wants is precisely what Tocqueville warns us about—a strong central government with unrestrained majoritarian democracy.

I fear that Putnam is right about the decline of civil society in the United States, even if I doubt his evidence, his definition, and his reasons. When Americans faced a problem in Tocqueville's time, they tended to form a group to solve the problem—and turned to government only when there was no other way. Nowadays,[37] we tend to form a group to lobby government to spend money or write a law. And the problems with that are Legion (it's not a typo, it's a reference). First, there are some problems government cannot solve—or at least, cannot solve without making things worse. Perhaps you remember squabbling with a sibling (or friend or cousin, for you only children) about a toy. You had it first, they took it away, and when both of you complain to your mom, she takes the toy away and puts it where you can't reach it. Now neither of you gets to enjoy it, whereas you could have reached a common understanding and shared it, so that you could both enjoy it.[38] Your interest was in having the toy to yourself (and let's be honest, you were going to enjoy it mainly because your playmate couldn't), but your mom's interest was in peace and quiet.

Likewise, government has different interests from ours. Primarily, it wants not to be disturbed, which for democratic governments means getting re-elected (and for authoritarian ones, not having strikes and

---

31 Probably not. But stay 20 feet away, just in case.

32 My guess is that it compresses the amount of information we have to retain—remember that whole "information cost" thing? By the way, that's how compression software works, too—find a pattern and remember that, then use it to reproduce the individual observations.

33 For those of you who studied Greek instead of Latin, it means "beforehand" or "from before."

34 "Duh." (Sounded a little sarcastic, too.)

35 Don't know what this is? Ask your grandparents. Or watch *O Brother, Where Art Thou?* Whichever is less painful.

36 And spawned a whole generation of American Government textbooks with colorful boxes highlighting how you can Get Involved!

37 This word brought to you in memory of the 2009 AP GoPo Reading, in honor of Eric Zeemering.

38 Remind you of something? Prisoner's Dilemma, perhaps?

protests). So when it tries to fix things, it has to fix them in popular ways. And sometimes what is necessary to fix the problem can't be legislated—take a look at the eternal quest for campaign finance "reform" sometime. The world might be a better place if we all stood patiently in line and treated others politely. But having government force us to do those things is counterproductive. The level of coercion and oversight it would take means first surrendering our freedom.

Second, and more important, is the effect it has on us. It discourages us from trying to *be* people who patiently wait our turn and treat others politely. I suppose the best example of this comes from Charles Dickens' *A Christmas Carol*.[39] If you remember, Ebenezer Scrooge is a man who puts his own interests—particularly his own material interests—ahead of the interests (and feelings) of others. When asked to donate to charity, his response is, "Are there no workhouses?"

Perhaps you, like most of us, aren't up on Victorian social welfare policy, but that's exactly what workhouses were. They were places where the poor—those who could not find work and could not find housing—could live and work as manual laborers for the government. As Scrooge's interlocutor[40] notes, they were not pleasant places, nor sufficient to allow the poor to do more than subsist. In essence, though, Scrooge's retort is that the government is looking after the poor, relieving him of the burden of caring.[41]

Perhaps all of this concern for the state of someone's heart sounds uncomfortably close to a Sunday school lesson, but I will remind you of the importance Tocqueville ascribed to the role of religion in democracy. And one of the reasons he gave for its importance is the same as one he gave in justifying the importance of decentralization to democracy: teaching us to consider others and their interests (precisely what Scrooge had to learn from his supernatural visitors). And unless you slept through the last chapter,[42] you'll remember that our government has become much more centralized, especially since the New Deal.

And this centralization has had precisely the effects Tocqueville said it would. It has increased what he termed "individualism," the tendency to withdraw from others. Certainly that is the complaint everywhere heard, that citizens have lost the "we're all in this together" ethic and replaced it with an "every man for himself" one. Most people attribute this to a decline in moral fiber, or to the lack of a great national emergency like World War II that conditioned a generation to self-sacrifice and concerted action. Again, we see correlation—but it would seem more likely that the self-sacrifice and concerted action we saw in WW II was possible because people had previously learned that behavior was appropriate to such times. I would also point out that WW II occurred in the middle of an era in which the national government centralized a great deal of power. Nor was this centralization solely due to the war—out national government expanded its powers during almost every war in our history, but WW II was the first after which the national government did not contract.

We owe a great deal of this centralization to the Progressive movement. The Progressives believed that government could make people better, and the will of the majority was just and right simply by virtue of belonging to the majority. Among the many reforms we owe to them are the Sixteenth Amendment, which allowed the federal government to tax citizens directly without apportioning the tax by state according to population, and the Seventeenth Amendment, which changed the election of senators from indirect (by state legislatures, whom "the people" elected) to direct ("the people" themselves). The former's purpose was to provide the federal government with the resources to engage in social engineering, the latter's to fight corruption by increasing the role of the noble common voter, who could not be bribed or corrupted like state legislators.

---

39 If you don't know this story, what rock in the Canadian wilderness have you been living under?

40 A fancy word for conversation partner—from the Latin, *inter* (between) and *locute* (speak).

41 Oddly, most people read *A Christmas Carol* as a call for *more* government social welfare policy. But perhaps that just supports my contention that we look to government policy as the first and only solution. Reading it as a call to personal effort to supplant inadequate government provision is more defensible. And if you're reading Dickens in your lit class, be sure to cite where you got that idea (i.e., me).

42 Or have already been tested over it, and assumed it was safe to flush down the memory hole.

The Progressives ridiculed as elitist Madison's distrust of the mob. They weren't "the mob," but "the common man," in whose heart beat justice and fair play. When they didn't, it was because someone had not properly educated them. All that was needed was for those who knew better [43] to explain it to them. They thought that democracy was itself inherently good—not a tool or a means to achieving good government, but an end in itself. "Democratic" was a form of approbation, not just an adjective.

The irony, of course, is the elitism hiding just behind the sycophancy. Even though people were inherently good, sometimes those who knew better [44] had to sometimes correct and educate them—for their own good. This was the motive behind the centralization Progressives [45] advocated, so that the strong hand of central government (guided, of course, by the wise, noble, and well-meaning Progressives) could show people the error of their ways and teach them where their true interests lay. The Progressives didn't want power over you for **their** sake; they wanted it for yours.[46]

The farce, of course,[47] is that people are no less corruptible than senators or state legislators. As Madison understood, public officials are people just like the rest of us, and we just the same as they. Instead of having party machines bribing senators, we now have senators bribing voters with pork to keep their jobs. And of course, interest groups bribing senators—since the federal government now controls so much money, it is worth interest groups' time and money to lobby for laws that benefit them. Madison shackled government so that it wasn't worth your time to try and get government to do something for you. You'd spend more time, money, and effort than if you just did it yourself.

And so we come again to Tocqueville.

If despotism were to be established in present-day democracies, it would probably assume a different character; it would be more widespread and kinder; it would debase men without tormenting them.

. . . It is absolute, meticulous, ordered, provident, and kindly disposed. It would be like a fatherly authority, if, fatherlike, its aim were to prepare men for manhood, but it seeks only to keep them in perpetual childhood;

. . . It provides their security, anticipates and guarantees their needs, supplies their pleasures, directs their principal concerns, manages their industry, regulates their estates, divides their inheritances. Why can it not remove from them entirely the bother of thinking and the troubles of life?

. . . Thus, the ruling power, having taken each citizen one by one into its powerful grasp and having molded him to its own liking, spreads its arms over the whole of society, covering the surface of social life with a network of petty, complicated, detailed, and uniform rules through which even the most original minds and the most energetic of spirits cannot reach the light in order to rise above the crowd. It does not break men's wills but it does soften, bend, and control them; rarely does it force men to act but it constantly opposes what actions they perform; it does not destroy the start of anything but it stands in its way; it does not tyrannize but it inhibits, represses, drains, snuffs out, dulls so much effort that finally it reduces each nation to nothing more than a flock of timid and hardworking animals with the government as shepherd.

I have always believed that this type of organized, gentle, and peaceful enslavement just described could link up more easily than imagined with some of the external forms of freedom and that it would not be impossible for it to take hold in the very shadow of the sovereignty of the people.[48]

Have we reached this point? Tocqueville's description certainly feels eerily familiar, as a direction if not yet a destination. As tragic as the flooding in New Orleans after Hurricane Katrina was, the first reaction after it was to turn to the federal government for aid. When there was a steroid scandal in baseball, the immediate

---

43 Also known as "Progressives."

44 Also known as "Progressives."

45 The people who knew better.

46 As Tocqueville once observed (in the preface to another of his great works, *The Ancien Regime and the French Revolution*), ones' love of centralized power is inversely related to his trust in his fellow man.

47 A farce is a farce, of carse, of carse . . .

48 Alexis de Tocqueville, *Democracy in America* (New York: Penguin Classics, 2003), 804–806.

reaction was to consider federal legislation. Banks play musical chairs with risky loans, and the federal government steps in to make sure the music keeps playing.

Of course, we can pile up confirming examples, and all we will accomplish is failing to falsify the hypothesis—we can't really prove that it is so. So let us simply say that it is possible, and let us assume for the sake of argument that yes, increasing centralization has turned us from independent citizens working together to **be** the government into dependent subjects **of** the government, seeking its favor. How can we fix this? My pet answers are repealing the Sixteenth and Seventeenth Amendments, for a start. Even if repealing the Sixteenth is too strong a medicine, limiting the rate of taxation (to a single digit number) and requiring a balanced budget would redirect a great deal of our attention to more local governments. An amendment restricting the commerce clause (to commerce, perhaps) would also accomplish a great deal, returning a lot of policy decisions to the local level.

What's that you say? You'll get right on that? True, these are somewhat tall orders for any of us individually (though that is something of the point). But in the meantime, take every opportunity you can to solve problems with your fellow citizens. When your efforts alone aren't enough, get some others together who could benefit from solving the problem. You may have to persuade them, you may have to come up with creative ways to avoid free-riding problems. But there are some great places you can go to practice, like serving on a jury or in a local government. I mean, your great-grandparents did it, and they never learned to set the clock on the VCR,[49] did they? So take Tocqueville's advice and engage in "a long series of small services, hidden deeds of goodness" and "a persistent habit of kindness." You might just end up with the love and respect of your neighbors.

---

49 "VCR" is what we called DVD players back when DVDs were plastic cassettes filled with magnetic tape. I think the Smithsonian still has one, if you want to look it up the next time you're in D.C.

Chapter 5: The Legislative

 We now turn our attention to Congress, the place the love and respect of your neighbors goes to die.[1] I do not wish to plead for sympathy for the devil—I come to bury Caesar, not to praise him—but there is something odd, perhaps disturbing,[2] about most voters' relationship with Congress. Congress is a body generally held in contempt, as evidenced not least by its prominence as the butt of jokes. It is rare to find a citizen with a kind word for Congress.[3] Yet we continue to elect our particular Congressperson. Opinion polls—for what they're worth[4]—tell us that we generally approve of *our* representative; it's everyone else's who are the problem. So it's not that we hate our Congressperson and seek to punish her[5] with the company of the rest of them. We love our Congressperson, but hate Congress. How do we explain this disturbed relationship?

I could give you the answer right now,[6] but then I'd have to come up with some other excuse for making you read about Congress.[7] Plus, it wouldn't fit the pattern of all the other chapters, which is important, and not solely for my OCD.[8] It is also important because it should help you organize the information, and therefore learn it better. It makes this an inquiry, rather than a recitation. And holding the subject constant (which we must), inquiries are much more interesting than recitations—witness the popularity of crime dramas over PBS[9] documentaries (and that many documentaries now try to mimic the "whodunit" theme). So yes, it is a conceit,[10] but it should be a useful one. And you're stuck with it, either way.

So let's first perform a vivisection of Congress to find out exactly what it is and how it works.[11] Because Congress has the sole legislative authority in the federal government, and because they are the closest to the citizens—the most representative, and the most responsive—our Founders considered them the most dangerous branch. Of course, the Founders took precautions to mitigate that danger, but let us first consider why they made it dangerous to begin with.

That is, Congress is the most representative because it has small constituencies and short terms in office, relative to other federal officers. The President represents the whole nation, whereas the size of the average

---

1 Coincidentally, it is also full of people who can't set VCR clocks.

2 Or even "oddly disturbing" and "disturbingly odd."

3 One poll published as I was writing this placed Congress in a tie with used car dealers for the amount of trust the public has in them (and thanks to Renee Reyle for telling me about it).

4 Not much.

5 Marsha Blackburn.

6 Rent seeking.

7 Union rules—they'd pull my textbook author union card.

8 Obsessive-compulsive disorder. You probably knew that, but I had to make sure. OCD. And union rules.

9 The Public Broadcasting Service; if you're not familiar with their particular brand of high-fiber, educational programming, you either grew up calling it the Canadian Broadcasting Corporation, or your parents didn't love you.

10 In the sense of an artifice which requires you to play along, rather than that of arrogance.

11 If that does not presume too much. (See, I told you Congress is an easy target.)

Congressional district is, well, 1/435th of that (guess how many Representatives there are in Congress). Small interests that are locally concentrated may elect a Representative; they have no hope of influencing, let alone determining, a Presidential election.[12] Federal judges are appointed, not elected, as are bureaucrats—and they are appointed to represent not people, but abstract ideas (justice and such). Representatives face re-election every two years; the President has a four-year term, and federal judges (at least those on the Supreme Court) serve for life, or until they start knocking over convenience stores in their spare time. This makes Representatives very responsive. If they displease enough constituents, those constituents will shortly have the opportunity to do something about it. Supreme Court justices can call voters' mamas all sorts of things, but the voters can't do a thing about it.

Of course, I have thus far referred to the House of Representatives, rather than the Senate. And I intend to continue that for a brief while yet. The Senate had a different purpose in the legislative branch, which we will discuss at a more appropriate point. First, though, we should consider why the Founders wanted a branch to be representative and responsive. And the answer is that it beats the alternatives. As we've discussed previously (unless you skipped Chapter 1), human nature does not make anarchy an attractive option. Some of us might be able to live together in peace without an authority over us to keep the peace,[13] but not nearly enough of us.

So we need an authority over us. The question then becomes to whom this authority should answer. Popular answers include no one (monarchy or tyranny), God (theocracy[14] or divine-right monarchy), a few (oligarchy), the noble (aristocracy), and the masses (democracy). In all of the others aside from democracy, a smaller group—a minority of greater or lesser size—controls authority, and may use that control to promote their interests over those of others or the polity as a whole.[15] When the masses are in charge, though, any pursuit of self-interest on the part of authority will at least promote the interests of most of the people. Of course, that raises another question: how "most" is *most*? We could say that everyone would have to agree, but then we are unlikely to reach many decisions. One member can hamstring the process, holding out to extract concessions in their favor from the others. So as a practical matter, *most* probably has to mean more than half, but not so much as all.

So once again we find ourselves at the mercy of another question[16]: how do we keep the most from pursuing their interest at the expense of common interest, or needlessly imposing cost on the rest? That is, the good we get from democracy is to let the larger part pursue its interest. But there are interests we must keep them from pursuing, if pursuing them too greatly damages the interests of the minority. The fact that we have more people in charge doesn't make such abuse any less likely. In fact, if you've been around a mob lately, you'll know that it probably makes it *more* likely. And the fact that fewer people are being hurt does not (or should not) make the abuse any more just. Otherwise, feeding Britney Spears and Paris Hilton to lions is okay, so long as enough people (and lions) enjoy it.[17]

If this begins to sound familiar, it should. It was to solve this problem that the Founders turned to federalism and the separation of powers (or did you miss Chapter 3, too?).[18] They wanted to get the benefits of democracy while avoiding or at least mitigating its less pleasant side effects. Thus they balanced the responsiveness of the House with the more insulated Senate: not only elected every six years (three times the length of a House term), but elected by state legislatures, rather than popular vote (*popular* referring to the population,

---

12 Technically, very little hope. If *everyone* else forgot to vote, they'd have a good chance, but that's not much to pin your hopes on. And of course, I am eliminating illegal means of influence, like bribery and extortion.

13 Though not, of course, without singing "kumbaya." A lot. While holding hands.

14 Technically, in a theocracy, God *is* the authority, and answers to Himself (like the king in a monarchy). In practice, however, earthly agents (clerics) rule and presumably answer to Him.

15 What was that term again? Horal mazard? No, that's not it . . .

16 Seriously, these things are worse than rabbits.

17 Hmm . . . maybe not the best example.

18 Yes, you have to remember stuff from other chapters. No, that is not an injustice.

not a criterion). Thus, the Senate was to provide a soothing semi-aristocratic ointment to the inflamed democratic passions of the House.[19]

However, the legislature is the most dangerous not only because it is the branch most closely connected to the masses, but also because of the nature of its power. It writes the laws. Now, the ability to enforce the laws (the physical power of coercion which belongs to the executive) may run it a close second. In the end, though, the legislature gets to decide what it is the executive can force people to do, and since it also controls the raising and spending of revenue, the legislature can make it worth people's while to follow their instructions. There's a limit to what you can physically force people to do, and a limit to the number of people you can physically coerce at a time—when you have half the country holding a gun to the heads of the other half. So long as you can print or borrow money, though, there is no effective limit to the people you can bribe to comply. Or at least, Congress hasn't discovered it yet.

Thus, the Philadelphia Convention spent a great deal of its time on structuring the legislative branch. In fact, the order in which the Constitution deals with the different branches gives a rough indication of how dangerous the Founders considered them, as does the length at which the Constitution treats them.[20] The first and longest article in the Constitution concerns the legislative power of the federal government. And that article splits the federal legislative chamber in twain,[21] creating the House of Representatives and the Senate.

The House of Representatives was (and is) elected directly by citizens. Each representative is elected from a district, with districts apportioned to states (who draw the district boundaries) according to state population. In fact, this is why we have a census every ten years; the Constitution requires it for the reallocation of districts. Until the government could conduct a census, it simply gave the number of districts each state would have, producing a House of sixty-five members initially. The Constitution specifies only that a district can have no fewer than 30,000 people in it, with the caveat that every state must have at least one. Congress regulates the size of districts,[22] and it decided in 1929 to fix the number of seats at 435 (the size it reached in 1912), rather than continuing to add seats to the House. As a result, the size of a district is what now varies. According to Title 2 of the U.S. Code, each state gets one seat, and then seats are allocated according to a largest remainders formula (though it is called the method of equal proportions).

Although the actual formula is somewhat different, the basic idea works something like this. Say we have a country with a population of 100,000 and a legislature with ten seats. Now imagine that this country has five states: A (pop. 30,000), B (pop. 25,000), C (pop. 20,000), D (pop. 15,000), and E (pop. 10,000). We assign each state the minimum of one district, and divide its population by the number of districts it now has. Since that's one district, each state's quotient is still the same as its population. We add the next district to the state with the highest quotient, which is A (at 30,000). We divide again, and now A's quotient is 15,000 (30,000/2), while the others' are still the same as their populations. The next district (the seventh overall) goes to state B (with a quotient of 25,000). In the next round, A's quotient is 15,000 and B's is 12,500, so C gets the next district (eighth overall) with a quotient of 20,000. In the next (and as it turns out, final) round, A and D tie, so each gets one additional district.[23] The final totals are three for A; two for B, C, and D; and one for E.

The actual formula makes finer distinctions than the rough one we used (dividing by the number of districts allocated), but the principle is the same. Ideally, each district would have a size of 10,000 (the quota, so to speak, for a district is 100,000 divided by 10, or 10,000). However, life is rarely so kind as to apportion

---

19 That's right, the Senate was originally democratic Preparation H. I said it.

20 It is named, oddly, "Article I." I thought they'd go with "Rufus," but I suppose they wanted to avoid confusion with a delegate by that name from Massachusetts.

21 An archaic way of saying "two." See *Robin Hood: Men in Tights*.

22 Though Madison proposed a constitutional amendment along with those adopted as the Bill of Rights which would have stipulated a system for enlarging minimum district sizes as Congress increased in membership; it was sent to the states, but has not yet been ratified. In fairness, we have grown so far beyond its minimums that it would change nothing if ratified.

23 Has there been but one district remaining, it would have gone to D, since it had not yet received an additional district, and A had—unless, of course, the law specified something else for that situation.

itself neatly, and we would still be left with the conundrum of having 2.5 districts in B and 1.5 districts in D. While the idea of sawing Congresspeople in half is often quite appealing, it is somewhat pointless in a practical sense, as half a Congressperson functions amazingly like no Congressperson. Thus, the formula helps us determine who has the greatest claim to the next whole seat, if our goal is to apportion in as equal proportions as possible.[24]

Once we have determined the number of districts dealt to each state, the fun really begins. As mentioned above, state legislatures are responsible for drawing district lines, and like everything else legislatures do, they often do so for fun and profit. The practice of drawing district lines so as to influence the outcomes of elections is known colloquially[25] as "gerrymandering."[26] There are multiple ends to which one may decide to gerrymander, but the means remain the same: to affect through careful placement of district lines the concentration in a district of a group with desired characteristics.

Let us begin with a fictional state, called Schmansas. Let us assume Schmansas is a nice, neat rectangle (if you prefer a square, call it Schmolorado). Let us further assume that Schmansas has four allotted districts. Simply looking at the state, we would probably make our first draft of the district lines as shown in Figure 5.1, bisecting the state on each axis (north/south and east/west) and dividing it into four smaller, proportional rectangles. It's nice, it's neat, and we can still make it home in time for dinner.[27] And since we used geographic features to draw the lines, no one can accuse us of any hanky-panky (or gerry-merry) with the concentration of this or that group.

But then, of course, it hits us like lightning[28]: the districts are geographically equal, but what about population? Because they are supposed to be as equal as possible in terms of population, not in terms of land area. Is the population of Schmansas likely to be evenly distributed, or at least clumped equally into four areas? Well, it is *our* imaginary state, so I suppose we could imagine it that way. But if we want to use it to understand the real world, though, it probably won't do us much good unless that assumption is a reasonable one. And in fact, it is relatively heroic. That is, it requires a great amount of strength to hold it up. For many reasons, ranging from our innate sociability[29] to convenience (it's either where our employers or our customers are, or both), we tend to live together in groups, clumped together with spaces between us. Which is, of course, a really complicated way of pointing out that cities have much higher population densities than suburban or rural areas.

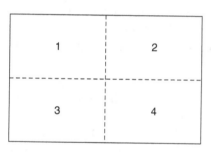

Figure 5.1 Hypothetical Districts in Schmansas

So if K—I mean, Schmansas has a couple of cities with suburbs, some smaller towns, and some farms (that is, if it looks like just about every other state of the union in that regard), then our geographically equal districts are likely to have very different population sizes. So we need to redraw them to take population density—and variation in it—into account. As long as we're looking at the concentration of people, though, why not look at the concentration of people who prefer one party to the other? It turns out, not only do we humans flock, we tend to do so with birds of similar feather.

There's something of a chicken-and-egg problem here, as we're not sure whether people have similar interests because they live in the same place, or if they live in the same place because they feel more comfortable

---

24 Which was, of course, the name of the thing. And yes, I'll file this whole discussion under "more than you ever wanted to know."

25 Yes, those geeky enough to say "gerrymandering" also use adverbs like "colloquially." They could say "on the street," or "by its rapper name," but we all know they'd just be frontin', yo.

26 His friends just call him "Diddy."

27 'Cause let's face it, reheats suck.

28 Suddenly, and leaving a burning smell behind.

29 Mad props to Aristotle on that one.

with people who have similar interests. There is probably something to both of them, to be honest, but for our purposes it is enough to know that we tend to find pockets of people who vote for the same party. So if we, the majority party in the state legislature, draw the lines to make sure that our supporters are a majority in as many districts as possible, we can maximize the number of House seats our party wins, even if the state is relatively evenly split.

We may not be able to get all of the districts. In fact, probably not. Consider, however, a situation in which all of our support is concentrated in one district, and we win that district 90-10, but lose the other three. If we can split that large concentration of support (and add little parts of other districts with our supporters), we can get two districts with smaller (but still safe) margins of victory—maybe 55-45. And voilá, we have doubled the number of seats our party wins. And if we let the other party do the same, then they'll have two districts where they don't have to spend as much time and money campaigning, and we'll have two districts where we don't have to spend as much time and money campaigning—and everyone goes home happy. We'll even have passed a "bipartisan" bill.

It is important to note at this point that, although it is often used to suggest equity, fairness, or justice, *bipartisan* is not a synonym of any of those, at least in regard to the public. It means that both sides got some of their interests addressed, but it does not mean that the number was evenly or fairly divided between those interests. Even less does it mean that the public's interests were among those addressed. Almost all elected representatives, for example, are usually in favor of raising their pay, but this is not necessarily fair to the public. After all, your plumber probably thinks his services are worth more than whatever you pay him (unless you tip your plumber and are an astoundingly good tipper). Not that plumbers have an especially high opinion of themselves—any one of us is likely to see the services we render as more valuable than the compensation we receive. If nothing else, we are intimately familiar with all the effort that goes in to it. Or maybe that wasn't you complaining about your grade on the last exam.

Thus it is that we begin to gerrymander.[30] And whether partisan or bipartisan, it allows politicians to influence the outcomes of elections, to the House of Representatives or to the state legislature. Since it boils down to motive—why did the legislature draw a line here?—it can be very difficult to prove any wrongdoing (that the lines do not merely divide up an area as expeditiously as possible). Of course, the stranger—or perhaps better said, the more unique—the shape of the district, the fewer the other motives which might have produced it. For example, in Mississippi after the Civil War, the legislature created one majority black district (a "shoestring" running the length of the Mississippi River) to leave the other five districts with white majorities. In the 1950s, Alabama changed the boundaries of the city of Tuskegee from a square to (as described by the Supreme Court in *Gomillion v. Lightfoot*) "an uncouth twenty-eight-sided figure," the effect of which was to exclude all black voters, and only black voters, from the city.

Lest we think racial gerrymandering a thing of the past, the Supreme Court heard two cases in the 1990s (specifically, *Shaw v. Reno* in 1993 and *Shaw v. Hunt* in 1996) regarding an oddly shaped district in North Carolina. The district's borders ran down the side of the interstate for several miles to connect two areas, creating a district with a black majority. The Supreme Court struck this down, concluding that strange shapes which include voters with only skin color in common violate the equal protection clause of the Fourteenth Amendment. Justice O'Connor, writing for the majority, remarked that the district bore "an uncomfortable resemblance to political apartheid."

You are perhaps too young, dear reader, to understand the comparison Justice O'Connor made.[31] Apartheid was the official government policy in South Africa for most of the twentieth century. Like segregation in the U.S. South, it was a set of laws requiring that the two races living in the country—native blacks and white

---

30 The American Government Textbook Writer's Union (AGTWU) requires that I tell you the origin of this odd word. Elbridge Gerry, when governor of the Commonwealth of Massachusetts, proposed an electoral district whose shape an enterprising editorial cartoonist embellished with wings and claws as the mythical salamander of alchemy. Soon, Gerry's Salamander became a gerrymander, thereafter adapted as a verb (much as has happened with the word "bling"). Whew! My union card is safe for another page.

31 Did the waist of my pants just move two inches toward my armpits?

settlers of English, Dutch, and German descent—be kept strictly separated, in jobs, in neighborhoods, in public accommodations, in short, everywhere. One facet of apartheid was the creation of "Bantustans," or "ethnic homelands" which were nominally independent countries within South Africa. Citizens of native African descent had their citizenship moved from the Republic of South Africa to one of these reservations.

The purpose in creating Bantustans, of course, was to isolate and repress an ethnic group. That was also the purpose of the "shoestring" district in Reconstruction-era Mississippi and changing the boundaries of Tuskegee in Jim Crow Alabama, if to a lesser degree.[32] And though the North Carolina legislature claimed a different motive—to ensure a racial minority could control at least one district, rather than to make sure it could control at most one district—the actions themselves are indistinguishable. The "shoestring" gerrymander, remember, had the effect of guaranteeing one district to a minority, too.

Probably we would all agree that gerrymandering is a bad idea, at least in terms of the common good (it may be very good for the interests of particular groups). It is also something we will find devilishly hard to eliminate; someone has to draw the boundaries, and they will always have an incentive to draw them to promote their interests.[33] Even if we built a computer to draw them, someone would have to program the computer. Until we can build a better person, we are left with the same old mousetrap. We can, however, hope to eliminate the most egregious cases. For example, the Supreme Court has invalidated some gerrymandering, as we saw above. In 2003, Democratic members of the Texas legislature fled to Oklahoma to ensure there would not be enough members of the legislature present for quorum.[34] Had the legislature been called into session, the Republican majority planned to pass a redistricting bill with particularly partisan gerrymanders.

Figuring out the electoral district to be represented is, of course, just the first step in figuring out who will do the representing. The Constitution leaves most of this to the states, in the absence of Congressional action. That is, the Constitution sets the requirements that a Representative must be twenty-five years old, have been a citizen of the United States at least seven years, and must be a resident of the state from which he is elected. Those who will vote for them must meet whatever requirements the state sets for those who vote for "the most numerous Branch of the State Legislature." Everything else is left for the states to determine, subject to Congress' ability to alter those arrangements by statute. Constitutional amendments have since prohibited states from using race (Fifteenth), gender (Nineteenth), payment of a tax (Twenty-Fourth), or any age above 18 years (Twenty-Sixth) as qualifications.

So, for example, in a typical state, all citizens over the age of 18, who have not committed a felony, are able to cast a vote. The fact that it is all citizens over 18 is the result of both Constitutional stipulations (the amendments mentioned above) and state law (removing property ownership requirements, for example, and requiring registration and residency). Disqualification on the basis of criminal conviction is from state law, and varies by state not only in whether it is a disqualification, but in the duration of the ineligibility and the means of ending it (whether automatic or requiring a hearing before a judge, for example).

Once the vote is cast, of course, the next question is how to count it. Again, states decide this, unless Congress overrides them. The most common electoral rule in the United States is plurality—the candidate with the most votes wins. To my knowledge, almost all states use this "first past the post" rule; the one exception is Louisiana, which has a majority run-off rule. If a candidate gets a majority in the first round, that candidate wins; otherwise, the top two finishers face off in a second round. Of course, the second round need not produce a majority in favor of one candidate or the other, but it is extremely likely to do so. In fact, it will fail to do so only when there is a tie, because the votes are split between only two candidates. Because we have a

---

32 Interestingly, the current Wikipedia entry on Bantustans describes them as "gerrymandering."

33 What was it we called that again? A floral bazaar?

34 *Quorum* is the number of members of a committee or legislative body which must be present for the body to conduct business; it is usually defined in by-laws or procedures.

two-party system,[35] the plurality rule tends to look a great deal like a majority rule. When two candidates split the votes, the one with more also has a majority.[36]

We elect the Senate in much the same way, except that their districts are the entire state. Each state has two Senators, and their terms are six years. They must be at least thirty years old, and have been a citizen for at least nine years. These differences were intended to make the Senate a more mature and less responsive body. Jefferson compared it to a saucer—apparently, it was once common practice[37] to cool tea in the saucer before returning it to the cup, and the Senate would likewise allow some of the heat of popular passion[38] from the House to dissipate before the product became law. Though these provisions do allow the Senate to function this way to some degree, changes in the election of Senators have reduced the benefits of bicameralism.

As I alluded to earlier, the Senate originally had a slightly different—or better said, larger—purpose. State legislatures elected Senators, and this indirect election not only increased its insulation from popular passions, but provided representation for the states *as states* in the federal government.[39] The Seventeenth Amendment, ratified in 1913 (and thus first having effect for the third of the Senate whose terms ended in 1914), changed this to popular election, so that citizens of the states directly elect their Senators. As I've mentioned, this decreased the insulation of Senators from popular sentiment.

I would argue, however, that it had a much more damaging effect in changing the constituency of the Senate from the legislatures to the populace of the state. For one thing, the vastly smaller size of legislatures (relative to their populace) and their institutional structure made them much more effective overseers of Senators' behavior. Essentially, citizens are likely to wait for another citizen to be the watchdog, since they'll enjoy the benefits whether they contribute to the oversight effort or not.[40] Legislatures are likely to assign the task to a specific committee.

More importantly, however, the change in constituency has affected the way Senators *vote*. Let's think about how that might matter for a moment. Elected officials will generally pursue the interests of those who elect them, so that they will re-elect those officials. Obviously, there is some margin of error (the officials may pursue their own interests, so long as they do not fear exposure[41]), and citizens may differ in their definition of their interests (leaving the official to sort out the morass as well as she can—but likely sacrificing some interests for the sake of others). The nature of the constituency may affect these; in fact, I've just presented an argument that legislatures can narrow the margin of error in their representation, by increasing the fear of exposure. Smaller groups are also more likely to have more homogeneity in their interests.

Let us hold those two considerations constant, however, and look solely at the effect of varying the nature of the constituency. How are the interests of state legislatures likely to diverge, if at all, from those of the citizens of their state? No, it's okay—take a few minutes and think it through. We'll start with the assumption that the citizens of a state have a given set of interests. We could define them, but the particular interests in the set aren't important—just the fact that there **are** particular ones in the set suffices, since we're not going to alter them. Whatever the personal interests of the state legislator, I think we can agree that she will want to promote the interests of her citizens. So although she may not hold them originally, or on her own, she will behave as if they were hers.

---

35 Other countries have more, but we never worry about our political party deficit, do we? Odd, that.

36 Of course, part of the reason we only have two parties is that we use a plurality rule—but I've got to save something for the chapter on parties. You heard me.

37 At least, in the Jefferson household.

38 If you don't believe passions run high, look up the number of fights that have occurred in the Capitol building as a result of things said in debate.

39 Knock-knock. Who's there? Chapter 3.

40 Free-basing? Base-jumping? What was that again?

41 Yep, you know the name for that. Rhymes with "latency pus."

So far, then, there is no difference between the interests of citizens of a state and their state legislators. One will hold those interests originally, and the other instrumentally—because they are the means to the legislator's interest in re-election (or "promotion" to higher office). Substantively—in the substance or nature of the interest—there will be no difference, or at least, we have discovered none yet. Does the legislator, however, have an interest which a citizen does not? We have already discussed one: by virtue of being a legislator, the legislator has an interest in re-election which the citizen does not share. Are there perhaps other interests which the position of legislator engenders, which the position of citizen does not?

I can think of at least one.

(Humming to self.)[42]

Just wanted to give you a chance to get there on your own. So let's see if you took it. Let us say that the interest the citizen has requires a regulation, or a government action of some sort. Does the citizen care whether it is the federal or the state government which takes the action? When you need a ride to the airport, do you care which friend[43] supplies it? You might care, if there's a friend to whom you're not comfortable being indebted. Or if you care about your friend's interests and feelings, and don't wish to always burden the same friend. But do we have either of those reactions to government? That is, do citizens feel an interest in preserving federalism?

I think the answer has to be "no," at least for most of us.[44] We have, as James Madison would tell us, an indirect interest in preserving a balance between state and federal governments. We don't read Mr. Madison, though, and because it is indirect, we do not feel it as strongly,[45] and our direct interest drowns it out.

For state legislators, however, it is a direct interest. For that matter, federal officers feel it directly, too, simply with the opposite polarity. Each would prefer to be the friend to whom we are indebted, so that we will vote to re-elect her. Thus state legislators care very much about whether a policy is decided at the state or federal level, as do federal legislators. Here we see the change the Seventeenth Amendment has wrought. Formerly, Senators would protect state prerogatives, and only nationalize policies where state legislators saw an interest in it.[46] Now they have an interest in expanding federal authority as much as possible.

So let's look at *South Dakota v. Dole*[47] again for a second (well, okay, for a few minutes[48]). The power to regulate drinking age[49] falls under the police powers, the general ability of a legislature to legislate for the health, safety, and welfare of its citizens. The federal government, as a government of enumerated[50] powers, does not possess these general powers. So there is no question that regulating drinking ages falls under state authority. Nevertheless, I don't have to know what state you're in[51] to know at what age the shape you're in[52] would be legal. How has the federal government been able to regulate without regulating?

Easy—it conditioned the receipt of part of the money it gives states to build and maintain roads on whether the state's drinking age was at least twenty-one. South Dakota sued, saying that the federal government had

---

42 Hard to tell. Could be the *Jeopardy!* theme—or "Scooby-Doo, Where Are You?"

43 Alison Parker or H. Vaughn May.

44 I mean, most of us can't **define** federalism, let alone detect an interest in it.

45 As John C. Calhoun would tell us, if we read him, either.

46 Which does happen—remember, solving collective action problems among states is an important purpose for having the federal government.

47 Not **that** Dole.

48 They'll only **seem** like hours.

49 If I have to explain to a bunch of college students what the drinking age is, either you're in a foreign country—like Utah—or the end of the world is upon us.

50 Delegated, limited—pick your favorite adjective.

51 Just that you are in one of the fifty states, as opposed to a foreign country—which, technically, California is not, no matter how much we wish it were.

52 If you're not thinking of an Eric Clapton song by now, shame on you. Know the classics, man. (Whoa. Déjà vu.)

the authority neither to regulate drinking, nor to coerce South Dakota to do so. The Supreme Court held that the federal government was neither regulating nor coercing South Dakota's regulation; it was merely presenting the states with a choice. Either states could raise their drinking age, or they could forego five percent of the federal highway funds they would otherwise receive. Since the states were free to choose, the condition did not violate the Constitution.

Let's think about the situation in which this places the states, though. They could all turn down the five percent of the funds, in order to protect their prerogatives in police power over potent potables.[53] If they all did, it might cause Congress to reconsider the condition, since it would result in five percent fewer roads than Congress evidently wanted (and Congress would take the blame for leaving the states with a budget shortfall). It would also allow the states to paint themselves as the protectors of their citizens. Some states, however, already have twenty-one as their drinking age, so for them, it is costless to comply (they already have done) but costly to decline (they have to make up the shortfall with higher taxes or reduced services). Suddenly, the picture for voters changes—other states are accepting the money, why are we having to pay more for our roads? Why should we bear the cost of standing on principle for the benefit of those who don't?

Sound familiar?[54] Can't quite put your finger on it? The states are better off if they stand together; they protect federalism and potentially force Congress to remove the condition on the funds. Each state individually, however, is better off letting others take that risk while it accepts the money and the condition; after all, if the others succeed in defending federalism, they will have defended it for everyone, not just those who bore the cost.[55] By creating a collective action problem,[56] the federal government has essentially made the states' decisions for them, precisely while appearing to do nothing of the sort. In other (and more immortal) words, they made them an offer they couldn't refuse.[57] The only recourse the few states who wanted to refuse had was to file suit in a federal court, to try and get the "divide and conquer" strategy itself declared out-of-bounds.

Interestingly, the German Federal Constitutional Court has developed a doctrine (*Bundestreue*, last seen cavorting near the end of Chapter 3) that forbids precisely this. A Senate filled with representatives of state legislatures, rather than individuals, would have *prevented* it. They could not place their constituents in such a position and expect to retain *their* positions at the expiration of their terms. A Senate representing individuals, however, can have that expectation. Furthermore, they have an interest in placing states in such situations, so **they** can the ones who are "doing something," the ones who are helping their constituents.

Now that we've looked at why we have a two-chambered legislature, let's look at how those two chambers organize themselves. First let's look at the tale of the tape, for some technical specifications.[58] The House is slightly more than four times the size of the Senate, at least in terms of membership (its ratio by weight is oddly unavailable)—the House has 435 members, the Senate 100. As we've discussed in relation to at least the House of Representatives, neither number appears in the Constitution. Federal law sets the size of the House at 435; the Constitution specifies a formula for the size of the Senate (two per state), but the number 100 is simply the result of using that formula (though probably enshrined somewhere in federal law itself). Senatorial terms are three times the length of Representative terms; the entire House faces election every two years. Only one third of the Senate faces election at a time—the terms are staggered so that the entire membership does not turn over at once. The Constitution (as mentioned previously) apportions Senate seats by state, and those in the House by population (see Table 5.1).

---

53 For both the *Jeopardy!* and Peter Piper fans.

54 Really, the whole thing should. We talked about this in Chapter 3.

55 And if you don't think risk is costly, talk to an insurance agent or casino operator. Or, if you have enough hand sanitizer, an economist.

56 Starts with a "p." Ends with a "risoner's dilemma."

57 I **told** you government is like the mafia—what, you didn't believe me?

58 Or "specs," as the cool kids (in the AV Club) call them; the really cool kids (in Auto Shop) call them "tech specs."

Table 5.1 The Legislative Tale of the Tape

House	attribute	Senate
435	size	100
by population	apportionment	by state (2 per)
2 years	term	6 years
Speaker of the House	leadership	President of the Senate

So far, so boring. You should have known a great deal of that from elementary school, if not Saturday morning cartoons.[59] The difference in the leadership structures of each chamber, however, is somewhat less susceptible to animation and musical interpretation. It also begins to give us some idea of the differences (and similarities) in how the chambers organize themselves. This last is an important thing to emphasize—the chambers do organize themselves to a great degree. Comparatively little of what we discuss on this topic is specified in the Constitution, or even in federal law. Much of it comes from rules which each house adopts for itself.

The posts of Speaker of the House and President of the Senate, however, are described in the Constitution. The House elects its Speaker; the Electoral College selects the President of the Senate, though only incidentally. The person elected Vice President of the United States[60] becomes, by virtue of holding that office, the President of the Senate.

Speaker of the House is a somewhat powerful position; it was once very powerful. As the House grew in numbers, the decision-making costs rose even more sharply. The solution to this was to delegate more decision-making authority to the Speaker, who functioned as the agenda setter for the chamber. I know what you're thinking, but that's an *Irish* setter. An agenda setter is (as anyone who's had the dubious pleasure of serving on a committee will tell you) the person who runs a meeting—who decides the order in which the group will consider the business before it, and manages their progress through those items (recognizing people to speak so that debate is orderly, etc.). I know what you're thinking[61]: if you dipped yourself in toxic waste and came out with those as your superpowers, you'd sue someone.[62] But these are actually quite stunning powers—you just don't know it yet. I can sense your doubt,[63] so please allow me to demonstrate.

Let's say that you and two friends are voting on what city to visit on your shared vacation. For financial reasons, you can only go to one city. Each of you suggests a city: you, Atlanta; Chris, Chicago; and Pat, Baltimore. Table 5.2 shows how each of you feels about those options. Your first choice is Atlanta, but you prefer Baltimore to Chicago. Chris prefers Chicago most of all, and Atlanta to Baltimore. Pat's favorite is Baltimore, followed by Chicago, then Atlanta. Note that each of your individual preferences is transitive; you prefer a to b, and b to c, and therefore a to c.

Table 5.2 The Voting Tale of the Tape

person	preferences	results	majority
you	a > b > c	a vs. b: a	you and Chris
Chris	c > a > b	a vs. c: c	Chris and Pat
Pat	b > c > a	c vs. b: b	you and Pat

The problem is that the aggregated preferences of your group are *in*transitive. They're not coherent, as you find when you start voting. When you try to vote on all three at once, each alternative attracts one vote; no alternative has more votes than the others (called a plurality), let alone a simple majority (50% + 1, which in this case means two votes). So you decide to pit each alternative against every other, pairwise. You may be familiar with this

---

59 If you don't know Schoolhouse Rock, what rock have you been living under?

60 Vice President—sounds like they get to be in charge of all the nation's bad habits, doesn't it?

61 I told you I'm psychic.

62 Me, I got psychic powers.

63 I was also bitten by a guy named Thomas who'd absorbed a lot of radiation.

round-robin procedure from youth athletic tournaments. It is known as the Condorcet procedure, after the French mathematician who devised it. The alternative that defeats all others in pairwise competition is the Condorcet winner.

Here, though, there is no Condorcet winner—when Atlanta is up against Baltimore, it wins with your vote and Chris'. When Atlanta faces Chicago, though, Chris and Pat vote for Chicago. But when Chicago faces Baltimore, you and Pat vote for Baltimore, and it wins.[64] But Atlanta beat Baltimore in the first round. Your collective preference is intransitive: the group prefers a to b and b to c, but prefers c to a. Thus, the voting outcomes cycle. Each alternative has a majority in its favor, and the outcome therefore shifts each time as the losing party proposes the alternative that causes one member of the majority to defect and form a new majority. So you never reach a final outcome; the vote never comes to rest.[65]

This is an example of a larger problem—one about which we will talk later[66]—but for right now, the important point is that the decision-making costs are functionally infinite (the voting never stops). One of the solutions to this process is to use institutional structure (voting rules and procedures, for example) to induce equilibrium.[67] So you and your friends decide to limit voting to two rounds, and that the group will delegate to whomever has been dipped in toxic waste the job of deciding the order in which you will consider the alternatives.

Suddenly your bath in hazardous chemicals looks like it will pay off. Simply by determining the order in which the alternatives face each other, you can determine the outcome. I continue to admire your skepticism[68]; nevertheless, it is true. Way. For example, you want to go to Atlanta, so you have Baltimore and Chicago face each other first. Baltimore wins the first round, but loses to Atlanta in the second and final round. World of Coke, here you come! You can already taste your chili dog from The Varsity[69] when it occurs to you: were you *really* the decisive factor, or were the others finally swayed by your descriptions of The Varsity's gastronomic delights?[70] Could you have made Chicago the winner, or even Baltimore? Yep. To get Baltimore, you have Chicago take out[71] Atlanta in the first round, knowing that Baltimore will win in the end.[72] Or have Atlanta beat Baltimore in the first round, so that Chicago can bury[73] them in the end.[74]

As you can see, then, being the agenda setter is no trifling thing. The Speaker of the House could, once upon a time, do even more. The Speaker decided which committee would consider a bill (and could assign bills to committees sure to kill or pass them), the rules under which a bill would be debated (and whether amendments would or would not be allowed—amendments that might build support or make the bill less palatable), and could force a bill out of committee, if the committee refused to report it (that is, keep a committee from killing a bill). Of course, as Speakers began to abuse these powers,[75] the House altered its rules to decentralize the power somewhat. Committees and party groups (often called caucuses) now exercise a great deal of these powers (though the Speaker is still influential in these decisions).

---

64 Obviously, this is make-believe. Who would ever take Baltimore over Chicago or Atlanta?

65 Such a resting point being known as an equilibrium.

66 When I say the words "Arrow's General Possibility Theorem," you will wake up and remember this example.

67 That resting place we were talking about (see footnote before last).

68 Psychic, remember?

69 Oh no you did NOT just wonder what The Varsity is. I can't look at you right now.

70 Emphasis on the syllable "gas."

71 It being Chicago, there's likely to be a tire iron and some brass knuckles involved.

72 Again, obviously hypothetical.

73 Don't worry, in Chicago, this doesn't impair your ability to vote.

74 And by "end," of course, I mean the end zone of Soldier Field.

75 With great power comes great responsibility; power corrupts, absolute power absolutely; these are both ways of saying that power represents . . . starts with an "m" . . . ends with "oral hazard" . . .

The President of the Senate, however, has much less power. The President of the Senate can only cast a vote if the floor vote is tied (since the Senate by definition has an even number of members, this is a real possibility). His other duty is to recognize people to speak (to run the floor debate, which the Speaker also does in the House). In fact, the President has so little to do that he usually isn't there at all. Instead, the Senate selects a president *pro tempore*, or temporary president, to run the floor debate. Well, "select" may be a strong word. The rule is that the longest-serving member present presides. And even that lucky person often defers to a newer member, to give them a chance to learn to run debates (the Speaker also often designates some lucky winner to do the recognizing of speakers on her behalf).

So what explains this difference in power and influence? Well, understandably, the fact that the President of the Senate is also the Vice President of the United States—and therefore an outsider, elected differently for a different term, and belonging to a different branch—has something to do with the reduced role of that office. But that doesn't explain why the president *pro tempore* doesn't exercise more power—or why the Senate hasn't developed a stronger office to perform the same functions. The fact that the Senate is so much smaller, however, does. The decision-making costs in the smaller Senate do not require as much delegation to make them manageable. Further evidence comes from the House itself—the increase in the role and power of the Speaker correlates with the increase in the number of members.[76]

Of course, by this point, I've already mentioned something I suppose we should investigate more fully. We've looked at the heads of the chambers, so now let's look at the bodies,[77] and how they organize themselves to work.[78] That's right, it's finally time to talk about . . . committees.[79] Generally speaking, committees are subdivisions of larger groups, to whom the larger group delegates authority to do something.[80] For standing committees, this task is the debate, consideration, and amendment of bills, as well as the oversight of bureaucratic agencies which implement and administer the bills which become laws. I've desperately tried to start the rumor that they are called "standing committees" because Thomas Jefferson, believing that people thought better and disagreed less when standing, created the rule that they could not have chairs at their meetings.

Sadly, that's not true; they are "standing" in the same sense as water sometimes is—they don't just run off, but stick around until you do something to make them go away. That is, once their chamber creates them, they remain until the chamber takes action to alter or disband them. Otherwise, they continue from session to session (without having to be re-created every session). They're like the default entry in a form. Most of the committees of which you would have heard[81] are standing committees: Agriculture, Ways and Means,[82] Ethics,[83] or Judiciary.

But those are not the only kinds of committees. In fact, some of the most famous committees[84] have been special or select committees. Chambers form special or select committees to consider special or select (that is, particular) issues that either fall between the competencies of the standing committees (and aren't likely to be durable enough to justify creating a standing committee of their own), or that are too sensitive for a standing committee. For example, the committees formed to investigate scandals are often select or special committees.

---

76 Remember, of course, that correlation does not mean there is a causal relationship—but it must be present to win (in other words, for there to be a causal relationship).

77 Metaphorically, not literally, of course. You can keep your mental images of Nancy Pelosi in a bikini to yourself, thank you.

78 If one can call what they do working. C'mon, you'd have been disappointed if I hadn't.

79 I've put it off as long as I can, I promise.

80 Sorry, I probably should have given you a couple of minutes, and you could have come up with that on your own.

81 Would have, if you watched CSPAN or CNN or PBS, anyway. You know, if you had no life. Like me.

82 Most committees have the same name in each chamber. Ways and Means, however, is the House committee that deals with revenue; its sister committee in the Senate is Finance. Remember that all revenue bills must originate in the House. You know, like we talked about before. In that other chapter.

83 Don't laugh.

84 Did I really just say that?

They are formed to consider a particular issue and to report what action (including legislation) the body should take. Once they conclude their consideration, they cease to exist. The most short-lived committee is an *ad hoc*[85] committee, a special committee formed to consider a particular bill, and which disbands when they report (or fail to report) the bill.[86]

There are also joint committees,[87] so called because they contain members from both chambers.[88] Just as special or select committees generally investigate, joint committees are usually administrative, and do not report bills (with at least one exception—keep reading). There is a joint committee, for example, that oversees the operations of the Library of Congress. Conference committees are a special type of joint committee that does consider and report legislation. In fact, they do nothing else. Since bills have to pass both houses, they go through two separate debate and amendment processes[89] in two separate standing committees (and perhaps subcommittees before that—that's right, our committees have committees). Imagine you ask two separate friends to proofread the same paper. Each is likely to produce a different set of suggestions, to catch a different set of errors. This is good; one friend thinks of things the other doesn't, or catches mistakes the other misses. But someone still has to produce a common draft to submit to the professor. In this case, that's you (or whatever paper mill you hired—and yes, that is cheating); in the case of legislation, that's the conference committee. They consist of members from the relevant committee in each house (the committees which first considered the bill), and their job is to reconcile the House and Senate versions of the bill to create a common text to send to the President for his consideration (after each house passes the reconciled version).

Of course, when the common text goes back to the floor of each chamber, they could take this opportunity to amend it, whether to restore things they wanted that the conference committee eliminated, or simply because they have a new idea, or simply because they have the opportunity. The chambers are unlikely to do this, however, for any number of reasons. For one thing, as a common practice, it would be self-defeating: changes not choreographed with the other chamber will require the conference committee to reconcile different versions again. They will likely strip the changes back out—after all, they know they have agreement in the committee on the version that doesn't include those changes. Having done nothing but caused the committee members more work, they may—remember tit-for-tat?—remove even more, or look on bills which the member who reintroduced the eliminated parts favors with a more jaundiced eye in the future. As individual members, they will probably be less likely to cooperate when that member needs support for her future efforts, and no legislator can pass legislation without the help of others.[90]

This would also be self-defeating in terms of the purpose of having conference committees—to create uniform versions of bills—or for that matter, committees in general. Committees produce two benefits: an increase in productivity and the development of expertise. They are, in other words, a division of labor.[91] Think of a person building a car; first she has to master metal working and die casting in order to create the parts (as well as fabrication in other media, like cloth for the seats, rubber molding for trim and seals, etc.). After making the parts, she has to pick up a different set of tools (and master another set of skills) to assemble the car. Different parts require different fasteners—some welded, some bolted, some clipped, some screwed. Each time she has to shift gears[92] between one job and another, she loses a few minutes (much as cars with manual transmissions[93] lose a little momentum every time the driver has to disengage one gear and engage

---

85 "For the thing."

86 These are popular for when Congress wants to pass a pay raise, so there is no committee left behind to take the blame.

87 Not that kind of joint.

88 See, I told you it wasn't that kind of joint.

89 Called "mark-up."

90 The general rule is, you don't pee in someone else's pool.

91 And if you're not thinking of *The Wealth of Nations*, shame on you! Know the classics, man.

92 If you'll pardon the pun.

93 You're not a real driver if you don't know stick. There, I said it. And no, that nancy-boy flappy-paddle nonsense doesn't count.

another). Not asking her to constantly shift back and forth from one to the other allows her to keep producing during those minutes; it increase productivity by eliminating friction, as it were.

It also allows her to develop expertise more quickly. That is, as coaches throughout your life have told you (or told people you were watching on the silver screen), practice makes perfect. The more you do something, the more practiced you are at it, the faster and better you are able to do it. You can do it with less thought (which takes time), and you learn ways to shorten the process. You arrange your tools in better order, and can pick them up without looking, for example. As a result, you are more productive, but in this case you also possess a specialized knowledge. You know the terrain like the back of your hand (you know, the part you see the most), and you can pick the safest or fastest path.

The same is true of committees. Dividing up the work of debating and editing bills increases the number of bills the body as a whole can consider (because the whole body, with its higher decision-making costs, doesn't have to consider all of them). It also means that the body can make better use of specialized knowledge its members already possess, or allow them to develop expertise in an area. Thus, when someone introduces a bill proposing a change in agricultural policy, the committee members are already up-to-speed on what the policy currently is, and have some idea of the prospective effects of the change. They can therefore evaluate the bill more quickly than another group of the same size.

Of course, one result of this is that committees are coalitions of those with the most at stake in an area. Or perhaps better said, they tend to represent narrow, specialized interests, rather than broad and aggregate interests. For example, members on the Agriculture Committee are likely to represent producer interests, rather than consumer interests. Consumer interests are broad and diffuse; every member has consumer of agricultural products in his district. So why stand up for them, when other members will? As a result, of course, no one does.[94] Instead, they protect the narrow and concentrated interests in their district. After all, no one else will protect those.

This difference between narrow, concentrated interests and broad, diffuse ones has important implications, as Mancur Olson[95] points out in *The Logic of Collective Action*.[96] Smaller groups—those with narrow and concentrated interests—have less of a hurdle to overcome in terms of free riding. As a result, those groups are more likely to form, and those interests more likely to be represented. Groups representing more general interests, however—those that, perversely, benefit more or even all citizens—are likely not to form, as everyone waits for others to bear the costs of organizing the group and lobbying representatives.

A previous theory of interest groups[97] had seen interest groups as important facilitators of democracy. According to this theory,[98] interest groups formed spontaneously, without any particular effort, and they formed in response to threats to interests, or opportunities to advance them. They also formed in size relative to the number of people with those interests. As a result, every interest had a group, and they would be successful in the competition for government favor in proportion to their weight (the number[99] of people for whom the group spoke[100]). Thus, interest groups helped us by transmitting information to government about the interest composition of the electorate. Even more galling, they had the nerve to claim that Federalist 10 was an encomium to this mediated majority rule (when the point of Federalist 10 is that no interest group should go unfrustrated, *especially* if they are large enough to be a majority).

---

94 Pensioner's dill weed? Knee-writing?

95 It's pronounced "man-sir." And he was a native of Nebraska. Not kidding.

96 And James Madison considers in Federalist 10, though in a different context.

97 Pluralism.

98 Pluralism.

99 Not the actual poundage.

100 Or claimed to.

What pluralism[101] could not explain (but Olson could) was the predominance of special interest groups, and the dearth of general interest ones (though many claim to be such—more on that below). Why, for example, were dairy farmers successfully organized to lobby for dairy subsidies, but the much larger number of consumers who would pay higher prices for milk remained absent from the competition? Where were the advocates for poorer families whose children would be more susceptible to rickets because milk was more expensive, and their family could afford less moo juice?[102] The fact that counterweights fail to emerge, and specifically of more general interests against narrower ones, encourages a practice known as rent seeking.

What is rent, you ask? Well, it's not a Broadway musical, that's for sure.[103] Here, the rent sought is rent in the economic sense. Now, I know what you're thinking[104]: what does what someone pays their landlord have to do with it? And the answer is: that is an example of rent, not the definition of it. Rent is the return to capital on its use. In the case of apartments, the landlord owns the physical capital—the building—and in exchange for using it, you provide a return to the owner of the capital (so it's rent in relation to the landlord, not in relation to the renter). I imagine that is in fact the origin of the phrase "for rent"—people advertising that you could use their capital so long as you provided them a return on it, whether that capital was for the production of transportation or of housing. That's why cabs are "for hire"—you are buying their services, not using their capital (they use it to produce the service).

In the context of Congress, however, the capital is not physical, but legal. After all, Congress does not produce machinery or housing (or anything particularly useful), it produces legislation. Rent seeking is lobbying Congress to pass a law creating a stream of benefits, and perhaps blatantly revenue, for you. You are seeking a piece of legislation that will produce a return to you when you use it. For example, you might get Congress to give you a monopoly in some business, or restrict the ability of others to enter the market and compete with you. As a result of that legal capital, you receive a stream of revenue in the form of the higher prices you are able to charge. The difference between your revenue in a competitive market and your revenue in the restricted market Congress created for you is the rent—the return on that legal capital.

The benefit does not have to be revenue, though. An environmental group may get Congress to pass a law prohibiting people from building houses on beachfront property that they own, or forbidding someone who owns a forest from logging in that forest; they might get a law requiring them to allow the public to use the beach or forest, or at least to pass through it. In these examples, the environmental group does not receive a benefit in the form of revenue, but in the use of the property (in particular, in getting to use someone else's property without paying for the use, whether as a scenic preserve or as a public facility).

Note that the environmental group probably claims that what it wants benefits everyone. This is not necessarily true, though the group may believe it honestly enough. For example, let us imagine that the forest is to have its numbers reduced for the construction of a rural hospital and roads going to and from it. The people in the area may well benefit more from better availability of health care than from the scenic beauty of the forest.[105] To get what it wants, though, the environmental group needs government action. Making what they want sound more like a public good helps justify that action, and helps drum up sufficient support to provoke that action. That is, few people will sleep well at night thinking that they want to take someone's property without paying for it. If, however, it is for a noble cause,[106] people are more enthusiastic supporting it, and resistance is lower (who can argue against a noble cause?). This does not mean that there are no public goods—far

---

101 That theory.

102 In fact, an earlier critic of pluralism noted that the pluralist heavenly choir of interest groups sings with a strong upper-class accent. This critic, by the way, had one of the best names in political science: Elmer Eric Schattschneider. Yeah, he went by "E.E."

103 That would be *Rent*.

104 Psychic, remember?

105 Or from that forest's contribution to the reduction of carbon dioxide and production of oxygen in the atmosphere.

106 True love, of course, being the greatest; "to blave" not so much.

from it. It does, however, mean that people have an incentive to present as public goods things which bear only a partial (or even passing) resemblance.

Let us, however, return to the subject of the government action. As noted above, Congress does not increase productivity, it merely shifts what is produced from one to another. And as you will remember, smaller groups are more likely to form. So let us say that there are 100 dairies in the nation (roughly two per state). If the dairies get a minimum price for milk set that brings them an additional $100 million, then they each get $1 million. There are over 300 million U.S. citizens, however, most of whom consume milk in some form or another. They're each coughing up a mere thirty-three cents (well, every third one kicks in an extra penny). So let me ask you: if you saw thirty-three cents—three dimes and three pennies—lying on the ground, would you bend down and pick it up?[107] Or more accurately, if you discover that amount missing from your pocket, do you search every couch you sat on during the past week? You might do the first; you probably wouldn't do the second. The difference? The cost to you to retrieve the money. Bending down to pick up something you've already found is relatively costless (depending on your physical condition, what you might be carrying, and how strong the seam in the seat of your pants is). Spending the time to find it and get it back when it has gone missing is much more costly.

And that is the problem with rent seeking. When the cost is dispersed over a large group, but the benefits are concentrated among a smaller group, the larger group finds it too costly to get the law generating that rent repealed. Think about it. You've lost thirty-three cents. Say you spend thirty minutes writing a letter to your Congressperson asking her to repeal the law. You're simply throwing good money after bad. You're down thirty minutes you could have spent doing something else. Heck, you could have made a good $4 (after tax) working as a barista at Starbucks for that half hour. You've spent a few cents on an envelope, and what's a postage stamp running these days? One letter won't change your Congressperson's mind, and thus won't accomplish your goal. You'd need a whole lot of letters. And you'd need them to go to a whole lot of Congresspeople—a couple hundred at least. And after all that time, effort, and postage, what will you have? Thirty-three cents. Hint: the stamp cost more. You should have put the shovel down and quit digging when the hole was just thirty-three cents deep.

And that, as I told you oh-so-many pages ago, is why we hate Congress, but love our Congressperson. Our Congressperson brings home the money-generating legislation for us; I mean, everyone benefits from that research on making pickles crisper[108] conducted in our district. It's all those other crazy projects in other districts—paying for public transportation, polishing the statue of Vulcan in Birmingham, Alabama[109]—those are the wastes of money. That darn Congress and its inability to control its blad—uh, spending. In fairness, of course, even if our district went all noble and refused to engage in rent seeking, we'd still be paying about the same amount for everyone else's pork. Ours doesn't add perceptibly to the total, when dispersed across the whole country.

Sounds like a collective action problem, doesn't it? Sort of like a tragedy of the commons. Which is one good argument for repealing the Sixteenth Amendment. That's the one that allows Congress to levy an income tax without apportioning it on the basis of population. It's what began the dramatic increase in the size of the federal budget, so that there was an even bigger pig trough (or commons), increasing the size of the group across which the costs may be dispersed. It's also an argument for constricting the construction of the commerce clause to solely interstate commerce, as that ability to regulate gives Congress even more opportunity to create legislative capital.

But, you object, Congress does so many necessary things. We can't limit its ability to spend wastefully without keeping it from spending when we need it to. To this there can be but one reply: nonsense. Congress managed to fund necessary expenditures for nearly 150 years before the Sixteenth Amendment. Or rather, to

---

107 You do if you were raised by my mother.

108 I kid you not, Congress subsidized this, in Pennsylvania, home of the Heinz Company. They make pickles, you know (check the label on your ketchup bottle).

109 Still not kidding.

fund the expenditures it was necessary for Congress to fund. States and private organizations provided other necessities. As an example, let me tell you a little more about that statue of Vulcan in Birmingham, Alabama. It was completed created in 1904, at a cost of $20,000 (in 1904 currency).[110] In order to pay for their emissary to the World's Fair in St. Louis, the Commercial Club of Birmingham held fundraisers.[111] That is, the citizens of Birmingham paid for it voluntarily and privately.

When it came time to repair and refurbish the statue, however, a lot had changed. When two years of attempts to raise the money ($12.5 million) fell short, the easiest thing to do was get federal money to make up the difference. So, in 2001, federal taxpayers contributed $1.5 million, and in 2002, another $2 million, for a grand total of $3.5 million (about a quarter of the amount).[112] There were about 130 million taxpayers in the United States at the time, so that's a little more than a penny each the first year, and a little more than a penny-and-a-half the second. Not worth your time to recover.

The amounts, though, are not the important thing. Notice instead how people's expectations had changed. Institutions affect behavior, and more than that, they regularize—they create habits. Those habits can be good (like exercising regularly) or bad (couch potato city). But good habits are generally hard to develop, and bad ones especially easy to slip into. If it were up for a vote, how do you think it would go between exercise and sitting on the couch a little longer—especially if we could make someone else do our exercise for us?

And we can always find a good excuse—I mean reason—to stay on the couch. The weather's about to come on, and we need to see that. Then we can go outside. Remember what I said about groups having an incentive to claim their particular interest was everyone's? Consider this quote from a *New York Times* article on the Vulcan statue.[113] The chairman of the Vulcan Park Foundation defended the federal money by comparing the statue to the Gateway Arch in St. Louis and the Statue of Liberty—"there are certain symbols and destinations in this country that rise above simply local interests, and deserve a place in the federal budget." We all think our individual interests are broader than they actually are. Honestly, how many of you had even heard of this statue before reading this?[114]

Precisely, and precisely why the Framers created a government of enumerated powers. The U.S. Congress was unusual in its time as a national legislature. When other nations have borrowed the design of U.S. institutions, they have generally omitted the enumeration of powers. A legislature of limited, enumerated powers is comparatively rare; most countries have generally enabled legislatures. A generally enabled legislature is presumed competent to pass any legislation, unless it is specifically forbidden to do so. Enumerated powers work precisely opposite—the legislature is presumed not to have the power to pass legislation, unless it has permission.

To give you an idea of generally enabled legislatures, remember the British Parliament and French National Assembly. The British Parliament operates under the doctrine of parliamentary sovereignty—that the Parliament exercises the full sovereign powers of the monarch. There is, therefore, only one restriction on the power of a Parliament: it cannot bind a future Parliament. There are, of course, other kinds of restrictions on Parliament, as we discussed earlier.[115] This follows Hobbes' justification for government: we transfer all of our sovereignty to the ruler in exchange for peace and order. We have no other claim on government, and any restrictions would interfere with it carrying out that duty.

Likewise in France,[116] the law being the expression of the general will (following Rousseau), there can be no thought of limiting it. The general will is by definition what is best for everyone, what people would want if

---

110 All of this information is courtesy of the Birmingham Historical Society (and their Viva Vulcan! book promoting the statue's restoration: http://www.bhistorical.org/education/Vulcan.pdf).

111 Including opera performances by the sculptor. Hey, apparently it worked.

112 The tattoo removal program in San Luis Obispo, though, was a paltry $50,000. Still not kidding.

113 From the July 19, 2001 issue.

114 More importantly, how many of you have heard of it *after* reading this?

115 What was that, Chapter 2?

116 Though I warn you never to even suggest to a Brit or a Frenchman that they have something in common, politically or otherwise.

they knew what they should want. Thus, forcing someone to follow the law is forcing them to be free. To limit the general will is nonsensical—it is limiting the good, saying that you only want to do part of what is best for everyone. The general will cannot (again, see the definition) be wrong.

Only with Locke's justification, that we form governments to protect our rights, do restrictions like the enumeration of powers begin to make sense. Only Locke recognizes that government may become at some point counterproductive. Or, as Madison so eloquently stated the problem, "In framing a government which is to be administered by men over men, the great difficulty lies in this: You must first enable the government to control the governed; and in the next place, oblige it to control itself."

And you thought all that theory stuff was pointless and irrelevant.[117] If institutions shape behavior, theories shape institutions. And, in places still unblemished by Cartesian philosophy, the practical has a great deal to do with it, as well. So let us turn to the branch most shaped by practical demands, the Tina Turner to Congress' Ike,[118] the executive branch.

---

117 Psychic.

118 Parents. Or Google.

Chapter 6: The Executive

All right, so I suppose I should explain that Ike and Tina Turner reference from the last chapter. I figure it ought to take us about a chapter (oh, say, this one). To begin with, the President holds a somewhat unusual position in our political system. The office of President is the one nationally elected office. I know what you're **not** thinking. You *should* have been thinking "what about the Vice President," but you weren't, because no one ever thinks of the Vice President.[1] And technically, what you weren't thinking is correct; technically, we do also elect the Vice President nationally. But we don't really vote to choose the Vice President—we choose the President we want, and take as part of the bargain whatever emergency back-up he's seen fit to select.[2]

On the other hand, how many of us actually vote for President? Raise your hand if you've voted for President.[3] It's okay; nobody's looking. Especially not that attractive person of the opposite gender over there. How many of you have your hands up? Well, you probably shouldn't. The thing most of us overlook—and which political parties encourage us to overlook—is that we don't actually vote for Presidential candidates in the general election. We vote instead for a slate of electors,[4] chosen by their party and equal in number to the total number of people in a state's Congressional delegation (representatives plus senators). These electors comprise the Electoral College.

Now I know what you're thinking.[5] Why do they call it a college? For the same reason institutions of higher learning are called colleges—though that may not be the reason you think. The word *college* doesn't refer to the buildings in which you attend classes, it refers to the faculty. The roots of the word—*co-* and *lege*—refer to being under a common rule. *Lege* is also the root of *league*, a group of people (or states) united (in a limited, legal sense) for a common purpose, agreeing to act together according to agreed-upon rules. That is how the first colleges formed; professors formed a group to offer courses together, each in their field. Thus, they could offer a better selection at a lower price than hiring a stable of private tutors.[6]

The Electoral College is also a group of people united under a common rule for a common purpose (as, for that matter, is the College of Cardinals that elects the Pope).[7] Their purpose, of course, is not to educate young minds more conveniently, but to select the President of the United States.[8] After we elect the electors in

---

1 Until it's too late. See *My Fellow Americans*.

2 Apparently even if it's Al Gore.

3 Or if you're sure.

4 Ballots used to list the names of the individual electors, and some still do (though in fine print below the candidate's name); others have "Electors for" in small print at the beginning of the entry, followed by the candidate's name in prominent font. Some don't mention electors at all on the ballot.

5 Psy—yeah, you're right, I need to quit saying that.

6 That's right, colleges are intellectual Wal-Marts. But don't tell your English or Sociology professor; it might break her heart.

7 If you have to ask "which Pope," you've already been excommunicated.

8 Well, and the Vice President, but no one cares about him.

November elections, they go to their state capital (currently in December) to cast their vote. These votes are then transmitted to the President of the Senate,[9] who is responsible for counting them. Some states—and according to the original intent of the institution—do not require electors to cast their votes for the candidate they promised to support. The parties who select them, however, usually make sure that party loyalists are the ones who serve. In fact, most parties use these positions as rewards for especially dedicated members, which means it is rare indeed for an elector to vote otherwise than promised. Some states, though, do provide legal penalties for "faithless" electors who abstain or change their vote. Odd that the same state legislatures have not provided penalties for faithless representatives who deviate from their campaign promises. In reality, though, such laws are mainly campaign statements by state legislatures—as noted above, the elector selection process is largely self-enforcing.

To be elected President, a candidate must receive a majority of votes in the Electoral College.[10] This is something of an oddity in U.S. elections, where plurality is the electoral rule for most (or at least a plurality[11]) of elections. A majority—and since it is unqualified, a simple majority—is 50% + 1 (**not** 51%; in every case except 100, they are still very different numbers, just as they were when we talked about this in Chapter 1). A plurality simply means "more than any of the others," which usually looks like a majority because we don't often have more than two candidates (and votes not for the one candidate are likely for the other). What plurality (often called "first past the post") means is a little easier to see if we imagine more than two candidates running for an office. Let's say the first candidate (A) gets 40% of the vote, the second (B) gets 35%, and the third (Frank) gets 25%.[12] Under plurality, A wins; under a majority voting rule, no one wins. Systems with majority voting rules usually solve this by having a run-off election between the top two finishers; reducing the candidates to two pretty well assures one will get a majority (unless they tie exactly). The Electoral College (which, remember, has a majority rule) solves this by having a run-off in the House of Representatives (where state delegations each cast one vote together).

The electors themselves are usually elected by plurality, as are Congressmen in both houses. States control the voting rules for all of these. In fact, the requirement of a majority vote for President[13] is the only voting rule specified in the Constitution (at least, for an office—the voting rules for over-riding Presidential vetoes and for proposing and ratifying amendments to the Constitution are also in the Constitution). But then, the Presidency is the only nation-wide election in the United States.[14] Other elected offices at the national level have smaller constituencies; in the case of Senators, a state (and formerly a state legislature), and in the case of Representatives, a district within a state.

This probably explains a least a little bit of why we have the Electoral College in the first place. The logistics of organizing a simultaneous, nation-wide election when it took days to carry news from one end of a state to another probably made the extra level of aggregation attractive. Sending all of the ballots to the national capital to count would have taken a great deal of time and effort (and allowed more opportunity for loss, theft, or alteration of ballots). That is hardly the only reason for the College, though, and not even the primary one. Much as the Senate was to provide a saucer to cool the passions of the House, the Electoral College was supposed to function as a buffer against the intensity and boisterous passions of popular elections. Remember, the founders did not really anticipate the formation of political parties. They intended these elections to choose the wisest, most considerate citizens, who would choose on behalf of their fellow citizens.

We can see this in the original voting procedure for the positions of President and Vice President. Electors were to write down the names of two people on their ballot, at least one of whom was from a different state.

---

9 The sitting Vice President, remember?

10 And to be Vice President, a candidate has to get a majority of Vice President votes—but we'll talk more about this later (and still no one will care).

11 Not only is it a joke, but it's a *math* joke. Trust me, your math professor just groaned on your behalf.

12 The ratios add up to a nice even 100%, as they should; in real life, rounding means that the total might be slightly more on some occasions.

13 Yes, yes—Vice President too.

14 Yes, except for the other one.

The list of everyone for whom they had voted (and the number of ballots on which each name appeared) was signed, sealed, and delivered to the President of the Senate for aggregation into a common, national list. The person with the most votes would be President, and the one with the second-most would be Vice President. This makes sense if the purpose was to find the two people held in the widest esteem.[15] When we add parties to the picture, as we did by the 1796 election, we get a President of one party (John Adams, Federalist) with a Vice President of the opposing one (Thomas Jefferson, Democratic-Republican[16]).

Parties, of course, failed to anticipate this problem, and did not do so well in their first attempt to fix it. In the 1800 election, the Democratic-Republican Party arranged for all of its electors to submit the names of Jefferson and his candidate for Vice President, Aaron Burr. One elector was supposed to name someone other than Burr, but apparently no one was clear on which elector exactly was supposed to do so.[17] Since no one wanted to accidently withhold their vote from Burr and leave the other party's Presidential candidate with the second-most votes, Jefferson and Burr tied for having the most votes. When Burr refused to yield to Jefferson (his ostensible running-mate), the election went to the (still Federalist-controlled) House of Representatives (where, remember, each state's delegation casts one vote).[18]

The point being, the Electoral College was meant in large part to make popular democracy somewhat less popular. Even today, though, when we have pledged electors, political parties, and no longer worry that popular passions will elect Brittney Spears or Justin Timberlake,[19] the Electoral College still serves an important function in Presidential elections, one that was also part of its original purpose. And oddly enough, the World Series is the best illustration of that purpose.

So let's think about the World Series, and especially how it is different form the Super Bowl, for example (aside, of course, from the difference in the sports that use them). That is, let's look at the structures of the games. What does it take to win the Super Bowl? Of course, the Monday afternoon[20] quarterbacks among us have immediately begun debating the value of offense over defense, and whether you need a franchise quarterback or running back more, and a great deal of other arcana. The cheap and easy answer, however—the proximate one—is (for once) the correct one: more points than the other team. Football decides its champion in one game, with four quarters, and whoever has the most points at the end of the game wins.

Baseball, however, doesn't merely go by the number of runs (points) a team scores, but when they score them. That is, in the World Series, it's not the team with the most runs, which wins, but the team, which wins the most games. Football, for example, could count points at the end of each quarter and declare the champion to be the team, which won the most quarters. In the World Series, it's not the total number of runs, but their distribution across games, which is important. You can't just have one good night against one pitcher; you've got to prove that your team is good enough to beat the opponent on more than one night, against more than one pitcher (and vice-versa: that you have more than one pitcher who can beat their offense).

Take the 1996 World Series, for example (please!). The New York (Gosh-Darn)[21] Yankees beat the Atlanta Braves. Well, they won the World Series, because they won more games. Atlanta outscored them (26-18) across the six games, had more hits, fewer errors, more home runs, a lower team earned run average[22]—everything

---

15 In fact, it's an early variant of a Borda count, which is something we will discuss later.

16 Which of course sounds creepy today; eventually, Andrew Jackson dropped the "Republican" part of the name.

17 Coordination problem, anyone?

18 The Twelfth Amendment soon followed, which changed the voting procedure so that electors cast separate ballots for President and Vice President (and eliminated the coordination problem). Told you we'd talk about VP votes. And that no one would care.

19 Think about it—there have been times when, had those individuals been on the ballot, they would have won. We call those times "When Brittney Spears Ruled the Earth" and "The Reign of the Boy Bands." (Shudder.) I need some hot cocoa to make these chills go away.

20 I know better than to think that college students see many Monday mornings.

21 I know: if you're going to cuss, go for the gold. But publishing standards (and religious beliefs) require something less offensive (and blasphemous).

22 I mean, what the frogurt? They totally got schnitzeled.

except more games. The Braves won the first two games by eleven and four runs, respectively. The Yankees won the next four, by three, two, one, and one runs, respectively (as shown in Table 6.1).

Table 6.1 The Tale of the 1996 World Series Tape

game	1	2	3	4	5	6	total runs
Atlanta	12	4	2	6	0	2	26
New York	1	0	5	8	1	3	18
Atlanta's margin	+11	+4	–3	–2	–1	–1	+8

Atlanta's smallest margin of victory was larger than the Yankee's largest, and therein lies the moral of our story, the lesson that helps us understand the utility of the Electoral College. Atlanta piled up all of its runs in two games. The Yankees spread theirs out over more games. The Electoral College essentially requires candidates to do the same, to spread their support across more games—in this case, the individual states—rather than concentrating their support in a few, very populous areas. They must demonstrate broader, rather than deeper, support. The Electoral College makes the margin of victory in each state irrelevant, just as Atlanta's margin of victory was irrelevant in the World Series. Narrow wins (the Yankees) count just the same as big wins (Atlanta).

To give you a rough idea—and this is a very rough idea—try to guess the fewest states whose electoral votes comprise a majority in the Electoral College. There are 538 electors: each state has a number of electors equal to the number of its Representatives and Senators.[23] So the fewest electors a state can have is . . . come on, you've got this one . . . three electors. The most . . . well, there's probably a mathematical upper limit,[24] but the most any state had under the apportionment after the 2010 census (remember, we reapportion House seats every ten years) was fifty-five (and that state was California).[25]

So what's your best guess? Five? Nope. Ten? Warmer. As apportioned after the 2010 census, the number is eleven.[26] More importantly, though, those eleven states are not very likely to vote together on much. You can probably guess the big three: California (fifty-five), Texas (thirty-four), and New York (thirty-one). Well, really, there's California, then the next big three: Texas, New York, and Florida (twenty-seven). Those three are relatively close in size, but the difference between California and Texas—twenty-one—would be tied for fifth-highest on this list by itself (and is close to the size of Florida). The next group of three are Illinois (twenty-one), Pennsylvania (twenty-one), and Ohio (twenty) , which leaves just four more: Michigan (seventeen), Georgia (fifteen), New Jersey (fifteen), and North Carolina (fifteen), for a grand total of 271 electoral votes. This is one more than necessary, but replacing one of the last states with the next largest—Virginia (thirteen)—leaves us one shy of a majority, so it is a minimum winning coalition.

Okay, so eleven—slightly more than 20% of the states—doesn't sound all that impressive. But there are two things you should note. First, it is highly unlikely that those states will all vote together against the other states. Obviously, there have been times when they have all voted for the same candidate. For example, in 1984, Ronald Reagan won every state except for this opponent's (Walter Mondale) home state (Minnesota) and the pretend state, the District of Columbia. It should be obvious that all eleven of our minimum coalition voted for the same candidate then. And in 1972, Richard Nixon also hit electoral Yahtzee by winning all eleven; in

---

23 You're right, that should be 535 (435 Representatives plus 100 Senators), but for purposes of electing a President, we pretend the District of Columbia is a state. Really, it's just teasing them with statehood. Like letting someone on a diet smell a fresh Krispy Kreme doughnut.

24 Given that each state (and D.C.) must have at least three, the most any one state could have is 388, but the population distribution that implies is . . . fantastical, if not frightening.

25 If you're worried about remembering that California had fifty-five electoral votes, you're missing the point. Like for the last six chapters. Go back and read the introduction again—carefully, this time.

26 Again, more recent apportionments may have changed this number slightly, but the important part is its size relative to the next number, not its absolute size.

fact, Nixon's opponent (George McGovern) didn't even win his home state (South Dakota), though he did win his VP candidate's (Massachusetts—did I mention his VP candidate was married to a Kennedy?).[27] Since 1968 (the last eleven Presidential elections), those eleven states have voted together only twice, and then only in the context of everyone else voting the same way.

Now, there's nothing magical about 1968, but the further back in time we go, the more our context changes. The political makeup of the states might have changed. Certainly, their population would have (and thus, the makeup of our minimum winning coalition). California, for example, was once very Republican, but is now very Democratic. Neither has it always been such an electoral vote behemoth—its population boom started during the Great Depression and took off after World War II. The South used to be "the Solid South," always voting decidedly Democratic as a bloc—but now fairly reliably Republican, at least in Presidential campaigns.

The important point is that while California and New York may have some things in common (entertainment industries, for example), and even Texas and California may some things in common (oil and information technology), there's not much that brings this group together as a whole. New York and New Jersey—fine. Ohio, Michigan, Pennsylvania, and Illinois—sure. Georgia and North Carolina—yep. But none of those groups have much in common with each other. New Jersey and Georgia barely speak the same language. Florida is full of people who resent the people from Ohio and Michigan that move down there every winter (and wear black socks with their sandals). California, Texas, and Florida might (and I emphasize *might*) develop a common position on immigration, but Michigan and New York[28] are unlikely to share it (and Georgia and North Carolina probably have a third perspective).

So now let's get to the rough part of the comparison: the actual comparison. Guess the minimum number of states a candidate would have to win if we used a majority of the popular vote instead. Ten? Nope. Five? Warmer. Three. Three states' voting age populations in 2000 were a greater number than the number of people who voted for *either* candidate in the historically close 2000 election. In fact, that population represented an actual majority (50.78%), whereas Al Gore had at most a plurality of the popular vote (48.38%), despite his claims to represent the "will of the majority."[29] Bush had 47.87%, a difference so small that we can't be sure it existed.

Of course, that's a rough comparison; not every person in a state is going to vote the same way. Most states, however, "lump" their electoral votes together in the Electoral College (and the decision is one states make for themselves), which produces the same effect. Only two states, Maine and Nebraska,[30] don't elect an entire slate of electors based on the state-wide vote. Those two states elect one elector in each Congressional district and two based on the state-wide vote. So Maine, for example, might have three electors of one party and two of another. This seems to give the more accurate representation of the amount of support in the state for each candidate, so why do the other states elect theirs as a bundle?

Well, what do you think? You should have the tools to answer this by now. Hmm. Well, what's the difference between a Congressional district in Wyoming and one in California under each system? The way Maine and Nebraska allocate their electors, there's no difference. Each district you win is worth one vote, and every state-wide contest is worth two. So take a state like New York with a liberal urban area (New York City) and a relatively conservative upstate (Rochester). A conservative candidate will focus on upstate districts, a liberal one on urban districts, each cherry-picking the low-hanging fruit, to mix metaphors. When the state's votes are all-or-nothing, it is no longer safe to ignore any area. Even if you lose in that region, the closer you make it, the more votes you have—and those still count toward the state-wide total.

---

27 And he won D.C. Note two patterns. First, D.C. always votes liberal, even when liberals don't. Second, the two electoral landslides of the last forty years both belong to Republicans. The sample's too small to claim any evidence of anything—to claim that it's a pattern rather than coincidence—but that shouldn't stop you from teasing your Democrat friends until they point that out. And since they're Democrats, that may take a while.

28 **That's** the real border threat—the northern border—but no one's watching there.

29 Displaying the keen mathematical prowess that led him to invent the internet, no doubt.

30 Nebraska is unique in another way, remember? Think unicamerally.

Let's put a little more flesh on these bones. Imagine the state has two districts, east and west. You—we'll call you Candidate U—know that you will win the western district and lose the eastern: 55-45 in the former, and 40-60 in the latter (each district having 100 people). Since (under the district-based allocation) you have to win the western district to get your elector in the Electoral College, there's no sense in wasting resources on a lost cause (the eastern district). In fact, you're not likely to do much in the western district, if you're sure that your margin of victory will hold up. (Of course, if either district is close, you'll pay a great deal of attention to it.)

Now let's switch to the bundle allocation. You've got to make sure of every vote you can. Even if the western district will stay 55-45 in your favor, the margin by which you lose the eastern district now matters. If it stays the same, you lose the state-wide vote (and all of the electors), 95-105. If, however, you can manage to improve your margin of loss to 48-52, you will win the state-wide vote (103-97). Suddenly, the eastern district is worth your time.

Of course, the two state-wide votes in the district-based system provide a little incentive in that direction, too, but not nearly as much as bundling the votes together. Think about it: there are 435 Congressional districts, each with one elector, and you only need 270 of them to win. If you could win twenty of California's, you wouldn't have come close to getting the whole state, but you'd have a significant consolation prize. You could give up on the other thirty-five, because you could make up for them in other states. When it's all-or-nothing, though, it's hard to give up the entire fifty-five, or the entire thirty-four in Texas' case, or the entire twenty-seven in Florida, and the state gets a lot more attention. So if you said it was a coordination problem, at least from the point of view of the states, you're right. Like the toys in *Toy Story* 2 trying to open the automatic door to Al's Toy Barn by jumping on the pressure pad, their votes have more weight, more effect, if they cast them together. And it is not from the benevolence of political candidates that we expect our policies, but from their regard for their own interests.

Now, if you've been paying attention, something else should have come to mind during that discussion, and that something is Chapter 4. And a smattering of Chapters 3 and 5. Because yes, a fair amount of lobbying for government favors goes on in Presidential elections (though it is the people of the state, not the states themselves, which gain that influence).[31] In fact, one of my favorite authors[32] once commented that anyone capable of getting himself elected President should on no account be allowed to do the job. Granted, he was talking about the fictional[33] job of President of the Universe, but the sentiment is accurate for most elected offices (and the larger the constituency, the greater the accuracy). If candidates have to promise benefits to different groups to get elected, they will either have to take resources from others (in the case of deficit spending, from future generations) to keep those promises, or they are going to have to break those promises (and perhaps, intended to do so from the beginning). To borrow from another Disney movie,[34] whether candidates woo voters with flowers and chocolates or with promises they don't intend to keep, they are not the sort of candidates who are likely to use the office as we would like them to, at least generally.[35]

This raises another, more basic question. What sort of favors can the President promise to deliver? After all, as Alexander Hamilton succinctly summarizes in Federalist 70,[36] the legislative branch has the power of the purse, but the executive has the power of the sword. The person with the bag of money can always throw a little swag your way, but what can the person in charge of making people obey the law do? She could turn a blind eye to your violations of the law, but that will only go so far. On the other hand, it would damage her ability to do her job. That is, everyone else would try to get away with the same thing, and she'd have a lot more

---

31 Do you taste that hint of Chapter 3?

32 Douglass Adams.

33 At least as far as we know.

34 *Beauty and the Beast*; don't pretend you haven't seen it.

35 Get that whiff of Chapter 5?

36 More on this later—like Chapter 7.

work to do (and a lot less legitimacy, and therefore authority, with which to do it). And anyway, most of us don't want benefits we have stolen; we want to have them by right, not fraud.[37]

And now we return to the Ike and Tina Turner reference: the changes across time in the power of the Presidency. Tina started out under Ike's thumb, but came to eclipse him. For the first part of its history (and little more than its first century), the Presidency took a back seat to Congress. There are, of course, some exceptions, most of whom are featured on Mt. Rushmore (Andrew Jackson is probably the only President to have played a major policy role who *isn't* memorialized in South Dakota). Generally speaking, however, the President was seen as a glorified clerk: Congress passed laws, and the President did as they told him. The President was solely the administrator, a manager, tending the legislative crops Congress planted.

That began to change with the most recent face on Mt. Rushmore, Teddy Roosevelt. Roosevelt saw the Presidency as a more important position. He argued that the "take care" clause ("the President shall take care that the laws be faithfully executed") was an independent grant of power to the Presidency, one that implied other powers (like the necessary and proper clause did for Congress). The important difference is in the reading of the adverb *faithfully*. Previous generations had read this to mean "faithfully to the intent or will of Congress" (as if there were some such discernable thing).[38] Roosevelt read it as "faithfully to the Constitution," meaning that the President had powers to defy Congress where he felt the Constitution required it.

Perhaps the best way to frame a discussion of the growth in Presidential power is with one of Roosevelt's favorite phrases. He called the Presidency a "bully pulpit." Now, to understand what he meant by this, it's important to know that Teddy Roosevelt was an anglophile.[39] So when he said "bully," he meant it as the British (used to) use it, to mean *great*, rather than in the American schoolyard sense of intimidating people into doing what you want (though it may be true of the Presidential pulpit in that sense as well; read up on Lyndon B. Johnson).

Which leaves us with the word *pulpit*, which does not mean reducing something to a moist paste through the repeated application of blunt force. Those of you who are regular church-goers probably already know this word, but for those of you who aren't . . . well, perhaps you've visited an old cathedral. Big, aren't they? Now imagine you're seated in a pew in the back, trying to listed to someone sitting in a folding chair at the front (right in front of the pews, facing them). If it makes you more comfortable, you can imagine that it's an entirely secular event. How easy is it to see the speaker? Since her head is at about the same level as yours, and there are several hundred heads between you (some probably wearing hats), it's pretty difficult, isn't it? She could stand up, but what about if everyone else does, too? If only there were a platform on which she could stand . . . yep, if you're remembering that old cathedral well (or if you'll bother to watch *The Curse of the Wererabbit*), there's a small bulge on one of the pillars, sort of like a pocket in which a person may stand—which is exactly what it is, because that's the pulpit.

What Teddy Roosevelt was saying, then, is that the Presidency is a great place in which to stand to get the attention of (and address yourself to) a large number of people. This was less true before Teddy and has become much more so since. In Roosevelt's time, public communication was just becoming possible on a national scale. Thanks to the telegraph, newspapers in every corner of the country could print news from every other corner of the country, including the ones on the other side of the continent. No more waiting for the mail to deliver a copy of a speech—you could print it the same day the President made it. And with advances in transportation, like the completion of the transcontinental railroad, the President could travel all over the country to deliver those speeches.

Of course, that platform is much higher today, or at least has a kickin' audio system. Innovations in communication and transportation let the President address himself to a much larger audience much more quickly (nearly instantaneously, in fact). This is the heart of Presidential power; if the President can persuade a lot of

---

37 Most of us. The rest run for Congress.

38 More on this in Chapter 9.

39 No, what you're thinking of is "pedophile." "Anglophile" means he was fond of British culture, literature, and such. Slightly less creepy.

voters across the country to see things his way, he can use them to pressure Congress to do what he wants. So if Presidents in the 1800s generally didn't do much policy advocacy, if they functioned more as Congress' glorified clerk, it was because they did not generally have the resources to do otherwise. They had less ability to bring public opinion to bear on Congress.

This may not fit well with our popular conception of the President as the man on horseback, the Leader of the Free World, who rides to the rescue of fair democracies in distress. Outside of the executive branch, however, the President has no ability to order anyone—and by "the executive branch," I mean only the federal one (which includes the federal bureaucracy, but no state officers). Congress writes the laws, and the President can't fire them (as he can members of the federal executive branch). If he wants their cooperation, he has to persuade them that it is in their interest, whether through reason, bribery, or threat.

Notice that I have not mentioned party affiliation in this, because it does not much change things. The President may have position or influence in his party which would give him leverage over a member of Congress from the same party, but not nearly as much or as often as you might think. As Richard Neustadt (the political scientist who pointed out that the President's power consisted largely of "the power to persuade") noted, "what our Constitution separates, our political parties do not combine." As you will remember[40] from the last chapter, Congressmen need their parties less than their parties need them.

Keep this in mind as we go through the catalog of Presidential powers.[41] Some of his powers are relatively stable, that is, their potency does not fluctuate much across time (or Presidents). Probably more, however, do depend on the amount of influence the particular office holder is able to bring to bear. And the most stable are probably the least potent, at least as compared to the high end of the more volatile powers' ranges.

Let us begin with the observation that the President in the U.S. system has two roles, roles that are often separated in other systems. These roles are head of state and head of government. The head of state is the symbol of the nation, especially in external affairs, and of national unity (especially inwardly). They often have functions as a representative of the nation as a whole (as opposed to simply the party that won the last election), both outwardly to other nations and inwardly as a neutral arbiter of sorts, who can step in if the system comes to an impasse. They are often ceremonial positions. The German Federal President, for example, is technically the person who nominates Chancellor candidates for election by the Bundestag, calls the Bundestag into session, represents the country in international relations, and dissolves the Bundestag when new elections are necessary. When necessary, he provides the "good offices" (serves as an honest broker) to facilitate coalition agreements among parties (to form governments).

In fact, where the head of state is a separate position, it usually either is a monarch in a constitutional monarchy or a president who takes the equivalent role in a republic.[42] The role of the Queen in the United Kingdom may be a useful way to understand the role of head of state. Formally, the government of the United Kingdom is the Queen-in-Parliament, with the Queen still in possession of all of the powers and prerogatives of her ancestors. In practice, however, power has shifted to the Parliament, leaving the Queen with only ceremonial functions—where *ceremonial* is not a synonym for *unimportant*. The Queen nominally chooses her Prime Minister, but she always chooses the leader of the majority faction (or more recently, coalition) in Parliament. The Prime Minister decides when to call new elections, though technically it is the Queen's decision. Though it would be legal for her to refuse, or to refuse to accept a Prime Minister's resignation, it would be unconstitutional.

The Queen's function as a symbol of national unity, however, is still very important (things can be both touchy-feely and true). She stands above the political fray—in fact, she does not even have the right to vote—and thus is the neutral arbiter in the political process. She is like the referee; if a party does something beyond the pale, hers is the voice that calls them to account. Her authority is more moral than legal (yet no less real).

---

40 Gotcha! We won't talk about this until Chapter 9.

41 Yep. That's what we're about to do. Luckily, it has free shipping on orders over $50, so you can finally get that Richard Nixon paper shredder you've always wanted. But you're still too young to see the Clinton section.

42 In a republic, the people are sovereign, and there can by definition be no monarch.

The Prime Minister, on the other hand, exercises most (if not all) of the political authority in the United Kingdom (even if nominally on behalf of the Queen). He is an example of the other executive role, the head of government. The head of government is the political figure, the one who **does** bloody noses (and have his bloodied in return) in the political arena. Heads of government generally oversee the administration of the laws, and often (in parliamentary systems) play a leading role in the writing of laws (because they are in those systems usually members of the parliament, as well as the executive). If the country were a sports team, the head of state would be the retired player who is "the face of the franchise," the good will ambassador—though with more of the profile of most chief executive officers or owners. The head of government would be more like the general manager and/or coach, usually with more of the power of the CEO or owner.[43]

The President of the United States combines both of these roles (though former Presidents often perform at least some of the head of state functions for sitting ones). So let's look at the powers of the President. Well, we can look at some of the most prominent ones, anyway. And by "look at," of course, I mean briefly outline.[44]

The President's head of state functions are probably—though not necessarily—the ones that spring to mind first. Let's try it: what's the first Presidential title that comes to mind? Was it "Commander-in-Chief"? Well, we'll pretend it was. If you thought of it, then you probably know that it means the President is the head of the armed forces of the United States[45] (though not of the states—who used to have them—unless and until the federal government called those forces into federal service). Now, we could stop there; after all, we've covered the fact. In fact, you probably know a little more fact than you used to, because we covered a related fact about state militias. We have not, however, thought about what those facts **mean**—why it's important to know them. So let's do that now. (Don't worry—we'll leave the state militias out of it for now.)

Why is it important that the President is commander-in-chief? First, let's think about what difference it makes. So we then want to think about the alternative: who would otherwise be in charge of the military? Probably a general, wouldn't you think? So how is the President different from a general? Some Presidents have been generals, though not in active service when they were President. But not all have been generals—in fact, not most. What other occupations have Presidents had before they were President? Yes, we mentioned general already. Several have been lawyers. Ronald Reagan was an actor; Herbert Hoover was an engineer. Jimmy Carter was a peanut farmer, and Harry Truman was a haberdasher.[46]

All right, what difference does it make if the person in charge of the armed forces is a haberdasher or peanut farmer instead of a general? Hmm. Generals rise through the ranks of the military. The military trains its members to apply force to remove obstacles. That is, in fact, what we need them to do. When lives are at stake, we want the Marines to take the shortest route, even if it involves using explosives to clear the path. In some cases, that is the appropriate solution, even the necessary one.

That is not, however, the necessary or appropriate solution in *all* cases. Take, for example, a dispute between an employer and an employee. The employer is rude, miserly, venal, thin-skinned, and short-tempered. When the employee politely suggests that he might be wrong about something, the employer summarily dismisses him—in violation of the contract they both signed. The employer may be a reprehensible human being, and the world might on balance be a better place without him, but the employee does not need to use a rifle to resolve this dispute. (He may **want** to, but that is a different story altogether—one no doubt written by John Grisham.) Instead, he has recourse to courts of law or arbitration to resolve the dispute peacefully.[47]

This is an important implication of having a civilian be President. Civilians are trained to use debate and arbitration to resolve disputes. Politicians learn to remove obstacles by negotiation and compromise—talking them to death, rather than shooting them—as well as by varying degrees of bribery. One reason to have a

---

43 Whew! Now I'm that much closer to my union-mandated sports analogy quota. That counts as two, right?

44 I saw that eye-roll. We have so covered some things briefly. Yuh-huh.

45 That, or you looked at the answer guide at the end of the chapter.

46 What, aside from a double-word score waiting to happen, is a haberdasher? Look it up.

47 No, you're right—this is the one John Grisham would write.

civilian in charge of the military, then, is that it makes the *overuse* of the military—its use to solve problems amenable to non-explosive resolution—less likely. (Note: *less* likely, all else being equal. That's far from saying it's impossible, though.) It may sound crazy to have someone whose professional talents run to fitting fedoras be the one to decide whether to annihilate two enemy cities, but there is a method to the madness: to make it more likely that the annihilation occurs only when necessary.

In the same vein, the President as chief executive serves as the representative of the United States to the rest of the world. The President receives diplomats from other countries (and, by formally receiving them, recognizes on behalf of the United States those countries status as sovereign states). He also sends diplomats to other countries to help him execute his duty to manage relations with foreign countries. More prominently, he (or those diplomats acting on his behalf) negotiates treaties with those foreign countries.

In the use of this power, the President is subject to one of the more important checks Congress has over his use of his powers. The President makes treaties with the advice and consent of the Senate, and two-thirds of the Senators present must concur on the advice and consent. We commonly refer to this as ratification, and some commentators (and by "some commentators," I mean "other textbooks I've used, which shall remain nameless") will tell you that this does not give the Senate much influence over treaties. You may be thinking that yourself. In truth, though, it is much more complicated; the amount of influence the Senate has varies according to the circumstances.

Let's use a spatial model to see how this works. In fact, let's use one from Figure 6.1, since they're handy.

We'll imagine a left-right policy dimension, and let's imagine that dimension is free trade (which, believe it

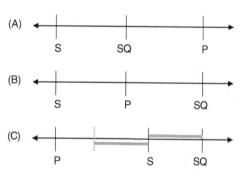

Figure 6.1 Spatial Relationships in Veto Decisions.

or not, tends to cut across party lines). As we move from the status quo toward the right, we decrease the amount of free trade; as we move left, we increase it (and decrease/increase it more the further we go in each direction). "SQ" will be our current position, the status quo; "S" will be the position the Senate would prefer, and "P" that which the President would.

Let's begin with (what we'll generously call) model A, in which the status quo is between the Senate and the President. The President makes the first move, proposing (by negotiating a treaty which effects) a change in the status quo. Then the Senate decides whether to accept or reject the proposal. Technically, the Senate can also amend, but let's make the simplifying assumption that they only have a veto—the right to block the proposal from going into effect ("veto" being Latin for "I forbid"[48]). This sometimes happens, especially for trade agreements; the Senate grants the President "fast-track" authority, meaning that they won't amend what he submits, but only vote it up or down (we'll talk more about this shortly).

Where on the line does the President prefer to locate his proposal? (Hint: it rhymes with "T.") Now, where *will* the President locate his proposal? Think about it for a second. He'd like to sign a treaty moving trade to point "P" on the line. If he negotiates that treaty and submits it to the Senate, though, what will their reaction be? Note that the outcome depends on neither on them solely, but on the combination of their decisions. The President can negotiate it, but it doesn't go into effect without Senate approval; the Senate can withhold that approval, but they cannot propose an alternative.

So if the President proposes "P," that would (if the Senate approved it) move the policy further away from what the Senate wants. Will they approve it? Well, if you are negotiating to purchase something, and the saleswoman responds to your offer by raising the price—proposing a point further away from your preferred point—are you likely to agree to the offer? I sincerely hope your answer is "no." The saleswoman may ask you to move your proposal closer to the starting price, but if she raises the original price, you really have no common ground. Negotiating further is a waste of time.

---

48 There being no truth to the rumor that this was Caesar's wife's response whenever he tried that "veni, vidi, vici" crap around the villa.

Likewise, the President—if he knows his position relative to the Senate's and the status quo—will not waste his time negotiating a treaty the Senate will not approve. Now, Presidents may sometimes negotiate un-approvable treaties, but that should tell us that they either made a mistake (it happens to the best of us) or had some other goal in mind, such as making a negotiating partner feel better, or embarrassing Congress by making them publicly reject a popular treaty (assuming it would have been popular).

Note two things about this. First, in this set of circumstances, the Senate's veto prevents a treaty from being proposed in the first place. This makes it hard to see the effect; it's hard to count potential treaties that were never negotiated (remember the dogs that don't bark?), and that makes it easy to underestimate the influence this gives the Senate. Second, these are not the only set of circumstances, and the strength of the influence depends on the particular set of circumstances—in this case, that the President and Senate want to move in opposite directions. If the debate is not about the direction of change, but the degree, the strength of the influence the Senate can exert becomes less.

So let us consider model B. The President wants more free trade than the current amount, and the Senate wants even more than that. What will the President propose? No, seriously—what do you think? We should probably work this question from the other end. What will the Senate approve, and of that, which is closest to what the President wants? The Senate prefers its position to any other, but anything between that position and the status quo still beats the status quo itself. And the Senate's position is not necessarily on the table; the President has to put it on the table. But the President knows that they prefer any position moving to the left of the status quo (at least until their preferred position), and that their choice is between the status quo and whatever he proposes. The Senate doesn't get to make a counterproposal, it merely decides to accept or reject.

The President most prefers his position, but will the Senate approve it? We know that the Senate (because the alternative is the status quo) will approve any point left of the status quo (and a little beyond, in fact). Since the President's preferred position is to the left of the status quo, if he proposes it, the Senate will accept it. Of course, they would *prefer* their position, but the President isn't offering it. He is offering his position, which is closer to theirs than the status quo is. And half a loaf is better than none.[49]

In the second set of circumstances, then—when the President and Senate want change in the same direction, but the Senate wants a greater degree of change—the Senate has no influence over the outcome. They may threaten not to approve the treaty, but because the President controls the choice available, he can be confident that they will ratify his position when he proposes it. Of course, here we have to remember the simplifying assumption we made at the beginning of this discussion: the Senate only votes the treaty up or down, and does not amend it. If we remove this simplifying assumption, then the President has to consider the possibility that they will amend the treaty to move it closer to their position. If, however, we add that much complexity, we have to consider whether we must add more.

So, for example, we should consider that amending a treaty is not costless for the Senate. We have (by simplifying assumption) treated them as a single mind, when in fact they probably have a good half-dozen between them.[50] They may have difficulty determining their aggregate position, and they may have trouble voting to insist on it. So while they may use the amendment power to move a treaty closer to them (in these circumstances), they may not be able to move it to exactly their position (and may find that accepting half a loaf is easier than baking a whole one).

Yes, I know: you are going to gouge out your eyes[51] if you have to read one more word[52] about the relative positions of the President and the Senate on treaties, and how that affects the policy content of the treaty. I can only encourage you to keep the gouging instruments out of easy reach for just a few more minutes.[53]

---

49 What does that mean? Well, if you want some bread, and someone offers you half a loaf, do you turn it down because it's not a whole loaf?

50 Okay, baker's dozen. But these are people who decided to run for Senate. And I'll remind you that Dan Quayle, Al Gore, and Joe Biden have all been Senators.

51 Don't try this at home. Or anywhere else.

52 Good news! You get to read several dozen more.

53 Or more, if you're a slow reader.

We have one more set of circumstances to consider.[54] At the risk of self-mutilation, we press bravely on to consider model C, where the President wants change in the same direction as the Senate, but desires a greater degree of it.

If you don't know what question I'm about to ask, you really haven't been paying attention, have you? That, or you read **really** slowly. So I'll be off waiting over here in literary limbo[55] for you to think about it and tell me the answer.

. . .

You know, the soundtrack in literary limbo involves a surprising amount of Crowded House, and not nearly as much muzak as you might expect.

. . .

Those of you who are big on parallelism or reasoning by analogy are probably thinking that the President will propose at the Senate's preferred point, since he could propose at *his* preferred point when that was in the middle. Since the Senate is now between the President and the status quo, you're thinking, obviously it's his turn to settle for half a loaf.

Obviously. But let's think about the reasoning there for a second. Although the President's preferred point[56] **was** between the Senate and the status quo, was that the reason the President proposed it? Because it was in the middle? In fact, the reason the President proposed it was because it was the best deal for him *that the Senate would accept*. It just so happened that the conditional best deal (the best with the condition that the Senate would accept it) was the same as his *un*conditional best deal.

However, we are not always so lucky in life. So what is the best deal (for the President) that the Senate will accept? Obviously they would jump at having their ideal outcome, but can the President do better? Yes, he can. Remember that the Senate chooses between the President's proposal and the status quo, so his proposal just has to be closer to them than the status quo is. But that says nothing about which side of them it is on. The President can propose a point between himself and the Senate, so long as the distance between it and the Senate is less than the distance between the Senate and the status quo.

In this case, the Senate affects what the President negotiates, but does not determine it. It exerts, if you will, a gravitational pull, but it is not the only force acting upon the position of the treaty. The Senate constrains what the President negotiates, but does not control it. And you should add here all the stuff we talked about earlier, concerning relaxing our assumptions about amending treaties.

We see, then, that the amount of influence the Senate has over treaties through its ratification power fluctuates according to (among other things) the positions of the President's and the Senate's preferences relative to the status quo and each other. Certainly other factors come into play—the popularity of the President, for example, may affect the Senate's willingness (or ability) to demand concessions or alterations from him. But then, this should hardly come as a surprise to you. I'm sure that, remembering our discussion of Teddy Roosevelt and cathedrals, you were already there. Well done. We have not yet, however, begun to bully pulpit. Neither, as we shall see, are we prepared to damn the spatial model as we move full speed ahead into the President's more domestic (head of government) powers.

Let's begin with the President's role in the legislative process. The President has **no** authority to introduce legislation to Congress. He may recommend a bill to a member of Congress, and ask that member to introduce it, but he may not himself initiate legislation—much like the Senate in the treaty process. In this regard, the President is relatively weak, at least when compared with most other democratic heads of government. The Prime Minister in Britain, the Chancellor in Germany, and the Prime Minister of France all have the ability to initiate legislation. As you might imagine, this gives them a much greater ability to influence the nature of the policy adopted, or where on the spectrum the policy moves.

---

54 After all, we must be thorough. Otherwise, I couldn't look at myself in the mirror in the morning. And you'll be able to, as well. Especially if you put that melon-baller down.

55 As opposed to doing the literary limbo, which may be the worst cruise-ship game ever invented.

56 I would abbreviate it "p.p.", but I am simply too juvenile to do so and not giggle every time I type it. You go ahead though.

Though the President lacks positive power in this context, he does have a negative power: the power to veto. So flip back over to Figure 6.1 for a second.[57] Change "P" to "C," and "S" to "P," and you can see how this allows the President to influence legislative outcomes. Sure, he never gets what he wants, unless Congress wants it, too. And, depending on *how* his preferences differ from Congress', the amount of the influence varies. As we saw with the Senate and treaties, however, this is far from meaningless, even though the President (as we only pretended with the Senate) really *can't* amend the proposals Congress makes.

Congress did attempt to allow the President a limited ability to amend—sort of—the proposals it sends him. The Line Item Veto Act of 1996 allowed the President to veto parts of bills, rather than having to accept or reject everything in a bill together. The vetoed parts would go back to Congress, who could override the veto on all of them together. The other parts (those not vetoed) then became law when the President signed them. Congress' motivation—to let the President stop them before they pork-barreled again—underlines our earlier point about the difficulty a group has determining, let alone "enforcing," a common position. The Supreme Court, however, held the Line Item Veto Act unconstitutional in 1997 (*Clinton v. New York*), precisely because it allowed the President to amend laws, rather than simply accept or reject them. This, they said, violated the procedure the Constitution establishes for passing legislation, particularly the separation of the power to alter legislation from the executive branch (to alter its text, anyway; as we'll see in the chapter on the *other* part of the executive branch, it still has some means to influence policy outcomes after the fact).[58]

So if the President can't directly influence the content of laws, why do we hear so much about the President and particular laws that he supports? Why do we refer to things as "the President's health care[59] bill"? The answer, my friend, is blowin' in the wind. As long as by "wind" you understand "Chapter 5," and by "blowin'" you understand "written." D'oh! It's time for another LSD[60] flashback! Surely you remember your accidental bath in toxic waste. Well, it turns out the President was in the bath with you.[61]

That is, the President functions as an agenda setter. Remember Teddy[62] Roosevelt's bully pulpit? C'mon, that was just like three pages ago. The President has incomparable access to the media, and if he starts talking about something, the media starts talking about it, their viewers start talking about it. And another name for their viewers is "voters." And if voters care about it, Congress wants to care about it, too. They will start to propose solutions,[63] debate those solutions, assign committees to study solutions . . . For someone who can't propose legislation, the President sure can cause the proposal of an awful lot of legislation. And as we mentioned before, he may also have his preferred solution ready to hand to a friendly Congressperson to propose on his behalf.

So we come at last to the final type of function the President performs. After so much discussion of the President's involvement in the legislative process, it would be easy to miss that he is, when we get to the heart of matter,[64] an executive officer. In fact, he is THE executive officer, the CEO, if you will.

What does it mean to say that the President is the chief executive? It means that he is responsible for executing the laws he and Congress agree to (or that Congress passes over his veto). When it comes to policies, then—the purposes laws try to establish—the fact that the President is in charge of implementing them gives him (or more often, his minions[65]) some influence over what outcome actually occurs. That's right: Congress is the principal, the President is the agent, and it's time to play America's least favorite reality game show spin-off, How Devious Is Your Agent? (For rules, see Chapter 2.)

---

57 We'll wait a moment if you need to secure any sharp objects out of reach before you do.

58 But I don't want to spoil the surprise.

59 Or bacon-and-waffles, or whatever else it proposes to regulate.

60 Long Since Deleted—you thought you'd never need to know it again, didn't you?

61 A problem which also came before the Supreme Court during Bill Clinton's term in office (*Clinton v. Jones*).

62 And yes, teddy bears are named after him. No, seriously. Long story, though.

63 Note that this is regardless of whether there is any actual need for a solution.

64 Turns out, it's about forgiveness (or at least, that's what Don Henley thinks).

65 Where "minions" is short for "bureaucracy."

The fact that the President is the chief executive, however, also gives him some powers not mentioned in the Constitution. Remember (from Chapter 5) that Congress has enumerated powers (listed, of all places, in Article I, Section 8) and implied powers (those necessary and proper to the use of the ones listed in Article I, Section 8—at least, according to the last clause of Article I, Section 8).[66] Congress also has inherent [67] powers, which are powers it has simply as part of its nature (that nature being "a legislative body," rather than "lazy and quarrelsome"). For example, Congress has the power to subpoena[68] people to give testimony. It has that power because it is traditional for legislatures to be able to gather sufficient information to decide, even if they have to force people to come answer their questions.

Likewise, the President has expressed powers (those actually mentioned in the Constitution, like treaty-making, the veto, and receiving ambassadors[69]) and inherent powers. Part of being an executive, for example, is the ability to give binding orders to your subordinates. So the President is able to issue executive orders to the bureaucracy.[70] Doesn't sound like much, does it? It never does. Executive orders are **not** law; they do not create obligations for all citizens. They create obligations only for those people who work in the executive branch, and only regarding their work. So the President cannot order all of us to buy Christmas presents—Congress would have to do that (and they don't *really* have the power, the Supreme Court just thinks they do). He probably couldn't order bureaucrats[71] to buy them, either, because it's not related to their work.[72] But he could order the heads of every department to have an office party at Christmas.[73]

So, as long as you don't take a job in the executive branch, you're safe, right? Well . . . since the federal government administers a lot of programs, and the people who administer those programs are minions,[74] executive orders can affect citizens (though again, it can't *order* them, like legislation can). George Bush the elder, for example, once issued an executive order that required appropriate agencies to withhold federal funds from any clinic or hospital who discussed abortion services with a minor without parental consent. He couldn't order the doctors and nurses not to (unless it was a federal hospital or clinic, such as those run by the armed forces or Veterans Administration), but he **could** order bureaucrats not to give them money if they did. Although executive orders generally cannot forbid or require the action of a private citizen, they may still affect citizens' willingness or ability to take an action.

There are at least two other interesting and important inherent executive powers. But you don't want to hear about those, which is unfortunate, since you're going to anyway. The first is executive privilege, the authority to withhold information from the other two branches. Again, the justification is in the nature of the executive. For example, it would hamper the President's ability to negotiate treaties if he had to report his every bargaining position to Congress. As we just discussed, Congress has the power to require people to share information, because they need it to reach a proper outcome. This is the inverse of that idea: the President can withhold information if necessary to do his job effectively.

---

66 By the way, the enumerated powers of Congress are found in Article I, Section 8 of the Constitution. And you thought you could forget.

67 Think about what the verb *inhere* means. If *adhere* is "to stick to something," *inhere* is "to stick *inside* something," meaning that it is inextricable (can't be taken out of).

68 So let's think about this fancy Latin for a minute; *sub-* is a prefix meaning what? Submarines go under water, subterranean caverns are under the earth . . . let's go with "under." And *poena*? Sounds a lot like "penalty" doesn't it? In fact, that's the root of the word *penalty*. So, "under penalty"—a subpoena is a command to do something (to appear, or to turn over evidence) under the threat of being penalized if you refuse. Which sort of makes it an offer you can't refuse.

69 Doing so officially recognizes a country, so while it seems like it just means he always has to have a coffee cake ready, in fact it is a grant of power to the President.

70 His minions.

71 Minions.

72 Unless Santa secretly works for the IRS, which come to think of it, would explain a lot . . .

73 Again, probably couldn't *call* it a Christmas party—that would probably violate Supreme Court precedent on the establishment clause (part of the First Amendment; we'll get to it soon enough).

74 Or, "I Can't Believe It's Not Bureaucracy!"

For example one potential problem of informing Congress of the details of negotiations is that it could make them public—especially if the information is to be used in consideration of a law—and that could constrain the ability of negotiators to take useful positions. Sometimes they might need to take a position that sounds bad to the public, only because it will lead to the right position later. Sometimes having their counterpart know public reaction to those positions might undermine the credibility of those positions. In fact, the first President to invoke executive privilege was George Washington, who refused (politely, of course) to give Congress records of the negotiation of a treaty, for the reasons mentioned earlier.

There are, of course, limits to privilege, as Richard Nixon discovered. He claimed that releasing the tapes of his conversations in the Oval Office would damage national security. The Supreme Court (in *U.S. v. Nixon*)[75] confirmed that yes, Virginia, there is an executive privilege, but it is limited to information that would hinder the executive's ability to do his job (rather than information which would enable his impeachment or prevent his re-election).

The other inherent power I will mention is the power to make executive agreements. Executive agreements look and smell a lot like treaties, but with some important differences. For one thing, the Constitution specifically mentions the power to conclude treaties, but executive agreements are an inherent power. And this reflects the key difference between them: the parties to each. Who are the parties to a treaty?

Yeah, I know: I lost you once I said "party." You're wishing you were at one now. But it's not that kind of party, the kind you go to with friends. What's the root of *party*? (Don't over-think this one.) No. It's not *art*. (Told you not to over-think it.) Rhymes with "art," though. Yep—it's *part*. So the parties to an agreement are those who take part in it, those who have a share in the common project.

So who are the participants (hey, check that out—it's got "part" right in the word and everything!) in a treaty? What types of entities create them to manage affairs between them? Some of you, of course, have been yelling "states!" for the last thirty seconds (more or less, depending on how fast you're reading). Some of you have been yelling much less correct things, much less polite things, or—if you've forgotten your medication—very incorrect and very impolite things. But the important lesson here (aside from the importance of taking your medication, and that yelling at inanimate objects like books is considered proof that you need medication) is that treaties are agreements between states, like the United States and the Federal Republic of Germany, or between Canada and Djibouti (I know it sounds fake, but Canada really is a country) (well, sort of).

Who then are the parties to executive agreements, and how are they different? Here's a hint: they're called executive agreements. So yes, they are agreements between the executives of the countries involved, rather than between the countries themselves. What difference does that make? Well, how long has the United States been the United States? (Hint: the answer rhymes with "pence heaven-teen weighty leaven.") How long has the current President been the President—the executive?[76] No more than eight years, unless there's been an amendment or coup. Since executive agreements are between persons, they're tied to those persons' terms of office; they're usually more transitory.[77]

Not only does the nature of the parties to an executive agreement place limits on its duration, that nature also limits their scope (all else being equal). That is, the executive can only bind **themselves** with their promise. In the United States, that means anything requiring funding the President can't promise, because Congress controls that. He can promise to ask, but that promise is worth less than a (credible) promise to deliver. And if the President does promise something outside his ability to deliver, it's much less credible. So for example, if the President promises not to test any nuclear weapons, it's credible: the President can order the people who conduct the tests (the military) not to test them. Congress can't. If the President promises to buy nuclear weapons . . .well, he has to get Congress to allocate the money first.

---

75 As opposed to *Nixon v. U.S.*, which involved Judge Walter Nixon's appeal of his conviction by the Senate after his impeachment for perjury. Which tells us two things: 1) if your name is Nixon, you may want to change it; and 2) the Senate **does** convict people impeached for perjury, just not charming Presidents from Arkansas.

76 As I write, the current President is Barack H. Obama (which, by the way, makes a great substitute for cursing—e.g., "Barack H. Obama, it's hot in here"). I started writing this during George W. Bush's first term. Maybe your President's last name is Clinton. Maybe you're reading this in translation from the Canadian, eh?

77 Of course there are exceptions. If it's a rule, it has exceptions (though there are some exceptions to that rule).

If this limited scope reminds you of executive orders, it should. They're related, right? They share at least one parent (the nature of being an executive). There is, however, one difference. Where executive orders do not have the force of law, the Supreme Court has said that executive agreements have the same status in federal law as treaties (which is to say, they are federal law).[78]

All of which begs one important question. If executive agreements are like treaties, but more limited in scope and permanence, why do Presidents ever use them? Why not simply negotiate a treaty, which will cement their outcomes more solidly and allow them greater scope? Well, put on your safety goggles and put the sharp objects away again, because we're going back to that diagram about the President, the Senate, and treaties.[79] Remember how the Senate sometimes had stronger influence, sometimes weaker (or even none)? Why was that again—how are they able to exert whatever degree of influence they are able to exert? It was because the Senate had to approve of the treaty (and could amend it, too). As a result, the President has to consider their preferences.

Executive agreements, however, are just between the executives of the countries. Thus, the Senate does not have to approve of them, nor may it amend them. Of course, if whatever the President is agreeing to do requires Congressional action, he'll have to take the preferences of both the House and Senate into account (instead of just the Senate). Otherwise, executive agreements can give the President more latitude in some situations. So there are situations in which one is more useful or attractive to the President, and situations in which the other has greater advantages.[80]

All right, that leaves us with one more category of powers: implied powers. Congress' implied powers are (ironically) explicitly granted, in the necessary and proper clause. The President doesn't have anything like that, does he? Well, if your name is Teddy Roosevelt,[81] he does. Article II, Section 3 says that the President "shall take Care that the Laws be faithfully executed," and his oath of office (in Section 1) requires him to "preserve, protect, and defend the Constitution." Roosevelt read these to imply the President had greater powers than those expressed in the Constitution or inherent in the nature of executive power. For example, although Congress possesses the (enumerated) power to declare war, Presidents have argued that their charge to faithfully execute the laws and to defend the Constitution allows them to wage war, even if not declared, in order to protect the United States or its interests.

I do not believe Abraham Lincoln made this argument specifically[82]—that the take care clause implied some additional set of powers he possessed—but his suspension of *habeas corpus* during the Civil War certainly provides an example of an implied presidential power (or at least, one for which the argument seems suited). Lincoln argued that preserving the Constitution (and the Union it produced) required him to take some actions in violation of it.

Of course, one could also say that letting Southern states secede—sacrificing the Union—would have preserved the Constitution, though perhaps at the expense of taking care that the laws of the Union were executed in those states. But this points us to a more fundamental issue of which we must not lose sight. Notice that the President has to make an argument, has to claim (successfully) these powers. We could spend a great deal of time cataloging different powers of the different branches, but in the end, it's not the catalog that matters. Words on paper are no more than that—they have to convince actors in the world to act, to support or oppose, in order to have effect. And while the catalog can be a useful guide, we must not mistake it for the underlying reality,[83] which has a frustrating (yet fascinating) fluidity to it. Which is even more relevant to our next branch, the judicial.

---

78 At least, that's what the distinguished gentleman at the Indiana University School of Law who taught me international law said. The relevant cases are *U.S. v. Belmont* and *U.S. v. Pink*—again, according to David Fidler, J.D., M.Phil, Calamaras Professor of Law (as I said, distinguished—also very kind, for the record).

79 So the President, the Senate, and a treaty walk into a bar . . . oh, I guess you've heard that one.

80 You wanted an absolute? Sorry, life doesn't deal in those very often. (I hear the Sith do, though.) Just getting the conditions down is a big enough task.

81 But then, if it is, either your parents needed to get a life, you know how to time travel, or you're an undead ghoul. Don't take this the wrong way, but I'm rooting for sick and twisted parents as the explanation for your presence, and not your violation of the laws of physics or consumption of blood or braaaiiiins.

82 Though if he did, then eloquently.

83 Also expressed metaphorically as mistaking the map for the land.

ANSWER GUIDE

Made you look!

Chapter 7: The Judicial

To illustrate what I mean by this—the necessity of belief to buttress the written word—let me ask you a question: why does the Supreme Court have the power of judicial review? I'm sorry—what? Judicial review? Judicial review is the ability of a court to declare a legislative or executive act null and void[1] if it does not comport with the Constitution. Trick question: how many courts have the power of judicial review? Just in the United States—that's not the tricky part. So how many? I bet you said, "one." And in some countries, you'd be correct. But not in the good ol' U.S. of A. In the United States, *every* court has the power to review legislative and executive acts for their constitutionality, unless the court's statutory charter explicitly forbids it.

Now, there's a reason why you said "one," and it's not entirely unreasonable. The U.S. Supreme Court is the **final**, though not sole, interpreter of what the Constitution says. In a common law system (such as ours), judges of lower courts follow precedents set in higher courts. In fact, this is the rule of *stare decisis*, which means (I am told) "let stand the decision." This is also called the rule of precedent, because it means that, where a court of competent jurisdiction has already decided a similar case, a judge should use the same legal rule in the case before her.

Of course, sometimes judges may not wish to use the same rule. Let us say that a lower court departs from this rule and introduces a novel interpretation of some part of the Constitution. The party aggrieved by this novelty may appeal to the next higher court, until the question (if necessary) finds its way to the Supreme Court (from which there is no appeal). Since the court of last resort[2] gets its way in the end, lower courts—anticipating the futility of deviation—generally apply the Supreme Court's precedent (at least, to the best of their ability—more on this later). Thus, it is usually Supreme Court precedent about which we hear (and care), and therefore, why the Supreme Court is the one you thought of.[3]

So we have learned that our question should have been "Why does the **judicial branch** have the power of judicial review," but we have not yet learned the answer. If you had to guess, where would you look to find out whether the judiciary—especially the Supreme Court—has the authority to do something? No, not there—and you leave my mother out of this. Hopefully, the first answer that came to mind is the Constitution. Hopefully, because that should be the first place we look to resolve an issue about the separation of powers. And where would we look first? I'm going to pretend you said "Article III," and that you said it because you remember our earlier discussion of the thumbnail guide to the Constitution.

And? Why are you still here? The Constitution (the U.S. one, anyway) is among the appendices, unless we forgot.[4] Use your thumb, a finger, or a random piece of paper, and you won't have to lose your place here. I think you can handle it. Don't make me come over there.

---

1 "nothing and empty" (of any force or authority).

2 This means the highest court, from which there is no appeal. On a more trivial note, the oldest public eatery in Berlin is Zur Letzten Instanz, which means "at last resort." Which makes sense when you learn that it is near the city court and began as a place for lawyers to grab a meal between cases.

3 But don't think about it too much. Justices don't usually appreciate your Valentine's Day greetings. You might get a lovely visit from the Secret Service, though. What do you mean, how do I know?

4 Even if we did, you can find it online at http://avalon.law.yale.edu/18th_century/usconst.asp.

Now, what did Article III say about judicial review? Are you sure? Nothing? But that doesn't make any sense. Let me check. (Pages rustling.) No, you're right. It doesn't say a word about it. Plenty of cases and controversies, but nothing about declaring things unconstitutional. So from where[5] does the Court get the authority to do that?[6] Let me see what we've got in the basement, aside from creepy family members voted "most likely to become a serial killer."[7] (Author does "disappearing down imaginary stairs" bit behind the sofa.) (A cacophony of sounds ensues, among which are distinguishable, in no particular order, the crack of a whip; a gunshot; the roar of a three-headed dog; the cheer of a crowd; a loud, piercing, desperate wail; and the rush and rattle of a train passing on elevated tracks.) (Sound of footsteps ascending a stairway; author emerges from behind the sofa, blowing dust off an ancient, leather-bound book).

Well, according to *The Book of the Dead*, the rite we need to perform—wait, what was the question again? Right, judicial review. Well, that's not in *The Book of the Dead*. For that, we need *Marbury v. Madison*. Different book entirely. *Marbury v. Madison* is a Supreme Court decision from 1803. But to explain how we get to it, first we need to go back a few years before that. Hop in the Way-Back Machine, Sherman! In the 1800 elections, Thomas Jefferson and the Democratic-Republican[8] Party captured both the Presidency (after a particularly caustic campaign) and a majority in Congress. The Federalist Party, as you might imagine, lost both of those. In the months between the election and when the new Congress and President took office, the old Congress and President (still controlled by the Federalist Party under John Adams) decided to secure their party's future via the only branch left to them: the judiciary.

The Federalist[9] majority in Congress passed bills creating new judicial positions in the federal judiciary, bills which the Federalist President (John Adams) signed into law. Adams then nominated men[10] to fill these positions, which the Federalist-controlled Senate confirmed. Adams' Secretary of State, John Marshall, then set the Presidential seal to the men's commissions, and was supposed to see to their delivery.

I say "supposed to," because some of the commissions went undelivered. Marshall sent one of his six brothers, James,[11] to deliver some of the commissions, and—after riding the area all day in apparently inclement weather—James returned those he had been unable to deliver to his brother's office. His brother was apparently at his *other* office, though. See, a few months earlier, Adams appointed his Secretary of State to fill a vacancy in the federal judiciary: Chief Justice of the Supreme Court. The Supreme Court met in Philadelphia at the time; it moved to Washington, D.C. in February 1801, the same month Jefferson took his oath of office. John may have been organizing that move while trying to oversee the delivery of the commissions. James apparently neglected to mention the remaining commissions, so they sat unnoticed on the Secretary of State's desk until Jefferson and his administration moved in to the executive offices.

Upon learning of the undelivered commissions, Jefferson instructed his Secretary of State not to deliver them, so as not to complete the appointment of at least that many of the "midnight judges."[12] It would be much easier to repeal the laws creating those offices if no one were in them. One of the men whose commission had

---

5 The old-fashioned way of saying "from where" is "whence." But I had a hard time using that word without adding "-eth" to the end of every verb.

6 References to your anatomy are inappropriate, Rep. Wiener. (Anthony Wiener, D-NY—google it, but stay away from the images.)

7 Yes, we know about your uncle.

8 That's right—the Democrats used to have both names. And you thought the reference to Satanic participation before was facetious.

9 Not to be confused with the Federalist Papers—those writing under the name of Publius all favored the federal constitution, but one of them went on to found a party favoring a more active and assertive federal government (Alexander Hamilton and the Federalist Party), to which another responded by helping to form a party favoring a minimally active federal government (James Madison and the Democratic-Republican Party).

10 And given the century, that word is in its particular, rather than its general meaning.

11 Hey, he had eight sisters. John Marshall was the eldest of fifteen children (eight girls, seven boys) and a cousin (second degree) to Thomas Jefferson (they had a great-grandfather, William Randolph, in common).

12 The rumor of the day had it that Adams was still signing commissions until Jefferson's term began at midnight, though historians say he stopped at a decent hour.

not been delivered—William Marbury, whom Adams had appointed as a justice of the peace for the District of Columbia—sued to get his commission.

He filed his suit directly with the Supreme Court, that is, in its original jurisdiction. What's original jurisdiction?[13] Hmm, I suppose we need a brief bit of exposition here. Courts can have two different types of jurisdictions:[14] trial and appellate. Trial courts are also called "courts of first instance," because they are the first courts to hear a case. Another way of saying this that they have original jurisdiction—the case begins with them. You probably got that from the "original" part. What this means is that they actually hold trials, trying (testing) the evidence to decide what parts are reliable and what parts not. These courts hear testimony, look at evidence—all the fun things you know from *Law & Order* (or *Perry Mason*, or *Matlock*, depending on how much time you spend with your grandparents). Often, juries—regular people, not specialists in the law—determine what evidence is reliable, with the judge providing appropriate guidance on what the law says.

Having determined the nature of the circumstances in a case, the court's next job is to apply the relevant law to those circumstances to produce an outcome. Here, too, juries often make the decision, again with the guidance and oversight of a judge. So first the prosecution must establish the circumstances: that someone is dead, that the cause of death was blunt force trauma from an American government textbook,[15] that the accused owned a textbook of that type, that the accused's copy has the victim's blood on it, that a witness saw the accused leaving the victim's office about the time he died, etc. Then the judge (or jury) must decide how to apply the law to those circumstances: whether they meet the definition which the law establishes for a violation (the one[s] of which the defendant is accused), and if so, what sanction is most appropriate to the offense. Generally, the law will provide some range of appropriate punishments, from which the judge or jury will select, based on the circumstances of the case (though sometimes legislatures will provide specific punishments, so as not to leave the jury or judge any discretion).

Appellate jurisdiction does not extend to matters of fact, but only to matters of law. So for example, if a trial court finds that the fingerprints on the barrel that killed poor, immigrant plumber Mario do, indeed, belong to Donkey Kong, then that becomes a fact in the record. Mr. Kong (and his legal counsel) cannot ask an appellate court to reconsider whether those are his fingerprints.[16] They may ask the appellate court to consider (notice the lack of the prefix "re") whether the trial court followed the correct procedure in so finding. If the appellate court decides that the trial court did not correctly apply the law—did not follow the procedure the law establishes—then it can send the case back to the trial court for them to try again, this time observing the rule as the appellate court explains it to them. Note that the subject matter is the law, not what actually happened. Appellate courts consider what the courts did, not what the defendant did.

The Supreme Court has both kinds of jurisdiction; some types of cases fall under its original jurisdiction, and some under appellate. Article III,[17] Section 2 defines the types of cases to which federal judicial power extends, and then names those falling under the Courts original jurisdiction. It then says that the rest of the list belongs to the Court's appellate jurisdiction, "with such exceptions, and under such regulations as the Congress shall make."[18]

The framers left a good bit of the details about the federal judicial branch to the discretion of the legislative: the number of justices, whether there would be a lower federal courts, and if so, what they would look like, just

---

13 You're right, it's not the alternative to "extra crispy" jurisdiction, and yes, you need to go to KFC less.

14 Have you thought about what *jurisdiction* means? *Juris* is law, and *diction* is to pronounce—so *jurisdiction* is the right to pronounce the law (to speak or declare it).

15 Don't try this at home—our hypothetical people are professionals.

16 Like most rules, this sometimes has an exception. At the state level, there are courts of original jurisdiction from which one may request an appeal *de novo*—basically, an appeal to start over with a new trial in the upper court.

17 You know, the one about the judicial branch.

18 Turns out, it's not just colleges in Ohio that get all precious about definite articles.

to name a few.[19] Among the first things the first Congress did (along with the Bill of Rights) was to pass the Judiciary Act of 1789. (Some titles for Congressional acts get recycled, because they concern the same subject and build on each other. For these—and Judiciary Act and Civil Rights Act are two of the most prominent— the date becomes an important distinction.) Section 13 of the Judiciary Act of 1789 enabled the Court to issue writs of mandamus.

The relief Marbury requested in his suit was precisely a writ of mandamus. Oh, right—you're wondering what a writ of mandamus[20] is. A writ of mandamus is an order from a court to a public official, ordering that official to discharge some nondiscretionary duty of her office. The nondiscretionary part is important in the context of the writ of mandamus; discretion, by its nature, cannot be compelled. That is, if it is something left to the official to decide, a court cannot order him to choose one thing or another. For example, negotiating treaties is a discretionary duty of the President. He may if he wishes, but no one may order or compel him to negotiate a treaty. He must, on the other hand, inform Congress[21] of the state of the union, though the Constitution leaves the schedule and manner to his discretion. In a word then, the difference between discretionary and nondiscretionary is the difference between "may" and "must."

Part of the decision in the case, then, was whether the Secretary of State had a nondiscretionary duty to deliver the commission. In holding that the commission became Marbury's property upon its completion (the President signing it), rather than upon his receipt of it, Marshall construed the duty to deliver it as nondiscretionary. Thus the remedy would seem to have been precisely a writ of mandamus, ordering Madison to discharge his official (and nondiscretionary) duty.

Of course, since this case was in the Court's original jurisdiction, determining that the commission belonged to Marbury required the Court to first establish the fact of the existence of the commission, and of its completion. This meant hearing testimony from witnesses, such as James Marshall (you remember: John's younger brother; John, the guy presiding over the proceedings). This brings to mind another legal concept relevant to this case: recusal.

The Latin root of *recusal* is, well—*refusal*. The term "recusants" described Catholics who refused to attend services or perform the religious rituals of the Church of England after the schism[22] with the Church of Rome. I really have no idea why they used the "c."[23] But as applied to judges, a judge should recuse himself from cases in which he has a personal interest, or of which he has direct personal knowledge. That is, if the judge could be a party to a case, or could be called as a witness, or has interests which the outcome will affect, the judge should refuse to hear the case. The point is to make sure that the judge is neutral, that the law and the facts decide the case.

John Marshall, of course, had direct personal knowledge of the case: he was the one who sealed them, and was supposed to have delivered them. His brother was a witness to the existence of the commissions—and testified by affidavit to their existence. Other witnesses included Marshall's former clerks in the Department of State. Indeed, the best witness, the one who knew which commissions had been signed and sealed, was the presiding judge. Marshall, however, did not recuse himself, which—along with some other oddities about the case—have led some[24] to suggest that Marshall contrived to have the case come before the Court, so that he could use it to declare the principle of judicial review. (Wait for it—we're getting there).

---

19 Hmmm…would that be…what was that word again…oh, yeah: delegation. Now why was it people do that again? (Hint: it gets hot and muggy in Philly in the summer, and air conditioning didn't exist.).

20 It's Latin, so I don't know how it's supposed to be pronounced, but I've always heard it as "man-day-muss," with the accent on the middle syllable.

21 Sorry—THE Congress.

22 Fancy word for "break."

23 Though, according to a bio on IMDB, Cary Elwes' ancestors were prominent recusants. Apparently, "As you wish" has not always been a family motto. (If you don't get that joke, you have committed one of the seven classic blunders: not watching one of the greatest movies ever made.)

24 See, for example, Susan L. Bloch, "The Marbury Mystery: Why Did William Marbury Sue in the Supreme Court?" *Constitutional Commentary* 18 no. 3 (2001): 607.

As Marshall framed it, the case (once the fact of Marbury's commission had been established) presented three questions: did Marbury have a right to his commission, did the law provide a remedy for the violation of that right, and was that remedy a writ of mandamus? Marshall answered the first two questions positively: the commission became Marbury's property when executed, not when delivered, and Section 13 of the Judiciary Act of 1789 provided a remedy: it allowed the Supreme Court to issue writs of mandamus in its original jurisdiction.

The problem, Marshall explained, was that Section 13 was unconstitutional. Thus, the law did **not** provide a writ of mandamus as the remedy. Marshall reasoned that, when a law conflicted with the Constitution, a judge was bound not to apply that law.[25] According to Marshall, Section 13 contradicted the Constitution; if you read[26] Article III, Section 2 of the Constitution, it says that the Supreme Court has original jurisdiction over a few of the types of cases listed there. Over the rest, as we discussed above, it has appellate jurisdiction, "with such exceptions, and under such regulations as the Congress shall make." Marshall (quite reasonably) read the grant of Congressional ability to make exceptions and regulations (such as allowing writs of mandamus) to apply solely to the Court's appellate jurisdiction, and the lack of a similar grant after the definition of original jurisdiction (quite reasonably) to imply the absence of Congressional power to modify original jurisdiction.

Thus, Section 13 of the Judiciary Act of 1789 was beyond the powers of Congress (according to the Constitution), and null and void. Mr. Marbury had a right, it had been violated, but the relief he requested was not actually there, and so the Court could not grant it. But in case you missed it, the Court alone could decide what did and did not violate the Constitution (and invalidate statutes and actions which were).

This last—the principle for which we remember the case—is no part of the holding. That is, it is not necessary for the Court to claim the sole power of judicial review to reach that conclusion. It is what lawyers refer to as *dicta*, short for *obiter dicta*, or "words along the way." Judges include *dicta* to win over an audience with appeals to emotion, for example, or to include contextual material to help readers understand (and accept) their reasoning. Since it does not form part of the reasoning, however, it does not form part of the precedent, the rule which judges will apply to resolve similar cases in the future.[27]

So…the judiciary has the power of judicial review because…the judiciary thinks it does, and everyone else plays along with the delusion?[28] Thankfully, we do have somewhat more upon which to base this institutional rule. In Federalist 78, Alexander Hamilton makes the case that the judiciary should have the power to declare statutes and actions unconstitutional because the judiciary is the "least dangerous branch."

Now, in a perfect world, your professor[29] has you reading Federalist 78 (and several other numbers). Check that: in a **perfect** world, no one had to require you to read them. With the understanding that we live in an imperfect world, I will proceed nevertheless to outline (and admittedly, embellish upon) Hamilton's argument. If you haven't read it, read it before or after this.[30] Preferably before—it's only a few pages, it won't take long, and I'll wait for you to get back. It should help you pick out the relevant parts (and see where I've embellished), and those are vital abilities to develop (and nothing develops abilities like guided practice).

Hamilton describes the relative powers of the three branches with three metaphors. The executive, he says has the power of the sword; as the executive, they have the ability and authority to force people to comply with their instructions. The legislature has the power of the purse; because they decide the sources of revenue (also known as "taxes") and the targets of spending, they can bribe (with subsidies or tax exemptions) or threaten (with taxes) to produce compliance.

25 And judges, by the way, had to determine what conflicted with the Constitution—put these together, and you've got judicial review!

26 WHEN—I mean, WHEN you read.

27 Jefferson complained for the rest of his life about the weight people gave to Marshall's *dicta*.

28 Much like a dollar is only worth a dollar because (almost) everyone thinks it is. If they ever snap out of it…

29 Or teacher, or mentor, or clinical psychologist, or parole officer.

30 If you are waiting for someone to make this a homework assignment—why? You have the opportunity to improve yourself, to understand something better, to see the world more clearly—and you're waiting on someone to make you?

In fact, Hamilton argues that this is the most dangerous power, precisely because its abuse is so difficult to detect (at least, the bribery part). One can usually tell when another is acting under physical duress, but with bribery, both parties want to conceal the offense. So the executive putting a gun to someone's head to get someone to surrender their liberties—frog-marching them down to the cathedral on Sunday—will usually be visible. At the very least, there will be stress responses visible in the abductee (sweating, anxiety, awkward movement). The person getting an extra thousand dollars in their grant (or getting the grant, as opposed to not getting it) on the condition they show up at the church door every time it's open could simply be that enthusiastic about the religion, rather than about the grant.

The judiciary, on the other hand, has merely the power of judgment: peer pressure, more or less. Granted, peer pressure can get people to do some really stupid things—fraternity initiations, mullets,[31] bottled water— but it is usually much easier to resist than bribery or physical coercion. Those who would use peer pressure to affect your behavior must first get you to care about their opinion, and then keep you caring about it. If they push too far, too fast, they lose their ability to affect your behavior. If those using bribery or coercion push too far, too fast, either they pay you more than they had to (and you'll be even more eager to take their calls), or they kill you (and everyone else will pick up much faster when they call).

So while the power of judgment may get people to do stupid things, it reaches its limits far more quickly than the other two (in most cases). Plus, because the judiciary gets you to care about their judgments by the quality of their reasoning (I mean, it sure ain't their dope robes or fresh bling), they have an incentive to make the best arguments they can. Their success depends on it.

Beyond that, even, the judiciary relies on the other branches to implement its decisions. For example, when someone at a dinner party informed Andrew Jackson of a Court decision contrary to his wishes (regarding removal of the Cherokee from Georgia), he supposedly replied, "Mr. Marshall has made his decision. Now let him enforce it." Like most such stories (including the one from which this book takes its title), it is probably too neat and tidy to be true. For one thing, there are no curse words in it, so it seems less likely that Andrew Jackson said it.[32] Moreover, it is rare that we manage to be so pithy on the spur of the moment (though it does sometimes happen).

Even if someone else composed it *post hoc* and merely attributed it to Mr. Jackson, we are not concerned with its historical accuracy so much as its usefulness in illuminating a point, which is this. If you disobey a court's judgment[33]—let's say the Supreme Court's judgment—what happens to you? Do the ghosts of John Jay, John Marshall, and John Roberts[34] haunt you until you have a change of heart? Do Elena Kagan and Sonia Sotomayor visit you at work and make you an offer you can't refuse, and rough you up in the back alley just to make sure you get the message? Does a small, well-dressed cricket appear and teach you how to be a real citizen?

If you answered "yes" to any of the above, seek professional advice (and if it was to the last one, make sure that professional is licensed to prescribe medication). The judiciary has to rely on the executive; U.S. marshals[35] would be the ones coming to your house, and they answer to the President. So, on the list thus far, if the Supreme Court wishes to strip-mine some liberties, it must either convince its intended victims to go along, or convince the executive to make more pressing appeals.

Of course, there is one more option on the list. The Court can also convince the legislature that it is necessary (or at least, expedient to the legislature) to bribe people into compliance. But in every case,[36] its legitimacy is

---

31 Business in the front, party in the back. (This mullet reference brought to you by Christopher M. Griffith, M.D., who would really like to forget he wore one in high school. Whoops.)

32 Jackson was apparently so proficient and profligate with his profanity that his parrot had to be removed from his funeral because of its foul language. (See what I did there? You're welcome.)

33 Remember, don't try this at home. Our hypothetical persons are highly tattooed professionals.

34 Poetic license—Chief Justice Roberts is, at the time of this writing, very much alive, and I wish him well. Especially if he'll otherwise haunt me from beyond the grave.

35 Not named after John; in fact, probably the other way around, several generations removed.

36 Yeah, that pun just happened.

the key to its success, either because it causes the executive or legislative to accept and apply rulings to citizens, or convinces citizens to go along of their own free will. In fact, it sometimes has to accomplish the same feat in regard to the legislative or executive, as the Court is also supposed to guard against their encroachments on individual liberty.

The Court is also passive; Marshall's activity in *Marbury* aside, justices do not normally prowl the streets, looking for injustices to put right. They are essentially powerless until someone turns on the Robed-Wonder-Signal. In fact, even that analogy goes too far; it implies that they then respond to the scene. Rather than Batman, the detective they most resemble is Nero Wolfe, sitting in his office waiting for others to bring the case (and information) to him.[37]

Not only does someone have to bring a case to the Supreme (or other) Court in order for them to act on it, but there are rules restricting who may bring a case, and what circumstances count as a case. The first of these limitations is standing. The idea of standing is to make sure that an appropriate person brings the case to the court. What makes them appropriate? Well, we have an adversarial legal system. Our courts expect each party to come to the courtroom prepared to fight (metaphysically, though bailiffs are present in case anyone neglects that distinction). If each side makes its best argument, and each side tries its best to knock down the other's, then whatever is left standing (no pun intended) must be reliable. It's sort of a crash-test or demolition derby model of jurisprudence—what's left is reliable because someone has tried his best to demolish it, but failed.

That, however, is the linchpin: his best. Standing helps ensure that each party makes its best argument, and tries its best to knock down the other's. There are three elements: injury in fact, causality, and redressability. Injury in fact means the person bringing the complaint must have suffered a real (though not necessarily physical) injury, or be in imminent danger of it. Causality means that the injury must be the result of the action of which they are complaining (which must also be authored by the person of whom they are complaining). Redressability means that it has lots of cool outfits that you can put on and take off of it, like a tuxedo, and mountain-climbing gear, and an evening gown, and a tennis skirt.

Really? You're just going to go on to the next paragraph like that last sentence never happened? Not cool. There's a pretty big difference between a justiciable case and an action figure.[38] Redressability means *dress* as in "dress a wound." Essentially, this criterion requires that a decision in your favor be able to redress your wound, or make you whole again. Of course, sometimes the "whole" is not terribly literal. Think of it as returning you to an equivalent, if not identical, state; you have the same bottom line, even if the numbers in the columns are different. An addition in one column compensates for a loss in another.

So, if someone severs your arm, that someone must compensate you for your pain and suffering. If surgeons are unable to reattach it, they must also compensate you for the loss of the use of that limb (throughout the remainder of your life). Each of these will vary by circumstance—how they severed it, whether you are Peyton Manning or Roy Halladay and it was your livelihood—but neither is able to actually put your arm back on, to put you back to exactly the same condition you were in.

So let's develop our axe-murder model of standing a little more and see if it can help us understand the other two elements. Let us imagine you are at a secluded cabin in the woods on a dark night. Hearing suspicious noises outsides, you decide to investigate on your own, without telling your companions what you are doing (or that you are going outside).[39] As you round the corner of the cabin, a shadow falls in behind you, noiselessly and outside of your range of vision. A twig snaps, you wheel as you are knocked suddenly to the ground, and a rough tongue licks your face. You disentangle yourself from your friend's black Lab, send him

---

37 No idea who that is? Read. (Without being coerced.) They're by Rex Stout, and they're very good. You could also watch the TV series that was on A&E. It starred Timothy Hutton and was quite well done—check and see if it's on Netflix.

38 or "doll," before they entered the marketability protection program (also known as MarkSec), along with prunes (now living in Nebraska as "dried plums") and Patagonian toothfish (in a condo on the beach in San Diego under the name "Chilean sea bass"). Oh, wait—I wasn't supposed to tell you that. Umm…you didn't read that last part.

39 You'd think you'd know the beginning of a horror film when you saw one. I never said it was a **good** decision.

off with a scratch behind the ears, and some words tainted by the irritation and embarrassment of letting a dog scare you. Turning to go back inside, you find yourself looking up at a massive axe-wielding maniac (henceforth to be known as "AWM").

As you flee through the woods, branches clawing at your face and brambles tearing at your clothing, you run mentally through the legal ramifications of your circumstances. You know the owner of the cabin, and you're here with his permission, so you're not trespassing, the maniac is. That injury, however, is to the cabin's owner, not you. (We assume the AWM isn't the owner, and doesn't have his permission to be here.)

Your foot hits in a depression, and you roll your ankle, spraining it. You wonder whether that injury is one you'll live to sue about—and then, you wonder whether you *can*. It's definitely an injury, but did the AWM *cause* it, or did your friend's Labrador cause it, since his random digging created the hole in which you rolled your ankle? You stop to google that question, and AWM catches up to you. (Google, by the way, has no idea what you're talking about, or wouldn't, if you had service in a place this secluded. But then, it's hard to type when you're in mortal peril.)

As the lunatic raises his axe to bury the head of it between your shoulder blades, an alien appears from nowhere and stops time. If it weren't for your hobbled ankle, and if you weren't frozen in time, you'd think about running off to get an injunction or two (to keep the AWM from chopping you, and the alien from probing you); the imminent injury is sufficient to provide standing. The alien finally looks up from his mushroom collecting, apologizes for interrupting, and disappears (which releases time to go about its business).

Just then, your friend's Labrador leaps from the bushes in your peripheral vision and pins the AWM to the ground. As you hobble off, you realize that instead of googling answers to abstract legal issues, you should have been phoning 911. Luckily, a deputy is close by, and he is able to relieve the poor Labrador and take the would-be murderer into custody. Unfortunately, the deputy is too late to save the brave canine, which dies of injuries the AWM managed to inflict while trying to free himself. The attempted murderer turns out to be a professor from a nearby liberal arts college (which explains why he kept referring to his axe as "extra credit").

So, let's assess the damages: your ankle, and your friend's dog, as well as your friend's domestic tranquility (trespassing on their property) and yours (being chased with an axe through a forest at night). You have two injuries: your ankle, and your domestic tranquility. The other damages are to your friend; you would not have standing to bring those issues before the court, unless the homicidal professor killed your friend, and you were her heir, or trustee of her estate.[40]

Your two injuries were the direct result of the maniac's actions. If you had been jogging at night and rolled your ankle, it would have been the result of your own action[41] (and I'm pretty sure you can't sue yourself—we'll talk about collusive suits later). But your flight, and the terror that left you less careful about where you stepped, were a direct result of the maniac's actions.

Injury-in-fact, causality—that just leaves redressability. And while the court can't undo the terror or the sprained ankle, it can order the responsible party to pay to restore your ankle (medical care) and to compensate you for your pain and suffering (from the ankle as well as the terror). Thus, a decision in your favor would redress your injuries. Of course, if the professor turns out to be destitute and without prospect of earning money in the future, you might get an IOU. If you and the professor reach an agreement on compensation on your own, it would moot the case—essentially, redress it before the court has a chance to do so, leaving a court decision in your favor irrelevant (and removing your standing).

In fact, this is an excellent segue[42] to some of the other limitations on the Court. Standing addresses whether you are the appropriate person to bring a case; the "case-or-controversy" limitations address whether

---

40 Although that would add another injury, depriving you of the companionship of your friend.

41 Though an enterprising personal injury lawyer (or "shyster," a Yiddish word I believe to be related to the German word "Scheißer"—"one who sh!ts"—which does provide an accurate picture of that occupation) could argue that the owner was negligent in failing to warn passers-by of the Labrador's digging spots, or to fill them in.

42 Pronounced "segg-way," in case you've never seen it in writing; it means "transition" (which, thankfully, motorized walkers seem not to have been).

there is a viable case for you to bring. Standing is a prudential limitation, one the Court adopts because it does not find it wise to hear cases without those qualities (as we discussed earlier—all that stuff about the adversarial legal process. Go on, take a look back if you want to; it's still there, and this will still be here when you get back). The case-or-controversy limitations derive from the text of Article III, and are thus called textual limitations.[43]

Turn to Article III. And yes, you should have seen that one coming. If you did, you're probably already headed for Section 2 (and thanks for paying attention). Even if you haven't been paying attention, it's a short trip from anywhere else in Article III, so head there now. Read the first paragraph. Go ahead; it won't take but about 15 seconds, and let's be honest, you weren't going to do much with those anyway.[44]

What words stand out to you the most? Granted, "admiralty" is a cool word, and I can see how it would grab your attention. It's even the name of a landmark building in St. Petersburg, Russia, through which Pierce Brosnan (as James Bond) drove a tank in the movie *Goldeneye* (big, yellow, arch, spire—that's the one). But what other words stand out—perhaps by virtue of their repetition? Yes, "citizen" appears a lot, and "state" too. But what words are the defining ideas of that paragraph? That, you know, might have been mentioned a couple of paragraphs ago?

As you are hopefully realizing, all of the objects to which federal judicial power extends are cases or controversies. Since this paragraph defines the extent of federal judicial power, and everything it lists is a case or controversy, if it isn't a case or controversy, it does not fall under federal judicial power, and federal courts have no authority over it. If it *is* a case or controversy, then it has to involve one of the parties or issues listed, or federal courts have no authority over it. But first, it has to be a case or controversy.

This means that there must be a live dispute for the court to settle. As a result, the Supreme Court (and other federal courts) will not hear collusive suits or hypothetical questions. What, you ask, is a collusive suit? It is, of course, a suit with airbags sewn into the lining, to protect you in the event of a collision. Have to be really careful with the huggers in your life, though. I once saw this guy's kid jump into his arms when he got home from work, and the airbag's deployment shot the kid through the back wall of the house.

Seriously? And the judges have been genetically engineered so the sound of airbags deploying occurs at a pitch they can't hear? If you're buying that, the only thing I can tell you is, obviously, SEND ME ALL YOUR MONEY. It will be a lot safer with me. You know, since you unquestioningly accept whatever you're told. 'N stuff.

Collusive suits are law suits[45] in which the parties collude, or work together. This should immediately set off alarm bells: if people are working together smoothly, what do they need a court to decide—which of them was the most cooperative? Technically, a collusive suit is one in which both parties want the same outcome. This means there is no dispute (living or dead) for the court to settle. Generally, the collaboration in the suit is to create the suit, to get the court to interpret a law (when there has otherwise been no injury to create standing).

The quintessential collusive suit, the example found in most constitutional law textbooks, is the case of *Muskrat v. U.S.* This involved Congress passing a law about the disposition of some land that partially contradicted a previous law on that subject. I know, you're yawning already. I, too, had much greater expectations for a case with a name that great. So let's see if we can't imagine a less boring example. Keep in mind, though, that we're talking about law, so don't get your hopes too high.

Let's say Congress passes a law allowing the military to require private citizens to provide room and board (in their homes) to at least one soldier, or to pay someone else to quarter that soldier on their behalf. Sound crazy? Read the Third Amendment. (Go on—think of the hours of fun you can have stumping your friends and family later, since you'll probably be the only one of them who will know what it says. Poor little Third Amendment; no one ever thinks of it.)

---

43 As opposed to texting limitations, which your professor should not have had to impose, or textual healing, which is neither a song by Marvin Gaye nor a New Age cure for librarians.

44 Uh-huh. *Those* were the 15 seconds when you were going to cure cancer.

45 Law suits are suits with laws sewn into the lining. Dude, you've got to stop falling for that.

Read it? Good.[46] Notice that Congress is allowed to do this, but only if we are at war. So let's assume that it's 2011 and we're still at war in Afghanistan—unless, of course, we're still at war in Afghanistan. Therefore, the military really has no need to quarter troops in private homes in the United States. They've got plenty of barracks and plenty of messes on plenty of bases, but they'd like to know, for future reference, if they could, even when the war involved is on a different continent. If someone challenged the law, the Court might look at the original intent of the amendment (Congressional debate, ratification debates, etc.) and decide that "in time of war" meant only war on U.S. soil (when there might be a need to quarter soldiers nearby).

Before the military decides to start charging people directly for the room and board it provides (or allowing people to provide it themselves), it wants to know that it can count on that law staying the same, and not being suddenly[47] declared null and void. So it approaches a local homeowner's association near a base, and makes them an offer: we'll send you a bill we don't expect you to pay, if you'll promise to sue us over it. We'll reimburse you for your legal expenses once the case is settled, and if you lose, we'll pay the bill we sent you, too. Then we'll both know better what to expect.

Assuming the association accepts, we have just imagined our first collusive suit.[48] Both parties want the same outcome: for the homeowner's association not to have to pay the bill. They both want to know if the law is constitutional, and they have contrived a dispute to test it.

If we step back for a moment, we've also created another type of case the Court won't hear, a hypothetical case.[49] A hypothetical[50] case is one that does not actually exist; it is a "what if" scenario. No one has an actual injury, we're just imagining they do. Therefore, there is no live (real, like this book, as opposed to imaginary, like your friends)[51] dispute for the Court to settle.

Collusive and hypothetical cases do not meet the requirement of being a case or controversy, and there are good reasons for the Court to refuse both even without the interpretation of Constitutional text. When people contrive a case, whether in reality (collusive) or in imagination (hypothetical), the cases are not likely to present the full range of possible circumstances. In fact, as they are created for a specific purpose, to highlight a specific question, they present an artificially limited view of the potential problems with a law.

To see what I mean by that, consider that the injury has to be created. The law (or action) might never actually harm anyone. Thus, it is rather like asking the Court a loaded question. Moreover, since the cases *are* artificially created, people could craft them so as to force the Court to give them the answer they want. It's like when people ask you if you still wet the bed. Answering "no" acknowledges that it has been an issue; answering "yes" says that it still is. Either way, the questioner gets what she wanted: your public humiliation.[52] The best response is the Court's: don't play that game.

Aside from the potential for manipulation, it also leaves the Court with the possibility that it will declare a harmful law constitutional, leaving it to cause unanticipated harm in circumstances like the ones contrived, but with additional information the contrived ones didn't include. In that case, the Court has approved the harm, facilitated it, rather than remedying it. It could overrule its previous decision, but that would harm the stability of expectations their decisions are supposed to foster. Either way, it's a bad outcome.

---

46 Unless, of course, your answer was "no," in which case I say "bad reader" and swat you on the nose with a rolled up newspaper. When newspapers are entirely digital, how will we housetrain dogs? Or will we just have to spend a lot repairing tablet screens and dog noses?

47 "Suddenly" relative to legal time, which runs surprisingly close to geologic time.

48 It's an important milestone in every student's life. Make sure to take a picture and send it to your mom. Or have it bronzed or something. Just make sure you print it out first; your phone won't react well to the bronzing process, even if you are thinking of making it look like it has a tan.

49 C'mon, let's have some mad props for educational efficiency! Read one case, learn about two—you can't beat that deal.

50 literally "under the idea," probably better translated "under the assumption," meaning that it rests on a pretense.

51 Yeah, that just happened.

52 No, this is NOT autobiographical. But I have been on the phone with your mother recently.

Imagine (you're not on the Court, you're allowed to do that) your doctor created a rule that, before he will see them, every patient must first take two aspirin and return the next day. Sure, it would help some patients, but those with puncture wounds will bleed more and develop infections in the meantime. If the patient is a child with a viral infection, they may return tomorrow with brain or liver damage. Neither patient may be able to return. The lesson? Just as doctors need to see the actual injury in order to properly diagnose, so do the Courts.

Even when there is a real dispute, it may not be live. Mootness and ripeness are two further considerations which the case or controversy requirements prompt. Justice Ruth Bader Ginsberg once described these as "standing in a time frame." She did not, of course, mean that someone was upright under a frame with the word "time" on it.

Let's go back to our axe-murderer hypothetical for a moment. Picture seeing a film strip or storyboard of the events we imagined, frame-by-frame. In frames containing events before any actual or imminent injury—when the lab was licking your face, for example—the case is not yet ripe. No one has suffered an injury; standing may yet develop, but it is not yet mature. If it were a flower, the bud would have appeared, but not yet opened. Once the injury is redressed, whether by settlement, court action, or the vicissitudes of fate, the bloom has faded, the petals fallen. In those frames of the film, the case is moot.

Notice that there is a live dispute only so long as there is an un-redressed injury. Before the injury, there is not yet a dispute; after, there is still a dispute until settlement (that is, until redress, so long as redress is possible). Only so long as a party (even if you aren't that party) has standing is there a case or controversy. Thus Justice Ginsberg's insight: ripeness and mootness are standing, in a time frame. A case is unripe before there is standing, and moot when there is no longer standing.

These limitations—prudential (of which standing is an example) and textual (case or controversy limitations, for example)—are largely self-enforced. In theory, the textual limitations come from outside the Court, but since the Court decides (according to *Marbury*, remember?) what those mean and which cases fall under those restrictions, it ends up being self-enforced in practice. There is one more such limitation on the Court, one theoretically outside of it but practically in its own hands, which we need to discuss before we move on to external restraints on the Supreme Court (and by extension, on lower federal courts).

And speaking of those federal courts, they point to the very limitation of which we have yet to speak. As you'll remember from Chapter 3 and our discussion of Justice Cabell's decision in *Hunter v. Martin, Devisee of Fairfax*, there are state courts, too. And as you may have deduced from that, there are state laws, as well.

Except for the Court's decision in *Martin v. Hunter's Lessee*, there are two ways state judicial systems could function as checks on the federal one. First, a case must present a federal question in order to fall under federal jurisdiction. That means a challenged act or law must violate the Constitution or federal law, or the case must involve the combinations of parties mentioned in Article III.[53] Where a case involves only a question of state law, such as when one citizen of a state sues another of the same state over a matter of state law, the case is outside federal jurisdiction. Of course, if one side chooses to claim federal courts have jurisdiction, it is federal courts (and in the end, the Supreme Court) which will decide whether the case falls within their jurisdiction. And so we must again rely on the Supreme Court to decide its own limits.

To give you an idea of how this might work, let's return to our example of the axe-murdering professor. Your suit against the AMP[54] would probably be in state court. You would file a civil claim, "civil" in this context referring to the body of law which deals with private wrongs of one citizen against another. Those private wrongs are known as "torts," or bad acts; when a lawyer refers to a "tortious act," they mean that the act in question belongs to an individual and has injured another individual in a way that requires compensation.[55] Civil law, in this sense, is the counterpart of criminal law, in which the state sues (we call it prosecution, not

---

53 Seriously? It was just a few pages ago.

54 Formerly known as "AWM." Hey, if you can keep up with Diddy, you can handle this.

55 So "tortious" is not necessarily "torturous"—the tort may result from torture, but it might be an accident. I'm pretty sure I know which one you think this discussion is.

to be confused with persecution, though the words are closely related in origin) an individual for harms done to the public peace, by violating the laws of the state.

So while you sue the AMP in civil court for the personal injuries he caused you, the state will prosecute him for attempted murder, assault, and whatever else is appropriate to his crimes against the state, which is responsible for maintaining good public order. And it will likely be the state, rather than the federal government, whose laws he has broken and whose wrath he will face in the courtroom. It will likewise likely be a state criminal court to hear those charges and decide his fate, as it will be a state civil court to hear your case. In both the AMP has violated state, rather than federal, laws (and the federal government doesn't really have civil law jurisdiction, with some caveats—see more below).

I say "likely" because both of these sets of offenses generally fall outside federal jurisdiction. The federal government is a limited government of delegated power (at least in theory), rather than a generally enabled government. In other words, it has only the powers the Constitution gives it (principally in Article I, Section 8, though in a few other places, too—especially some amendments). It does not have what are known as "police powers," general and broad power to regulate for the health, safety, and welfare of its citizens. **That** power remains solely with the states (at least, theoretically—remember Chapter 3?). Thus, civil law (defining and remedying injuries to the health, safety, or welfare of one citizen, committed by another) and most criminal law (injuries to the health, safety, and welfare of the general body politic, especially its interest in peace and good order) are matters of state law.

That is, of course, unless something creates a connection (or nexus[56]) to federal jurisdiction. Although Congress cannot regulate murder (or attempted murder), it can regulate it if it occurs across state lines, or if the victim is an employee of the federal government. So if you were a U.S. Department of Agriculture food inspector or if the attempt on your life was one in a series of attacks that stretched across state lines, the AMP might face federal charges as well.

In this example, though, there is likely no conflict between the federal and state charges, because one does not prevent the other. The AMP may face all three cases (state civil, state criminal, and federal).[57] The only question would be which of the criminal cases (state or federal) went first. (Because the burden of proof is a little lower in civil cases, litigants have an incentive to wait until criminal proceedings are finished. A criminal conviction on the record goes a long way to establishing the civil case.)

What if the case turned on whether it was state or federal law that applied? In other words, what if the case asked the court hearing it to decide the extent of state (and therefore, by distinction, federal) jurisdiction? Except for *Martin*, state courts could use this (and to be honest, for good or ill) to limit the Supreme Court by deciding something fell outside of its jurisdiction. After *Martin*, however, the Supreme Court would likely review that decision (if the losing party thinks they'd do better under federal law), and decide for itself where its limits are (again, to be fair—for good or ill).

Martin weakens the ability of others to limit federal judicial power in another, perhaps more important way. Return to the world of Justice Cabell's decision in *Hunter v. Martin, Devisee of Fairfax*. If state supreme courts could produce alternative interpretations of the Constitution, it would encourage a sort of regulatory competition.[58]

In a properly constituted market, businesses compete for customers. To gain custom, the business must offer a better product, a cheaper product, or both. If Wal-Mart is selling Justin Bieber's[59] latest...no, I can't call those "albums." Let's say they're offering his latest *recording* for $10, and they could sell it for as little as $7

---

56 So if you saw *Star Trek: Generations*, now you know why that was the name of the other dimension: it was a connection between all times and places. And if you're one of the few who saw that movie, you're probably not allowed to have sharp objects or shoe laces, so at least now you've got that silver lining.

57 Yes, you read that correctly. One action can create multiple legal liabilities, in multiple jurisdictions. Double jeopardy relates to the legal liabilities—you can't be tried twice for the same offense—not to the actions (which may create several offenses).

58 Remember Tiebout? (I don't hear any chicken clucking...go back to Chapter 3 and try again.)

59 or whoever the latest overrated and under-talented pop star is—One Direction, for example

while still making a profit, then Target will offer the…*product* in question (can't call those "goods," either) for $9, and more people[60] will buy from Target. So Wal-Mart will lower its price to $8, or match the $9 and add an extra incentive (like a black velvet painting of the Biebs and his pet monkey).

Eventually, competition gets each to offer the customer as much as possible for as little as possible, and encourages them (and others) to keep looking for ways to offer more and lower prices as much as possible. Consumers, as is hopefully obvious, benefit; they get more stuff for less money, making them wealthier. Which is why, of course, businesses hate properly constituted markets; they keep profit margins low and require a lot of effort. Businesses spend a lot of time and money trying to get government to eliminate, or at least handicap,[61] their competitors.

Back to the world of jurisdictional competition. If other courts can offer different interpretations, some will be better for individual litigants, and some worse. Litigants will choose the jurisdictions with better interpretations, and move their cases to those jurisdictions when they can. We see this in corporate locations, for example. Many credit card companies locate their headquarters in states with laws and legal precedents more favorable to creditors, and require in their card agreements that disputes be settled in that state.

A court's influence depends on having cases brought before it, so a court with poor interpretations would, in a sense, go out of business. It would have few cases, and thus little influence. To put it differently, interpretational competition would limit (say it with me—for good or ill)[62] the ability of state or federal supreme courts to constrict individual liberty. Any court that abused its power to create overly restrictive precedent would find less and less opportunity to apply that precedent. *Martin* means there is only one supplier of Constitutional interpretation.[63]

All right, that enough time in the Land of Make-Believe. There are also come external, political checks on the Supreme Court and its ability to interpret the Constitution. Remember Hamilton's point[64] that the Court has to rely on others to give effect to its decisions. This means the Court has to rely on its reputation, and has an incentive to argue as well and fairly as it can. Because we want its decisions to be more about truth than political expediency, the checks the other (political) branches have with which to influence the Court are few and costly.

First, Congress. Congress can start the amendment process, to change the wording of the Constitution (and thus, the Court's interpretation). Proposing an amendment requires two-thirds of each house to vote in favor of the proposal, and three-quarters of the states (through their legislatures or special ratifying conventions) to ratify the proposal. Those are high decision-making costs, and as you might imagine, Congress does more barking than biting with this threat. Three amendments—the Eleventh, Fourteenth, and Sixteenth—overturned Supreme Court decisions (regarding whether the federal government could force states to allow people to sue them in their own courts,[65] whether freed slaves could be citizens,[66] and whether Congress had to do math before taxing income[67]).

---

60 or whoever (or whatever) buys Justin Bieber…stuff.

61 To see what this looks like between individuals generally, see the movie *2081*.

62 Why do I keep saying that? Well, most things are not all good or all bad. Sometimes judges make the right decisions on principle, even when it goes against their personal interests or preferences. In fact, we hope they always do, but there's a reason we expect them to recuse themselves from cases when they have a stake in the outcome. Sometimes, however, the correct outcome might be a curtailment of individual liberty, and if competitive pressures limit the judges' discretion, they may not be able to curtail it judiciously (see what I did there?).

63 In other words, the Supreme Court owns Boardwalk AND Park Place, and they can charge you whatever they want if you land there.

64 For crying out loud, that was in *this* chapter!

65 *Chisholm v. Georgia*, 1793.

66 *Scott v. Sandford*, 1857.

67 *Pollack v. Farmers' Loan & Trust Co.*, 1895.

Congress, however, also determines the number of justices on the Supreme Court. FDR[68] used this (as President) to threaten the Supreme Court into changing its interpretation of the commerce clause, among others, to make federal power large enough to accommodate his New Deal programs (which the Court had repeatedly and almost uniformly declared unconstitutional, when it had the chance). This may sound odd, given that this is a *Congressional* power, but Congress was essentially FDR's purse poodle at this point in history.

On one of his radio shows, FDR mused that his reform legislation—the only things, of course, which stood between the United States and utter ruin—kept getting held up while people challenged them in court. If only there were some way to speed up the process and make everyone's lives better **now**. You know, maybe it's the workload in the courts.[69] Those poor old men on the Supreme Court, for example; most of them were in their sixties and seventies. Maybe he, FDR, should help them out. Maybe he'd ask Congress (remember: purse poodle) to add another justice for each retirement-age justice who didn't retire. The he, FDR, could appoint some strapping young justices, with the vim and vigor to move more cases through. Surely the work would go faster.

Notice the sleight-of-hand: it wasn't the Court's decisions, it was the time they took to hear the case and reach those decisions. And, like lifting a sofa, more and younger lifters will make the work go faster. Except, of course, that these are decisions. More people having to agree means it takes more time, not less. Even in lifting furniture, too much of a crowd on a single piece reduces productivity (as they jostle for handholds, have more feet and directions to coordinate, etc.).

Since seven of the justices were over the age FDR considered appropriate, it meant he would be appointing seven new justices, making the total number sixteen. If he appointed seven loyal people, he'd start out with almost a majority on the Court behind him (see below on this—though as Congress' parliamentary purse poodle policy proves, FDR was good at getting what he wanted). The circulating of opinions, the slow-motion written debate, might take longer (unless the seven newbies really were mindless sheep), but FDR would likely get the decisions he wanted.

The threat worked; a few justices who had generally overturned challenged New Deal legislation started voting to uphold it against challenges that it exceeded Congressional authority. Justice Owen Roberts is often blamed (or credited) with the "Switch in Time That Save Nine," but the biggest about-face was Chief Justice Charles Evans Hughes. Hughes had written a majority opinion severely chastising Congress for exceeding the commerce power and for delegating its authority to the President in violation of the separation of powers not long before the President's radio musings; not long thereafter, he wrote a majority opinion which expanded the commerce power in line with the President's wishes (essentially delegating judicial authority to him, in violation of the separation of powers).

Congress also has the ability to alter the Court's appellate jurisdiction. Think back to *Marbury* (hint: it's in this chapter). Remember the clause in Article III on which Marshall hung his decision? "In all the other cases before mentioned, the Supreme Court shall have appellate jurisdiction…with such exceptions, and under such regulations as the Congress shall make." It means what you think it does—Congress has the authority to alter and regulate the Supreme Court's appellate jurisdiction (though not, if you remember your *Marbury*, its original).

If you're wondering if the Congress has ever tried this (and I hope you are), the answer is "yes." Actually, the answer is "they haven't tried, they've done."[70] The Court's discretion in accepting appellate cases, for example, is founded on Congressional statute.[71] Doesn't seem to prove much though, does it? I mean, the **real** test is if the Court goes along with something that **doesn't** make its life easier. Sleep easy, though; the answer is "yes" there, too.[72] The classic example is *Ex parte McCardle*, a case from Mississippi during Reconstruction.

---

68 Franklin Delano Roosevelt, and not at all Fervent Destroyer of Rights.

69 Note that if there were that many cases, not everyone was better off (since they had sustained injury sufficient to sue).

70 They did, Yoda. They did not try, they did.

71 28 USC 2071 delegates to the Court authority to make rules for the conduct of its business.

72 What the Court doesn't take kindly to, though, is Congress trying to tell it how to interpret the Constitution (see *City of Boerne v. Flores* for the Court's verbal pimp-slapping of Congress for telling it how to interpret the religion clauses of the First Amendment).

Mr. McCardle was a journalist, and the general in charge of the military district[73] didn't appreciate some of Mr. McCardle's editorial statements about the general (a General DeWitt, coincidentally also the name of a general involved in *Korematsu v. U.S.*, but probably not the same one, since *McCardle* is from the Civil War era, and *Korematsu* from the World War II era).[74] So the general decided to hold McCardle in custody without charging him with anything (in others words, to throw him in jail to shut him up and punish him).

At this point, I need to introduce the concept of *habeas corpus*. A petition for a writ of *habeas corpus* (I'm going to be all legal-hip and call it "habeas" from here on, though I suppose "habe-cor" would be even more hip, and less legal) asks a court to inquire about the reason an authority is holding someone in custody. If they have no (good) reason, the court then orders the authority to release the prisoner. This writ of inquiry from the court began traditionally with the reason for the inquiry: "you have the body of this person in your custody," and it became known by its first two words. Of course, most legal and scholarly proceedings were in Latin in the Middle Ages (even in England), so those words are "habeas corpus," or "you have the body."[75]

Perhaps fearing (perhaps rightly) the tendency of military authority to deal with smart-mouthed civilians and their complaints about civil liberties by thoroughly removing said liberties, Congress had passed a statute allowing prisoners in the areas under military control to appeal habeas decisions directly from the local (probably military) court to the Supreme Court (bypassing the rest of the state or federal system). Mr. McCardle made such an appeal, and the Court scheduled and heard oral arguments in the case. While the Court was deliberating (remember, that can take months), Congress repealed the statute that had allowed the appeal, apparently deciding that locking them up and throwing away the key was the way to handle mouthy separatist rebels.[76]

So, you're the Supreme Court, and Congress has just removed your jurisdiction over a case—what do you do? The Court might have argued that, since they had already heard the case, they could bring it to conclusion and issue a decision. You know, like you do when you try to rationalize to your parents whatever they just caught you doing (unless, of course, your parents never forbade you anything, in which case you have my condolences; however, since in that case I doubt you've had the self-discipline to read this far, you probably don't know that).

The Court, however, chose to act honestly and responsibly. The Constitution, they said, quite clearly gives Congress the right to remove their jurisdiction, and as Congress had done so, they could no longer consider the case nor deliver a verdict. The Court, regardless of how they felt about it, pulled on their big boy pants and did the right thing—even when it meant having wasted a good deal of their time, even when it meant seeing a man remain in prison solely because he had said (well, printed) something a person in power didn't like. Obviously, their parents loved them enough to teach them self-discipline and respect for rules.

We do, by the way, have some indication that the Court was not happy about the circumstances of McCardle's imprisonment. As part of their opinion acknowledging that Congress had the right to repeal the statute which gave them jurisdiction, the Court pointed out to McCardle that the usual, longer road of appeal remained open. Congress might have closed the drive-thru, but the counter was still open.[77] The thought of a bunch of former rebels being suddenly released, through a Court decision saying the military regimes were violating their rights and thereby seeming to support the claims which had gotten the prisoners imprisoned in the first place, may have prompted Congress to delay the proceedings by removing the shortcut Congress had earlier provided.

---

73 For those of you who are Yankees or otherwise ignorant of U.S. history, Reconstruction was the period of military rule in the South after the Civil War.

74 If you don't understand why this makes it unlikely, you need to review your history or your biology. The difference in time between the two is more than the expected life span at the time. So either "DeWitt" is what they call every general in the Supreme Court (like the CIA Agent Lynch in *The A-Team* or Darren on *Bewitched*), or that's one cranky military family.

75 Which is probably a happy accident, as the "writ of you have the body" sounds like a really cheesy pick-up line.

76 No word on whether the general had failed them for the last time, or if they found his lack of faith disturbing.

77 I'm paraphrasing.

Then again, maybe it was Tuesday, and the cafeteria meatloaf made one of the Congressmen cranky.[78] Remember, that's the beauty of collective decisions: you don't know why it happened, since each person voting for it may have a different reason (including no reason) and maybe not the one they're willing to tell you. You only know that it happened.

Last but not least on our list of ways Congress can mess with the Supreme Court is lower federal courts. The only court the Constitution establishes is the Supreme Court. It leaves lower federal courts to the discretions of Congress. So if Congress were having a major snit-fit (and while we might like to think such behavior is beneath them, they have often demonstrated that kindergarten-level maturity can be a challenge for them), it could theoretically threaten to abolish the rest of the federal court system and let the Supremes handle every single federal case. They would probably die of old age before they got through a year's worth, and that's **not** a crack about their average age. They'd probably retire, and the President (with the advice and consent of the Senate) would appoint nine new ones—and Congress might not like handing him this gift. Plus, they'd probably have to put the rest of the federal courts back before anyone would take the job.

In the meantime, of course, the colossal back-up in the judicial system's pipes would have raw suits and cases flooding all the voters' yards. I don't imagine having to step through an inch-deep pool of class-action suits just to get to your car would leave many voters kindly disposed toward Congress at the next election. In fact, they might start hunting them in the streets.[79] So we'll call that the nuclear option: you may destroy your opponent, but you end up with radioactive fallout that makes your office uninhabitable (at least for you).

The one thing we haven't mentioned is Congress' usual power, the power of the purse. Although Congress does set the budget for the federal judicial branch, it cannot lower Supreme Court justices' salaries, and even raises occur only with significant delay (so that even if promised in order to influence the Court, the raise could be repealed well before it took effect, making it much less tempting). After all, we generally don't want a political branch interfering in judicial proceedings. We want them decided by right, not by popularity.

Speaking of popularity, the President has even less ability to check the Court. You may be thinking of impeachment, but that power belongs to Congress. They have used it rarely with Supreme Court justices (or with Presidents). In fact, I can think of only once, and another time when they threatened to do it. Even someone as brazen as FDR didn't try to get them to use impeachment. Impeachment would require that the justice have committed some serious crime or have become mentally infirm. (Not in the "that's a really weak argument" sort of way, or John Paul Stevens would have had a shorter career; rather, in the "wearing foil hats to prevent time-travelling squirrels from the thirtieth century from hearing your thoughts" sort of way.)

We were speaking, however, of the President. The President can exert influence on the Court by…uh…well, he *is* the one who appoints them. Presidents try to use this to influence the general ideological makeup of the Court, but this has two weaknesses. One, it happens on the front end, and the President cannot influence them once they're on the Court. So he has no idea what cases they might see, and no way to encourage them to a particular outcome. Two, and more importantly, Presidents suck at doing this. The good news is, they suck for a lot of reasons, ones that aren't necessarily personal (though personal limitations may be present, too).

Let's think for a moment about why it is so difficult for Presidents to (for lack of a better word) judge prospective judges. They usually do not personally know a great number of qualified candidates (if any), so they have to get to know them. How do they do that? I suppose they could ask them out to dinner, but that's a lot of awkward small talk, and as any veteran of blind dates (or avid *Bachelor* viewer) will tell you, you don't necessarily get to know someone well on the first date.

Instead, Presidents will look at evidence from potential nominees' legal careers. If they are federal judges, Presidents (or their aides, more likely) will read their decisions in important cases (or cases the President is aware of and considers important). If they are law professors, the President (his aides) will read their law

---

78 Though I don't think there **was** a cafeteria then, but you get the point.

79 Much like you have to drive a holly stake through a vampire's heart, or kill a werewolf with silver, peasants have traditionally smeared laxatives on their pitchforks when hunting Congresspersons. After all, politicians are full of it, and nothing gets rid of it like laxatives.

review articles and any public speeches. If the potential nominee has been a federal prosecutor, they may look at what cases she chose to prosecute, and what arguments she made about what the law says in those cases (in briefs submitted to courts, especially appellate courts—remember?

So obviously, if this book has seen the light of day, my potential nomination is well and truly borked.[80] But think about what people are writing in each of those situations. More importantly, consider why they are writing. Federal judges do not make decisions based on what *they* think the law *ought* to be, they make them on the basis of what *the Supreme Court* has said it *is*. Otherwise, they will be overturned on appeal to that Court.[81] Likewise, prosecutors do not say what they think the law *ought* to be, they look for an interpretation which will win the case in front of them.

Law review articles and speeches point out how previous decisions might ought to have been decided differently given those circumstances, but they will not face those circumstances. They will face new and different facts and questions. Remember the *seriatim* opinions? Though the law professor may make an argument the President agrees with, he may have reached that decision through a different process—one that will produce a different outcome with differences in circumstances (or what seem like slight differences in the question asked).

Law professors often make points just for the intellectual fun of the argument, or just to get something published, because it is only talk at that point. As a Supreme Court justice, you deal with real people, not hypothetical replays of cases or changes in theory. Considering actual consequences—some of which she might not have hypothesized beforehand—to actual people sometimes alters the decision a justice is willing to make. In fact, it often should; the actual case represents an increase in available information over a hypothetical situation, and it is entirely reasonable that more information will shed new light.

So even if FDR had been able to appoint seven new justices, he might not have gotten the majority he thought he would. Let me give you an example. Dwight Eisenhower is the poster child for 1950s conservatism, from his proper bearing to his golf game to his close-cropped hair, at least two of which he honed in his previous life as a general (Gen. Dwight D. Eisenhower lead the invasion of Normandy[82] in World War II). When asked if he had any regrets about his eight years as President, Eisenhower reportedly replied, "Two, and they're both on the Supreme Court."

Mr. Republican had managed to appoint a chief justice, Earl Warren, who presided over a strong liberal shift in the Court. In fact, the "Warren Court" is as much a byword for '60s liberalism as Eisenhower is for '50s conservatism. How did that slip past Eisenhower? Earl Warren was governor of California before his appointment. I know what you're thinking, but he was a *Republican* governor of California. Warren was the running-mate for Thomas Dewey, the Republican nominee in 1948, and Eisenhower offered him the position of solicitor general in his eventual administration (with an eye toward a Supreme Court seat) to prevent splitting the delegates at the 1952 Republican convention (which nominated Eisenhower, with Sen. Richard Nixon—also of California—as his vice-presidential candidate).

Eisenhower evidently had a great deal of personal respect for Warren, whom he described as a person of character and integrity. Democrats apparently felt much the same way: the Democratic Party in California nominated Warren jointly with the Republicans for his third term as governor. If you remember the median voter theorem, then you should be able to see why Warren presented a significant challenge to Eisenhower's campaign. (If you don't, it's probably because we won't cover it until Chapter 9. Just remember this example for when we get there—or go take a peek now.)

---

80 No, I did not make that term up. The Senate has to approve nominees to the Supreme Court, and it used law review articles to scuttle the nomination of Robert Bork, whom Ronald Reagan had nominated. Being rejected because people—well, Senators—took issue with opinions you had expressed became known as "getting borked." No, I'm not kidding.

81 Something which admittedly seems to bother the Ninth Circuit a great deal less than other federal judges. The Ninth Circuit is in California, so perhaps they have some interesting prescriptions, or think the rest of us are waiting on them to free us from our hang-ups.

82 As featured in *Saving Private Ryan*.

Eisenhower's other supposed regret was Justice William Brennan, a Democrat—but also a staunch Catholic. Liberal groups opposed Brennan's nomination, fearing (publicly) that he would be guided by his religious beliefs (and thus, the pope) rather than the Constitution when interpreting laws. Similar fears had accosted Al Smith, a Democratic governor of New York, who was the first Catholic to run for President (in 1928, against Herbert Hoover). Smith lost, and lost the 1932 nomination to FDR.[83] Brennan, however, was appointed, and proved a staunch liberal during his time on the Court (much, presumably, to the dismay of the conservative who appointed him).

So in the end, the other branches check the Supreme Court in the use of its power in rough proportion to the amount it has. The Supreme Court can only interpret laws, but Congress and the President have little or limited ability to stop them. Of course, those interpretations can often have a large effect, but only because we let them. The Supreme Court's power, in other words, is a lot like the Bogeyman's: they have only the power we give them.

Our next chapter, on the other hand, discusses a part of government which always seems to have more power than we want it to have, but never as much as it needs. We ask the Supreme Court to oversee a division of power between branches of the federal government and the state and federal levels of government to protect our freedoms. We also reunite those executive, legislative, and judicial functions and place them in the hands of the bureaucracy. That unholy chimera[84] is the subject of the next chapter.

---

83 Interestingly, between those runs as nominee and for nominee, Smith served as the president of the company that built the Empire State Building.

84 A chimera is a mythical fire-breathing beast (mentioned in the *Iliad*) which had the head of a lion, body of a goat (often depicted with a goat head protruding from its back), and tail of a snake.

Chapter 8: The Bureaucratic

Let's get one thing straight right now: bureaucracy is boring. There's no way to sugarcoat it. It's right there in the name: "rule of the desks." Have you ever seen a desk at work? (I mean, a desk when **it** is working—you've probably seen plenty when you are at a place of employment.) Inert, only noticed when it fails, usually in need of dusting, often made of material which was once alive . . . there's a reason[1] the prequel episodes of *Star Wars* were so bad. The story was, at its heart, about bureaucracy. Even lasers and science fiction mysticism can't make that wooden heart beat.

Poets and other philosophers[2] have often pondered: can bureaucracy be so boring and needlessly complex that even bureaucrats can't understand it? The answer, of course, is "yes." As proof, I give you the Internal Revenue Service. Once you get past the 1040EZ form—and one day you will—you will find that the forms and instructions all seem to be translations from Chinese of the original Sanskrit copies of Egyptian hieroglyphs as depicted in Norse runes (who, of course, had it from the original Vogon). When you find yourself in those circumstances, do not despair: the IRS has a helpful helpline to help befuddled taxpayers. Best of all, however—and proof that bureaucracy can be too complicated and mind-numbing even for those involved in it—should you find yourself being audited, the fact that you did what the IRS advised you to do *is no defense whatsoever.*

That's right. You cannot rely on the IRS' own advice about how the IRS applies the tax codes.[3] This is a pretty clear admission that the tax codes and the IRS' administration of same are so hopelessly byzantine that even the IRS won't guarantee it understands them. Unless, of course, it's auditing you, in which case the auditor understands it perfectly and you (by definition) not at all.

Still reading? I know that leading with that caveat is hardly good marketing. I want you to go into this prepared for the challenge. Forewarned is forearmed.[4] You may have found parts of other subjects in this book tedious, you may only be reading this because someone is making you,[5] but the bureaucracy is pure, concentrated boredom. At some point, you will find your eyelids drooping to the lullaby of a ceaseless, droning hum of acronyms, and stilted jargon and obsessive technicality. Resist! Make sure you have your countermeasures handy: coffee, tea, electric current, fingernail tongs, waterboard . . . whatever it takes, hang in there.[6]

---

1 Other than Hayden Christiansen; and yes, "bureau" technically refers to "office," not "desk." But there is a reason why a piece of furniture is so associated with offices as to share a name.

2 In the immortal words of Samuel J. Snodgrass.

3 At least, the last time I checked. If anything has changed, however, I would wager it is that they no longer offer the advice.

4 As in "armed beforehand," not "equipped with four arms." And no, "armed beforehand" does not refer to having four hands, either. Get unhooked on phonics.

5 I'll be honest, that hurts a little.

6 At least three of those are things you should never try at home (or anywhere else). If you can't figure out which three, seek professional help.

The first question we need to ask about the bureaucracy is where it fits in the typology of government functions. You know (or you'd better by now, unless all this writing has been in vain)[7] the legislative, executive, and judicial branches[8] and their functions: writing the laws, implementing the laws, and interpreting the laws, respectively. Which of these does the bureaucracy perform? Some of you already know that the bureaucracy is part of the executive branch. I suppose the rest of you (at least, those of you paying attention) do now. Or . . . *now*, depending on how long it takes you to process. So the bureaucracy must be involved in executing the law. Executing the law means making sure that people follow the law. So what do they have to do to make sure people actually follow the law?

Let's pretend Congress passes a law that all knitters must knit two pairs of woolen socks a year as their contribution to national security.[9] Seems straightforward enough, at least until you start to think about it (which applies to most of life, by the way). You are a field officer for the bureaucratic agency in charge of implementing the law. You have to make sure every knitter in your district contributes his socks. What do you need to know?

Come on, you ought to know the drill by now. I'm going to stall and write silly things until you take a little time to think it through. (Author hums "You Ought to Know by Now" by Billy Joel.) What's the first thing you need to know? You can't tell if everyone who is supposed to has submitted their socks until you know who is supposed to surrender their hosiery handiwork. So who is a knitter? If you're not a knitter, the law does not apply to you, and you are not in violation of it if you do not produce the socks. The first thing you need to know is on whom the law imposes an obligation, so that you can then assess whether they meet that obligation.

There are some easy answers at either end of the spectrum. The grandma who owns thirty sets of knitting needles, has a room full of leftover yarn, and is on a first-name basis with all of the clerks at the local yarn store: sure. Prisoners, mental patients, toddlers, and anyone else not allowed to play with pointy objects: no. But what about the people in between? Do just people who already know how to knit socks count, or do beginners have to learn? Do people who *could* learn count? Or does the law apply to people who knit professionally, who sell wares at craft shows, rather than to the occasional knitting hobbyist? Anyone who's ever bought a pair of needles and a ball of yarn, even if they haven't knitted since that one class ten years ago?

Remember, we haven't even gotten to what counts as socks, or how to submit them (so that you can track compliance). One question at a time, though. We'll start with what we have. How do you define "knitter" in the law? Now, as a student, when you need more definition in the terms of an assignment, your first instinct is probably to ask the teacher. Certainly years of a bureaucratic educational system[10] have taught you to first fear ambiguity, then to exploit it to your benefit.[11] In fact, just asking every possible question can become a game to harass your teacher until he gives up on asking you to do anything, can't it?[12] And you thought we didn't know.

The point is, you don't want the trouble (or responsibility) of thinking for yourself.[13] Neither do bureaucrats—they just want to do their jobs. In their case, however, they have no one to ask. In the first place, Congress is not capable of greater detail, or they would have given it. Remember, it is a body of 535 people (well, there are a few

---

7 Again: ouch.

8 And you may still know Dasher and Dancer, but if those are stage names, that's pretty creepy.

9 The security of the bottom lines of woolen yarn manufacturers, nationally.

10 Educating people systematically since 1970! Those of you who were homeschooled will probably have little inkling of the spine-chilling horror that ought to induce, but then, you have other issues to call your own.

11 You could give me your word as a student, but it's no good—I've known too many students.

12 Be honest with yourself, if not with me. You've either done that yourself, or sat by as someone else did it, hoping you would benefit without having to actively sully your hands. Short term, you saved some effort. Long term, you'll never know what you missed. The funny thing about work: it usually produces something.

13 Probably. Then again, that type of person isn't likely to be reading this voluntarily. So sort yourself accordingly. I'm just playing the odds.

more who get to participate in debates, but they have no vote).[14] The greater the detail in which they must agree, the more time and effort it will require for them to agree. Go back to our pizza-ordering example (not physically, just in your memory) and imagine if you and your friends had not only to agree to the types of toppings, but the particular brands and sources for each one. You'd spend a lot of time agreeing to a pizza which no one would want to go to the trouble of baking for you and which would cost too much, even if you could. You've been to Starbucks. Think about the incredible level of persnicketiness people have about their orders. Now imagine trying to get them to agree on the one type of drink Starbucks was ever again going to make. Someone has a strong opinion on everything, because everyone has a strong opinion on something.

High decision-making costs aside (yes, **that** was the term you were trying to remember), there's a second (and related) reason they can't ask Congress: Congress is their boss. Sure, the President is too, but Congress decides on their budget. Bosses delegate tasks to reduce demand on their time, so they do not want to spend three weeks nailing down every last possible quibble in their instructions. They expect you to use your brain to interpret their instructions appropriately. When your boss asks you to "take care" of a customer, she usually doesn't mean "see that his body is never found" (unless you work for the mafia, which we've already established is a purely fictional organization, so there's no need to take care of me for writing about it). Try pestering your boss with innumerable requests for clarification of every last detail, and you'll be fired in a few weeks, if not days (or hours, depending on how big a pest you make of yourself).[15]

Because the government can't fire you, but you can fire it, the bureaucracy can't just say "well, it's common sense." Common sense isn't all that common, and extensive, detailed procedures and records of following those procedures to the last jot protect bureaucrats from accusations that they have been unfair. To go back to our national security socks hypothetical, it is only fair that citizens know whether the law applies to them, and if so, what they need to do to satisfy that obligation. This leaves us still asking our original question: where do bureaucrats find those details and rubrics for sorting situations into "applicable" and "not applicable," "satisfactory" and "not satisfactory"?

The answer is the bureaucracy. Congress delegates "rule-making" authority to the bureaucracy, and the resulting regulations—the little bits of law that fill in the details—are published in the Code of Federal Regulations (C.F.R.). Statutes, or the laws Congress makes which these details complete, are published in the U.S. Code (U.S.C.).[16] Citations for these look like this: 54 C.F.R. 299. "54" is the number of the title (like the chapter of a book), and "299" is the section of that title (like the paragraph in a chapter of a book). It's the same for the U.S.C, just different initials (and thus, a different stack of books) in the middle.

Thus, the bureaucracy has legislative power, the ability to write definitions and procedures to complete the laws. It has executive power, the ability to apply the law (which is why it needs to know the definitions and procedures). At least it doesn't have any judicial power, right? I mean, that would be bad.

So let's go back to our socks example and see how it ends, now that we've gotten all the gaps filled (pretend we spent time defining all that stuff; it'll make you feel like a *real* bureaucrat!). According to the definitions, Mrs. Bennett is a knitter in the sense of the law, and she therefore owes two socks, which must be of appropriate size for an average adult foot and have her production number embroidered in the heel. Mrs. Bennett turns in such a pair of socks, but you hear through the grapevine[17] that she didn't actually knit them herself (though she could have). Instead, she traded with a friend who needed a baby blanket; her friend is especially practiced at socks, and she at baby blankets.

Has Mrs. Bennett therefore violated the law? The precise wording of the statute would probably be helpful, so let's see if we can come up with some. "In the interest of national security, to ensure the warmth of foot

---

14 Well, no vote on the floor. A House rule (all five are in the House) allows them to vote in committee. They represent places that aren't states (the District of Columbia) or are U.S. protectorates (Puerto Rico, American Samoa, U.S. Virgin Islands, Guam).

15 So yes, ironically, the one place that was supposed to teach you to think for yourself (school) has become the poster child of places where you learn to completely avoid it. That, friends and neighbors, is the magic of bureaucracy!

16 No, that refers neither to the Trojans nor the Gamecocks. It's not football that the three USCs have in common.

17 It's what we old people had instead of social media.

necessary to the conduct of military operations regardless of climate or latitude, each knitter in the United States shall produce, under penalty of fine not exceeding $500 and seizure of all woolen yarns the knitter may possess, two pair of socks made from wool yarn of suitable gauge and durability." Following appropriate procedures—more on those later[18]—your agency (we'll call it the National Knitted Votives Dispensary[19]) has filled in all the details, specifying the acceptable yarns, defining who qualifies as a knitter, and establishing a submission policy (among other things).

Mrs. Bennett has done all of these things, but your agency says she has not produced them herself. She claims the law does not require her to do so. Although *produce* can mean "to fabricate," it also means "to bring forward or supply." For example, parties in legal disputes are required to produce evidence for their claims. They are forbidden, however, to fabricate it,[20] and may only bring forward to the court evidence which already exists.

Someone has to interpret the law, decide whether Mrs. Bennett's actions violated it, and if so, what penalty to apply. Your agency, of course, is in charge of implementing the law, of making sure that everyone follows it. Hmm . . . this sounds like a job for the NKVD! Who else knows the details so well? Has spent more time figuring out what the law means? And indeed, the IRS not only investigates cases of tax fraud or evasion, it holds administrative hearings to determine the innocence or guilt (and appropriate penalty) of the accused. That's right; they exercise judicial power, too.

At this point, a question should be forming in your mind, and the answer is no, we are not almost finished. The answer to the next question is yes, I do know a Mrs. Bennett. She is a friend of mine who taught me how to knit, though that's where the contact with reality stops (in terms of the resemblance with the fictional Mrs. Bennett). Wait! Go back to that last question—the one in the back there that hasn't finished forming yet. Yes, we just said that the bureaucracy has executive, legislative, and judicial powers. That's it—put it right there next to those faded memories of previous chapters.

Hmm. By this time, you ought to be yelling at me about how we've spent so much time (since, say, Chapter 3 at least) talking about the ways the Constitution separates those powers to prevent their abuse. Yeah, sorry about that. Hope you weren't in a very public place near attractive people of the opposite gender or someone else you wanted to impress in a quite different manner than that little outburst just did. Dude, yelling at a book just makes you look *mental*. And not in the "I can see the future" way. Oh no, wait, in that way, too. So if anybody's offering you pills right now, just remember to hold them under your tongue and spit them out when no one's looking. On the plus side, you probably just got a lot more personal space. (You're welcome.)

So why would we reunite all those powers we spend so much care separating in order to protect our liberty? They've all got solid solo careers, so why are we getting the band back together? If those powers united are dangerous, won't the resulting unholy bureaucratic chimera[21] threaten our liberty? Is anybody else reading this in movie-trailer-voice-over-guy voice? The short answer (to both of the last two questions) is yes.[22] Now, we do have some institutional provisions to try and prevent that abuse (and we'll talk about them shortly)[23], but one thing we have to keep in mind is the first rule of wing-walking: don't let go of what you've got until you have a hold on the next thing.

That is, the shortcomings of bureaucracy, especially as we now organize it, are self-evident truths. The question is not whether bureaucracy is perfect, but whether we have a better alternative. Rather, the question is what the alternative is, and then whether it is better. Would you like $100? You probably said yes, because the alternative

---

18 I can feel your excitement from here!

19 Google those initials if you don't recognize them. This is why it's important to know your history: the world is so unintentionally funny. For example, being trapped in Elba, Alabama becomes a chance to sympathize with deposed French emperors, rather than the annoying result of an educational system (or gene pool) which has left a population incompetent to operate a fast food franchise.

20 If this is not a crime in your legal system, your legal system *is* the crime.

21 The chimera is a mythological creature which is part goat, part lion, and part snake. Seems a reasonably accurate portrait of the bureaucracy. I mentioned it at the end of the last chapter. And yes, "unholy" and "bureaucratic" are redundant.

22 Also, by the way, the long answer.

23 "Shortly" in the sense of "soon," not "briefly."

is nothing. When the alternatives are nothing and $100, you don't turn down the $100 because it isn't as much as you want. It beats the alternative you do have on offer, even if you wish the alternative were $1,000,000.

First, though, we should get a better idea of the solution we have currently, so we'll know if whatever alternatives we might concoct would be better. Let's begin with that first question: why would the Founders, so concerned to separate these powers, enable a part of one branch to recombine them? There are two immediate answers, both of which embroider on this: they didn't. That is, the Founders did not create the bureaucracy, nor specify its powers. It does not appear in the Constitution; Articles I through III are the legislative, executive, and judicial branches, and increasingly little is said about the relevant branch as you progress through those articles. Article IV is about states, Article V is about amendment, Article VI about debt, supremacy, and swearing,[24] and Article VII is about ratification.

The only hints of bureaucracy are references to "all executive officers" in Article VI (they're doing the swearing[25]) and to "other public ministers," "such inferior Officers," and "the Heads of Departments" in Article II (which outlines the method of their appointment). The Founders[26] saw what we would call the bureaucracy as those "other officers"—the office workers, the postal carriers, the customs officers. These were the people helping the President do his job, which they also saw as helping the other branches get their work done. Remember the "take Care that the Laws be faithfully executed" line? He was supposed to do what Congress said.

Of course, as any smart boss listens to his administrative assistants, he was allowed to object (through the veto) to things he thought would go badly. After all, he was at the practical end of matters, unlike Congress, and thus had information available to him which they did not.[27] That is why he could refuse to sign a bill and return it with his objections, explaining to the boss why the new policy they thought up wouldn't work as they hoped. If the boss overruled him, though, he still had to faithfully execute the law.

This leads to our second bit of embroidery. The bureaucracy did not re-combine the powers of all three branches when it was created. The delegation of judicial and legislative functions occurred much later. That gerund ("delegation") also provides a clue to why it happened. Remember, delegation is one way to reduce transaction costs, including decision-making costs. We've already discussed the reasoning behind the delegation of legislative power: Congress does not have sufficient time to write laws with sufficient detail. The finer the detail, the more points they must decide, the (exponentially) more time and effort it takes them to reach a decision. Better to delegate that function to a smaller body, one which already has the requisite expertise (also saving Congress the cost of obtaining that information).

Over time, the federal government has expanded. It has taken more and more issues as its own, and these issues often grow more complex when they must apply to a whole nation rather than a single state. Some, of course, grow less so, which is why we created the federal government in the first place. National defense, treaty negotiation, and free trade between states were all a lot easier to solve at the federal level. In fact, if you remember our discussion of treaties, incorporating more local voices is an impediment. The same can be seen in national defense; local interests cause Congress to protect bases and procurements which interfere with the national interest in minimizing the cost of providing that defense.

Vocational education, however, is probably less easy to solve at the national level. Preparing students with the necessary skills for local industry is a fine idea, but which skills those are—which skills local industry needs—can vary greatly depending on what those local industries are. Although Congress may know that it wants to promote vocational education, it does not likely have sufficient time to thrash out a set of detailed rules which accomplish its goals in so many separate, different circumstances.

Instead, it sets a general framework (as we've discussed—or do I need to bring up the wool socks again?) and delegates filling in the details to the bureaucracy. This is the rest of our second embroidery upon our

---

24 Of oaths, though the debt and supremacy have probably prompted a great deal of the other kind of swearing.

25 Of an oath to support the Constitution.

26 Remember, when I use that term, I necessarily use it loosely—"the Founders" were a large group of people with a broad spectrum of opinion.

27 Information asymmetry? Why yes, it is, and it will return to haunt us soon.

answer about the Founders. Even today, when the bureaucracy has been delegated legislative and judicial power (in addition to its executive function), it has not been delegated the whole of those powers. It cannot write laws, it can only make rules that fill in the details of the statutes Congress passes.[28] It cannot decide the interpretation of any law, but only narrowly proscribed ones. They are not courts, but like courts, and highly specialized ones at that. Other people hold the reins, the bureaucracy just pulls the cart.[29] If governmental powers are bags of potato chips, then sure, they get chips from all three bags, but they get the broken bits and crumbs left in the bottom of the bag.

Let's pause a moment and catch our breath (or wake ourselves up and wipe off the drool, since we're talking about bureaucracy). Here's where we've been: the bureaucracy has small parts of the power of each of the other three branches. This was not part of a calculated design, but a response to increased decision-making costs as the federal government grew in power and responsibility.[30] The bureaucracy's job is to make sure laws are implemented correctly—that people follow them with the appropriate results.

Now, here's where we're going. We want to look at the evolution of the bureaucracy, and then at the incentives which shape bureaucrats' behaviors. We also want to look at how Congress, the President, and the Supreme Court oversee (and check) the bureaucracy's use of (the parts of) their respective powers (which they have delegated to it). Last but not least, we want to look at the variety of bureaucracy, how we vary its structure to respond to different goals. In other words, we want to disaggregate a little the word "bureaucracy," which we are likely until then to treat as an undifferentiated mass. Somewhere along the way, or at the end if not before, we'll return to whether that mass is benign or cancerous, and what might be done about it, if necessary.

In the beginning was the bureaucracy, and the bureaucracy was with the President, and the bureaucracy was the President.[31] Obviously, that's not meant to imply the same relationship or status as the immortal words to which it alludes. After all, I just spent a chapter (and a paragraph even more recently) explaining how the President does not have the god-like powers we often ascribe to him. I'm just borrowing some poetic cadence, and not very well at that. (And yes, *that* is the metaphor: borrowed power made less and poorly used.)

Still, the bureaucracy is an executive agency, which means it acts on behalf of the President. And it has been with us since the beginning of the republic. Back then, however, the most numerous officers in the bureaucracy would likely have been postmasters and customs officials. The Cabinet—our name for the President's closest advisors, who are also the heads of various parts of the bureaucracy—consisted of the Secretaries of State, War, and the Treasury, along with the Attorney General. That is, the President chose trusted friends or political allies to act on his behalf (and under his instruction) in relating to foreign nations, protecting the nation militarily, collecting and disbursing money, and representing the United States in court proceedings to which it was a party.

The Attorney General was something of an outlier in the following regard. The Secretary of State oversaw the operation of embassies and ambassadors abroad, the Secretary of War the organization of the military (the army and navy), and the Secretary of the Treasury the activities of customs officers, assessing and collecting taxes and duties. All of them oversaw some number of people as part of a department. The Attorney General, however, had no agents below him, no department. He might have employed a clerk, as any other lawyer would have, but he was simply the federal government's lawyer.[32]

The important thing is that these were people the President trusted to do these jobs well, since they were doing them on his behalf. As principal, the President had to worry that his agents might take advantage of the authority he delegated to them to enrich themselves or otherwise abuse their power. This would make him

---

28 So if you've been wondering why bureaucracies lobby Congress—or if you just started—this is part of the answer: to get statutes for which they want to fill in details.

29 So if you're thinking that explains the mulish attitude of many "civil" servants, you're right.

30 As Uncle Ben would remind us, the two are—or ought to be—inseparable.

31 Did anyone else hear thunder just now?

32 This is no longer true. The Attorney General now oversees the Department of Justice, but has kept the original title (as opposed to "Secretary of Justice"). The Solicitor General, an officer of the Department of Justice, now represents the United States in court.

look bad,[33] damaging his reputation (a definite agency loss—they were supposed to make him look capable, not incompetent). The first Presidents tried to minimize this danger by appointing to these positions (Cabinet members, postmaster, ambassadors, etc.) people they could trust, either because the President knew them, or because he trusted someone else who vouched for them.

That, at least, is how the Presidents saw it. To those on the other side of the experience—those who hoped to become postmaster, and perhaps even had a talent for organizing and delivering receivables, but who did not know anyone who could vouch for them to the President—it seemed more like a bunch of good ol' boys, whether or not they ever meant any harm. Even from a more neutral, public-interest perspective, "who you know" doesn't seem like much of a filter for deciding who should perform public duties. Perhaps the most able candidate was unknown to the President or his circle of trust. Worse, perhaps none of those in a given locale who happened to have the confidence of someone who could vouch for them were, in fact, any good at the job. In other words, the set of people about whom the President had sufficient information to ease his agency loss concerns and the set of people capable of performing the job well might not overlap much, or even at all. If the goal is to get the best candidate, artificially restricting the pool to those about whom the President (or his circle of trust) has sufficient information to trust seems a poor way to achieve that goal.

More than that, the "good ol' boy network" violates fundamental American mores about fairness and merit. The norm that one should earn on her own merits what she receives, and that merit should receive its due, is hardly new. In fact, one might argue that it is lately placed on life support, as a result of advanced age or neglect. The idea of benefitting from whom you know, from connections rather than ability, smells distinctly (and disgustingly) aristocratic to democratic noses.

Of course, modern democratic noses get a little sniffy at calling the U.S. "democratic" at that time. You have probably heard (or read) catty comments, especially in high school civics texts, about how the United States wasn't *really* a democracy until the 1920s or the 1960s. In the early years of the republic—and note that it was called a democratic republic, not a republican democracy—states had property, gender, and other restrictions on voting.

That is, women were not allowed to vote, nor were slaves. The former was often considered the ward of her husband or male relatives, as she supposedly lacked the cool and disciplined powers of reasoning, or the iron nerve necessary for the hurley-burley of public affairs. Apparently, people hadn't met many women. The latter, slaves, could not vote, as the law considered them property, and many people again (incorrectly) doubted their ability to comprehend such complex matters. Again, ignorance rearing its ugly head is perhaps the most generous explanation, and these slanders have been well and truly debunked since.[34]

However, neither were all of the AWMs (adult white males) able to vote. Even if one had reached the age of majority with sufficient paleness and body hair, he still had to own a sufficient amount of property. Culturally, this probably resonated with the idea of being sufficiently established so as to be independent, free (or at least insulated) from the financial influence of others. It also implied that one had sufficient material resources at stake to take the matter seriously; you were less likely to be flipping a coin in the voting booth with real, tangible interests at stake. (For some reason, we humans seem especially susceptible to trading away our abstract, intangible rights—say, to inheritance—for concrete, material benefits—like a bowl of stew.)[35]

Let's look at that from the other side of the coin again. Another way of saying "those with sufficient material resources" is "the wealthy." Granted, "wealthy" is a relative term, both to the conditions of others and the thing valued.[36] A person who is materially poor relative to others in the United States would be considered positively swimming in it in some other countries, where automobiles, refrigerators, electricity, and indoor plumbing

33 Nor is this purely hypothetical—it happened to Ulysses S. Grant when he was President.

34 Sort of—it turns out, we're all weak-willed and stupid and unfit to operate a government. Gender and race have nothing to do with it.

35 A tale as old as time, a song as old as rhyme (or at least the Book of Genesis).

36 If you don't understand, read "The Gift of the Magi" by O. Henry.

are still mere pipe dreams.[37] A person who could become materially wealthier as a corporate attorney finds that she is richer in self-respect and family relations as an undervalued professor. The point, however, is that relative to the context of the time, the United States was an expansive and inclusive democracy. Seen from here, it smells more like aristocracy (much like that whole bureaucratic selection process we were discussing).

Over time, these restrictions changed, and the process started relatively quickly.[38] By the 1820s, states had relaxed or removed property requirements so that a much larger proportion of the population was able to vote (still free adult males, though). This need to reach and organize a larger number of voters prompted changes in the bureaucracy, too. Presidential candidates (and their parties) needed to overcome several collective action problems.

We'll talk more about them (and in greater detail) in the next chapter, but here's the trailer: free-riding and coordination. Like-minded voters needed a way to identify which electors shared the perspective and would vote for their desired candidate. For that matter, they needed to coordinate on which candidate they all found best (or least objectionable). Once they decided how to coordinate their actions, they had to make sure everyone showed up and voted. After all, a prospective voter could get the same benefit while staying home, so long as all the others didn't free-ride.

Overcoming these takes a great deal of effort, and effort isn't free. The parties needed a way to compensate people for their work organizing those masses of voters on the local level. Since the party could not observe whether those receiving the payment actually fulfilled their end of the bargain, the best compensation would provide appropriate incentives to overcome that moral hazard.

The answer came in the form of Andrew Jackson's "rotation in office" system. Jackson was anti-elitist and found it offensive that only the well-connected had access to government jobs (and their steady paychecks). He thought a democracy's public offices should be open to more people. Not only would the salary mean more to those not already possessed of ample resources, it would bring government closer to the people, giving more people the chance to participate directly in the administration of their government, rather than kowtowing to their supposed "betters."[39] The rotation in office system—appointing people for shorter terms—would limit the damage of a bad appointment. In fact, since the person would soon be subject to someone else in the same role, it would encourage them to think of the precedent their actions would set.

As an added bonus, this stone nabbed a second bird: the President could use these positions as compensation for all those party workers whose efforts got him elected. And they would only get that compensation if their efforts were successful (with the local vote totals to show it). This gave some entrepreneurial spirits enough incentive to work (and work hard) on behalf of the party or candidate.

Sounds great, doesn't it? It addresses the increased collective action problems of a larger electorate. It solves those problems in a way that also makes the system more democratic and less aristocratic. Instead of whom you (or your family) know, the criterion for success is effort. So this produces a much more pleasing aroma for our democratic noses.

Still, there's something off about it. What could possibly be wrong with this solution? So . . . how many occurred to you? I've got two. Go ahead, write yours down, and let's see if we came up with the same ones.

First, think about teachers whose performance is judged by their students' performance on standardized tests. There are a lot of problems with that—students may do well *because* of their teacher, or *in spite* of her. Likewise, they may do poorly because of her, or in spite of her best efforts. It seems like giving the teacher a stake in the outcome would make sure she has the right incentives. Since the outcome depends on the other party (the student) as well, it gives her bad incentives.

---

37 I couldn't resist the pun. More seriously, the good news is that places where this is true are becoming rarer, if not yet rare. See Hans Rosling's TED talks on public health.

38 For an excellent theoretical depiction of that process, at least generally, read *Democracy in America* by Alexis de Tocqueville. And yes, I've mentioned him before. Or should I say be-*four*?

39 Jackson bore a scar on his face—you may be able to see it in the engraving used for the $20 bill—he received from a British officer when he was a child. The officer thought Jackson was not polishing his boots with sufficient fervor. No word on whether the officer had six fingers. Understandably, he was not fond of people who thought their status awarded them privileges.

Put yourself in the shoes of a teacher who has worn herself out, expended her considerable expertise trying to help a class of students master algebra. Now imagine a student—you can probably name at least one, and he might be in the mirror—who simply doesn't give a rat's . . . posterior. He could get better if he tried—the teacher is doing everything to make it easy for him—but he doesn't care enough to make the effort. His Playstation is much more important; only geeks make an effort at school. In the long term, he'll bear the consequences of that decision, but in the short term, it will be his teacher.

Faced with a class of those students, the teacher would do better to pack up and move now. She can put her effort into finding her next job, rather than wasting it on someone too apathetic to make use of it and *then* having to dredge up even more effort to find a new job, with a dismissal on her record. Even if the consequences are not so dire, why should she expend all of her effort, be perhaps the most meritorious of teachers, only to get no raise, or even a reduction in salary, as her reward?

Let's say that (unlike yours truly) she isn't psychic, and didn't see that coming. She now finds herself looking at the Scantron sheets and thinking that the patterns which the shaded bubbles form are all wrong. Then it occurs to her: they're done in (No. 2) pencil. Pencil erases, and she's got both an eraser and a No. 2 pencil of her own. Those patterns don't have to stay wrong, and then her effort would get the reward it deserves. From here, of course, it's a short trip to the teachers who don't care enough in the first place, and want to change the patterns to hide their lack of effort, not show it. In fact, the Georgia Bureau of Investigation found that forty-four of the fifty-six schools in the Atlanta Public Schools system had done exactly that on a standardized test in 2009.

The rotation-in-office system, whose detractors refer(red) to it as the spoils system, encouraged corruption in much the same way. The local organizer only got the spoils of victory if his candidate was actually victorious. This depended on whether other organizers did they work well, too. It also depended on whether people actually voted as they promised they would. He could make the payoff more certain by offering inducements (like money or alcohol—a friend of mine remembers his father handing out fifths of whiskey behind polling stations on behalf of a party) to get people to the polls and to cast their votes as he wished. He could make it easier, and just vote for them if they never showed up (or had inconsiderately died before voting).

To see the other problems, let's go back to those teachers and their students. The problem began with using as a filter a criterion (student scores on standardized tests) which has at best a partial relationship with the qualities desired (good teaching). What does helping a candidate get elected say about your qualifications to be, say, ambassador to Ireland? If we apply ourselves, we could probably find a few to stretch to fit, just as we could probably relate the ability to run a standardized-test cheating ring to some of the qualities of being a good teacher. The ability to persuade, coordinate, and organize people, for example. Thinking outside of the box, people skills—there are all sorts of clichés we could use to paper over that gap. In the end, the stretching we do is just proof that we know the gap is there.

So surely there were things in Dan Rooney's biography as the owner of an NFL[40] franchise which qualified him to be ambassador to Ireland. His ability to make campaign donations meant he knew how to motivate people. His Irish heritage meant that the locals would be able to pronounce his name. He might be able to establish a rapport with the long lost cousins his ancestors left behind a century before (give or take). My point is not that Dan Rooney was a horrible choice for the post—for all I know, he was great at it, or at least perfectly serviceable. At the very least, he didn't start any wars or cause any scandals.

My point is not that he was a poor choice, but that this—who helped someone get elected—is a poor way to *make* the choice. It's like picking whom you will marry based on her[41] ability to do karaoke. You might get lucky, or you might find the perfect spouse by blind luck. But you're counting on exactly that: luck. Either that, or it's a job that almost anyone can do (and the divorce rate says it's not that easy).

Take another example. Switzerland[42] has four official languages (German, French, Italian, and Romansch) and very different local cultures to go with them. A recent ambassadorial appointment was a former product

---

40 That stands for National Football League, in case you've just woken from a half-century long coma.

41 Or his; I'm not judging.

42 That may be what former Cowboys coach Barry Switzer calls his ranch, but that's not what we're talking about here.

manager and marketing executive for Microsoft and Expedia. She was the first person to take her oath of office on an electronic reader, rather than a physical book, and she made a charming video introducing herself and her family to the Swiss, which she posted on YouTube. In that video, she said exactly one word in each of Switzerland's languages, except for Italian, which got a second one when she ended the video with "ciao!" (The others, of course, were the greetings which opened the film.)

Now, maybe her team building skills from her time as product manager for Microsoft will prove invaluable in her new role of relating to people outside her building. No, wait, that's the marketing. Let's try again: her experience shepherding Microsoft products to market will help her create smoothly operating, problem-free relationships.[43] I imagine there is someone in the State Department who is an expert on Switzerland, its regions, their languages, and their cultures. I bet she even speaks a couple of those languages, and I bet she would use some choice words from all of them to express her feelings about being passed over for the job in favor of someone who literally doesn't even speak the language.[44]

That, too, seems to offend our American spirit of fairness and rewarding merit. Someone who has worked hard to earn the qualifications for a profession should not see someone else promoted ahead of them based on non-related qualifications. Moreover, it does not seem likely to produce the best results. Like the previous system, the sets of people who are able to help run a successful campaign and who are able to run a successful post office may not overlap, or may not do so sufficiently to produce enough good administrators. Although there may be heart surgeons who play chess well, you don't choose someone to perform open-heart surgery based on how well she plays chess. You especially don't choose Bobby Fischer or Garry Kasparov, despite their brilliance at chess, because neither has (or in the late Mr. Fischer's case, had) any training in surgery, let alone open heart surgery (at least, to the best of my knowledge).

It seems that we do not want administration of the laws to be democratic (done by those who are popular) or aristocratic (done by those who are noble, which is often mistaken for "wealthy" or "connected"). We want meritocracy, the rule of those who are deserving, who have the appropriate qualifications. In fact, what we really seem to want is technocracy, which means the rule of robots who enslave mankind through entrancing dance beats. And if you believe that, then I know a Nigerian prince who'd like to borrow your bank account. For charity, of course.

Technically, technocracy means the rule of those with expertise. We use the term "meritocracy" to describe the civil service reforms to the bureaucracy (the rule of offices, remember?), but since the qualification which makes them deserving is their expertise, or skill,[45] at the job, our meritocratic bureaucracy is predominantly technocratic.[46] The Pendleton Civil Service Reform Act of 1883 was the first to introduce these ideas for some federal bureaucratic positions. It required those positions be filled based on merit, as demonstrated in competitive examination of the candidates (for the jobs, not political office). It forbade the dismissal or punishment of the officers in those positions for their political allegiances or acts (or omissions, such as not donating to the President's campaign.

Interestingly, the Pendleton Act was at least in part a response to the assassination of President James A. Garfield in 1881. A crackpot named Charles Guiteau convinced himself that a speech he delivered twice to small audiences had been crucial to Garfield's election (in 1880). He demanded appointment as ambassador in consideration of his efforts on behalf of President Garfield.[47] When his persistence in pressing his case personally got him banned from the White House (with a lovely parting threat from Secretary of State James G. Blaine[48]), Guiteau stalked and shot President Garfield, fatally wounding him. On the day of his execution, Guiteau danced

---

43 After the second or third try, when the Swiss finally learn how to work around the bugs.

44 We don't, by the way, appoint most ambassadors this way anymore. We had to reserve the crony appointments (Wikipedia politely calls them "non-career appointees") for countries which are close friends or tropical islands or world-class ski resorts with world-class chocolate.

45 Except that their skills are not the ones which pay the bills, but the ones which correctly invoice and collect payment.

46 Chanting that last bit may very well empty your mind. Or at least your bowels.

47 Who most certainly was not an orange tabby addicted to lasagna.

48 Yes, there were other politicians whose names did not involve "James" or an initial "G."

to the gallows, singing a poem he had written that morning. In spite of all of this, Guiteau refused any defense based on his insanity. Sadly, none of this makes him terribly difficult to imagine as a bureaucrat.

Now that our TMZ: History[49] moment has passed, let's get back to the bureaucracy. The Pendleton Act was one of the first fruits of the Progressive movement. The Progressives (later a political party) advocated a rationalization of government, as well as an increase in the responsiveness of government to popular majorities. They saw the power of government as a force for good, at least when constrained by an enlightened will of the majority. This led them to champion a great number of reforms, but in the context of the bureaucracy, it was civil service reform. Part of that was meritocracy, ensuring that people capable of performing the duties held those positions. Another part was applying reason to the training of those officers and the division of their duties.

This was known as "scientific management," a term apparently coined in 1910 by future U.S. Supreme Court Justice Louis Brandeis in his arguments in a court case, the *Eastern Rate Case*. Brandeis argued that a railroad (regulated as a public utility) should not be allowed to raise its rates, as it had requested, because the need for the increase came not from increased costs, but from poor management. He called as an expert witness Frederick W. Taylor. Taylor had begun his working life in a Pennsylvania steel mill. His experiences there led him to think about how best to organize work, so as to maximize productivity. Taylor called his method the "shop system," though be apparently knew a good marketing strategy when he heard it, and used Brandeis' phrase when he published his book on the subject, *Principles of Scientific Management.*

Essentially, managers were to break jobs down into specific tasks and then distill rules and instructions on how best to accomplish those tasks. They would then select those best suited to perform those tasks, and train them using the rules and instructions. In the abstract, that may sound a great deal like the division of labor which Adam Smith described more than a century before. The difference is in how that principle is applied—consciously (with intention and thought) and systematically (thoroughly and according to a repeatable pattern).

To see the difference, let's consider cleaning your apartment with your roommate as an example. You each take your own bedroom; one of you takes the bath and the living room, and the other the kitchen and dining room. You've divided the labor, so you'll be done faster than if one of you were cleaning all six rooms. If you keep that same division of rooms, you will get even faster, as you develop expertise—you'll find better ways to organize the tasks so as to reduce time between them, to make use of the same rag while you have it, rather than having to go back and get it, or rewet it, or getting another and having more to put away.

Now let's say you have a nosy neighbor named Winslow. Winslow is watching you clean your apartment,[50] and his out-of-control obsessive-compulsive disorder compels him to come over and offer some suggestions. Instead of dividing the work by room, divide it by tasks. One of you vacuums and dusts, the other mops and puts stray objects back where they belong. One of you cleans porcelain, the other glass and mirrors. Moreover, Winslow has been watching you for a while—see previous footnote—and suggests that the one of you who *doesn't* have allergies do the dusting and vacuuming.

He has also catalogued some of the expertise each of you has developed while dividing the work by room, so the other can start at the same level of productivity. So he leaves instructions on how to complete the tasks, and in what order. For example, he says to dust first, then vacuum—all the dust you brush up will be on the floor for the vacuum to pick up. Squirt toilet bowl cleaner around the underside of the rim first, then spray mildew cleaner in the shower, then clean the sink and mirror. By the time you're done with the mirror, the toilet is ready for scrubbing; by the time you're done with the toilet, the shower is ready to finish. Plug the vacuum in to the outlet in the hallway, and you'll be able to reach all the rooms without stopping to move the plug to another outlet.[51] Thanks to Winslow,[52] you and your roommate are much more productive (if also somewhat more sleepless, as you worry about to what other tasks—such as disposing of bodies—he has devoted this much thought).

---

49 Not to be confused with the original TMZ: Las Vegas, or the other spin-offs, TMZ: New York, TMZ: Navy, and TMZ: Los Angeles Navy.

50 I know—how creepy is that?

51 Hey, I never said it was a big apartment.

52 That is, by the way, what puts the "W" in "Frederick W. Taylor." And yes, he **is** the same Frederick Taylor who (with his brother-in-law) won the first men's doubles championship at what would become the U.S. Open.

Thanks to the Progressives, the ideas of this Frederick and another (Frederick II of Prussia, known as Frederick the Great) became part of our model of bureaucracy. Frederick the Great, who died the year before the U.S. Constitution was written, reorganized his bureaucracy so that each department had a specialized task and answered directly to him. He wrote specific rules (or procedures) directing in detail the daily activities of higher-level administrators (and had them written for other administrators). He promoted people based on talent, not title. If that sounds like Weber's ideal bureaucratic form, there's a reason for that.[53] The Prussian bureaucracy was the one he studied, and, because of its successful history in modernizing Germany, its forms the ones the Progressive reformers in the late 1800s and early 1900s turned to for a model.

Let's think about that for a second. What made the Prussian model so effective was that every department head answered to Frederick II. For one thing, Frederick II was renowned for his preternatural energy. The Prussian bureaucracy worked best when it had a very active king directly engaged in monitoring the departments—reading daily reports, always current on what the departments were doing. When kings were unable to exercise that level of control, the bureaucracy became much less efficient.

Aside from his unusual ability to maintain such a workload, we also have to consider another way Frederick II was unique: he was King of Prussia. All right, so that didn't make him unique in history—Prussia had several kings—but it means that the head of this model has characteristics which may be unique to the context of a monarchy. In fact, the model depends on the ability of the head to command both the information and issues facing the departments as well as the departments themselves. In the first instance, Frederick's great energy was needed, and U.S. presidents may have that same quality. In the second instance, while the president is the head of the bureaucracy, Congress is also able to exert some control over bureaucratic departments, and neither can command the state bureaucratic agencies also involved in many federal programs. Put more generally, the Prussian monarchy had no division of sovereignty or of power, while the United States has both. To the extent that the efficacy of that hierarchical Prussian model depends not just on an energetic head, but a unified one as well, we might expect it to function poorly in the United States.

Let's look more closely at what that model is, as Weber[54] describes it. But first, let's describe Weber. Max Weber—Karl Emil Maximillian Weber, when he was in trouble with his mother—was a German social scientist of the late 1800s and early 1900s. I say, "social scientist" because his work belongs to several modern disciplines: sociology, political science, and economics (just to name a few), which are all social sciences. Among the things he studied was authority, how it worked and what made it legitimate. He defined three types of authority, according to their sources: traditional, charismatic, and legal.

Traditional authority relies on custom; most monarchies work this way (certainly the British one). We believe they have authority because they traditionally have. Charismatic authority comes from special qualities which the person in authority has. We believe we should do as they say because they are blessed, or wise, or special. You see this a lot in cult leaders (and Jedi masters). Legal authority is based on the rule of law, and thus is administered in a particular way: through a meritocratic bureaucracy.

There are essentially three core features of a meritocratic bureaucracy. First, it has a hierarchical division of labor. So far, so . . . what's the opposite of earth-shattering? Organizations, especially large ones, are often arranged hierarchically, and usually so as to divide up labor. So what are *those* things—hierarchy and division of labor—and why are they so common?[55] A hierarchy is an organization by rank, from greatest to least. In the case of hierarchies which organize people and their activity (rather than organizing concepts or knowledge, for example), the ranking is from greatest to least authority, and there are fewer people in each rank, usually with a single person at the top. The armed forces, for example, are organized this way, and the commander-in-chief is alone at the top rank. Generals answer to the commander-in-chief, colonels answer to generals, majors answer to colonels, captains to majors . . . you get the idea, and we're not even out of the officers yet.

---

53 Actually, it's amazing, since we apparently haven't talked about Weber yet. Sounds like you've stolen my psychic powers. Well played.

54 Pronounced "vey-bear," emphasis on the "vey."

55 Though please do not confuse "common" with "only."

Along with this hierarchy comes a division of labor, and that often in two dimensions. The primary division of labor is vertically, into columns (the divides run vertically). For example, the President is head of the bureaucracy, just as he is commander-in-chief of the armed forces (which are part of the bureaucracy). Most members of the cabinet are the heads of the next level of bureaucracy: the cabinet-level departments. If you try to think of the "Department of _____", you'll probably name one of these (unless you say "Motor Vehicles," which is a state agency): Agriculture, Defense (the armed forces, remember?), State, Justice, Treasury, Education . . . there are a lot. As you might guess from those names, each of them is responsible for administering the law in those areas.

So while the executive branch as a whole is responsible for implementing all of the law, that large, common task is divided into smaller parts. This is what we mean by "division of labor," and as Adam Smith tells us in *The Wealth of Nations*, it has at least two benefits. First, it makes the tasks easier. Each department has only a part of the whole, reducing the amount each one has to master, as well as the confusion that would likely result from each part trying to do the whole. That is, clear delineations of authority keep them from stepping on each others' toes, not to mention reducing the confusion for citizens. Imagine if every department regulated taxes—there would likely be several sets of rules, which would certainly conflict in some way. No one would be able to tell what they owed, or what the government owed them. How could they obey a law that simultaneously told them they had to do something, they were forbidden from doing it, and they could do so only under certain conditions?

The second benefit is specialization. As each department works on the same issue over and over, they develop greater expertise. They find better solutions, and they can more quickly assimilate changes, because they already know the relevant context. Think about your own experience with things you do a lot: you learn how to make them a little more productive (like Winslow), you learn how to minimize or replace parts that don't work as well—you find ways to do it better. At least, I hope you do, for your sake. Someone who mindlessly repeats the same actions without some sort of reflection or thought is perilously close to being some*thing* rather than some*one*.

So the division of labor makes the group as a whole more productive, and the resulting specialization makes each part more productive, too. Moreover, this process repeats: within the Department of Agriculture, different agencies are responsible for even smaller parts of agriculture. The Food Safety and Inspection Service checks agricultural products for their safety and quality (thus the "USDA Grade A"[56] you find on meat, eggs, and other produce); the Forest Service manages the forested land the government owns, often in conjunction with the National Park Service (a part of the Department of the Interior); the Agricultural Marketing Service helps farmers sell their produce, and the Animal and Plant Health Inspection Service guards against the outbreak of contagious diseases in farm animals and crops (as the Centers for Disease Control, part of the Department of Health and Human Services, does for diseases among the human population).

As some of the parenthetical comments note, divisions of labor sometimes overlap. This points us to a problem with the second characteristic, so let us table that connection until we've found out what that second characteristic is.

Sorry, I was waiting for the drum roll.

Still no drum roll? All right. The second one is a set of consistent, abstract rules. Let's start at the end and work our way to the front. Rules, of course, are instructions which bureaucrats are required to follow. Since bureaucrats administer laws which affect people, the rules are there to make sure they apply the correct law to the correct circumstances, producing the correct outcome.

What does it mean to say that the rules are abstract? We often confuse "abstract" with "vague," because we often experience one when we encounter the other. "Vague" means "unclear or undefined," while "abstract" means "drawn away from." Obviously, the two are related; as you step back from something, you lose some definition. On the other hand, you gain perspective, which is also part of seeing something clearly. Think of it this way: when you see someone up close, you see the things that define them as an individual. When you

---

56 The USDA is the U.S. Department of Agriculture. Now you can sleep soundly at night.

step back, you see the things that define them as human. The first shows you them as an individual, the second shows you the category, the things that individual has in common with others.

So the abstract rules are meant to function that way, to determine actions and direct outcomes in categories of circumstances. Of course, every set of circumstances is unique, and sometimes determining which category into which a particular set fits can be difficult. This is where abstract rules can seem vague—when circumstances have relevant characteristics from more than one category. The abstract categories may be clearly defined, but reality is much more complex, and it is not always clear to which category those circumstances belong.

That leaves us with the word "consistent." We often use this word to mean "constant" or "never varying." It literally means "to stand still or firm," but we need to think of that in at least two senses. In the immediate sense, it means stable or unchanging. Part of what allows a structure to stand still and firm, however, is when its parts fit together seamlessly. When a building has gaps in its foundation or support structure, it's not likely to remain still. In the same way, the instructions for determining outcomes according to categories must be stable (not changing quickly or substantially) as well as not leaving gaps between categories. Every set of circumstances should find a category. Having cases fall between categories destabilizes the whole structure.

The third element is a career system, which is to say that people are appointed and promoted based on merit. Rather than what service you had performed for party or presidential candidate, you are hired based on your suitability for the position. You have to take an exam to assess that suitability.[57] Your promotion depends on further assessment of your performance. In other words, if you were capable and competent, you could make a career out of it. Your continued employment depends not on the changing political fortunes of candidates, but on your own talents (as in most other careers).

As a result of these, the application of the law should be equitable, expertly, and efficiently done, so that every citizen receives the outcome Congress has prescribed for whatever category in which the citizen finds herself. Of course, reality often disagrees with theory, and it has a way of winning whenever they conflict. In a hierarchy, information is supposed to flow up and commands down the chain of authority. In reality, information and commands are sometimes distorted by passing through so many stops along the way, inhibiting the coordination that the top is supposed to provide. Worse, those responsible for passing information up the chain do not always have the same incentive to pass all information along. They may omit information which reflects poorly on themselves, or which might negatively affect the assessment of their work.

The division of labor requires coordination to reassemble the divided parts into a coherent whole. The different branches of the chain—and it is more of a cat-o'-nine-tails[58] than a single chain—don't generally have means for sharing information horizontally. It has to go up to a common node, then be routed correctly back down the correct channel. The node may not know that the two disparate parts *need* to communicate, let alone which info needs to go where. That aggregation is supposed to happen at the top, but the top cannot always process and redistribute a sufficient volume of information quickly enough. Thus, people often receive conflicting instructions from different parts of the bureaucracy. For example, although several of the 9/11 terrorists where on the FBI's watch list, the FBI[59] didn't know where they were. The INS knew where they were—they mailed some of the terrorists their visas—but didn't know the FBI considered them dangerous (and needed to know where they were).

Reality being so much more complex, the consistent, abstract rules don't always function that way, either. Inevitably, unforeseen cases present themselves, which either fit in no category or fit equally in more than one.[60] Surely you've had the experience of filling in a form and being asked to check a box, only to find that you can't tell which box is the appropriate one to check. Sometimes it's because you know the technically or literally appropriate box (or the closest one you can find) gives a false impression, and sometimes because more

---

57 The Civil Service Exam was introduced as part of the Progressive reforms of the bureaucracy. It was suspended for most domestic positions in 1981, but it was reintroduced in 2015. It continued uninterrupted for the Foreign Service.

58 Dude, know your medieval weaponry.

59 Which stands for Federal Bureau of Investigation, and not Female Body Inspector (no matter what redneck t-shirts may tell you).

60 Remember our connected problem between the first and second elements above?

than one box is appropriate, depending on the exact definition of its label or which part of your circumstances you consider.

So reality is messy, nothing is perfect, why even try? I should point out that we have ideals not because we reach them, but so that we will reach **for** them. We do, however, live in that messy reality, and the reality of it is that these imperfections and shortcomings in the system emphasize why it is important to restrain power, to limit its potential for abuse. So let us now consider some of the ways the other branches are able to monitor the bureaucracy.

First, how does the executive branch check the bureaucracy in its use of the authority delegated to it? Note that this misuse is an example of something we have encountered before (agency loss, though the principle may vary). Note too that regardless of which branch is the principle, they each have the ability to check any abuse, not just that of the power they have delegated. The executive's means are fairly straight-forward: the President can fire them. That, of course, is a stick, and the President does have a carrot, even if it is considerably smaller than the stick. The President can also use his ability to affect the Congressional agenda in their favor, pressing for more budget or more authority for them.

Yeah, you're right; it's not much, especially compared to the firing part. Of course, the bureaucracy answers to the President anyway. He can require reports or briefings from them, and he meets regularly with the heads of the top-level departments. This allows him to monitor the bureaucracy's activities, if not perfectly.

The judicial branch has two technically different options, depending on whether it is the judicial authority or that of the other branches which the bureaucracy has abused. When a bureaucratic agency functions as a court—when the IRS holds a hearing to determine if someone has committed tax fraud or not, for example—the affected citizen can appeal that decision, as if the agency were a federal trial court. It is slightly different when the judiciary checks the abuses of other delegated authority. It does this the same way it checks the abuse of those powers by the principals. Affected individuals can initiate cases in federal district court. Of course, this is (remember Hamilton's argument about the "least dangerous branch"?) still passive; they can act only when someone brings them an actionable case.

This leaves us with Congress. Settle in; this may take a while. And really, it makes sense that it should. The legislative power is the most subtly abused,[61] and Congress is delegating the use of it to members of a different branch. Congress' abilities to check the bureaucracy begin with the facts that Congress writes the statutes which authorize bureaucratic action, and they write the budgets which fund their activities. So even though the bureaucracy technically answers to the President as part of the executive branch, Congress has a fair amount of leverage over it. Congress could write reporting requirements into the agency's authorization, or they could simply ask for reports when they want them. Either way, unless the President explicitly orders the bureaucracy not to comply, they have a strong incentive to do as Congress asks. Technically, they have that incentive regardless of what the President orders or doesn't, but when he doesn't, his stronger incentives (firing) aren't there to override the ones that Congress provides.

Consider the example of *INS v. Chadha*. This case involved a challenge to a legislative veto, provisions Congress includes in some authorization statutes. The legislative veto allows Congress, in whole or in part (depending on the particular statute), to overturn decisions which it has delegated to a member of the bureaucracy.[62] Congress had allowed the Commissioner of the Immigration and Naturalization Service (INS)[63] to waive deportation for some foreigners who, having overstayed their visas, also met some other criteria (gainfully employed, no criminal record, etc.) Mr. Chadha had remained in the United States past the expiration of his student visa, but met the other criteria. The Commissar waived deportation and allowed Mr. Chadha to stay. For reasons unknown, the House of Representatives vetoed that decision, reinstating Mr. Chadha's deportation.

---

61 Or do we have to go back to Chapter 7 and review Federalist 78?

62 Sound like their protecting against agency loss? You bet. In fact, this whole section is about that. Didn't we cover that earlier?

63 Now the Director of Citizenship and Immigration Services (CIS).

Mr. Chadha challenged the constitutionality of this legislative veto, and the Supreme Court (in *INS v. Chadha*—see how that works?) agreed that the practice violated the constitutional principle of the separation of powers. Justice White[64] wrote a dissent lamenting the thousands of legislative vetoes which would now be invalid. As it turns out, he need not have worried. Congress essentially ignored the Court's decision. Remember, the Court has to have someone who has been injured and is willing to sue over it. The people most often injured by a usurpation of executive power like the legislative veto, the ones who would usually suffer an injury and have standing, rely on Congress for their budget. It's rather like suing your boss: you can do it, but you probably want to have plans for your next job lined up. Your boss may not fire you, but they can make you wish they would. Bureaucrats who antagonize Congress end up with smaller budgets and more onerous red tape.

So we see several things: one of the means Congress uses to check the bureaucracy (legislative veto); that while this means officially comes through Congress' power to write authorizations, it works unofficially as well, through Congress' power to write budgets; and that the judicial branch really is limited by its passivity (in terms of cases) and by the support (or lack thereof) of the other branches. All of this from one example—now that's efficiency. By the way, it also shows you how you can use connections between ideas to help you both understand and recall them.

Let's pick back up with red tape, though. This again comes through Congress' statutory power, its ability to write the rules that create and empower the bureaucracy. It is a general term for a whole variety of tools, but what they have in common is that they increase accountability. For example, paperwork requirements—stacks of onerous forms—not only tell bureaucrats what they need to know to resolve your case properly, they also provide evidence of what the bureaucrat does, and the basis on which they made those decisions. This creates a paper trail, which allows oversight at least in retrospect.

Think about how knowing there's a record of your actions changes your incentives. If you knew your professor had access to your social media, would you be more careful in explaining why you're late turning in your paper? Because for someone who just lost a grandmother, you look awfully cheerful in that Instagram post from that frat party. Paperwork, then, is the antique form of social media and surveillance cameras.[65]

Likewise, bureaucratic actions sometimes require multiple levels of approval. If you've ever received a *physical* check (something else which seems more and more antique, though ironically not in a valuable way) from an organization or business of sufficient size, you might have noticed more than one signature on the check. On the *front* of the check, so no, not counting your endorsement on the back.[66]

Now, maybe you've written a check yourself, or at least someone do it in an old movie or a museum or something. How many people does it take to sign a check?[67] For most of us, one is enough. Requiring another person to sign it as well makes it less likely that the funds will be disbursed fraudulently or incorrectly. The other person at least has the chance to notice that you're buying a lot of gym memberships from your cousin George, but never seem to go to the gym. At that point you're either busted, or you've got to expand the scam to buy off a new accomplice. And if it's the latter, then you're closer to being busted, because the more people who are involved, the harder it becomes to keep a secret. If for no other reason, there are now twice as many people with suspiciously lavish lifestyles, and so twice the opportunity for someone to notice.

In other words, that second signature helps discourage agency loss on behalf of whatever group is the principle. The whole group can't sign every check—it would take way too long, and checks would have to be huge.[68] So they delegate to reduce the transaction costs, but require more than one agent to agree, so that

---

64 In college, Justice White was a runner-up for the Heisman Trophy. He was a running back, and the fourth overall selection in the 1938 NFL Draft. In his later years, he was not fond of the nickname he had in college: The Whizzer. This was also the name of a WWII-era superhero (like the Flash), but I imagine it sounded much differently applied to a man of advanced years.

65 Except that paperwork is at least twice the hassle and none of the fun—and pointless to hide in stuffed animals.

66 Though I appreciate the smart-aleck spirit.

67 It depends on how fast he skates and how well he lip reads.

68 How huge are they? Just don't let them body check you.

they monitor each other (to some degree). The same is true of the requirement for multiple authorizations (or signatures on forms) for bureaucracies.

Congress still has a few tricks up its sleeve.[69] Not only does it get bureaucrats to watch each other, it gets us in on the act. Public comment provisions, for example, act as fire alarms. Public comment provisions are part of an agency's authorization which require it to publish proposed regulations before they take effect and receive the public's comments on them. The public may or may not have edifying comments to make—you've seen comments on Facebook or Internet news stories—so the purpose isn't to improve the regulation. Remember, we called this a fire alarm. How do those work? (And no, you don't need to go pull one and find out from personal experience. Not unless there actually is a fire.)

You've seen the little red boxes on the walls, but you've never really thought about them (except maybe when you wanted to get out of an exam or an assignment you weren't prepared for—but don't try that at home; it comes with criminal charges). You see a fire, you pull the lever, and a signal goes out, warning people who are likely to be affected and alerting people (the fire department) whose attention is needed. Think about life without fire alarms. What would the fire department do—drive around looking for smoke? That seems an incredibly inefficient way of doing their job. Aside from the fact that not all fires produce sufficient smoke to be seen from a distance until most of the building is engulfed, how likely is it that they would happen to be near a fire when it breaks out? if they stay in a central location, they can minimize the time it takes to get to any random fire. If they are driving around, they may be at one edge of their district when they see smoke at the other.

Regardless of the happenstance of location, driving around still makes fire suppression more costly and less effective. If we instead keep the fire fighters ready in a central location, and send a signal to let them know when and where they are needed, it will cost them less time and produce better results (since they'll get to the fire sooner and have a better chance to save more of that building or of surrounding ones). Public comment provisions work much the same way. Congress stays in a central location (metaphysically speaking), and if we see a problem in proposed regulations, we send Congress a signal letting it know when and where its attention is needed. Like the Bat Signal, which I guess makes Congress Batman. Or just plain batty.

Citizen suit provisions work in a similar fashion. Also known as "qui tam"[70] suits, a citizen suit is one brought by a citizen on behalf of the government as well as on her own behalf. (If you read the footnote, you probably guessed that already.) That is, the citizen may act as the (United States, in this case) district attorney, filing suit on behalf of the government, and raising the government's interests. That citizen must generally also have standing on her own.[71] This allows citizens to bring problems to the attention of the executive (and then judicial) branches, but the principle is the same as with public comment provisions: distribute the monitoring (and the costs of it) so that those well-placed to observe can alert those capable of acting. Qui tam provisions usually allow a citizen to bring a violation to the attention of the U.S. district attorney. If the district attorney does not initiate proceedings within a specified amount of time, the citizen may then proceed to file a suit on their own behalf as well as that of the government. (Remember, standing usually does not allow you to raise the rights of others—that's what the Congressional statute in the authorization adds.) The most common examples of these (or at least the ones most familiar) involve whistleblowers and pollution.

Of course, none of this is an exhaustive list of the ways the different branches—especially Congress—find to keep an eye on the activities of the bureaucracy. That would be a longer and even more boring book. Speaking of which, numerous scholars have studied the bureaucracy and its relations with the other branches, so if you're really interested (and the medication hasn't taken effect), I'm sure you can find more details in your local college or university library. Why you'd want to is beyond me; perhaps a loss of the will to live, or the

---

69 It lost the other sleeve in the War of 1812. It's not what you think—it was a strip poker game. Unless that's what you were thinking. In which case, seek professional help.

70 Pronounced "key tahm," and short for "qui tam pro domino rege quam pro se ipso in hac parte sequitur." (Gesundheit.) It's Latin, of course, meaning "he who appears in this matter on behalf of the king as for himself."

71 See *Lujan v. Defenders of Wildlife.*

need to be in a coma for a few years for tax reasons. You should, however, now have an idea of how such checks work and the powers on which they rely.

So let's look at some other variation by type. Just as the type of check the branches have depends on the power on which it is based, so the type of agency (in terms of how it integrates into the bureaucratic hierarchy) varies with the purpose which the agency is intended to achieve. These categories are (as were those before them) analytical types. That is, these are categories which we make up and impose on reality because they help us organize (and thus, better remember and apply) our knowledge. These categories do not exist, physically or legally. Congress and the President **do not** create these categories, nor define an agency as belonging to one of these categories, nor by such a definition grant an agency the relevant characteristics. Just so we're clear on what we're doing here.

Let's begin with the garden variety, the cabinet-level department. We met these a few pages back—remember the Department of Agriculture, and the "Department of _____"? These are probably the most common type, certainly the most familiar. These agencies are part of a department whose head is a member of the President's cabinet. Yes, the name is thus somewhat tautological (or circular) in reasoning. These are the parts of the regular hierarchy: member of agency answers to head of agency, head of agency answers to an undersecretary of the department, the undersecretary answers to the secretary, and the secretary to the President. Being a part of the cabinet means that the heads of these meet with the President regularly and often.

Sometimes, however, we have administrative tasks which don't work as well in that framework. Some bureaucratic agencies are independent regulatory agencies.[72] Think of all the controls we just discussed. We mean them to protect us, and often they do. But they are also capable of being used to influence the bureaucracy to do what is politically expedient[73] rather than what is correct (or best for us all). Take the Federal Reserve for example. Congress or the President could use their ability to influence the Fed to print money and inflate the economy just before an election. Everyone feels better off at first, so they vote to retain the people (or, well, politicians, which may not be the same thing) whom they credit for their prosperity. The necessary contraction—the "hangover"—comes after they are safely elected. So instead of regulating the economy to make everyone better off, the Fed could be influenced (whether by threats of firing or budget reduction) to regulate for the benefit of elected officials to whom they answer.

I should tell you that this idea is called the political or electoral business cycle and there is little evidence of it every happening. Part of that is because we took precautionary measures such as the ones we're about to discuss; part of that is because the timing and other details of the political actions are very difficult to get right. The economy doesn't have much in the way of fast-twitch reflexes. Whack it in the knee with some deficit spending or an interest rate increase and something will happen. It's just hard to tell what or when, because "the economy" is the name we give to the aggregation of (in our case) millions of separate, individual decisions. It's more cat- and lemming-herding that any sort of elegant machine with dials for fine and precise adjustments. So even if they have tried it, it might not have created the effect they desired in the timeframe which they targeted.

At any rate, it will serve well enough for out hypothetical. The Federal Reserve ("the Fed" for short) regulates the supply of money in the economy. This exerts a sizeable influence on borrowing and lending, as well as prices. If the Fed were a cabinet-level department, elected officials (Congress and the President) would have the means and the motive to push them to regulate the money supply so that it benefits them. We want, however, for that regulation to occur for the benefit of everyone. We want the health of the economy to guide decisions, not the health of someone's re-election chances. How can we make this happen?

We could, of course, just let them do it without any oversight from political authority at all. But that just shifts the moral hazard from Congress and the President (don't use your influence to corrupt the Fed's judgment in your interest) to the Fed (don't let your own interests corrupt your judgment). Our real question is,

---

72 You are welcome to abbreviate that as "IRA," as long as you don't confuse it with your accounting notes, or take to Great Britain.

73 No, that is not a special travel website for politicians.

"How do we give the bureaucrats the right incentives and not give anyone else the wrong ones?" The answer is, we remove some of the leverage Congress and the President have, and weaken the rest.

How do we do that? In the case of the Federal Reserve, we give them long appointment terms, and make them removable only for cause (committing a crime or demonstrating mental incapacitation). They don't have to worry much about facing re-appointment (and thus needing to be in the President's good graces) or about their continued employment if they ignore the President's "advice." To insulate them from Congress, we give them their own resources, so that they do not need to seek anything from Congress. In the Fed's case, they raise their own money through their activities (fees for their services and interest on financial instruments they hold). This helps align their interest with the public's (the better the economy, the greater their funding) and reduces the ability of the political branches to influence their regulatory decisions.

Other agencies are also described as "independent," but they are independent of something else. Independent regulatory agencies are independent of (or at least insulated from the influence of) the political branches. Independent executive agencies are not independent of control, but independent of the regular bureaucratic hierarchy. That is, they are taken out of the normal chain of command to reduce (or eliminate) . . . wait a minute, you should know enough to put this together. Why would we want to remove an agency from the normal chain of command and make it directly accountable to the President (or Vice-President)?

Not coming to you immediately? It's okay. Take a minute. Still nothing? Well, let's approach it from a different angle. Have you ever played the game "telephone"? For people of a certain age (mine), it was known as "grapevine." A group of people sit in a circle, and one of them whispers a sentence in the ear of the person to her left, who whispers it in the ear of the person next to her, and so on, around the circle. Each person says (and hears) the sentence once. When it gets back to the person who started it, she says what she hears out loud, and then says what the original sentence was. They usually don't match well. If you've ever heard (or worse, been the subject of) a rumor, you know how the story grows and changes each time someone repeats it, until it bears no relation to the truth (if, that is, you weren't the subject and bothered to find out the truth).

So when information is passed from person to person, it can become distorted. In the case of information flowing up (reports) and down (commands) a hierarchy, this creates agency loss. Information is distorted or delayed, and errors result. One way to reduce this is, at least in some cases, is to take out the intermediaries and have direct communication. I qualify this with the limitation to some cases because using it in all cases is impossible, and that very impossibility is what makes bureaucracy necessary. Not every agency can answer directly to the President, or there wouldn't be enough of his attention to go around. When necessary, however, it can reduce agency loss. For example, after the Soviet Union[74] launched the first (artificial) satellite into orbit, President Kennedy[75] took the agency in the Department of Defense which was working on rockets and spaceflight and made it an independent executive agency, answering directly to him. This indicated how seriously he meant his promise to be the first to the moon, and it also increased his ability to see that promise fulfilled.

That leaves us with only government corporations and our special guest. Government corporations are also independent, technically. The government functions as the shareholders, as it were, with a relatively independent board of directors running the company. In the case of the post office—the United States Postal Service, which used to be part of the regular bureaucracy—there are nine governors, with the Postmaster General being the tenth. These are appointed by the President (with the advice and consent of the Senate) to terms of seven years (since 2006; when the post office was reorganized as a government corporation in 1970, the terms were nine years).[76] The British Broadcasting Corporation (or BBC[77]) is another example, as is the Public Broadcasting Service (PBS) in the U.S.

---

74 Crack a book, Judy. Or get thee to a Wikipedia! (Shakespeare joke. Again: open book, insert brain.)

75 Please don't ask which one.

76 Incidentally, when I looked this info up on the USPS website, it mentioned that five of the governorships are currently (as I am writing) vacant—so get your applications in now!

77 Or "the Beebs," at least before certain Canadians forever tainted that shorthand

The British term for this type of bureaucratic arrangement, however is much better than our bland "independent government corporation." They call them quasi-autonomous non-governmental organizations, or "quangos." "Quasi-autonomous" means that they are somewhat or partially independent; "non-governmental" means that they do not perform governmental functions, like applying laws or creating regulations. Instead, like other corporations, they produce a product and compete in the marketplace (or don't, if the government gives them a monopoly, like the USPS' monopoly on first class letters).

Now this raises a question—or really should have by now, if you have brain activity above that of a kumquat.[78] Why does the government, which by definition does *governmental* things, need something to do *non*-governmental things? We already have a lot of organizations and individuals who do non-governmental things, in a whole lot of contexts: the market, the family, society . . . why does the government need to do them, too? It's not the nature of the work. Though there **are** such things as natural monopolies, or goods and services where more than one supplier is destructive or wasteful, they are relatively rare. In fact, if you think of the two examples we've given (carrying messages and broadcasting), there are any number of private entities willing to provide those services. FedEx and UPS (United Parcel Service) deliver things, too, and I'm confident that they would be happy to add first class letters to their services. We certainly do not suffer from a shortage of people willing to broadcast entertainment **or** news, whether television, radio, or streaming video on the internet. So we're not talking about public goods here: companies successfully exclude those who do not pay (or make viewers watch ads, which is payment in time, irritation, and subjection to marketing instead of in cash).

We conclude, therefore, that government doesn't (usually) so much *need* to as *want* to do these non-governmental things. So why do they want to? Think about sending a package by UPS. If you're going to send it to the other side of your state, does it cost the same as if you're sending it to the other side of the continent? Maybe you've never sent a package by UPS, but the answer is "no."[79] It takes more resources (fuel, manpower, etc.) to move something a greater distance, and UPS charges you accordingly. Now, does the cost of mailing a first class letter change depending on whether it's going cross-town or cross-country? Again, maybe you've never done that either,[80] but no, the price does not change.

Here we see part of Congress' purpose: to connect every citizen to every other on the same terms. It costs less to add one more letter to a truck already going to a big city (in fact, it costs almost nothing more than what it was already costing) than it does to take a letter to a tiny, out-of-the way town in the middle of nowhere. (We'll call it Waynesboro.) To get a letter to people living in small, isolated towns—most of the Dakotas, Montana, Idaho, or Alaska, for example—you'd have to pay for the whole trip, because no one is going there anyway. That would be one expensive letter.

Instead, Congress creates a corporation and instructs it to provide that service for the same price. This helps create a connection between each and every part of the United States, allowing people everywhere to communicate with each other, at least by mail. The same is true of PBS. It's not that the market won't or doesn't provide broadcast entertainment. It's just that it won't (or isn't likely to) provide it in the manner which the government desires.[81] So Congress creates a corporation to make sure the good or service is available on the terms Congress wishes.

That leaves only our special guest, and our special guest is . . . state bureaucratic agencies! No, they're not a separate *type* of bureaucracy, but they are separate. Sometimes the federal government asks state bureaucracies to manage federal programs (especially when the federal government doesn't itself have the power[82] to regulate the matter directly). Tocqueville—remember him?—pointed to this administrative decentralization as part of the

---

78 It's a vegetable. I'm hoping you're not.

79 If you're thinking of the "shipping and handling" on things you order, keep two things in mind: first, "and handling" goes to the person shipping it, and the percentage of the total going to that may vary; second, businesses may charge a flat average amount and let the differences average out across orders. Those more likely, it's the amount of handling they get to keep which varies.

80 You young people and your new-fangled social media . . .

81 Which is it to say "full of educational fiber and cultural vitamins!"

82 As enumerated in . . .

institutional arrangements which allowed democracy to survive in the United States. He described them as so many hidden reefs, which absorbed and deflected the centralization of power. They are so independent of the federal bureaucracy that they answer to a different sovereign, but they are often part of the administration of federal programs.

Now we are come to the close. You may have forgotten my promise[83] to discuss the prognosis for a body politic infested with bureaucracy, but I haven't. I left myself a note. Still, we're not quite there. First we need to consider an important question, one I believe to have first been asked by James Q. Wilson. You have probably had interactions with bureaucracy in your life (the Department of Motor Vehicles (DMV) and your local Board of Education or school board are two very strong candidates), and I'm very confident you've had interactions with retail establishments (from the mall to fast food). How would you describe the difference between those two sets of experiences?

Obviously, actual mileage varies, and I have no way[84] of knowing your answer. I have a strong impression, however, that you have had a rather mixed set of experiences in both categories. Some were pleasant, some were unremarkable, some were unpleasant. Yet I also suspect—I mean, sense—that you remember more strongly the pleasant bureaucratic experiences and the unpleasant retail ones, precisely because most bureaucratic experiences peak at "not unpleasant," while retail experiences bottom out there.

This brings us to Prof. Wilson's question: why are those experiences different? Why do the experiences of customers vary between the DMV and McDonald's? Your first answer—if you bothered to think at all (and if so, well done you!)—is that people don't have any choice about going to the DMV, while they can choose another fast food restaurant. That's true, but the DMV does have some competition, at least between its own local outlets (and to some degree, with other forms of transportation which don't require a license). People will go to a different DMV location if the service is better. Likewise, McDonald's sometimes exists in locations where it has little or no competition. You've stopped at some of those interstate exits. Sometimes it is open during hours when its competition isn't. Neither seems to change their service systematically (although things do vary—every store has its bad days).

Nor can the differences be explained by the amount of regulation or the size of their operations manuals. McDonald's has federal regulations to follow as well as its own mammoth and comprehensive procedures binder. Safety? No. First, food-borne illness is at least as great a danger to the public. Second, how many people do you know who've failed to obtain a driver's license? To judge by the level of expertise and concern for safety evidenced by most drivers in the United States, we give driver's licenses away as prizes in cereal boxes.

Nor can we point to the career system, or to education. Both have a career system; McDonald's is quite proud that many people who begin at the counter or the grill progress to manager, regional manager, and even franchise owner. Neither requires a college degree. McDonald's even operates Hamburger University, where it trains its managers. So why is it that McDonald's can get people through the drive through in 90 seconds or less on a regular basis, when that same amount of time doesn't suffice to even take your number and find a seat to wait to be called to the counter at the DMV?

We've been trying to get down to the heart of the matter, and I think it's about incentives.[85] Consider the McDonald's employee first. If she[86] finds a way to get customers through the drive-thru 20 seconds faster, what will happen to her? She may get a raise, maybe a promotion (or on the list of people to consider promoting in the future). Now consider our DMV-automaton. If she thinks of a way to get people through her line faster, what happens? If it works, people switch to her line; if her supervisor makes everyone do it (and I emphasize the "if"), then people start going to the "fast" DMV location. She might get a commendation, but mostly all she'll get is more people in her line. If it doesn't work, she'll have a demerit on her record for not following the proscribed procedure. Unless someone loses life or limb, the McDonald's employee will probably just be told

---

83 Or threat.

84 Aside from my psychic abilities, of course.

85 With apologies to Don Henley.

86 Tiffany.

to quit doing that (and only fired if she persists in the failure). The bottom line: employees in the private sector are encouraged to innovate, while bureaucrats are discouraged from it.

Prof. Wilson had some other useful insights to share on bureaucracy. I mentioned before that red tape—massive amounts of paperwork—is linked to oversight. Not all jobs are like that. For example, a supervisor can observe whether a mechanic is working on a car, and can observe whether those effects are successful (the car runs properly or it doesn't). Most manufacturing is like that, too. You can see if the worker is operating the machinery, turning screws, stirring the batter, or sorting the candy. You can also see their product and proof their work. Prof. Wilson created a rough set of categories for tasks, based on the interaction of two criteria: whether one can observe the work or input (the worker's contribution) and the product (and therefore the quality of the work). So the categories are when both are observable, when one is but the other isn't, and when neither are.

As we said, manufacturing tends to be the first. For some tasks, however, we can observe the product, but not the work that went into it. Art is often this way, for example. You can observe the product (the painting, for example), but you have no idea if he spent hours of actual work planning and creating, working and re-working, or if he simply had a fortuitous series of spills on his table cloth at breakfast. Homework, by the way, falls in this category. A professor can see that there **is** a product, but does not necessarily know how much (if any) work it represents.[87] This presents problems for those charged with evaluating the work. They can evaluate a product, but not how much credit the person submitting it deserves.

Likewise, there are tasks where an evaluator can observe the work you do, but not the product. Think of a salesperson, for example. You can observe how much work the salesman does—knocking on doors, discussing with clients in the showroom, and trying to drum up business. You can see that he is busy. You cannot, however, see what product comes from that effort. You can perhaps count sales or their monetary value, but you have no idea if the salesman's efforts increased or decreased those numbers. Even if they correlate, it may be that the sales would have been greater, if not for the salesperson's off-putting overzealousness. A police officer walks a beat, but it is difficult to observe the intended output: crimes that don't happen.

Many bureaucratic tasks (though not all) fall into the fourth category: neither the work itself nor the product is measurable or observable. Take, for example, Hillary Clinton as Secretary of State. (Or take John Kerry now.) The Secretary of State's job is to conduct our relations with foreign countries. So if you see her at table having lunch with someone, is she a) having lunch with a friend; b) soliciting campaign donations; c) doing her job? the three aren't easily distinguished from each other simply on the basis of observation. Likewise, the quality of the output is difficult to observe. Sometimes stress in a relationship can be strategic and constructive, and sometimes what is popular is not appropriate, so the success of those efforts to conduct relations with foreign countries is difficult to judge, as is what part the Secretary played in producing them.

If you remember from our earlier discussion (of wool socks), the bureaucracy needs clear definitions in order to do its job. It needs criteria which can be assessed objectively, which can be measured empirically. Empirical measurement gives us as close to a truly objective measure as we can get because it references an underlying physical reality which, although we may experience it subjectively, remains constant. Its characteristics depend (at least to some degree) on the object itself, not on the subject observing it. For example, we can probably agree that there is a long, wooden object with a tapered, cylindrical shape in my hand. We may experience it differently—one may find it pleasant, another unwieldy, a third threatening, a fourth confusing, depending on what references we (the subject of the sentence) bring to it (the object of the sentence). If, however, you wish to disagree that it is a solid, real object[88]—no matter whether you wish to call it a bat, a shillelagh, or a poorly designed walking stick—I can bludgeon you with it and allow you to experience its reality directly, and more importantly, to share that experience (that it is real and solid, even if it hurts you more than it hurts me).[89]

---

87 Sure, that thought **never** occurred to you.

88 Or if you let your enthusiasms interfere with our common enterprise (for crying out loud, watch *The Untouchables*).

89 Also the most constructive way to communicate with post-modernists.

This should help us understand the obsession bureaucracies have with "measurables." They need something to demonstrate that they have done their jobs, and that they have done them fairly (so another observer doesn't "just have to take their word for it"). Your teachers (and increasingly, professors) are often in the same trap. It's hard to capture teaching as it occurs; it occurs in lots of ways, in lots of times and places, many of which aren't planned. Even a video of someone speaking to a class doesn't necessarily document that they *taught*, just that they spoke.

Likewise, the connection between that activity and output is hard to observe. The students do well or poorly on the exam. Was it because of or in spite of the teacher? Or were the two things completely unrelated to each other? So measurables become important. Administrators require that teachers file lesson plans, to show at least that they did some planning. Teachers have to engage in "assessment," attempting to document their efforts and results. At some point, the efforts to document become self-fulfilling—I filled out the form, and **that** is my job, rather than the just the physical residue of it.

As bureaucratic administration becomes a greater part of life—as more of our life is governed by administrative or legal authority, rather than our discretion or judgment—we come to focus on measurables as a good in themselves, forgetting to ask whether or to what extent they actually measure what they're supposed to, and why we should care about those things. Because some of the best things in life are not empirically measurable—in fact, most of the things that make life enjoyable or even bearable—we risk reducing ourselves to a solely material existence, not to mention creating particularly perverse (in a rational sense) outcomes.

Reality, of course, usually doesn't come in extremes, or in only one flavor at a time. It usually presents itself as a mixed bag of more or less. We have, however, finally come to our last question: is the administrative mass benign, and is there an alternative. As with most such questions, you should probably answer that yourself. I would merely add some thoughts with which to flavor your stew. Bureaucracy is like alcohol: at times, it is necessary, and in appropriate amounts it can be beneficial. Overindulgence or reliance on it, however, is unhealthy: it kills brain cells, damages livers, destroys personal relationships, and reduces society to materialism. Well, bureaucracy probably doesn't cause liver damage, at least not directly. As with so many things in life, it is not inherently good or bad. That comes from our decisions about how and when to use it, as with any other tool.[90]

I fear that we have ceased to ask those questions. We don't want to be bothered with *being* the government, we just want it to happen. We can, however, change how and when we use bureaucracy, in order to get the best out of it. We can use it at more local and less national levels, where people are more likely to share knowledge that can't be reduced to a measurable. They might, for example, know that although a family appears to qualify for aid, they don't really meet the spirit of the law—or vice versa. Of course greater flexibility of that sort also involves greater discretion for the members of the bureaucracy, discretion which might be subject to abuse. Again, however, reducing the scope to a more local level also allows greater oversight by the public; they know where the official lives.

Relying less on law to structure our interpersonal relationships would also reduce some of the burden placed on bureaucracy. Asking it to do less means reducing less of life to "measurables," but it also means asking more of us in terms of those relationships. We might have to build a positive relationship with our neighbors, so that they will be willing to oblige when we ask them to party a little more quietly. We might have to become more tolerant, more willing to yield our (perceived) right for the sake of our neighbor. We might have to develop discretion and judgment about how and when to ask, and what a fair compromise might be, considering the rights and interests of the other. And most difficult of all, we have to have the courage to speak with our neighbor knowing the conversation might be awkward and require effort, when we could just let the police talk to them for us, or let our lawyer talk to theirs.

Yeah, that sounds better.

---

90 And yes, bureaucracy is a giant tool.

Chapter 9: Voting

Since we're talking about awkward things that require effort, now seems a perfect time to discuss voting. I'm sure that, if you have attended any sort of educational institution in these United States (and maybe even if not, if you're just a big fan of public service announcements), you have been deluged during your obligatory yet perfunctory civics lessons with messages about why you should vote. In fact, you've probably gotten the same message as part of the subtext or as commentary in other classes. The self-righteous acolytes of benevolent government want you to vote and legitimate government's power over you. You can't object to what we have decided, because you voted.

I'm not sure at what age one first becomes aware of put-up jobs and confidence schemes, but I suspect it correlates strongly with the age when one notices that the saccharine[1] truisms and platitudes drip-fed to them in school do not well match the world outside their window. After being told so often and unrelentingly that one **should** vote, one should begin to question why the message is so fervently pressed. The answer, of course, is that (a) progressives **need** the stamp of popular authority to legitimate their decisions, and at the same time, (b) people in the United States generally don't vote.

This is true whether looking at the United States alone or comparing it to other countries. Before you engage in self-flagellation to abate your shame as a citizen, let's consider whether or not this is the moral failure we've been told it is. Maybe we should consider some evidence. First, though, let me put all of my cards on the table. We're going to look at why people do (or don't) vote before we consider whether they should or not. I will in the end make an argument that you **should** vote, but for different (and stranger) reasons than you may yet have heard.[2]

So first, let's look at voter turnout in the United States. The highest turnouts tend very strongly to be in elections where the office of President of the United States is on the ballot. The next highest are also national elections, the midterm elections (even that—*midterm*—is a reference to the presidential office) in which the House of Representatives and one-third of the Senate are on the ballot without the President. Elections featuring only state-wide offices as the highest level on the ballot are next, again higher when the executive (governor) is up for election and lower when only legislative seats are involved. Last, and oddly least, are purely local elections (city or county).

According to the International Institute for Democracy and Electoral Assistance (IDEA),[3] since the Watergate scandal, voter turnout (as a percentage of voting age population, a distinction I will clarify shortly) has been between 47 percent and just over 55 percent. Midterm elections have been between 34 percent and 39 percent. According to the Tennessee Secretary of State,[4] solely state elections (held in August) have turnout of around 30 percent in years when there is a gubernatorial election and around 15 percent when only legislative seats (our

---

1 Wikipedia (currently) says that saccharin "is an artificial sweetener . . . 300–400 times as sweet as table sugar, but has a bitter or metallic aftertaste, especially at high concentrations."

2 Have you come to expect anything else?

3 www.idea.int.

4 Hey, I'll look up my state, you look up yours. Besides, all politics is local. But you can find this data at sos.tn.gov; the page you're looking for is "Election Statistics by Year."

legislature is called the General Assembly) are in play. According to the Davidson County Election Commission,[5] turnout in solely local elections is more volatile, running from single digits to around 30 percent. To give you an idea, a December 2002 runoff election for the Metro Council had a turnout of 3 percent. Just a month before, in November 2002, the turnout for the general election was 50 percent in the county. Of course, that election had state and federal offices on the ballot, so it does not reflect interest in local elections alone.

I should also note that the statistics from the State of Tennessee and Metropolitan Nashville are not given as a percentage of the voting age population, but as a percentage of registered voters. They are thus somewhat higher than they would be otherwise.[6] So let me now explain the difference. Or rather, let us think of our way through it. What's the difference between the population of people old enough to vote and the population registered to vote? Well, in some cities[7] people not old enough (or not alive enough)[8] may be registered to vote. The more common relationship, however, is that there are people old enough to vote who aren't registered. Now why would that happen?

In order to vote, you have to register. Some people simply aren't interested in voting at all, ever, and so have no interest in registering (and therefore don't). Those who wish to register, however, have to fill out a form and show proof of their identity and residence. They may have to take off work to go down to the county courthouse and do this. With a life full of other pressing demands (working to pay a mortgage and feed and clothe themselves and their family), that errand often falls to the bottom of the list, if not off it entirely. Some people of age are also disqualified from voting because of a criminal conviction; some states do not allow those convicted of serious offenses to vote, though whether and for how long vary by state.[9] Some people don't register because names for jury duty have been and may still be chosen from the list of registered voters, and they hope to avoid jury duty.

So if we want to study what factors effect an individual's decision to vote or not, we don't want to start out by eliminating a factor which we know has an influence: how easy it is to register. If we want to know how many did vote as a percentage of those who might have, we have to make sure not to ignore some who might have. Because registration is costly, fewer people do it. This means that turnout as a percentage of registered voters will look better (or at least higher) than it actually is, because the denominator is already reduced.

When I say, then, that most people in the United States don't vote most of the time, or that people generally don't vote, you can hopefully see that this is empirically true. You may be wondering why people don't vote, but I think the better question may be why people **do** vote. Since the bulk of voting opportunities pass untaken and unmourned (if not entirely unnoticed), what explains the ones which *do* get taken? As it turns out, not voting is relatively easy to explain; voting is the miracle which requires explanation.

Bear with me for a moment. Let's examine some of the reasons to vote which you've surely heard over the years (or months, depending on how long you've been paying attention). My personal favorite is the "Vote or Die" campaign to which Piffle or Puffle or Piddle or Puddle or whatever he calls himself now subjected us in 2004. Several music stars (according to Wikipedia) joined together for the 2004 election to form Citizen Change, a "political service group," which aimed to increase voter turnout. Of course, when P. Diddy, Mary J. Blige, Mariah Carey, and 50 Cent tell you to "Vote or Die," it can be something of a mixed message. Is that a threat? I mean, Carey sometimes seems unbalanced enough to make you wonder.

At the very least, however, it is a logical fallacy: a false dichotomy. Spoiler alert: you die in the end. While I certainly hope that end is far away, physical death is one of the very few certainties in this universe. Years of unwitting experiments have shown that voting in no way hinders or alters that outcome. Those are not the

---

5   Nashville and Davidson County have a metropolitan government; *metropolitan* means the city and county governments are a single, combined entity. The website for historical election returns is www.nashville.gov/Election-Commission/About/Historical-Information/Election-Returns.aspx

6   That's right—and one of them was 3 percent.

7   (Cough) Chicago (cough) Cleveland (cough) Memphis (cough) . . . do you have a lozenge? I seem to have an oddly municipal cough.

8   Hey, they're just trying to be inclusive of the metabolically challenged.

9   Remember, states make most of the rules about voting. The federal government certainly provides some general stipulations and restrictions, but states write them.

two alternatives on the table (thus, a false dichotomy). Choosing not to vote does not cause the Grim Reaper to get a text alert with your location.[10]

Granted, that's a pretty silly one, but it's so ludicrous[11] I just can't resist making fun of it. The fact that it existed for one election (when George W. Bush was running for re-election) and has been dormant since tells us I probably was not the only one laughing. That, or it tells us something about the attention span of Hollywood and the press, or perhaps something about the partisan motivation behind its non-partisan façade. Or more likely, a little bit of all three, and a few more besides. So let's look at a more common set of tropes. (Don't stop me if you've heard these before, or we may never get done.) You must vote in order to make your voice heard. You must vote in order to change what's going on, to decide the future of our country, or your future. You must vote or you lose your right to complain about government.

There are about three themes bound up in that list, so let's start with the funniest: you have to make your voice heard. Friends and neighbors, there are a lot of good and necessary things voting accomplishes—I told you, I'm going to explain why you **should** vote[12]—but making any sort of "voice" heard is patently not among them. Start with this: what voice? Do people know how you voted? Only if you tell them, and studies show that you don't actually have to vote to tell people you did. You may not even tell them accurately *how* you voted, had you done so. The point is that the act of voting is **secret**. If that is a voice, it's one you hear in your head. Your voice is much more heard on Twitter, Facebook, or (gasp!) in actual conversations with other people.

Even if we *did* know how you voted, it (remember, the act itself, not your discussion) would be a very muddled mumble. In the last election, I voted for Gary Johnson. Do I agree with every policy he advocates? Hardly. Do you know which ones I support—you know, the message my "voice" is supposed to be enunciating? In any election, do we know why someone votes for a candidate? Candidates are a bundle of policies (and neuroses),[13] and you don't get to edit them or choose which of the policies you're supporting and which not. Are you voting for that candidate's position on abortion, or in spite of it, because you value another position more? Or are you really saying not that you prefer that candidate or her policies, but that you dislike her less?

So voting "to make your voice heard" is irrational, to put it mildly. It is not audible, and it carries no coherent or identifiable message. If your goals were to communicate your ideals or political positions, there are just two words: epic fail. Just promise me you'll break it gently to your English or Sociology professor.

Let's move to the next least substantive: gaining the right to criticize. In our particular circumstances, that's nonsense, too. The First Amendment guarantees the right to peaceably assemble and petition the government for a redress of grievances. It doesn't condition that right on anything: not on sobriety, sanity, or previous condition of voting. We want, however, to consider voting in general, in the abstract, not just in the United States. Besides, this "you can't complain because you didn't participate" argument is meant more to shut people up and end debates (with the moral superiority of the voter unassailably triumphant). Again, there is a moral argument for voting, but shutting people up and feeling smugly superior when you can't otherwise answer their substantive arguments isn't it.

So let's address it on its own terms. Morally, it is only when you vote that you give up your right to complain. If we agree to decide something by voting, only a sore loser complains when the outcome isn't what they want. When we vote, we act together, and we have all of us thereby authorized the outcome. We can't then take back our authorization and declare the outcome invalid or wrong because it wasn't the one we wanted. Establishing which was the valid or right outcome was the purpose of voting. We're breaking our word if we don't peacefully go along with the outcome as we promised (and would expect the others to do had we won).

If we never agree to participate, we never agree to be bound by the collective outcome. Only then do we have the moral right to object to the outcome, to complain that it is unfair, invalid, or wrong. We never agreed to be part of the decision, never agreed to be bound by what the group decided, to take that outcome as our own. We did not author the decision, and it therefore does not constrain us. Logically, if we wish to preserve

---

10   Besides, we all know he's still got a landline.

11   But not Ludikriss—I have no idea if he was involved.

12   You're not there yet.

13   See the 2016 Presidential Election, for example.

the ability to complain, we can only do so by making clear that we are not part of the decision, by purposefully not voting.

Think about what we're saying otherwise. I'm a libertarian.[14] My preferred candidate never wins. My vote doesn't change that. So am I supposed to vote, so that I can be told to shut up, because I agreed to this contest that I never had a hope of winning? Or because I refuse to give my consent to something I know I won't agree with, I have to shut up, because I had my "chance" to win, even though that chance was like a subatomic particle, so small and so fleeting in its existence that we usually aren't even aware of it? We're going to have to start building bigger closets to keep people in.

So one is unintentionally funny, and the other is self-serving and insulting. How much better can the third cliché be? I know, I can't wait to find out, either! This is the one about influencing the outcome of the election, and believe it or not, it has more substance to it than the others, though still not nearly enough. Sort of like a lottery ticket that has a little promise of money, but not nearly enough to be your retirement plan.

In fact, let's start with lotteries, which economists and other people who can do simple math refer to as "taxes on stupidity." If you're reading this, there's a good chance you haven't won the Powerball jackpot.[15] Then again, if you're breathing—heck, even if you're not—there's a really good chance you haven't, because the chances of winning are really, really small. Granted, if you do win, you get a couple hundred million dollars, give or take.[16] A winning ticket is worth a lot, just shy of whatever the net amount you take home is. A non-winning ticket is worth . . . well, the paper it's printed on. Before you know whether it's a winning ticket (and unless you're cheating, that should be before you buy it), how do you know if it's worth buying?[17]

$$E(u) = p(b) - c$$

p: probability of desired outcome
b: value of desired outcome
c: cost of engaging in activity

Figure 9.1 Expected Utility of Voting

The aforementioned economists (et alia) have a handy formula for figuring out the value of something under conditions of risk, chance, or probability. It should be somewhere around here, labeled "Figure 9.1" or some such. Found it? Good. It reads like this: the expected utility of an action is the benefit it may produce, weighted by the probability with which it produces that benefit, minus the cost of engaging in the action. Let's see how that works with the lottery. The last time I checked,[18] a Powerball ticket costs two dollars. The jackpot (the last time I checked) was $222 million.

We should note that this figure ($222 million) represents the nominal value of the jackpot paid as an annuity. Because future money is worth less than present money, the jackpot you would take home (before taxes) would be $151 million, if you chose to take it all up front (and since future money is worth less than present money, you should). That gives us two dollars as the cost of buying a ticket[19] and $151 million as the benefit. Why isn't everyone buying a lottery ticket?

Right: we don't get the $151 million, we just get a chance at getting it. How likely is the ticket we buy to be the jackpot winner?[20] The last time I checked, Powerball gave the odds of a jackpot-winning ticket at 1: 292,201,338 (or slightly better than one in three hundred million). If you divide one by 292,201,338, you get a decimal with eight leading zeros: .000000003422298, at least to the places the calculator on my iPod can handle. If we weight (multiply) our benefit by that probability, the result is 0.5168 dollars—so let's just say

---

14   NOT a librarian. Not that there's anything wrong with that. Also—duh. What book were you reading?

15   If you have, have you considered how good it would make you feel to endow a chair in political science for an under-appreciated associate professor?

16   And the state **will** take.

17   Assuming, of course, that the paper isn't more valuable than the purchase price, but that's a pretty safe assumption. That, or the lottery will be bankrupt quickly.

18   June 28, 2016.

19   It's a little more complicated (and higher) than that, but we can ignore that for now. I'll explain when it becomes relevant.

20   Yes, there are other prizes, but including them makes things a lot more complicated and makes the result not at all different.

fifty-two cents. The jackpot is worth $151 million, but the very small chance at winning the jackpot is only worth fifty-two cents, or slightly more than Curtis Jackson. That's why economists call state-run lotteries taxes on stupidity. No one stops to do the math, and people exchange two dollars for fifty-two cents.

Maybe the probability weighting is throwing you for a loop. I don't want you to think I'm stacking the deck here, so let's go over it another way. I say the lottery ticket is worth fifty-two cents. In the end, the ticket has only two possible values (nothing and $151 million), neither of which is fifty-two cents. The problem is that you don't know which one it is when you buy it. Since almost every single one of them is worth zero, that's probably what yours is worth. That's what the fifty-two cent value is telling you. Or maybe another way to think about it will help. Imagine there are 292,201,338 tickets sold. One is worth $151 million, the rest are worth nothing. On average, each ticket is worth fifty-two cents, but no ticket *is* average.

In case you're wondering, not much changes if we use the nominal value, other than that we pretend future money is more valuable than it is. Even using $222 million as the jackpot, the value of the chance at winning is slightly more than seventy-six cents. Of course, with a higher jackpot, more people buy tickets, and your chance of having the whole jackpot to yourself goes down.

Back to voting. We need to know what the benefit of voting is, what the probability of getting that benefit is, and how much it costs to vote. How much it costs seems like it would be the easiest answer. It costs nothing to vote, at least not the same way as it costs two dollars to purchase a lottery ticket. We left a few things out of that calculation, though. I should have written "the cost of a ticket" rather than "the cost of buying a ticket," because the cost to buy one includes the cost of a ticket, plus more. If you remember our discussion of registering, you may start to see it. It takes time and effort and other resources to vote. We didn't think about the time and gasoline spent going to the convenience store to buy the lottery ticket. That time and gasoline could have been used for something else, so that too is a cost.[21] We no longer have these resources, because we have spent them. In the case of lottery tickets, most people are usually passing by where they purchase them, or add them to another trip they are making anyway, so the amount of this cost (called an opportunity cost; see the most recent footnote) which the tickets add is probably low and safely ignored. In the case of voting, however, most people are not already going to the polling place anyway, and must make a special trip. Remember, too, that the same is true of registering to vote.

Let's say it takes an hour of time and a gallon of gas between the two trips (registering and voting). Federal minimum wage is currently $7.25 per hour, and Google at the time of this writing gives the estimate of the average price of a gallon of gas as $2.33. I'm going to round that down to $2.25, just to make the math a little easier. In time and gas, then, we have to spend $9.50 to vote, all else being equal. It could be less; we might not have much else to do with our time, and we might ride a bike to the polling station (and courthouse). It could be more; election day could be the day you are giving birth (or being born, but then you're not eligible), or have a family medical emergency, and you could drive a car that measures fuel efficiency in gallons to the mile, or live far away from the polling station (or courthouse).[22]

Now, what's the benefit to you of casting the deciding vote in an election? I'm sure it depends on the election. Most people would probably pay more to decide who the President will be than they would pay to decide who their mayor or city council member will be, but then, people also buy lottery tickets. What I mean by that snide comment is that your mayor and council (or equivalent) have much greater influence on your life than the President could ever dream (or fear). Local property taxes, zoning, codes and ordinances, roads, education, trash, water—most of what affects you most closely is close to home. That should make it more valuable to you. But we'll stick with the President.

You may have a hard time figuring out how much you'd really be willing to pay. First, you know you really can't, so it's easy to plop in any astronomical number in order to outbid everyone else. (Maybe that's the way to pitch it: how much would you pay to keep someone else—remembering that "someone else" includes Hillary

---

21 We talked about this before—remember how we can't spend the same fifteen dollars twice? It's called an opportunity cost, the value of a use of a resource which you forego in order to use it as you do.

22 I keep referring to the courthouse as well on the assumption that you must go there to register.

Clinton, Donald Trump, Paris Hilton, and that creepy drunk guy down at the end of the bar—from being able to decide?) You don't have to worry about the other uses of that money which you're foregoing, because you never have it in the first place. On the other hand, it's also hard to figure out what something like that might actually be worth. You can probably get a pretty good idea of how much you'd enjoy a car, a trip, or a video game. You can usually try at least two of those before you buy, and you can certainly get a decent estimate based on previous, similar experiences. It might turn out to be a little more or less than you thought, but at least know what ballpark you're in. With deciding elections, we're all a little out of our depth.

Maybe we can get an idea by looking at how much of their personal money candidates are willing to spend on their campaigns. According to their June 2016 Federal Election Commission filings, Hillary Clinton has donated almost $900,000 to her campaign, and Donald Trump has donated a little more than $395,000.[23] Of course, he also loaned his campaign more than $45 million, but Hillary hasn't loaned hers any. Not that she wouldn't; she loaned her 2008 campaign (when she lost the nomination to Barak Obama) a little over $13 million. We don't know if Trump's campaign will be able to repay him; Hillary's doesn't seem to have repaid her. So we can say she was willing to spend $13 million to be nominated, and he is willing to lose $45 million to be elected.

What you should be thinking at this point is, "There have got to be better ways to spend $58 million." And you are right. But if you held that decision in your hand, we've got pretty good evidence that you candidates will pay (even if they have to borrow to do it) at least $10 million for it. Just to be careful, we'll take that lower number ($10 million) as our market value for ability to decide the election.

That just leaves the odds, the probability by which we must weight that benefit. The first thing we need to know is how many votes decide the outcome in an election. How many do you think? Nice try. It depends on the electoral system. In the plurality, or first-past-the-post system, the rule is that the candidate with the most votes wins. Now, you may be thinking that a lot of votes may go in to having more than the next candidate. Those votes may influence the *totals*, but how many are necessary to create the *difference*? It's the difference, not the totals, which matter. It's like the idea of the winning run in baseball or the winning goal in football (soccer) or hockey. There's one run or goal that puts you ahead of the other team to stay. Now, which one that is can change during the game; you don't know until the end which one (or which chance at one) it was. Nevertheless, at the end, though many might have done, only one decided the outcome. If we knew which it was at the beginning, we could have skipped the rest of the game, just as if we knew which vote would be decisive others wouldn't have to bother, and if we knew which lottery ticket had the winning numbers, we could skip all of the other tickets we buy trying to find it.

Hopefully, you are currently giving me the stink eye, wondering why I'm talking about plurality electoral rules, when we're talking about Presidential elections, which we have known since Chapter 6 don't work that way. Thank you for your skepticism, your attention, and your stink eye. You are right. Presidential elections are decided by majority vote in the Electoral College, and most of us will never hold that ballot in our sweaty, common paws. Plurality is a majoritarian electoral rule, however, and the same is true of all majoritarian rules: one vote decides the outcome, whether it is the one which gives a candidate more than any other, or more than half. Even with the interference of an additional level, the vote in the state whose electoral votes prove decisive of the majority is the winning vote, and only that one vote. Since it doesn't change anything, and the statement is easier to understand without all of the additional clutter around it, it seemed best to approach it as a simple plurality vote.

So it's one vote, but out of how many? As I write, the most recent (2014) estimate of the voting age population from the U.S. Census Bureau is 239,874,000. First, the three trailing zeros should set off alarm bells telling you that it is probably an estimate, since life rarely produces numbers so well-rounded. Of course, the good, decent statisticians at the Census Bureau are honest about that and call it such, but you can still learn to be wary of others who are less scrupulous. Second, we should keep in mind that some of those may not be deterred from registering by the difficulty, but by legal disqualification, which we may or may not be willing to remove. Third, we want to make the math easier. So let's take a nicely rounded estimate of 220 million people who *could* register, and therefore could

---

23   So like most things he says, Trump's claims to be self-financing his campaign were exaggerated, to say the least.

vote. Your vote is then one of 220 million possible deciding votes, so there's a 1 in 220 million chance that it will decide the outcome. Our probability is then 0.000000004545, which is slightly better than Powerball.

When we use that to weight our benefit ($10 million), we get 4.545 cents. Let's again be generous, erring on the side of caution, and round up to call it a nickel. Now what was that cost again? I know I left it around here somewhere . . . we went with $9.50, didn't we? Ouch. If we're voting to change the outcome of an election, we're paying about $9.50 for something worth about a nickel. If two dollars for fifty cents was a tax on stupidity, what the Habakkuk is trading $9.50 for a nickel? An admission of imbecility? That might explain a lot out our elections, come to think of it.

However, I think we should perhaps take a step back and remind ourselves why we're looking at this. What we can say is that if you're voting to change the outcome of an election, that's not a particularly rational decision. We can add to that the fact that the local level, which is where our odds of determining an outcome are highest and the potential impact on our lives the greatest, is the one where we vote the least. If we were voting to make a difference, we would be voting most there. So either that's not the reason why we're voting, or we're colossally deluded.

Honestly, I'm not sure we can rule out the latter. In fact, life tells us that most social phenomena have more than one cause, but let's stick with the idea that we have a different reason. What other reason do we have? What do you mean, that was the last one on the list? Whoops. Can you think of any other we might be overlooking? There's a whole category we're missing, and maybe you've been screaming some of them for the last several pages. Again, you've got to watch that screaming at inanimate objects, especially in public. The only thing it will get you is heavy sedation.

Maybe you thought of them, but don't want to admit to it because they sounded too touchy-feely. "People fought and died so I could do this, and I want to honor them," or "It's my civic duty," or "Because I'm proud to live freely in a democracy," or even "Diddy will kill me if I don't." Wait, no, not that last one. We've already ridiculed that one back to the public relations hell which spawned it.

You probably thought that would happen with these touchy-feely ideas, too. I'm happy to disappoint you. Just because something has to do with emotions or feelings doesn't mean it is invalid, false, or untrustworthy. Of course, when other people use emotional appeals, they're usually trying to manipulate you. So there's a good reason to be cautious, but the fact that emotions can be awkward and thus, like most awkward things, that people find them easier to deal with through ridicule is not that reason.

I call this category the "warm fuzzies." That is, for some people, the very act of voting produces a warm, pleasant sensation somewhere in the vicinity of their heart.[24] For some reason, they feel better about themselves when they vote, whether because they have honored the memory of loved ones and heroes, or they feel as if they are a part of something larger than themselves, or maybe lived up to at least part of their end of the democratic bargain. For me, I appreciate the reminder that I am part of something that creates bonds not just across to the friends and neighbors I see at the polls, but forward to my children and grandchildren, and back to my parents and grandparents. (I think they call that a "community.") For a few moments, the world is a friendlier, more welcoming place. Granted, it's the warm fuzzies, not the screaming hot plushes. It's a warm glow which fills a moment, no more. Importantly, though, it is also no less.

Let's see how that changes our calculus. It still takes $9.50 of resources to vote; physics and economics haven't changed, and resources are still both necessary to do things and scarce. If, however, I vote because voting gives me the warm fuzzies, what are the chances I'll get that benefit if I vote? Don't overthink this one. It's a certainty; the odds are one out of one. Of course, the benefits are lower. No one pays $10 million for the warm fuzzies; for the screaming hot plushes, maybe, but not the warm fuzzies. What would you pay for something that gives you the warm fuzzies? Maybe we could use comfort food as a proxy. It's the same idea. You feel alone and homesick, so you eat a meal that reminds you of home. It's not the meal itself you value, so much as the warm glow that makes you feel better.

---

24 For a beautiful song, find "Somewhere in the Vicinity of the Heart" by Shenandoah and Alison Krauss on iTunes (or wherever you're getting your music these days). If you're watching the video on YouTube, the guitarist is NOT Jeff Foxworthy. The drummer, however—full disclosure—is my wife's second cousin, once removed.

There's still a lot of variation there, though. Would you pay five dollars for that? You'd pay at least that for your favorite pizza, right? Or a hot dog and a Coke that remind you of your family grilling out on summer days at the lake?[25] Or a bowl of chicken soup just like the one your grandma made you when you were sick? Five dollars is probably a conservative estimate for the pizza at least, but maybe for the others as well, by the time we add the warm fuzzies to them.

Plug all of those values in, and E(u) = 1(5)–9.50, which equals –$4.50. That's still a negative number, but we're a lot closer than we were before (–$9.45). Some people might pay ten or twenty dollars for their favorite food from home, so those people whose fuzzies are warmer or fuzzier will vote. That's not everyone, though, so let's keep the value at five dollars for now.

Changing the purpose changed the probability, and that former probability was the weight which dragged the sum down so significantly. Changing the purpose also changed the benefit, making it significantly less (just as the odds were significantly greater). The resulting sum, however, was much larger. Do you suppose there are other things we could change, or other ways to change these things?

Start with the cost. In 1993, Congress passed the National Voter Registration Act, which is better known as "motor voter." Among other things—and most Congressional acts are chock full of other things among which to be—it required states to allow people the opportunity to register to vote when they were getting or renewing their driver's licenses. Remember the cost of our lottery tickets, and how it made a difference in the opportunity cost if we weren't making a special trip just to buy the ticket, but were buying in the course of completing other errands? It meant that the additional resources being used to purchase the ticket were not much greater than the ones they were already incurring. This additional cost is known as marginal cost, and the motor voter act reduced it for registering to vote. You are already at a government office, so it only takes the additional time to complete the voter registration form, omitting the further additional time and effort to go to the Election Commission separately. This makes it easier (less costly) to register, and thus more likely that people will.

States have taken other actions to reduce the cost of voting, sometimes with the (more or less) gentle prompting of Congress. Absentee ballots are usually available for voters who will be unable to reach their polling station on election days. A more recent tactic is early voting, which allows voters to cast their vote (usually at one central location) in the days before an election, often including Saturdays. This allows voters to choose a more convenient (less costly in time and effort) time to vote. Although there are still some logistical problems to overcome, online voting would also reduce these costs for many voters. As the cost becomes lower, it becomes more likely that the warm fuzzies are warm enough and fuzzy enough for the benefit to outweigh it. Some states even try to enhance the warmth and fuzziness, by giving "I Voted" stickers, for example.

Of course, in all of this, we have taken the voting rule as a given. That was what determined our odds; one vote produced a plurality or majority, and thus determined the one seat. If we alter the voting rule, can we change these odds, and allow more of the benefit to survive weighting? Not if we stay with the warm fuzzies as our purpose; odds don't get better than certainty. So can we make voting to influence the outcome more rational? IDEA reports that turnout (as a percentage of voting age population) in the Federal Republic of Germany, in the same timeframe for which we looked at turnout for the United States, has been between 65 percent and 84 percent, and most often between 70 percent and 75 percent.

Like the United States, Germany is also a federal republic.[26] I mentioned Watergate as a break point for the United States, and Germany also had a political scandal that affected trust in government at about the same time. On April 24, 1974, federal authorities in Germany arrested a close, personal aide of their chancellor at the time, Willy Brandt. That aide, Günter Guillaume, had been sent with his wife in 1956 from the German Democratic Republic to infiltrate the West German government. His arrest led Chancellor

---

25 Yes, advertisers have long known the power of the warm fuzzies.

26 So its official name is accurate, unlike that of the German Democratic Republic (the former East Germany), which was neither a republic nor a democracy. It was definitely, however, German—it had the highest productivity and some of the best products of the former Communist bloc.

Brandt to resign from that post a couple of weeks later, citing his own negligence in not knowing his aide was a traitor and spy.[27]

Unlike the United States, however, the Federal Republic of Germany is a parliamentary (fusion-of-powers) system rather than a presidential (separation-of-powers) system. As you may (*cough* should) remember from Chapter 2, that means the legislature (the parliament, or more specifically, the *Bundestag*[28]) elects the executive, which is then theoretically dependent on the legislative branch.[29] In practice, this often means the legislature becomes dependent on the executive, because the executive controls the agenda (and especially decisions about when to call elections, if the parliament does not have a fixed term).

More relevant to our current concerns, however, is the fact that this means German legislative elections are also executive elections, since the composition of the legislature will determine who the executive is. (Hint: it's usually the leader of the party with the most seats.) Since we saw a relevant pattern in U.S. turnout (that executive elections tend to have higher turnout), we should keep this in mind as one potential cause.

Germany also has a different electoral rule. Germans actually cast two votes, the first for a candidate in their district, and the second for a party (and not necessarily the same one as that of the candidate). The first vote is used to determine, by plurality, which candidate will represent that district. These directly elected seats are half of those in the Bundestag. When the winners of each constituency are known, the percentage of seats each party has is compared to the percentage of the second votes the party received. The remaining seats are then distributed[30] so as to make the proportion of seats each party holds as equal as possible to their proportion of the second votes. If a party has a greater percentage of seats from the first votes than from the second, it keeps them, and parties must get at least 5 percent of the second votes[31] to receive any of the additional seats. Seats from the second vote are filled from a list the party publishes before the election, starting with the first name on the list.

The second vote system, by itself, is a proportional electoral rule, as opposed to a majoritarian one. Proportional rules tend to produce more representative results, because they tend to make more parties competitive. Under a majoritarian rule, there is one seat, and only one winner.[32] Proportional systems have multiple seats in a district, so there is a prize for finishing second or third.[33] On the other hand, it also decreases the connection between the voter and the representative. Your vote goes to a party; the representative owes her seat to the party placing her on the list, not to your vote. In a purely proportional system, there really is no one designated as *your* representative in government.

The German electoral system is a hybrid of the two, capturing both the stronger connection (or representation) which the single-seat district determined by plurality offers and the greater representativeness of the electorate as a whole which the proportional system offers. Now, back to dancing with the one what brought us. Does this different rule change the calculation of the utility of voting? For people who vote because it gives them the warm fuzzies, it may increase the warmth or fuzziness a little. Even if it is the act of voting itself which you value, the more effective and less quixotic it is, the better you'll feel about it. I realize we haven't yet established that it is more effective, but you'll see it better if we look at it with the other purpose, affecting the outcome.

---

27 The Soviet Union was apparently miffed with its East German allies for causing this resignation, as they considered Brandt someone who would deal with them fairly.

28 Federal Assembly.

29 If you don't realize by now that we're talking about Germany and not the United States, which clue did you miss? The context? The fact that the name of the parliament is *der Bundestag*? All of Chapters 5 and 6?

30 These calculations are actually done at the regional (*Land*, or what we call state) level, and they are actually allocated according to quotas which are sensitive to the changing number of seats as each one is allocated. It's easier to think of comparing percentages at the national level, and the effect is mostly the same, but if you want to know more about it, take a class in comparative politics or, if the one near you doesn't discuss electoral systems, a class on electoral rules.

31 Or win at least three districts directly.

32 Yes, Highlander, there can be only one.

33 Before you think that having more than one seat in a district is un-American, remember that each state (a Senatorial district) has two seats in the Senate. We just elect them in separate elections, one seat at a time.

The real change comes if we look at people who vote for that reason. Although the prize may be lower, since control of the district's seats is split, you are much likelier to get some prize. Note that although we removed it to simplify the math, lotteries do this too. Except here there is no jackpot, only lots of smaller prizes. Let's focus on those odds for a second. We said that only one vote determines a plurality or majority election. How many determine a proportional one? Well, to some degree, each vote cast alters the proportion of votes; the question is whether it alters it enough to cause the allocation of another seat.

If we elected all 435 members of the House of Representatives proportionally, from a single, nationwide district, your vote would have 435 chances to be the one which moved your party from "not enough for a seat" to "enough for a seat." Dividing 435 by 220 million gives us 0.00000198, which is still not a high probability. It is, however, significantly higher than the other; it has three fewer leading zeros. That means our odds have improved by three orders of magnitude, which is a pretty strong improvement. Depending on how much smaller we see the benefit being (and since there's a chance to be the seat that creates a large enough share to pick the executive, that gets complicated quickly), but it seems likely the weighted benefit will be closer to exceeding the costs.

Rather than simply reduce the costs of voting, some countries also try to increase the costs of not voting. They have what is known as compulsory voting. This compulsion can take many forms. It usually is not physically escorting people to the polls, at least not in an actual democracy; that would be far too costly. Instead, the punishment can range from a small fine to loss of government benefits (such as income support like what we call welfare or unemployment benefits). Indeed, there may be a sliding scale from fines to loss of public aid to imprisonment (though again, that last one is usually beyond the pale in a democracy).

This all sounds so very frightening, so let's look at the example of Australia. Yes, Australia has compulsory voting. According to the Australian Electoral Commission,[34] if you do not vote in a federal election, you will receive a notice in the mail asking you to either provide a valid reason[35] or pay a twenty-dollar fine (in Australian dollars, of course). If you fail to respond, you will be required to pay up to $180 (again, Australian) plus court costs. As an added bonus, you'll have a criminal conviction on your record.[36]

If we assume that one Australian dollar is worth one U.S. dollar,[37] then you can see how this changes our calculus. Because we don't have to pay twenty dollars if we vote, we add twenty dollars to the expected benefit. This already outweighs our estimate of the cost, rough as it surely is. In fact, it's a little more than twice that estimate; I gain $10.50 plus any direct benefits of the act itself when I vote.[38] If every two-dollar lottery ticket were also a five-dollar voucher for something else you want or need, you'd be stupid not to buy them, wouldn't you? If they were vouchers for textbooks, for example, you could buy lottery tickets and get your textbooks for 40 percent of what they otherwise cost. That's a 60 percent discount, regardless of what happens with the jackpot, and its odds are again certainty (one out of one).

Compulsory voting addresses a different part of that voting calculus. We looked at the individual calculation, but remember our prisoner's dilemma. There is a public as well as a private good produced in voting. Voting keeps politicians accountable so long as someone does it. Our party's candidate, presumably our preferred candidate, wins so long as enough of us vote (and our party represents a plurality). As long as enough people vote, we get these benefits, whether we contribute to producing them or not. When we do the individual calculation of our private costs and benefits, we do not consider these public goods (with our party being the public in the second case), because we get them (or don't) anyway.

As a result, we each have an incentive to let everyone else vote while we don't. Except, of course, that we discover maybe not enough of us are willing to be suckered, and not enough people are contributing to production,

---

34 www.aec.gov.au.

35 "I was in a coma" or "I was giving birth to a future taxpayer" are presumably valid. I would guess that "stopping the zombie apocalypse" or "the waves were just too gnarly, mate" probably aren't. Then again, it is Australia, and one shouldn't make assumptions.

36 And remember, Baskin-Robbins don't play.

37 Currently (July 8, 2016), Google says $1.00 (U.S.) will get you $1.32 (Aussie).

38 Though knowing you are forced to vote may make the warm fuzzies cooler and scratchier.

so the goods go unproduced (or insufficiently produced). If this sounds familiar—you should be screaming "free rider" by now—it should. And it will sound familiar again in the next chapter,[39] so stay focused.[40]

Compulsory voting address this free riding problem, just as the other measures we've talked about address the individual cost-benefit analysis. Think of Australia's twenty-dollar fine as a tax on not voting; it's trying to get people to contribute their share to producing the public goods of voting by changing their incentives. Of course, this raises all sorts of other questions, not least among them whether a coerced vote presents an accurate picture of peoples' preferences. If the alternative is wasting twenty dollars, I may just blindly mark a candidate, so as to make voting cost me as little as possible.

That undermines the goal of producing accountability, doesn't it? If elected officials know people are voting randomly, or based on anything other than the quality of their work, then they have no incentive to do their work well (other than personal pride). Think about it: if grades were distributed randomly, how careful would you be to do your best work? Someone who didn't turn the assignment in could get an A, and someone who completed the assignment perfectly could get an F. If there's no relationship between quality and outcome, you'll either find out with what it does correlate and do that instead, or you'll do whatever the heck you want to do.

Do voters vote based on an official's performance? Magic Eight Ball? "Signs point to no." This is where I get to introduce you to a term which sounds oxymoronic, but isn't: rational ignorance. We suspect it of being an oxymoron because we conflate *rational* with *intelligent*. *Intelligent* means that you learn and understand well. *Rational* means that your choices align with (are likely to produce) your goals. If you are ignorant of the subject on which a question examines you, you may rationally give a very unintelligent answer, as it cannot produce a score lower than zero, and might produce one above that, even if sheerly accidentally. Granted, since the ability to reason is learned, the two ideas may be highly correlated, and some level of intelligence may be necessary in order to apply the discipline of reason. So you have a point; they do at least feel like contradictory terms.

So what is rational ignorance? We've discussed the rationality of voting, but we've said nothing about whether that voting was informed or not. An informed vote is one for which the voter knows very well why he cast it. I mentioned earlier the example of someone voting blindly. What if someone covers her eyes and pushes a random button to vote? She has literally no idea why she cast the vote; in fact, it was chance rather than she who cast it.

Let us imagine she instead spends the necessary amount of time to find out exactly which candidate best matches her preferences so that she can vote for it.[41] She will then cast a very informed vote. But how much will it cost her? How much time and effort does it take to find out which candidate most closely matches your preferences? Well, first you need to figure out in sufficient detail what your preferences are. Once you've cleared that hurdle (and no, "I want, like, good candidates to win and stuff" does not suffice), how do you find out what a candidate's preferences are?

The good news is that they generally make lots of such information public. The bad news is that they have every incentive to make those statements as vague (or even contradictory) as possible, in hopes of seeming like a match for as many voters as possible. You've got to sort through the tangle, parsing which are consistent with each other, which are consistent with the candidate's actions (which are much harder to observe). You've got to figure out whether the candidate voted for that bill because it really does support the rights of indigenous peoples in Antarctica, or because he was trading votes to get support for some other issue, or if there was some amendment or addition to the bill which created some benefit for his district.

Remember, you're going to have to do that for every issue, for every candidate. That could easily become a full-time job, one which does not come with a paycheck. Nor does it come with a metaphorical paycheck. Is a well-informed vote any likelier to be the one to decide the election? No. It may make the warm fuzzies a little warmer or fuzzier; if you vote to do your civic duty, you'll presumably get a little more pride out of knowing you did it well. Just not that much more. Time spent trying to make your vote more informed pays out very little or not at all.

---

39 For those of you who have trouble with simple math: Chapter 10.

40 And classy. Always classy.

41 Unless you have some evidence which would cause us to assume that political candidates are human.

Small wonder, then, that most voters are rationally ignorant. We like to make fun of people who don't know for whom they just voted, or why, or who vote for dead candidates, but we forget to ask if it's reasonable to expect them to know much about a candidate. Some voters use heuristics, or information short cuts, to make decisions about candidates. They could rely on a party label, on endorsements from interest groups, or on the opinion of someone they know whom they consider informed. Some vote based on which names seems familiar, or take some other cue (the candidate's occupation before running, marital status, religion, etc.) as an indicator of what qualities and preferences the candidate has. Some flip a coin, or let their children (or goldfish) pick. It tells us something that poll workers are carefully instructed not to answer questions about candidates or how to vote; it tells us that people ask them.

In the end, the picture is probably a lot more complicated. We usually have more than one motive or purpose for voting, so both conceptions of what value those variables take are working in us, and (as hinted before) may even compound: the slim chance to make a difference may warm our fuzzies. I would urge you to think of voting as a small investment in our common enterprise, and to let that small investment lead you to becoming an active shareholder, one who invests time and effort in that common enterprise. If you're already involved, of course, it lowers the marginal cost of informing yourself. Voting is the democratic equivalent of day trading; it's unlikely to pay off, and it should not be the sum of your involvement, but a deposit.

Okay, the after-school special is over; back to the regularly scheduled programming. We've talked about voting, so let's widen our scope to encompass the context in which voting occurs: elections. There are (at least, in terms of public elections) two types of elections, primary and general. Primary elections are elections within a party to determine who will represent that party in the general election. The general election commands a large number of other elections, directing their strategic deployment . . . yeah, you'd better not have been swallowing that. General elections are elections to the office; they are the ones which determine who will be president, governor, senator, or representative.

State laws govern how state parties (and the national organization of our political parties is simply a coalition of state parties for the purpose of electing a U.S. President) arrange their primaries. Though human (and politician) cleverness knows no bounds, there are generally three kinds of primary. A closed primary is one in which you must be a member of that party to vote. An open primary is one in which you must simply be a registered voter, and may choose in which party's primary you would like to participate, regardless of whether you are a member of that party, another, or none whatsoever.

A blanket primary is a somewhat more confusing creature. It is like an open*er* primary, where you don't have to be a member, and you don't have to choose just one party. Blanket primary ballots list all of the candidates running for nomination for each office, grouped together by office. So if five Republicans, three Democrats, two Libertarians, and two Greens are all seeking their respective party's nomination for governor, they will all be listed under the office of governor on the ballot. Voters can pick one (and only one) per office, but the candidates the voter selects can be from different parties. Voters may choose a Republican in the gubernatorial primary, a Democrat in the Congressional primary, and a Libertarian in the state legislative primary. Each of those votes then counts in the appropriate party's primary to determine their nominee.

Some states use this as both primary **and** general election. Okay, it's not some, it's just one: Louisiana.[42] Drawing on its rich[43] French heritage, Louisiana uses a majoritarian electoral rule. All of the nominees are in the general election. If any one candidate for an office gets an outright (50% + 1) of the votes, she wins. Otherwise, there is a run-off between the top two finishers.[44] In Louisiana, it is sometimes called the "jungle primary," perhaps because of Louisiana's muggy and buggy climate, or perhaps because the candidates jump out from unexpected places and attack each other on every side.

---

42 The first person I ever met from this state, a very attractive young lady named Tracy, said that the correct pronunciation of its name is "Lousy-anna," and no one has ever told me otherwise. Physically threatened me if I said it again, but never contradicted.

43 By which I of course mean "deleterious and retardant."

44 Metro Davidson County recently switched to this method for electing mayors, and it produced the highest turnout in a local election in recent memory (I think it was around 32 percent).

I know I said there were three kinds of primary, but now it's time to talk about the third-and-a-half kind. Some state parties use caucuses[45] to decide who their candidates will be (or in the case of Presidential primaries, whose partisans will be sent to vote at the national convention). A caucus is a group gathering to debate and decide, and the party and other groupings which legislators form in their legislative bodies (where like-minded legislators gather to debate and decide their strategy) are called caucuses, as well. In electoral caucuses, local party members get together and vote with their feet.[46] Members stand in different parts of the room and explain why the others should vote for the candidate they support. People who are convinced stand behind them. Others move around listening to the arguments until they are convinced, or until they see which candidate has the most support. The process continues until there is a clear winner.

The closed primary is more intuitive for us. The party is deciding who will represent it; it makes sense that you'd have to be a member of the party to do that. Letting people who aren't members participate in that decision just seems to give them a chance to make mischief in the party's business. In fact, open primaries do allow voters to try and get a weaker candidate nominated in other parties' primaries, so that their party's candidate has a better chance of winning the general election. So why would parties voluntarily choose to have an open primary?

Oddly, it is so that their own candidate has a better chance of winning the general election. Are you confused, or are they? Let's see if we can clear that up. First, parties may opt for open primaries so that independents (also known as "people who vote in the general election") can help choose their party's candidate. How does that help choose a candidate more likely to win the general election? Thanks for asking. You've said the magic word, so now the duck pops down. The duck, in this case, is a short[47] digression on the median voter theorem.[48]

Imagine that political preferences are one dimensional, running on a spectrum from left to right. Now imagine that voters are dots. As we move down the spectrum, we stack the voter-dots in the places on the spectrum where their preferences are located. At the very extremes, we expect to have very few dots in each stack. As we move toward the middle from each extreme, the stacks get slowly taller, then quickly taller. We find the tallest stack in the very middle then, immediately surrounded by stacks of similar heights.

The picture we have drawn (hopefully) looks like a normal distribution (as seen in Figure 9.2). In a normal distribution, the mean, the mode, and the median are all the same. The mean is what we usually refer to as "the average," but all of them are averages, or measures of central tendency. The mean is the total value of all cases divided by the number of cases. In this context, if we assigned point values to each position on the spectrum, we could sum the total value of the political preferences across voters (in this instance, each voter is a case), divide by the number of voters, and find the value which best summarizes the value of voters' political preferences.

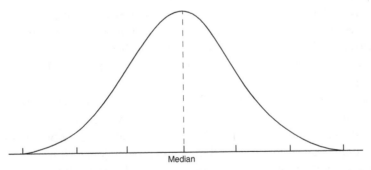

Median

Figure 9.2 The Normal Distribution.

---

45 No, that's a callous. No, what you're thinking of now is caulk. Neither of those is a caucus, though callouses are probably involved. Caulk might be.

46 I told you callouses are probably involved.

47 Hah! In your dreams.

48 The median voter theorem first appears in *Tales to Astonish Non-Economists* No. 21, or as it is more widely known, *An Economic Theory of Democracy* by Anthony Downs.

The "best summarizes" is linked to the "central tendency." It gives the value at the center, around which the others tend most to cluster. Think of it in terms of clouds of dust swirling around a dense center of coagulating dust, whose gravity attracts the swirling dust (and attracts it more strongly as the dust gets closer). That makes the central tendency our best guest of where to find any particular bit of dust; the sum of the distances from the middle to each other point is smaller than the sum from any other point to the rest of them, so using that value as a guess is likely to be off by the least.

The mode gives the central tendency for the frequency of values. To find the mode, you count the number of times each value appears among the cases. The mode is the value which occurs most. For example, the modal (the adjective form of *mode*) previous occupation in Congress has traditionally been "lawyer" (and probably still is—there's nothing like familiarity with the law to make you think that you can surely do better than that). When a mathematician describes a frequency distribution as "unimodal," it means that it has a single high point, or one value which occurs most frequently. Of course, some frequency distributions may be bimodal, having two values which share the highest number of occurrences.[49] Our distribution of voter-dots is unimodal, and the tallest stack is also the one at the mean value.

The median gives us the central tendency of the range (or spatial ordering) of the data. If we line up the cases in order of their value from least to greatest, the value in the middle is the median (or, if there is an even number of cases, the mean of the two values in the middle of the range). Knowing the middle of the range is sometimes more important than knowing the mean. For example, a lot of students where I work want to become successful (by which they mean famous and wealthy) musicians. Let's think about the mean income for musicians. For the ones you probably know (the ones who are famous), that income is high to very high. However, you have to remember all of the other musicians, the ones who have to find supplemental jobs to support their musical career. If we take the mean income, the relatively few very wealthy will overwhelm the much more common low values and produce a deceptively high mean.

Imagine a bar full of musicians. Most of them are probably the waitstaff, because they are making almost nothing as a musician. Let's say there are nine of them, and each makes $1,000 a year from gigs, so the mean income is also $1,000. Now Eric Clapton walks in. Although (like any musician or actor) his income varies from year to year, he's averaged almost $7 million per year over the last twenty years.[50] The mean income of the musicians in the bar just went from $1,000 a year to more than $700,000, if Mr. Clapton is having an average year.

Hearing this, you decide you want a career in music, since an average musician makes $700,000 a year, and you can be at least average. This is where the mean (the central tendency of the value) is misleading, because of the presence of an outlier (Mr. Clapton, whose income is wildly more than anyone else's in the room). It might be more helpful for you to consider the modal income ($1,000), or the median. If we lined up the salaries from least to greatest, the one in the middle . . . well, ten is an even number, so the mean of the two in the middle would be (drumroll, please) . . . $1,000. Our mode and our median are the same, but this is not normally distributed, because the mean is not.

Of course, that example is a little extreme. If we really arranged every musician from least income to greatest income, we'd probably find someone who makes just enough from studio work to get by, but not in the manner to which he wished to become accustomed. The mode would probably be the waiters and waitresses wishing they could find enough studio work to quit their supplemental job, so it would be in a different place, too. The same is true of major sports, writing novels, and acting (and plenty of other jobs that seem lucrative), so the point is not to shatter your dreams of stardom.[51] The point is that each of these measures gives us a shorthand description of the whole batch of information, and like any summary, it can be misleading.

---

49 We sometimes call these modal points "humps," since the graph falls away on either side. This, of course, makes Bactrian camels bimodal and dromedaries unimodal. Oh, yeah . . . math humor and biology humor together. Savor it.

50 According to the interwebs.

51 Though you probably should start taking those dreams with a little salt.

In the normal distribution, then, the middle value of the range (the median) is also the most frequently occurring value (the mode) and the value closest to all the others (the mean). In terms of our model of normally distributed political preferences, we are assuming that moderate positions are most common, and that immoderate opinions are rare (and the more immoderate, the more rare). Now, this seems a fairly reasonable assumption. We do not have many people in the United States arguing for the imposition of a Communist dictatorship and the abolition of private property. Nor do we have many arguing for re-establishing the British monarchy, or even an American one. For all their bluster—which has a reason we will discuss later—our political parties actually agree on a lot of things. They have an incentive[52] to hype their small differences to the point of absurdity. For now, let me remind you that Barak Obama and John McCain mentioned some of the same people as potential cabinet[53] appointments in their 2008 town hall debate, and that in 2004, John Kerry and George W. Bush differed only in who should be implementing strategy in Iraq or the economy, rather than on what those strategies should be. However, we reach the same answer to our question regardless of whether we assume this, or that the electorate is bimodal and the middle ground only sparsely populated.

Back to normally distributed political preferences. The party memberships, of course, do not generally cover the bulk of the middle, but are concentrated around the middle of their respective halves. (Imagine underneath the whole curve a small, blue normal distribution curve with its median on the dotted line just left of the center of the larger curve, and a red one just like it on the right side as depicted in Figure 9.3.)

To win the general election, candidates need to be near the center of the whole, the median voter. We assume that voters prefer candidates whose position is closest to their own. If there are only two candidates, candidates move closer to the median voter; this maximizes the number of voters for whom they are the closest alternative. Think about one candidate just to the left of the median, and one at the midpoint of the right half. A line halfway between them would show the border between the voters closest to the one on the left, and those closest to the one on the right. That line, however, would be a quarter of the way down the right-hand slope, meaning that the left-hand candidate would have a large majority.

In response, the right-hand candidate has to move toward the median. When she is just to the right of the median (as close as the left-hand candidate is), the candidates will each be maximizing their vote total, given the placement of the other. They won't quite get to the median voter. The point is to win, not to make it a lottery, and if they are so identical as to both be at the median voter's position, they are both the same distance from every voter, and voters will select based on other (random) attributes.[54]

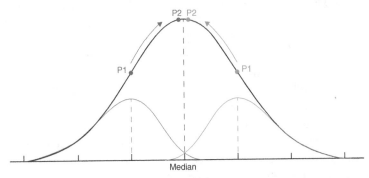

Figure 9.3 Median Voters: Primary Versus General Elections.

52 Remember that part about a free riding problem in voting? Again, later.

53 Hey, you know what that is! (You do, right?)

54 Granted, some do that anyway, whether from apathy or due to the difficulty of accurately discerning a candidate's position. Hey, it's a model; if it were exact in every detail, it would be reality. But reality is a little too large to fit in a book or a classroom. You can put a model in your pocket or your backpack, but the entire universe is a little much to schlep.

This is what the median voter theorem tells us: in a plurality system, candidates will be pulled toward the very center of the political spectrum, because it maximizes the number of voters to whom they are closest in terms of policy preferences. This tells us why we often see elections as a choice between the lesser of two evils, or as a former professor of mine liked to say, the evil of two lessers. The candidates usually try to be as vanilla as possible. Vanilla isn't most people's favorite flavor, but it usually isn't that objectionable, either. People will take it, if it's what's on offer.

Going back to our original question, this is why parties sometimes prefer open primaries. If only their partisans select the candidate, they are likely to select someone at the median of their party. While this pleases the most people in the party, it produces a candidate well away from the median voter in the general population. Allowing independents, who are closer to the median, to participate in the primary allows them to influence the choice toward a candidate closer to the median of the general population.

In other words, unless the party's members are very sophisticated voters—willing to choose a second or third preference because that preference has a better chance in the general election—then winning your party's primary can cost you the general election. In order to win in the primary, you have to stake out a position near the median of the party. You then have pull up stakes and hike toward the median of the general population in the general election. Your party's voters feel as if you have betrayed them. Independent voters will (rightfully) be suspicious of which position is your actual one. If you don't, however, then you may be long remembered for leading your party to landslide defeat.

You often see candidates performing this difficult dance. They speak to the center of their party in the primary, then suddenly revise their positions to make them more moderate once they secure the nomination. This should help us understand why Barak Obama, to give but one example, had very negative things to say about the North American Free Trade Agreement in the primary, when he had to appeal to the core of the Democratic Party (including labor unions). It should help us understand why he began to describe it in much more positive light once he secured the nomination. Just watch an election, especially a Presidential one sometime. Once a candidate has the nomination—and keep in mind, this may occur sometime before the convention—they will become more moderate. This can also be another advantage for incumbents, but we haven't gotten there yet.

Let's go back to the "least offensive flavor" idea. If the two candidates are trying to out-bland each other, why doesn't a third candidate enter the race as grape sorbet or rocky road? (We probably have had the occasional rum raisin.) Here the median voter theorem helps too. Look at Figure 9.4. Imagine our two candidates eyeballing each other across the divide of the median voter. If we place a third candidate behind the left-hand candidate, in the middle of the left half of the population, then the electorate will split halfway between the two leftward candidates, as well as at the median voter. Since the right half is bigger than either of the two pieces of the left side alone, the right-hand candidate wins.

In other words, that third candidate splits the vote for the candidate next most attractive to his voters. In voting for their first preference, they cause their third preference to win. Even though they prefer the leftmost candidate first, they prefer the candidate just to the left of the median to the one just to the right of the median. Since that second preference is more likely to win than their first, they strategically transfer their vote to the one closer to the median. This is the wasted vote phenomenon. Their most preferred candidate appeals to too few voters to win, whether they vote for him or not. Instead, they focus on the candidates who have the top two vote totals, and attempt to influence the gap between them—either to widen or to narrow it. A vote which does not address that gap is, the voter believes, a wasted vote.[55]

The plurality rule, then, focuses votes on the top two parties. This makes it very difficult for third parties to establish themselves. People are hesitant to vote for them until they show they can win, and they can't win because people won't vote for them until they do. So the median voter theorem not only helps us understand why the two major parties generally look so much alike in terms of candidates and policies in

---

55 Of course, in terms of determining an outcome, most of them are wasted. Think of this as buying a ticket for last week's lottery as opposed to this week's lottery. You already know the one from last week lost; at least the ticket from this week has a chance, even if it is small.

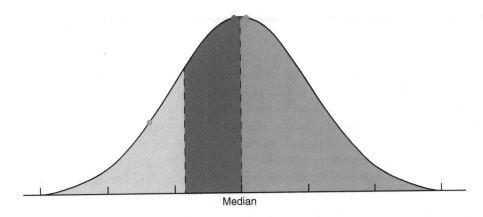

Figure 9.4 Effect of Third Party Candidate.

each election, but also why there are only two of them. It helps us understand why the Republican Party used its organization in many states to help get the Green Party candidate, Ralph Nader, on the ballot in several states in 2004.[56]

We started all of this by wondering why parties would choose open primaries when it allowed for their opponents to influence their choice toward weaker candidates. We then said it is to allow independents to influence their choice toward stronger candidates. How can both be true? Well, we're talking about probability, not certainty. And the likelihood that open primaries help is much greater than the likelihood that they harm. For opposition voters to successfully sabotage the party's primary, they have to meet some rather difficult conditions. First, the opposition party's primary must already be decided, or their partisans will want to help decide that contest first. Sometimes parties have candidates running unopposed in primaries, often because they are incumbents.

The second and third conditions, however, are much more difficult. The opposition voters have to both organize enough of themselves to be able to exert sufficient influence on the other primary, and they have to coordinate their vote on the same spoiler candidate. You should have already recognized these as two collective action problems. Getting enough of them to vote is a free riding problem. Casting those votes for the same candidate is a coordination problem. As a result, even though we fairly often see the first condition, we rarely see all three of them. Although I know of several stories about people attempting this, or at least talking about it, I've never heard of an instance where it was successful, even in this age of social media (which should make the coordination easier, at least).

In some states, parties have made that convergence even less likely by combining the closed and open primaries. Called a semi-open primary, it allows independent voters—those with no party membership—to choose in which primary they will participate. Those who are members of a party, however, must vote in their own primary. And there you have it: a solution to a problem no one had, proof that fear of a thing is stronger than the thing itself.

It also removes one of the more general benefits of an open primary, or the reason why some states might require parties to have open primaries. Some localities are so dominated by one party that the nominee of the dominant party will be running unopposed in the general election. If other voters cannot influence that nomination, they will have no ability to affect the selection at all; the party can essentially impose its decision on the rest of society. Of course, they could always simply join that party. One-party rule, however, doesn't have a very good reputation, and for some very good reasons.[57]

---

56 They probably did in 2000 as well, and it is equally likely the Democrats helped get Pat Buchanan, a candidate to the right of George W. Bush, on some ballots that year, too. Of course, the great irony is that instead of splitting votes on the right, Pat Buchanan's inclusion on the Florida ballot seems to have unintentionally helped Bush. Confused by the design of the ballot, some voters intending to vote for Gore apparently voted for Buchanan by mistake. Bush won Florida by only 537 votes, so the mistake could have altered the outcome.

57 Boreal blizzard. No, that wasn't it . . . listen, if it really isn't coming to you, just think about what happens to the idea of democratic accountability if you can't be voted out of office, because there is no opposition to take your place.

Enough about primaries. Let's talk about general elections. In terms of electing federal officials, we elect the entire House of Representatives and one-third of the Senate every two years. We elect the President every four years. So every time we vote on a President, we're also electing all of the Representatives and some of the Senators. Halfway through the President's term, we have an election just for the House and the next third of the Senate. We call the first presidential elections; presidents are divas that way, always wanting top billing if they're involved. Okay, while there may be some truth to that, we are the ones who call them that, probably because the Presidential office is the only one we elect in a single national election, even it if is organized through the states (and blocks of electors). The second type of federal elections we call midterm elections, because they occur halfway through his term.[58]

In Presidential elections, candidates of the same party as the winning Presidential candidate who are running for other offices tend to get an electoral boost. People tend to vote for candidates of the same party (straight ticket) rather than switching between parties across offices (split ticket). We call this electoral boost the President's coat-tails, which the other candidates ride into office. If you've ever seen a tuxedo with tails, imagine the President wearing one with tails so long they trail the ground behind him.[59] Now imagine candidates for the House, Senate, and state positions standing on them, and the President pulling them forward as he walks.

In midterm elections, however, the President's party tends to lose seats in Congress. As we've already discussed, turnout is lower, so some people who helped the President have those coattails through their votes aren't there to swell the ranks. If the candidate won last time 55 to 45 percent, then the 13 to 15 percent who stay home because there's no President on the ballot more than account for the candidate's margin of victory. We tend to think this is a protest vote, because people are upset by something the President has done, and take it out on his party, since he's not on the ballot. We forget that it may not be a change in preference, that it may be a difference in who is voting, rather than how they are voting. Again, though, it is probably some of both, in varying amounts at varying times.

Another regularity we observe in elections generally is that incumbents tend to win. As you may know, an incumbent is someone who holds an office. When we talk about them in elections, it means someone running for re-election to the office they currently hold. If they hold one office but are running for another, they are not an incumbent in terms of that election. Elections for offices without an incumbent running are referred to as open seats. Because incumbents tend to win—the re-election rate for the House and Senate varies, but it's generally around 95 percent—parties tend to save strong candidates for open seats, and run token opposition against popular incumbents.

Why is it that incumbents win re-election so often? One potential explanation is that we as voters do such an excellent job of choosing elected officials that they cannot find better. When you've stopped laughing, I'll add that opinion polls on how satisfied the public is with the performance of public officials would cast some doubt on that.[60] On the other hand, we might need to investigate those polls a little more thoroughly. Given that turnout is low, and more people claim to have voted than actually do, it could be that the 20 percent in the poll who are happy or satisfied were also the ones who elected the official in the first place, and the rest is sour grapes from those who lost or didn't vote at all. That is, if turnout was 35 percent, 20 percent would have been well more than half. That leaves 15 percent who voted for someone else and 65 percent who didn't vote at all, in other words, 80 percent who weren't thrilled with the candidate to start with.

We should also consider that the question asked in the opinion poll is different from the one asked at electoral polls. The question at the polls is usually which of these two do you like better. That's a relative value; you may not like Taylor Swift, but that doesn't mean there isn't another[61] singer[62] you like even less. Again, think of

---

58   See, even that has to be about him. Diva.

59   Imagine we could go back in time and get Abraham Lincoln's tuxedo coat, then take it further back in time to James Madison. (Lincoln was 6' 4", while Madison was 5' 4". Together, they are proof that size really is irrelevant, and good things come in all sorts of packages.)

60   Or, as the kids say, "throw some shade." Sorry—as the *kidz* say.

61   Iggy Azalea.

62   Is that too strong a term for them? "Artist" didn't really feel right, either.

the prevalence of the description of elections as the choice of the lesser of two evils, and not just in this book. The result of elections is not always or even usually the candidate we like most, but the one we dislike the least. That has some advantages (believe it or not),[63] but if we choose the least distasteful candidate, we still find them distasteful. No surprise, then, that we say so in opinion polls.

More than just the difference in the questions and the mathematics of how many vote, there's still a question of why the choices on offer are usually so disappointing.[64] How many candidates would you be willing to buy a used car from? Part of it is surely the fact that people entrusted with power are still first and foremost people, and likely to succumb to the moral hazard[65] of holding power. Part of it may be that we are far more familiar with the spectacular failures than the successes. We may only be counting the dogs whose barks we hear.

Part of it, though, has to go back to civil society and civic virtue. A good, decent person who tries to do the **right** thing will always be publically pilloried for not doing the **popular** thing (popular with whatever group is doing the pillorying). That is, we do not ask whether the public official made a reasonable decision given the information at her disposal, we do not ask whether it was factually the right decision, we ask whether we like the decision. Since any decision angers someone and reason is no defense, we are asking these people to put themselves in the most painful position possible. We want them to make difficult decisions wisely and well, then ignore our calling them names and abusing their name and character, then pretend they eventually heard us say "thank you" when it worked out well. That's a whole lot of work for no payoff. If they are irrational enough to sign up for it, we can hardly expect them to make rational decisions—that, or they had a different purpose than serving the public.

Back to incumbents and why they do so well. There are some quick and easy technical answers, and we're getting to them. But there is one more thing we must consider: the stupidity of voters. Maybe incumbents aren't popular, they just have inertia. Voters don't know what incumbents' service records are, or whether they've done a good job, they just know the world hasn't exploded yet. Now, maybe that's because of the incumbent's efforts, maybe in spite of them, and maybe the two (efforts and outcome) are completely unrelated. Voters may engage in the logical fallacy of *post hoc ergo propter hoc*—"after it, therefore because of it"—in the most general of contexts. World still spinning? Check. Incumbent must be doing something right, then. Never mind that they elected Lex Luthor and it has taken Superman's best efforts to defeat Luthor's plans to stop the world from spinning.

This general anesthesia under which voters function is an important backdrop to all of the causes we're going to discuss. None of them deal with the quality of the incumbent, but solely with her ability to make a dent in the numbness of most citizens when it comes to public affairs. First, incumbents usually have an advantage in name recognition. Because they are in office, they have usually run a campaign before, so voters have had at least one heavy exposure to their names. This makes it more familiar than the typical challenger's. While in office, they often have public funds available to stay in touch with their constituents. They can't use these to campaign, but they can use them to let you know what they're doing for you. I remember the name of my state representative[66] from when I was in graduate school. I can't tell you (and never could) what his[67] party affiliation is, or what policies he[68] supported (I used to have some idea of that). To this day, around twenty years later, I can still tell you that his[69] name was Mark Kruzan, because I got mail from him on what seemed like a weekly basis with his name plastered across it everywhere.

---

63 It encourages moderation, which is as beneficial in politics as it is in the consumption of alcohol, food . . . okay, just consumption in general, but especially alcohol.

64 Maybe this is just a function of writing this during the 2016 campaign.

65 Boreal blizzard . . . what were you thinking? (Or should that be "drinking"?)

66 Mark Kruzan.

67 Mark Kruzan.

68 Mark Kruzan.

69 Mark Kruzan.

Incumbents can also build name recognition through media. Of course, doing this explicitly is what they do in a campaign. As a public official, however, they will be quoted in news stories, photographed cutting ribbons for new shopping centers and reading to second graders at the local elementary school, and answering questions on television or radio call-in shows any time they can swing it. Since they are public officials, they will be asked to do those things a lot more than people who aren't. They are minor celebrities, so they will be asked to attend events to attract attention and media coverage. People meet them, see them, and most importantly, hear their name repeatedly.

In fact, celebrities often make good candidates, because they already have name recognition. Ronald Reagan, Clint Eastwood, Arnold Schwarzenegger, Sonny Bono, Jesse Ventura, Al Franken, John Glenn, Jack Kemp, Heath Shuler, Jon Runyan, even Hillary Clinton and Donald Trump already had name recognition on which to draw. [70] Four were actors, one a musician (and actor), one a wrestler (and therefore, actor), three were professional athletes, one the spouse of a prominent politician, one an astronaut (and the first American to orbit the earth), and one a mediocre real estate developer with a talent for self-promotion.

Aside from bare name recognition, incumbents are also positioned to perform favors for voters. If you visit the nation's capital, call your Representative's office first. They will usually arrange a tour of the Capitol for you.[71] Is Grandpa having trouble with his Social Security check? Call your Representative's or Senator's office, where underpaid staff are waiting to lodge a formal inquiry with the Social Security Administration on the Congressperson's behalf. Difficulty with a visa so that family from the old country can come visit for the big reunion? They've got that, too. This is called casework, and it is an important, appropriate, and exhausting part of an official's job. It also means that voter will (or should) remember them with gratitude for their assistance, a gratitude they are not likely to feel toward a challenger who was in no position to help them.

Likewise, public officials can use their influence to pass measures benefitting their constituency particularly and block ones which threaten it. Of course, representatives should generally promote and protect the interests of their constituency. Here, we're talking especially about amendments or additions to bills that include specific benefits for their constituency, usually in the form of federal spending. That's right, we're talking about pork.[72] Politicians now call these things "earmarks" or "riders" in an attempt to escape the negative public opinion "pork" and "pork barrel spending" attracted.[73] The principle is the same. Voters see bringing public funds to be spent on them (and not on others) as "winning."[74]

For example, getting an Army base built in your district (and keeping it there) brings jobs, not only building the base but staffing it, and it brings soldiers who will spend their pay in your community. Preventing the base's closure because it's a naval base on the Mississippi (which hasn't needed defending since approximately the time we purchased Louisiana from the French) helps keep those funds flowing. Likewise, keeping your district from being the location for the spent nuclear fuel storage facility is locally popular and in your district's particular interest, if not in the common interest.

By the way, there is a defense of pork,[75] as reprehensible and repugnant as pork may seem. Remember those high-friction gears that make it difficult to make laws? Well, pork is also pork lard, and smearing it on those gears gets them to work a little more smoothly. It's the grease that keeps the system running. When you have to get a coalition together around a bill, you have to give people a reason to join that coalition, so that you have sufficient (and sometimes, sufficiently well-placed—remember committees?) votes for it to pass. One would hope, of course, that the innate merits of the bill would suffice; if enough people are going to benefit from it, their representatives should be in favor of it.

---

70 Mark Kruzan. Just kidding!

71 Thanks again to the nice folks in Rep. Blackburn's office. (See how that works?)

72 Shut yo' mouth! Just talkin' 'bout pork.

73 "Rebranding," just like the prunes and the Patagonian toothfish.

74 No word on whether tiger blood is involved, Charlie.

75 The public spending for particular districts, not the other white meat, which obviously needs no defending. Especially when smoked and pulled or sliced. Barbecue and bacon are, to borrow from Ben Franklin, proof that God loves us and wants us to be happy.

Remember what we said, however: politicians are not thanked for doing what benefits their constituency, but for doing what is popular (even if it is damaging in the aggregate). Between voting for a good bill and voting for it with pork that lets you cut the ribbon on a new bridge, there's really not much of a decision. And sadly, it is a short trip from there to simply voting for whatever comes with a stretch of highway, or a bridge, or whatever other tangible thing you can parade before your constituents.[76]

There is something of a tragedy of the commons at work. If all representatives could agree not to seek these side payments, the budget (and the common good) would be in better shape. However, each one's side payment by itself is a small contribution to the consumption of the budget; her one bit of pork isn't the problem. If she alone declines to bring home the bacon to her district, the budget is still over-consumed, and she has no positive gain to show her constituents.

Congress tried to enlist the President as an enforcer to keep them from indulging in succulent pork. They passed the Line Item Veto Act in 1996, which allowed the President

> ... to cancel in whole any dollar amount of discretionary budget authority, any item of new direct spending, or any limited tax benefit signed into law, if the President: (1) determines that such cancellation will reduce the Federal budget deficit and will not impair essential Government functions or harm the national interest; and (2) notifies the Congress of any such cancellation within five calendar days after enactment of the law providing such amount, item, or benefit.[77]

Unfortunately, the Supreme Court (quite reasonably) found that this violates the Presentment Clause, which says that the President may accept or veto bills, not parts of bills. That is not to say the line item veto (which was restricted to lines of pork, essentially) was a bad idea, just that it would require an amendment to the Constitution, rather than a regular statute, to allow it.

There are at least two more benefits to being an incumbent. As an incumbent, you are in a position to influence (or even control) the rules. We've already talked about gerrymandering, but elected officials make other rules, too. For example, there are rules which determine what a potential candidate must do to get on the ballot. There will usually be some rule allowing a candidate nominated by a party whose candidate for some specified office received at least some threshold percentage of the vote to have automatic access.

Other parties, on the other hand, have to go through quite a bit more to get their candidate on the ballot. Again, the details vary, but they will have some time frame in which to collect a relatively large number of signatures on a petition. These have to be valid signatures, usually meaning from a registered voter, so you also have to collect some identifying information. Any duplicate signatures or invalid signatures are eliminated.[78] Just like the bipartisan interest in gerrymandering, this means that incumbents of both major parties have fewer viable challengers. Either their party chokes them off and makes them wait their turn, or the difficulty of getting on the ballot otherwise does.

The state (which consists of incumbents) did not always control ballot access in the same way. Originally, each party printed its own ballot. They did this on different colors of paper, so that illiterate voters could know what ballot they were casting. Of course, it also meant party observers could see if voters were voting as they had promised, by seeing what color paper they put in the ballot box. It also made splitting your ticket pretty well impossible. The common ballot, with all (approved) parties' candidates on the same ballot and therefore requiring voters to mark their choices, was a Progressive reform.[79]

---

76 Incidentally, though not coincidentally, relatively large amounts of West Virginia have Robert C. Byrd's name on them. Also not coincidentally, he was a Senator from West Virginia for over fifty years.

77 www.congress.gov/bill/104th-congress/senate-bill/4.

78 Mickey Mouse might be a registered voter in Orange County, Florida, but he probably isn't registered where you collected that signature.

79 It is known as the Australian ballot, because it was another electoral innovation of Australia. Because Australia is entirely peopled with criminals, who are used to not being trusted . . . or something like that.

It was meant to damage party machines, just like the Seventeenth Amendment, and it did. Party machines provided social services for the poor and assistance with assimilation for immigrants (who were also usually poor). They did this in exchange for the votes of those they helped. Having ballots on different colors of paper meant they could see if the people they aided kept their side of the bargain.[80] The Australian ballot, on the other hand, kept the machines from knowing if their clientele defected. Of course, it also gave the government control over who got on the ballot, and made literacy an obstacle to voting. Nothing's perfect, right?

As an incumbent, you also likely already have a war chest. Whatever money you collected as donations for your last campaign, but which you did not spend, is still on hand for your next election. This means you usually have a head start on fundraising. In fact, you've probably been adding donations over the years you've been in office. After all, you've know when you'd be up for re-election since you were elected. Your opponent has probably not been as prescient, and has spent less time knowing he would be his party's nominee.

Speaking of which, that reminds us of a benefit of being an incumbent which we've already discussed. As the median voter theorem showed us, not having to face an opponent in a primary allows you to stake out a position near the median immediately. You do not have to stake out one position at your party's median, convince them you mean it, then convince independent voters in the general election that you only sort of meant it. And that was yet another additional advantage, beyond the last two. What's the total at now?[81]

Back to the money for a second. Why is it that politicians always seem to have their mind on their money, and their money on their mind? Why is money so important in elections? Two (familiar) words: information cost. Candidates need you to know their names and what things for which they're willing to stand. They need you to have a reason to go vote, and to cast that vote for them. We talked about informed votes earlier. Spending time and effort to inform ourselves doesn't really pay off for us, so candidates need money to spend to replace the time and effort we don't.

This is what also explains mudslinging, or negative ads. Mudslinging is generally unpopular with voters; it usually does not increase their opinion of the candidate who is personally attacking his opponent, and may decrease it a little. Two factors related to campaign finance, however, help explain why and when it happens. The first is that money is scarce, and advertising costs money. People remember negative (or attack) ads more readily than they remember positive ones. Psychologists confirm that we remember negative comments about people after hearing them once, but have to hear a positive comment four times before we remember it.[82]

So, when a candidate is behind and running out of money, they can get close to the same bang by denting their opponent's reputation for about a quarter of the bucks it would take to polish theirs (all else being equal; that is, assuming they have one capable of being polished). As long as the damage the backlash causes to their standing is less than the damage the attack ad causes their opponent, as long as the opponent loses more ground than they do, it will close the gap between them.

Of course, negative ads appear at other times, too, not just late in the campaign when the candidate is broke and desperate. These other times are a result of campaign finance laws. The McCain–Feingold Act (or Bipartisan Campaign Finance Reform Act) of 2002 limited the amount and frequency of donations to individual candidates. Rather, it increased or added limits; some already existed. It could not, however, limit donations to 527 groups, which are political advocacy groups identified by the section of the tax code[83] which governs them.

These groups are meant to be vehicles for citizens to organize and advocate on issues they care about. As it turns out, some citizens care about who gets elected, and organize and advocate on behalf of their preferred

---

80 Don't make me cough it out. You know whose dilemma this is.

81 I count six. No wonder they win so much.

82 We ought to find people's successes, their good behavior, inspiring and their failures regrettable lessons from which to learn. Instead, we seem to find their success threatening and their failures comforting. Doesn't speak well of us, does it?

83 Wait for it . . . in a stunning upset, it's Section 42! No, of course it's Section 527.

candidate. They cannot, however, coordinate their campaigns with the candidate's, or they become an extension of that campaign and the McCain–Feingold limitations apply to them.[84]

Since they cannot coordinate with their preferred candidate, it is difficult for them to run a positive campaign. They may emphasize something they appreciate about the candidate but which actually harms his position with the broader electorate. A mayor running for governor, for example, would not want supporters from his city crowing about how he has stuck it to the rest of the state for their benefit. Or a Democratic governor of a liberal northeastern state may want to save his support of gun rights for the general election, because it will hurt him in the primaries. Because the group cannot communicate with the candidate's campaign to resolve this problem, they shift to an area where they don't need to be "on message": what's wrong with the other candidate. Any flaws they find seem likely to be helpful to their cause by damaging the other.

Except, of course, when they do more damage to the candidate who voters think is making them, rather than the opposing candidate, whom the group intends to damage. Again, timing matters. Going negative early in a campaign, for example, seems to increase the damage done to the candidate doing the attacking (or on whose behalf the attacks are made) and reduce the damage done to the victim. 527 groups may try to highlight as a flaw something which voters actually find attractive. Loose cannons are still likely to fire in any direction.

Let's take a moment to step back and look at where we've been. We began by examining the individual and the process of voting. As you may have noticed, we've not been able to talk about that without talking about collective action. You may not have noticed, which may be a testament to how ubiquitous and omnipresent the need for collective action is. Since it's everywhere, we take it for granted; it's part of the background of everything we do, so we no longer notice it. Of course, it may also be a testament to your ability to be oblivious. We'll choose up sides and argue about which one is right in the next chapter, the one about political parties.[85] Go ahead. It should be just the other side of that page . . .

---

84 Another provision from the McCain–Feingold Act is the one requiring candidates to personally indicate their endorsement of messages from their campaigns. If you'll notice, those tend to be nasty only when they're behind and low on funds. The ones without that statement (which include those from 527s) tend to be nasty all of the time.

85 In case you missed it last time, or if you're an amputee trying to count on your fingers, or if you're just too darn lazy to find the Table of Contents, the next chapter is still Chapter 10 (though Chapter 42 gave it a run for its money).

Chapter 10: Political Parties

So this is the party chapter. Huh. Somehow, I thought it would be a little more festive. Why do we have parties? No, *political* parties. We have regular parties to celebrate, to enjoy the company of others, to have a good time. Do any of those sound like the reasons we have *political* parties? Didn't think so. How can the same word refer to two such disparate things? Well, the root is "part," as in participate, partisan, and partial. In that sense, it means to be involved in some common enterprise among a group which is less than the whole. A party refers to a group of people traveling together, as they often did (and still do in some places) for safety. Of course, people often tried to have fun on those journeys, to make the dreary, plodding time pass more quickly. *The Canterbury Tales*, for example, are supposed to be the stories told by a group of people traveling together on a pilgrimage to Canterbury. They told stories to entertain themselves. This is where we get the entertainment context of the word "party": people having a good time together.

The gathering together, forming a "team" to overcome opposition, is where we get the political context. People choose a side and band together for mutual aid and support in reaching a common goal. A partisan is someone who has chosen a side, who identifies with and acts on behalf of some group less than the whole in number (or faction, as Madison would say). This is why "partial" can refer both to not being the whole, but some fraction thereof, as well as to having sympathy or preference for one side over another.

Now that we have cleared that up, we still have our original question: why do we have political parties? Why do we need to take sides and work together with some in order to overcome the others? Can't we all just get along? The beginning of that answer is in Federalist 10. Because we are different people, we have different interests. Those of us with similar interests are "united and actuated by some common" interest. How is it, though, that we come to be united? Why do we fight as a group for a common cause, rather than as individuals for our personal interests? Many are stronger than a few, whether we're talking about hand-to-hand combat[1] or counting votes. As we know, however, organizing individuals into a "many" (or in other words, collective action) is costly. So what exactly prompts us to organize in politics?

We've discussed previously that the Founders (certainly Madison) saw factions as an incurable disease of the body politic, one whose symptoms had to be controlled, lest it kill that polis. So why were two of the authors of the *Federalist Papers* directly involved in forming the first two political parties? They did not anticipate the formation of parties. Not only are they nowhere mentioned in the Constitution, but several of its original provisions make no sense in the context of partisan competition. For example, the President was originally the person who received the most electoral votes, and the Vice President the person who received the second most.[2] This works well to give us the first and second preferences of the group as a whole, if there are no competing subgroups.

And for the first two Presidential elections, it worked splendidly, because there was little to no partisan competition. Everyone wrote George Washington's name on one ballot, and whoever received the largest share of the other ballots finished second and was Vice President. Washington himself was resistant to the idea of splitting the body politic to gain advantage. He was perhaps the last vestige of the national unity which the American Revolution had inspired, when the common cause was colonists ("us") versus Britain ("them"). As that pressure to join or die faded, once the cause was achieved, other divisions resurfaced.

---

1 With the obvious exceptions of Chuck Norris and Bruce Lee.

2 Each elector cast two votes, which had to be for different people.

In the 1796 election, John Adams of the Federalist Party (which favored a stronger national government) received the most votes. Second place, however, went to the leading candidate of the other party, Thomas Jefferson of the Democratic Republicans (yes, that was a thing, and they favored decentralization and a weaker national government). To give you an idea of how well this worked out, consider that Adams and Jefferson had worked together on the Committee of Five (in the Continental Congress), which was charged with producing a declaration of independence. The committee decided on an outline, Jefferson completed a draft following that plan, then Adams, Ben Franklin, and the two other members[3] helped edit it. I don't know if you've ever been part of a process like that, but hurt feelings and resentment often result. Yet Adams and Jefferson became good friends.

Until, that is, they had to share the White House after having faced off against each other for the Presidency. Their time sharing the executive branch worked as becoming roommates often does with friends: it alienated them and made them bitter rivals. It was not until years later that they renewed their friendship, and even grew closer than before. Seeing at the time the mayhem and dissatisfaction the electoral process had caused, Congress proposed (and the states ratified) an amendment to the Constitution to make separate the votes for President and Vice President.

So parties were unanticipated and undesired. How then did we get them? We did not have parties to speak of in the days of the Continental Congress. As a near-contemporary points out, "the States, in the confederation, had but few and feeble motives to form combinations, in order to obtain control of its powers,"[4] because the Continental Congress had no power over individuals or states.

> But very different is the case in their existing confederated character. The present government possesses extensive and important powers; among others, that of carrying its acts into execution by its own authority, without the intermediate agency of the States. And, hence, the principal motives to get the control of government, with all its powers and vast patronage; and for this purpose, to form combinations as the only means by which it can be accomplished.[5]

So democracies need parties, combinations of people, in order to exercise power (and a government which cannot exercise power is no government all).[6] To understand why this is so, let's put ourselves in an imaginary legislature which has just formed and in which parties do not exist. We need to pass laws which establish freedom and order among our citizens. Let's say we are also an extremely small legislature: you, me, and George. Now we have to find a bill[7] that makes at least two of us happy so that we can pass it.[8] Issues are complex, and we will usually be trading off some of our interest in either freedom or order against a greater share of the other (or, if you really want to complicate it, some part of another interest). To make the process easier to understand, let's pretend we're dividing up a dollar, so that the amount of "money" we receive is actually our satisfaction with the bill and its trade-offs.

Would you care to propose a bill?[9] Remember, the division of the money is a proxy for our satisfaction with the balance of conflicting interests. Most people playing this game in a classroom[10]—where they face the public yet silent judgment of their classmates, and know they really don't get any money anyway—propose splitting the pot of money into even thirds: one third for you, one third for me, thirty-three percent for George.[11]

---

3 Roger Sherman and Robert Livingston.

4 John C. Calhoun, *A Discourse on the Constitution and Government of the United States*, in Ross M. Lence (ed.), *Union and Liberty: The Political Philosophy of John C. Calhoun* (Indianapolis, Liberty Fund, 1992), 163.

5 Calhoun, 164.

6 If you have questions, take them up with Somalia.

7 A proposed law, not Bill, a fourth person who wants to be in our legislature.

8 Why two of us? Well, what's a simple majority (more than half) of three? Also, if it **is** Bill who makes the other two of you happy, I'm not judging. But please don't pass him. In any sense of the word.

9 Again, a bill, not to Bill. Still not judging; one of those just isn't relevant.

10 Duh; is there some other place you'd be playing this game? (And yes, I use the term "game" lightly.)

11 Leave Bill out of this.

Thing is, George turns to me and proposes that we split it between us: half for him, half for me, nothing for you.[12] Since half is greater than a third, I accept.[13] What do you do?

If you're not as good at math as George, you lean over and suggest you and I split it. If you offer me the same 50 percent as George offers, I have no reason to change my vote. So you propose 40 percent for you, and 60 percent for me, and nothing for that devious cheat George. Forty percent beats the zero you were getting, 60 percent beats the 50 I was getting, so we have a new majority (around a 40/60/0 split). Done? Hardly. George is still just as devious and just as mathematically dexterous. He turns to you and offers you a 50-50 split, leaving me out (50/0/50). He's better off, you're better off, and I can't throw any shade—wasn't I the one just explaining that 60 beat 40?

Blame may not be on the table, but a new offer can be, so I turn to George and offer him 60 percent, with 40 for me (and none for you—a 0/40/60 split). 60 is more than 50, 40 is more than zero, so we are both willing, and we have another majority around a different proposal. And yes, we can do this all day. You should recognize the problem by now. Or do I have to remind you of our fictitious vacation in Atlanta, Baltimore, or Chicago? Of course, we could delegate power to an agenda setter to make it stop, but that just gives power to that person.[14] We're only in favor of that if the person is someone we know to be just and impartial, or someone we know to be partial to us. Since the former is in short supply, we'll need to vote on whom to put in that position. Oh, crap; here we go again.

We could go about this one other way.[15] We're probably going to vote on more than one bill. If we keep defecting from each other, none of us will ever trust the others' promises of support. It would make sense for those of us (and here, let's think of a legislature of a more realistic size, like three hundred) who have a lot of common or similar interests to agree to pass each other's bills. In fact, if we get enough of us together, we can just tailor the bill to those in our coalition. Since we have some similarity in our preferences, it will be closer to all of us. Remember our left–right spectrum with values assigned to each point?[16] Imagine it goes from one to ten, in whole numbers. If we add up all the numbers, the sum is fifty-five, so the mean is 5.5. If we just sum the left half of the numbers, the mean is three (fifteen divided by five); the mean of the right half is eight (forty divided by five). If we know that we have a majority on one side, we can put the bill at the median of our half, rather than the overall median (making it 2.5 units closer to us, on average).

If we cooperate, if we form a combination, we can get more of what we want enacted. Of course, that cooperation is subject to the prisoner's dilemma, but the shadow of the future helps restrain us. If we defect, we lose all of the better deals we could have gotten on future bills, too. With our incentives to defect curbed, we form a stable legislative coalition. Cycling is no longer the problem it was, because we all rank one alternative (offers which divide our coalition) last. This is the origin of political parties, and the first reason why we have them.[17]

Of course, for this to work, we have to have a majority of the legislators in our party. If you are the legislators who are consistently left out of this stable coalition, your first goal (after forming your own party) is to unseat some of the other party's members in favor of candidates with preferences similar to yours, who will therefore get you closer to having the majority.[18] If you have the majority, you want to preserve or increase your numerical advantage. So how do you get more candidates with preferences similar to yours elected? The problem with electing legislators is not cycling; there is only one vote. Alternative candidates are not offered

---

12 Isn't that just like George? I know, right?

13 Yeah, you saw that coming. Don't act like you're surprised.

14 Seriously, leave Bill out of this.

15 To give credit where credit is due, the following discussion owes a considerable debt to John H. Aldrich, *Why Parties? The Origin and Transformation of Political Parties in America* (Chicago: University of Chicago Press, 1995).

16 Dude, that was just the last chapter.

17 For a real example of life without institutions to prevent cycling, see Josephine Andrews, *When Majorities Fail: The Russian Parliament 1990-1993* (Cambridge, Cambridge University Press, 2002).

18 Note that it is the party as stable legislative coalition which allows us to speak of **the** majority, rather than **a** majority, because it stabilizes the composition of that majority.

one at a time so as to re-arrange support from one majority to another. They are offered all at once, and so are vastly more likely to suffer from not having a majority at all, rather than not having a stable one.

Not a problem—we're using a plurality electoral rule, so somebody gets elected. While that is true, it misses our actual problem: that candidate represents a small (and perhaps very small) portion of voters. If all of us with similar preferences split our votes between three or four candidates, while the other side coordinates theirs on a single candidate, they make it much more likely that their candidate's total will be more than any other candidate's. If you've seen *Toy Story 2*, think about the scene when the toys are trying to get into Al's Toy Barn. The automatic doors have a pressure-sensitive pad which activates them. The toys' combined weight provides insufficient force to trigger the sensor, so they start jumping to increase the force. It still doesn't work, because they are jumping at different times. Whey they coordinate their actions and jump together, they trigger the sensor, and the doors open. Same thing here, just replace "toys" with "voters," "jump" with "vote," the sensor with the plurality rule, and Al's Toy Barn with the legislature (more or less).[19]

This is the second purpose which prompts the formation of parties, the one which prompts their extension beyond the legislature itself and into the electorate. If voters can form stable electoral coalitions, coordinating their votes on a single candidate, they can increase the chances of a candidate with preferences more similar to theirs winning. The more such candidates who win, the more likely it is that they form a legislative coalition large enough to be the majority. There is also something of a prisoner's dilemma here. Not only do we have to agree on the common candidate, we then have to actually keep our promise to vote, and to vote for that candidate (rather than defecting to one we like better, and splitting the vote).[20]

Even if we overcome the problem, voting for the candidate we promised, we still have the first, going to vote as we promised. You and your fellow travelers have agreed to a candidate whom you all find second best. Are you going to feel quite as warm and fuzzy about voting for someone who is the least objectionable? The more excited you are about a candidate, the more likely you are to pay the time and effort it takes to vote. The more apathetic you are, the more likely you are to prefer other uses of that time and effort.

In fact, even if you are enthusiastic about the candidate, you may easily have alternate uses for those resources, which you prefer to voting, especially since it isn't likely to change the outcome. If your party is a majority, it probably isn't by a single vote. So you can spend those resources on the other uses, let everyone else vote, and get a better outcome: the same candidate plus the product of the alternate use.

If you haven't spotted this as a free riding problem yet, where have you been? Because of course, every voter in your coalition wants to get that better outcome, and not enough show up to vote, so you get your least preferred candidate, the one from the other party. Parties help solve this problem, too. They could do it through enforcement, sending party thugs out to force members to the polls, or sending them the next day to "re-educate" those who didn't show up to the polls. That is likely to be very costly, however, not to mention illegal and immoral. It is also likely to negatively affect party membership, which is why we tend to see it only in immoral autocratic regimes which only have one option when it comes to parties, and it really isn't an option.

Instead, parties in democracies respond with mobilization efforts. Some of these are very practically oriented, such as sending busses to pick up voters at retirement homes (or anywhere else a concentrated group of voters with transportation challenges might be). More noticeable, however, are the tones parties and their candidates use. Although the parties are not, in perspective, that far apart on a lot of issues, they do their best to make the difference seem as wide and gaping a maw as possible, so that their partisans see the prospect of the other side winning as more repellant. There's often not a whole lot of difference between what the two parties do once in office, but they make every election seem as if it is a cosmic contest between good and evil, one

---

19 Somehow, it feels as if the voters should be jumping on candidates, but maybe that's just a subconscious response to the quality of most politicians.

20 Though occasionally, the plurality that selects candidates for Presidential elections can select a candidate who alienates the rest of the party, calling this promise into question. Apparently (to borrow from Justice Robert Jackson) party membership isn't a suicide pact, either.

which will determine the fate of the universe.[21] When the stakes are that high, the alternate uses of your time don't look as attractive as saving the universe does. The risk that the other side could win is simply too great.

I mentioned in a previous chapter[22] (and referenced above) that the outcome wasn't likely to hinge on your vote. When we think it is more likely, that is, when an election is close, turnout goes up. So parties will try to make the odds as well as the stakes look greater. It becomes a contest of good and evil, and your vote is crucial to determining whether good triumphs or falls. Everything is a crisis of the highest order.

There are, of course, consequences for using fear as a mobilizer (or motivator). How many times can we fear for the world before we figure out it just keeps spinning regardless? Like the boy who cried wolf, the parties find their credibility in ruins, and they have to go to greater and greater heights to overcome the desensitization they've caused.[23] Not to mention, of course, the actual wolves which go ignored because of their false panic. Moreover, once you've cast an election as good versus evil, and told voters their vote was too important to do without in this critical struggle to defeat evil, they are not likely to understand if you then compromise with the other side. Nor will they understand if you need time to study a problem to find a practical solution. This was a crisis of truth versus perfidy, justice versus injustice—delaying only increases the injustice, and compromising allows evil to prosper.

As a result of all the labeling and rallying, however, parties produce some by-products which have some use in elections. Identifying a candidate's party is a fairly low-cost way of increasing your information about that candidate's preferences. Seeing a "D" or an "R" next to a candidate's name won't tell you everything they stand for (if a politician can be said to stand for anything); there is a great deal of variation within parties, even if the pep-rally atmosphere tends to obscure it. That single letter, however, significantly improves the accuracy of your guesses about what policies the candidate favors. It at least lets you know which side of the spectrum you're working with. One letter is very low cost for that quantity of information. Voters can use it as an heuristic, a way of making a decision with little information.

You may have heard of someone using a "rule of thumb," a rough guide to making decisions. It will not always produce the correct or best decision—remember, you're working with limited information, and the part you don't know could radically alter your decision, if you knew it—but it is a way of making a quick and good enough decision with the information you have. Sometimes we cannot wait for complete information, or cannot get it at all. Why? You know the answer: information is costly to obtain. The origin of the term "rule of thumb" gives an indication of exactly how rough a guide it is. In the Middle Ages, English common law allowed a husband to beat his wife with a stick, so long as the stick was no greater in diameter than his thumb. Setting aside the immediate horror of this first sort of roughness to the guide, we see the second roughness, meaning "not fine or detailed." The law did not define the thickness of the stick in precise and consistent units, to the extent these existed. No one had precise measuring instruments with them, even if they could have read them or done the math. It was a way to distinguish, based on the limited information available the person making the decision, what was legal and what was not.[24]

---

21 When really not much at all is affected. Be honest, name one way your life was tangibly different the day after a Presidential election, as a result of the election. More appropriately, name one way four years in your life under one President was different than four years under the President before or after, because of the change in President.

22 You may remember it; it's the one just before this one. (That's Chapter 9, if you are unable to operate a table of contents.)

23 Much like drug addicts.

24 Leaving aside, of course, what was moral and what immoral. Sadly (and shockingly), this probably seemed a reform to improve the lot of wives by limiting their husbands' brutality to "reasonable" levels. Progressive liberals should now be torn between denouncing that brutality and denouncing the use of modern moral standards to judge a different time and culture. They probably *aren't* torn, because they happen to share the modern sensibilities in question—after all, we've progressed since then—and it's only wrong to judge another culture if you're not a Progressive. Regardless, using force to bludgeon someone weaker into getting your way is wrong, whether you use a stick or a ballot box. It's bullying, pure and simple and wrong, no matter the time or the place. This shows us again the moral hazard involved in possessing overwhelming force; unrestricted by institutions (formal or informal), husbands metaphysically abused their advantages and physically abused their wives. We see, too, the operation of both informal (morals, social opprobrium) and formal (laws) in altering that behavior (or failing to do so).

We sometimes form bad heuristics, too. We can mistake our partial information for being more complete, or mistake it for being representative when it is in fact highly unusual, or even misperceive and misinterpret what information we do have. These produce prejudices, stereotypes, and superstitions. Like any other tool, they require constant re-evaluation, questioning whether they still work, or if they ever did in the first place. Use them cautiously.

Back to our letters "D" and "R." To give a positive example, you may have seen people in supermarkets or grocery stores flicking one end of a watermelon or smelling a cantaloupe. They are trying to use limited information—the sound the flick produces, the strength and flavor of the odor—to find the best produce. No one has full information about the quality of the part of the melon we eat (the inside) until they cut it open. Since they can't do that without purchasing it first, they are using an heuristic about the sound or smell to choose melons which are more likely to be ripe or have better flavor. I have found, for example, that bags of clementines smell of ammonia shortly before mold becomes visible; the smell lets me make a decision with little information (a sniff). Party labels, the "D" and "R" which inform us about a candidate's allegiances, function as the same sort of smell test.

Last (and honestly, least), party labels provide some means for collective responsibility. The idea is that it is difficult to know which individuals are responsible for a bill becoming a law. We've discussed this before in some chapter. Let's say that sixty-five of a one-hundred-person legislature approves a law. Are all sixty-five at fault? Maybe. We do not usually get a chance to punish more than one of them at the ballot box, however. And that may not be fair; they may have used their agreement to moderate the bill, keeping it from being worse, and thus deserve our praise and our vote toward re-election, not our criticism and removal for office. Similarly, they could have been the sixty-fifth person, who just agreed in order to get something for our district, since the bill was going to happen with or without them.

In this sense, public trust or confidence is something of a common pool resource. All of them contributed in some measure to consuming a little of that trust by producing the bad bill, but none of their individual contributions was sufficient by itself to cause the overconsumption of it. They have each written a check drawing on a common account; individually, the checks are small and well below the balance. Together, they are a sum greater than the balance. They each wrote their individual checks at the same time as the others. So which one is the check that caused the overdraft? All, and none. But we can only punish individually, so it must be none.

Except, of course, that we have the party label. Whichever party was in the majority is responsible; now we have an "all" to punish. Except, of course, that we don't. We usually re-elect ours, and vent spleen at the party generally. Because party discipline[25] is low in the United States, it often doesn't make sense to punish everyone in that party. In the United States, parties usually need their incumbents more than their incumbents need them. It is candidates, individuals, who are on the ballot, not parties. Parties help organize and fund campaigns, but at the end of the day, it is the candidate who decides to run, and if so, under which party's flag. As a result, parties often allow or even encourage their legislators to vote with their constituency in mind, rather than with the party, where voting with the party will cost them re-election to their seat.

In parliamentary and proportional systems, this is usually reversed. In most parliamentary systems, it is the parties who decide who will run. In the United States, candidates may seek the nomination of a party. In the United Kingdom, candidates must have the nomination of a party to even stand in the election. To give you an example, Joseph Lieberman was a popular U.S. Senator from Connecticut, and Al Gore's running mate in his 2000 bid for the Presidency. In 2006, he was defeated in the Democratic primary in Connecticut for re-election to his Senate seat. He ran as an independent in the general election and won. In the United Kingdom, another party would have had to nominate him, and even had a smaller party done so, he would have been less likely to win, because voters want to contribute to deciding which party will be in the majority (and thus, which party's leader will become prime minister).

---

25 The ability of a party to get its members in the legislature to vote as the party wishes. Thankfully for all concerned, it involves no paddles and only metaphorical whips. (And the whips in the metaphor aren't even those kind of whips. They refer to whippet hounds, used in fox hunting to herd the quarry.)

This focus on parties is only stronger in proportional systems (and keep in mind, systems may be both parliamentary and proportional), where voters usually cast their votes for parties, rather than for candidates. In a party list system, the candidate owes her seat entirely to the party. Parties make a list of candidates, and voters vote for parties. Parties get seats in the legislature in proportion to the votes they receive as a percentage of the total number of votes cast. They then seat candidates from the list, beginning with the first one on the list, until they run out of seats. In a party list system, the candidate owes her seat entirely to the party, and the party's control of its list (and the order of names on it) makes party discipline high. There is no competing constituency interest. So in our hypothetical one-hundred-person legislature, the sixty-five legislators voted in favor of the government's proposal because the government is made up of their parties' leaders (and it probably is a coalition government). If we do not like it, we know exactly the parties to blame (and thus, to punish electorally). Conversely, if we like the law, we also know which parties to credit (and thus, to reward electorally).

I mentioned (parenthetically) that the government is a proportional and parliamentary system[26] was likely to be a coalition. This is because proportional electoral systems tend to produce more than two parties. Plurality systems tend to produce two parties. You already know why this is so, unless you skipped Chapter 9.[27] In a plurality system, the candidate with the most votes wins. As a result, voters seek to influence the difference in votes between the candidate in first place and the candidate in second. Voting for a candidate with less support means having to get that candidate's vote total ahead of the second-place candidate, and then getting them ahead of the first-place candidate. Since the second-place candidate is already in second place, he is best placed to overtake the leader, and since the first-place candidate has the most votes, she is best placed to win. If the voter prefers the first-place candidate, he will add to her vote total. If he prefers the second-place candidate to the first-place—even if he prefers others over the second-place—he will vote for the second-place as his best chance of defeating the first.

This concentration of votes on the two most prominent candidates results in two prominent parties. The lack of this incentive means that votes are more dispersed; because the third-place party will probably get some seats, there is a prize for finishing third or even fourth. Voters do not feel their votes are wasted if they cast them for a third or fourth party, and so we see more than two effective parties. Other factors influence this as well. For one, a single, nationally contested office (such as the President of the United States) tends to concentrate votes on fewer parties, because only one party candidate (and thus, one party) can win. Federalism can allow regional parties to thrive, even if they have minimal success at the national level. The same is true of geographically concentrated ethnicities or nationalities, which often prompt the adoption of federal forms of government. In the United States, we see a federal system, but one with a plurality rule and a nationally elected office. We also see two effective parties. In Canada, we see a plurality rule, but not nationally elected office, and federalism along with at least one geographically concentrated ethnicity, the Quebecois. Canada tends to have three or four parties in its parliament. The United Kingdom has plurality, no nationally elected office, and no federalism, but it has multiple geographically concentrated ethnicities (Welsh, Scot, Northern Irish), and so tends to have about five parties in its Parliament (at least, recently).

If you've been paying attention, you've noticed that I have often qualified the term "party" with some version or near-synonym of the word "effective." I tell you that we have effectively two parties, or two major or prominent parties, or two effective parties in the United States, the Democrats and the Republicans. I have already mentioned at least two others, the Libertarians and the Greens, so (if you have been paying attention and can do simple math) you should already know that we have at least four parties. In fact, we have a lot more: a Socialist Party, a Communist Party, and National Socialist Workers Party, a Constitution Party . . . if the number of parties we have is anything by which to judge, we have taken Jefferson's admonition about pursuing happiness all too literally. But then, they're not that kind of party, are they?

---

26 Again, just to make sure we're clear: notice that these describe separate, if complementary, aspects of a system of government. "Proportional" describes the electoral system, the way votes are translated into seats (and candidates into incumbents). "Parliamentary" refers to the structure of power in the government, whether it is divided between separate institutions or not. ("Federal" would describe another aspect, whether power is divided across levels or not.)

27 I know; you were just about to read it.

Well, most aren't. Britain does have a Beer Lovers' Party, and Germany has a Pirate Party (which has actually won some seats in regional elections). My favorite is still Canada's Rhinoceros Party. They advocated switching to driving on the left-hand side of the road (as they do in Britain), but they planned to phase it in gradually, staring with lorries.[28] They declared war on Belgium after Tintin (the eponymous character in a Belgian cartoon) killed a rhinoceros, but offered to cease hostilities if the Belgian embassy sent over a case of Belgian beer.[29] They proposed to make illiteracy Canada's third official language. There's more; I highly recommend the Wikipedia entry on them.

All of these parties get winnowed by their chances to win. As their popularity and electoral rules make it more likely that they will finish with some sort of role, the more effective they become. The rules influence how close to first they have to finish to have some role, and their popularity influences how close to first they do finish. As a result, in the United States, we have two effective parties, parties which play a role in government.

The influence of popularity was self-evident. We are talking about something called popular elections, after all. Maurice Duverger[30] is famous for stating the relationship with the electoral rules, though he regarded it (probably rightly) as something already discovered. Asked to state a law of political science as regular and dependable as the laws of physics, he offered the statement (since known as Duverger's Law) that plurality electoral rules tend strongly to produce two effective parties. He considered the corollary that proportional systems tend to produce more than two effective parties to be slightly less well established, but still a very regular empirical outcome.

We discussed how plurality rules tend to produce more wasted votes in relation to the median voter theorem in Chapter 9. We also discussed how this influences them to at least campaign (and to some degree to govern, since they eventually face re-election) toward the median voter. This produces very similar positions, even if (as we discussed in this chapter) they have an incentive to make their small differences appear much greater than they are—as the difference between right and wrong, or good and evil.[31] Let's take a moment[32] to look at that left–right spectrum and see if we can get a feel for the ideologies of our parties, and how they stand in relation to each other.

The first thing we must do is add a dimension to our left–right dimension. There is more than one axis along which parties and ideologies differ; in fact, there are at least three useful dimensions for classifying ideologies and policies, though we often collapse them to one. Let's rename our left–right dimension the economic axis, with positions along it indicating how much it is appropriate for the government to intervene in the economy, according to the ideology. From the center, such intervention (minimum wages, hiring restrictions or requirements, taxes, for examples) is less favored as we move left, until we reach the extreme end, at which an ideology holds that no intervention is appropriate. As we move from the center right, intervention in the economy is more favored, until we reach the extreme, where the government completely controls the economy.[33]

We must yet add a vertical dimension.[34] The vertical dimension is the extent to which government should determine social relations. The bottom end is no government involvement in social matters (such as defining

---

28   "Lorries" are what we south of the border call "semis" or "tractor trailers" or "eighteen wheelers."

29   Which, proving that Belgians are capable of subtle humor and great civility, the Belgian embassy promptly did.

30   He was French, so it's pronounced something like "doo-vare-zhay," not "doo-ver-jer."

31   Again, focus on what they do, not what they say. Words are cheap; actions cost something. A Democratic President and Congress bailed out Wall Street, supposedly the bastion of the Republican Party. Republican George W. Bush pushed for and signed into law an education bill sponsored by Ted Kennedy (the poster child for liberal Democrats at the time). Democrat Barack Obama used a health care system produced and instituted at the state level by a Republican, Mitt Romney (and Romney later campaigned against that plan). A Republican instituted waterboarding as an interrogation tactic, and a Democrat who campaigned on the brutality and uselessness of the tactic merely reduced (rather than eliminated) it. Do I have to keep going?

32   Okay, a lot of moments.

33   If you remember our discussion of decision making rules (and why wouldn't you?), there is a relationship here. Think of this as deciding the degree to which economic decisions are made individually versus collectively, where government intervention means a greater degree of those decisions are made collectively (through government).

34   Lest we put Descartes before the horse. (Pen drop; exit stage left)

marriage, regulating speech, or legalizing marijuana), and the top end is complete government control of social issues. Of course, the two are not so clearly separated in real life. For example, taxes make consumption less attractive. Given that consumption often relates (even if it shouldn't) to social status, and that discouraging work can encourage engagement in social relationships (like family and friends, or volunteering), you can see that they are intertwined, at least in terms of consequences. More directly, some taxes—on alcohol and cigarettes, for example—are specifically adopted to discourage consumption, because their consumption produces social ills, rather than to raise revenue (though they do that, too).

At the intersection of these two axes[35] we find the true moderate, someone who believes in moderate regulation of both economic and social issues. A former U.S. Attorney General[36] once compared moderates to dead skunks as the only two things found in the middle of the road. This seems more than a little inaccurate—road kill consists of much more than skunks,[37] and it is found at least as frequently on the side of the road as in the middle. As we discussed previously, our electoral system tends to reward moderation. In fact, most do, but plurality does so to a greater degree than proportional.

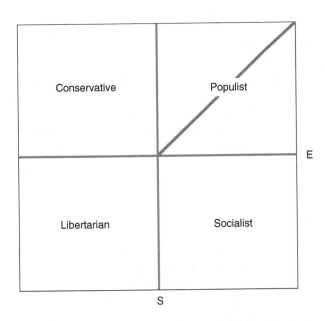

Figure 10.1 The Two-Dimensional Ideological Spectrum

The upper right quadrant (as depicted in Figure 10.1) favors more government intervention in both social and economic issues. This ideological quarter is populism, so called because it favors giving the majority whatever it wants. Since most people seem quite happy to tell others how to live their lives as well as what to do with their money—or have you never gotten unsolicited advice on these subjects?—this means favoring government intervention in both areas, to make you behave. Foreigners, gays, and artists are all disturbing, and must be removed for the sake of communal unity. If they can't behave like everyone else, or speak the same language, they have to learn to do so, or leave. Everybody ought to have a job, so while the young have to pull their pants up and turn their hats around, we have to keep employers from employing foreigners just because they cost less. After all, everyone has to be able to afford homeowner's association dues and keeping their lawns cut. But just because employers have to pay more for labor, they can't charge more for their products.

Yeah, that's probably enough. You probably get the idea: populists want to use government to make everyone behave the way they're supposed to (as decided by populists). If we drew a line bisecting the quadrant from the origin[38]—dividing it into two equal triangles, with the bisecting line as the hypotenuse of both—those above the line would be those who define how one ought to behave in terms of tradition. Those below it (but above our "E" axis) would tend toward defining "ought" in terms of social justice, rather than (social)

---

35 "Aks-eez" is the plural of *axis*, not the plural of *axe*, the thing you use to chop down a cherry tree (at least, if you want to become President as a result). Sadly, both plurals are spelled the same. Yay, English!

36 John Ashcroft.

37 Deer, possums, squirrels, John Ashcroft's political career, raccoons, dogs, cats, some birds and (in some parts of the country) armadillos are on the menu. Possums are probably the most frequent fatalities, at least in Tennessee, though that's a guess based on anecdotal evidence. Still, possums faint as a defense mechanism, so they are less evasive than the others, in general. Plus, when armadillos moved into Tennessee, the locals referred to them as "possum on the half-shell" when they saw them on the side of the road, perhaps indicating that possums are the first to come to mind. Or that opossums and armadillos have the same basic silhouette. Whichever.

38 The spot where the axes intersect.

tradition. This is the area in which we would find progressives, early twenty-first as well as early twentieth century versions.

Diametrically opposed, in the lower left quadrant, we find libertarians. Technically, this should be the liberal quadrant, in terms of classical liberalism, which is how the term is used still in Europe. In the United States, however, what we call liberals are the result of a liberal party absorbing a populist party, producing what we distinguish (in the United States) as modern liberals. The merger of those two ideologies pulled those liberals into the lower right quadrant.

Classical liberals, or libertarians, value individual liberty (thus both of their names). They want as little government as possible (though defining that point proves it to be something of a moving target). At its extreme, it becomes anarchism, the belief that no government at all is best, that any use of force is illegitimate and therefore invalid. There is, however, a great difference between the central parts of each quadrant and their most extreme points. Bottom line: classical liberals do not believe in letting everyone do whatever they individually want to do—that's anarchism. Classical liberals believe in having as much liberty for each individual as possible, that government should only regulate behaviors which have negative effects on others—which produce real, not imagined, injuries.

Modern liberals, who are in the (lower right) socialist quadrant, argue that economic opportunity affects how much one actually *is* free to do as one wishes. Someone who cannot afford to lose his job is at the mercy of his employer, who may demand all sorts of unreasonable things of his employee so long as his employee has no other option for employment. Of course, sometimes the shoe is on the other foot, as when the best and most popular athletes are free agents. Then the employee has leverage over the employer, because the employer cannot easily find someone who will do the job (either on the field or in marketing) as well. More common, however, is the situation in which the employer can find similarly capable people who would take the job for less (or with all of the onerous impositions: think Bob Cratchit) because it beats their current alternative (unemployment and no income). Thus they favor intervention in the economy to keep employers from having too much power over employees, and to keep as many people as possible from the powerlessness of poverty.

Of course, since the majority of people are employees rather than employers, and most of us aren't as wealthy as we think we ought to be (or in comparison to the neighbors), you can see how these positions have some affinity with populism. Hopefully, you can see from the previous paragraph that they are focused on empowerment, which is related to liberty. Think of it as the ability to make good use of your liberty. At the extreme of this ideological quarter we find communism. You've probably heard that term used quite a bit, but rarely accurately. Communism advocates intensive government intervention in the economy, abolishing private property so as to empower everyone. Interestingly, this empowerment is supposed to lead to the government withering away and dying off, as people live in harmony together (having achieved a harmony of all of their interests through the abolition of private property). You may recognize this as anarchism, the extreme of the libertarian quadrant. In practice, however, it looks like the extreme of the populist quadrant, which we haven't discussed yet (and won't just now, either).

That leaves just the upper left quadrant, nationalism. Ideologies in this quadrant tend to favor more economic freedom, but stricter social control. That social control often focuses on (or through) an ideal of what people should be like, and usually defines "society" in terms of a nation (and thus, ethnicity). Think of descriptions of ladies and gentlemen that you often hear: a gentleman always does X, a gentleman should never do Y. Now substitute some nationality for the lady or gentleman in the commandment, and imagine using government to make people observe their manners. This should bring to mind a word we haven't used yet: conservative. Just as classical liberals and modern liberals (or social democrats, in Europe) are in the corner of the libertarian and socialist quadrants, respectively, so conservatives are in the corner of this quadrant nearest the origin.

Conservative, on its own, just means to keep what is worth keeping, to not make rash exchanges of what theory says should work for the what practice already shows does work. We test first and move slowly, to avoid unforeseen pitfalls. Change should be slow and considered. To see the benefits of this approach, consider the Hippocratic Oath. Doctors take this oath, and its first tenet is "first, do no harm." The Food and Drug Administration moved slowly in approving thalidomide as a treatment for morning sickness until it could test it and make sure it was safe.

Pregnant women who could afford to rushed to other countries to buy it, and experienced what the FDA eventually found: though thalidomide is very effective at controlling morning sickness, it causes birth defects (generally missing or underdeveloped appendages). For the drawbacks to this approach, see the history of civil rights in the United States, but especially the "Letter from the Birmingham Jail" by Martin Luther King, Jr.

Of course, the things we wish to retain are often rooted in social traditions, and society seen at a national level. Change is disruptive, and should be governed and regulated, so that we preserve good social order while it happens. In fact, this valuing of social order is common to the top quadrants, just as valuing freedom is common to the bottom ones. At the extreme of nationalism, we find authoritarianism, the desire for the principled knight on horseback to restore order and national pride, which the bickering and dithering of elected officials either can't save, or are the very things endangering order and pride.

Where the ownership of property is highly concentrated, the strongman restores order and protects economic liberty, because it leads to prosperity, and that prosperity is highly concentrated in his supporters' hands. Since Deng Xiaopeng, China has become more nationalist and less communist. There is a combination of nationalism and socialism, however, and it is the extremity of populism: national socialism. You may not have read enough history to understand why that extreme (like all of the others, frankly) is so blood-chilling. You have probably heard the word "Nazi" tossed around, probably far too casually.

You may not, however, understand that the word "Nazi" is shorthand, an abbreviation, for the National Socialist German Workers' Party (in German, the Nationalsozialistiche Deutsche Arbeiterpartei, or NSDAP). In German, the first syllable of "national" is pronounced "nahts," and the "i" on the end (pronounced "ee") makes it a member of that group, or an adjective (sort of like the "n" on the end of "American"). So whereas socialism seeks to organize the economy to protect workers of all nations, national socialists want to organize the economy and society for the benefit of their nation, at the expense of others if need be. Their national is special, deserving of special protection.

People often claim that Hitler was some rhetorical genius, that he wove some spell on his audiences. The truth is less mystical and much more frightening. Hitler was somewhat spastic in his movements, and he had an Austrian accent that most Germans found (and find) somewhere between amusing and annoying.[39] It wasn't how he said it, it was what he said. He told the public that their troubles weren't their fault, that government (in his hands) would make Germany great again, would restore them and their nation to their rightful prominence in the world. He would create social order and economic prosperity, and get rid of those who didn't fit in and wouldn't get in line. He would squeeze those who had been getting more than their share of the benefits, the rich exploiters who owned capital.

We all like to hear that it isn't our fault, that we deserve better, that someone else will take care of it for us. Think of every diet pill you've ever seen hawked on television: it's not your fault, you deserve better, this one pill will solve the problem for you. Or every beer commercial you've ever seen: you deserve a reward for your hard work, and this beer will make your life full of attractive people, laughter, and good times.

The attempt to control both social and economic spheres produces a type of government known as totalitarianism.[40] A totalitarian government is one which encompasses all of society, or the totality of life. All relations must run through the government. If individuals form relationships directly to other individuals, they create smaller societies, which may come to command their loyalty. The state, however, must be the only entity to which the individual feels loyalty, or at least, that loyalty must always come before any others. If it does not, then citizens will not act as they are supposed to, and society will not be able to achieve its promised (and deserved) glory.[41]

---

39 I'm not saying they are right to view it that way, just that they do. (But they are.)

40 Hannah Arendt seems to have been the first to use this term. See Hannah Arendt, *The Origins of Totalitarianism* (New York: Harcourt, Brace, Jovanovich, 1973).

41 Fed. 10 should be echoing in your head: "the public good is disregarded in the conflict of rival parties," so government must "break and control the violence of faction." Note, however, that this is only an echo; Madison rejected the totalitarian solution to the problem. Plato, however, strongly endorsed it in *The Republic* (in fact, he created the first model of a totalitarian government).

The only way to avoid this, of course, is for the state to organize all facets of life. The state will assign you a job, the state will assign you a spouse, the state will decide what you need, the state will lead you in calisthenics so that you will be fit for service to the state. In fact, that may provide a better window: all that an individual does should be in service to the state, whether it be matrimony, procreation, education, labor, recreation, worship, art, or any other part of human existence.

As we have already discussed, the social and the economic are intertwined. Complete control of one requires complete control of the other. Complete control of the economy, for example, means that the state determines your job and your wages. This means, it must determine your education, to make sure you are fit to your duty. You job and your wage have an effect on your social standing in most societies. Even in a Communist state, some jobs are more important or prestigious than others, more directly related or more central to economic control, have more rewards and more status. That status then creates a social power. But more than this, the state must control the social, as well. If left free to think, speak, and associate as you will, you may form other loyalties, and this will interfere with economic control. As a result, Communist governments tend to be totalitarian, as well.

The intertwining of economic and social issues should play out the same for nationalist extremism, as well. Most modern authoritarian governments have seemed comfortable emphasizing national character and patriotism (loyalty to country) only to the extent necessary to squelch questions about their place as rulers. That is, they are not often so extreme in their nationalism, but find it a convenient and cynical tool to promote their ends, which are personal enrichment and empowerment, rather than national interests. To some extent, this is because a king needs a country rich enough to support him. If he is so shortsighted as to squeeze too hard, he reduces the wealth from which he skims.

I would hazard a guess, however, that it reflects something else as well. Vaclav Havel describes a similar circumstance, which he refers to as post-totalitarianism, in Communist Czechoslovakia. Communist ideology had become a cynical practice, used to justify the rule of the rulers. The real sin was to question that rule. I think perhaps we let ideology carry us to extremes—if an idea is good, more of it must be better, and even more of it best—only to find out that each extreme requires the sacrifice of some other value. In fact, it requires the complete sacrifice of all other values,[42] which we call "values" for a reason—they have some. I value freedom, but it does not exist without some sort of order. When we discover the horror of life without those other values, perhaps we learn not to let them carry us too far, lest we exceed the precipice.

I can think of one historical example of nationalism taken to the extreme, but I am not so familiar with it as to even be sure that it is such an example, let alone that it confirms the idea that complete social control implies (and requires) complete economic control. The example I have in mind is Napoleonic France. I suspect Napoleon found it necessary to exert a great deal of control over the economy, both to ensure citizens lived up to their duties, as well as to ensure the availability of resources for his army as they attempted to bring the glories of the French nation to all of the poor, suffering nations around them.[43] I will leave it to you to consult French history sufficiently to confirm or contradict this guess.

Well, that certainly led to some dark places. It turns out humans together are stronger, but no less human: well-intentioned, misguided, fallible. Ideas, like fire, can warm us and protect us, but with too much fuel, they can destroy us. That reminds me; I've still never explained to you the title of this book. George Washington is supposed to have said (or written) that government, like fire, is a dangerous servant and a fearful master. Historians have found no records of Washington actually making this observation, and attributions of it to him are (if I remember correctly) all well after his death, suggesting that someone simply borrowed his name to add authority to their own statement.

Still, it makes the perfect example of what we were just saying: someone lying about the authorship of a statement to get others to accept it more readily. I imagine they felt the message so important as to justify the

---

42   Remember Hobbes and his sacrifice of everything for the sake of order?

43   For a great song expressing the exhaustion this nationalism caused, listen to "Done with Bonaparte" by Mark Knopfler (from the album *Goldenheart*).

falsehood. Regardless, I offer it to you on its own merits: that government is meant to serve us, but because it is power in the hands of humans, we must be ever vigilant to keep it within its proper and useful bounds, lest we become its servants. And since we have been talking about some of the dark materials of democracy, about the danger and necessity of people united and actuated by some common impulse of passion, let us continue in the next chapter with other mortal instruments: interest groups.

By the way, if you're interested in more reading on classical liberalism, try *On Liberty* by John Stuart Mill; if the more modern libertarianism appeals to you, try *Anarchy, State, and Utopia* by Robert Nozick. If you're interested in modern liberalism, *A Theory of Justice* by John Rawls will probably appeal to you. For conservatism, you'll want Edmund Burke, *Reflections on the Revolution in France* (on the subject of the French Revolution, though, I highly recommend *The Ancien Regime and the Revolution* by Alexis de Tocqueville). For communism, *The Communist Manifesto* by Karl Marx and Friederich Engels is your best bet (Marx's *Capital* is not for the feint of heart). If you'd like to hear the positive case for political machines, I recommend Jonathan Rauch's *Political Realism: How Hacks, Machines, Big Money, and Back-Room Deals Can Strengthen American Democracy.*

Chapter 11: Interest Groups

Interest groups, like parties, have a deceiving name. Parties are in fact no fun, and interest groups are rarely interesting. Unless, of course, they are advocating for (or against) one of our interests. Even then, though, they're hardly fascinating. Except, of course, in the way we have a morbid fascination for car wrecks. Try to tap into that interest while we're discussing them. Just don't clog traffic while you're doing it.[1]

Why do we have interest groups? They are quite explicitly what James Madison named a faction, "a number of citizens, whether amounting to a majority or minority of the whole, who are united and actuated by some common impulse of passion, or of interest, adversed to the rights of other citizens, or to the permanent and aggregate interests of the community." So what do all those words mean?

Start with "a number of citizens." That's simple enough: some amount of people. It doesn't matter if the group is small, or even if it consists of a majority of the citizens ("whether amounting to a majority or minority of the whole"). What matters is that some common interest brings them together, and that they pursue that interest together ("united and actuated by some common impulse of passion, or of interest"). In fact, the interest doesn't have to be actually in their interest; notice that Madison first lists a common impulse of passion. An interest would be a considered position, something you have investigated and found to be to your benefit. An impulse of passion is a momentary fever, something you don't take time to consider fully. Like the sirens calling sailors to the rocks in the Rhine, however, it may only appear to be in your interest, right up until you discover your ship wrecked. The point is that they want something, whether rationally or not, and they are prepared to purse that happiness by combining forces.

So far, so inspirational: people are coming together to pursue their common interests and desires. Does anyone else feel the need to teach the world to sing, possibly in perfect harmony, or to buy the world a Coke? Turn the kumbaya down a few notches, Judy, and look out, Sunshine, because here's the punchline: their common interest or desire is common to them, but not to everyone else. In fact, the happiness their group is pursuing damages either the common interest of another group, or interests which are common to everyone, shared by the community as a whole.

Think of a football team. Each player has individual interests; let's say putting up impressive individual statistics, whether for pride or for leverage in contract negotiations. Each player also shares in the interests of the team as a whole, winning games. If the players pursue their own interests, the team usually loses. Or, as Madison said, "the public good is disregarded in the conflict of rival parties." They sacrifice what is good for the whole team to what is good for them individually.[2]

Note too that there can be direct conflict between one interest group and another. They may want something that comes from someone else, whether by physically transferring a resource from one person's hand to

---

1 Rubbernecker.

2 This, by the way, is why Lionel Messi is indisputably the greater football player than Cristiano Ronaldo. One makes his team better by (literally) passing up chances for individual glory, while the other sees his teammates as existing only to hold the ball for him briefly while he runs toward goal so they can pass it back to him.

another's, or whether by sticking them with bill. Surely you've noticed toddlers who only want a toy because someone else has it, or people who are only interested in dating someone if they're already dating someone else. Aside from sociopathy, however, there's always someone who has something you want (a Ferrari, a nice house, inner peace), and somebody who wants something you have. This is the principle that makes markets, from stock to flea, when exchange must be voluntary. What about if, instead of having to offer them something they want in return, you can just have someone take it from them and give it to you?[3] In other words, that's economics—what about politics?

Well, in democratic politics, they just have to have more votes than you do. Then they can take your family home from you, because they'd rather have a shopping mall (or a pharmaceutical plant[4]) there. We all have a little tyrant in us, and if we get together with a bunch of like-minded people, then it ceases to be just our crazy pet peeve and becomes the public interest. (We very easily forget the difference between "everyone" and "everyone I know.")

Take me, for instance. I am a convinced libertarian, and I wish to preserve as much individual liberty as possible. Yet I know what bits of autocracy would tempt me, against all reason or justice. If someone were to propose a ban on SUVs,[5] I would know that I ought to oppose it. It would, however, severely test my principles. There are places where drivers need that type of vehicle, but those places are far from the shopping malls and strip malls and warehouse stores and downtown streets where they roam in packs.

For most of the people who drive them, they are pointless. Minivans would be cheaper, more fuel-efficient, and provide at least as much utility. Most people who drive SUVs have no idea how to handle an oversized vehicle, and drive (and park) them in ways that endanger (or at least impose burdens on) other drivers. People drive them because minivans aren't cool or fashionable, and because their tiny selves feel more secure behind the wheel of a behemoth.[6] Banning them, especially selectively,[7] would probably (certainly arguably) benefit the rest of us far more than it would damage those who buy them.

See how that works? Suddenly it's "us" and "those," and lots of reasons why we should get what we want at the expense of what they want. In the marketplace, those of us annoyed by SUVs could just collect money and pay people not to drive them, or car manufacturers not to make them. That, however, would take a lot of money, even before we get to the sudden increase in the number of people who are going to drive or produce SUVs if we don't pay them.[8] We could, instead, spend the same money forming an organization, and a whole lot less lobbying government to pass and enforce a law getting rid of the pestilential things for us. Then the SUV drivers (and manufacturers) get stuck with some of the cost, and all of us (them included) split the cost of enforcing the ban through our taxes—which means that none of us much notice the change in our tax bill.[9]

Notice that our argument went from "SUVs annoy me" to "SUVs pollute disproportionately, and most people drive so poorly as to endanger others, so SUVs are a danger to everyone else and the planet as a whole." Why do we start framing our desired policy in the public interest, rather than as simply a private interest? For reasons psychological, economical, and political. First, psychological: we see private interest as less legitimate

---

3   One day, we will let my sister forget the time our father overheard her (as a child) tell one of her siblings, "You may as well just give to me, or I'll go and cry to Dad, and he'll make you give it to me." Politics begins early.

4   See *Kelo v. City of New London*, 545 U.S. 469. Or wait for the next chapter.

5   That's short for "sport utility vehicle," though they barely qualify as one of those (at most). A more appropriate referent for the acronym would be "sub-urban vanity."

6   Yeah, it's not just middle-aged guys with muscle cars who over-compensate; petit soccer moms do it, too.

7   For example, allowing them to operate in areas with a high percentage of unpaved roads, with rugged terrain, and exempting the smaller ones, which are essentially compact cars with greater ride height.

8   We would essentially be setting up a blackmail scheme on ourselves, and mailing the incriminating information to everyone. While that would ruin a normal blackmail scheme, this one is even more perverse.

9   Rent seeking? Good call. Magic 8-Ball, will we hear more about rent seeking in this chapter? "Signs point to yes." Will I mercilessly ridicule AARP in this chapter? "Bet on it. Heavily."

than public interest. When the two conflict, the public interest ought to have the greater claim. This makes our cause something right and moral, something that should happen, rather than just our own petty want.

Second, political: the public interest expands our potential support from cranks annoyed by the silly automotive decisions of others to everyone, including the people the change will burden. If it's for their own good, not only do we have greater legitimacy (the psychological reason), we have a claim to everyone's support, including theirs. We have a much larger constituency, making our demands politically stronger, and we simultaneously sap some of the strength from their defense. We have increased our chances of having enough money and votes to make a difference.

Third, economical: the greater the number of people affected, the greater the sum total of the damages which our ban would ameliorate. This makes it more likely that, when assessing the benefits relative to the cost, our policy will have a net benefit. Sure, we'll have to spend money enforcing the ban, but it will save us even more money in the reduction of pollution and accidents. Society will gain more than the SUV enthusiasts will lose, especially if we are able to enact a selective ban (since some of them will not be losing at all).

Some of you may own or drive SUVs (or wish to), and you have spent the last several paragraphs fuming that we'll just see about this ban, because SUV drivers will band together[10] and fight back. You'll not only defeat that stupid ban, you'll make everyone else subsidize your fuel bills. After all, in the event of a Canadian invasion, SUVs will become a vital to our national defense. How else will we get into the hills with our guns, jet skis, memory foam mattresses, Lean Cuisines, and juicers so we can form a resistance?[11]

This is precisely what David Truman says you should do.[12] According to Truman's theory, pluralism, the formation of one interest group provokes the formation of a countervailing one. People organize interest groups to promote their interests, or they organize them to protect their interests from threats (including from other interest groups pursuing their interests). According to pluralism, this is a good and necessary thing in a democracy. The groups represent the interests of citizens, and they compete to obtain policy reflecting those interests. The more broadly shared an interest is, the greater the membership and support for that group. The greater their membership[13] and support,[14] the greater their success. Thus, adopted policy should fairly represent the balance of interests among the public.

Peachy keen![15] Everything is awesome. We're part of the team. Except, of course, that this is built on a couple of assumptions about which we should perhaps not be so sanguine.[16] First, some supporters have more support[17] to lend[18] than others. As E. E. Schattschneider pointed out, people with long last names are really good spellers. Also, "The flaw in the pluralist heaven is that the heavenly chorus sings with a strong upper-class accent."[19] Getting government to pass policies requires resources, two of which are money and time.

---

10 Another pet peeve: people using "ban together" when they mean "band together." Dropping the final consonant implies a few things: people don't read anymore, and they don't listen all that well, either. And the people to whom they listen in large part either enunciate poorly or listen to the same defective echo chamber. I remember watching (and listening) as a sports announcer fumbled the phrase "to get on track," meaning to be back on the proper course, and then hearing it morph over the following months until announcers began saying "to get untracked" as if it meant the same thing—though going off the rails (getting untracked) is precisely the opposite, and considered disastrous, rather than beneficial. We are stupid lemmings. At least, that's what my T-shirt says.

11 You've got the citronella candles, right Caitlin?

12 David Truman, *The Governmental Process: Political Interests and Public Opinion* (New York: Knopf, 1951).

13 votes

14 money

15 Hey, it was published in 1951. I'm allowed to use vintage exclamations for vintage theories. But you can keep your poodle skirt.

16 Not to mention another question. If interest groups are what represent our interests, what are Congresspeople for? (No, the answer is not "target practice." It's a rhetorical question. The point is that we already have a mechanism for aggregating and representing interests.)

17 money

18 donate

19 E. E. Schattschneider, *The Semisovereign People: A Realist's View of Democracy in America* (New York: Holt, Rinehart, and Winston, 1960), 35.

These resources are not evenly distributed. In fact, the wealthy usually have more of both, at least in terms of spending them on this pursuit.[20]

The second problematic assumption is that all interest groups are equally likely to form. This relates to wealth in part, too, but it goes beyond that. The wealthy (at least, as defined in terms of money, and relative to the rest of society) are also fewer in number. Even taking resources out of the equation—a large number of small donations may equal or even surpass one large donation—smaller groups have an easier time overcoming the challenges to organization. It takes time and effort; if we all do our part, that time and effort will be small for each of us. We'd prefer, however, that someone else do all the organizing and lobbying. That way, we have no cost—they bear all of it—and we still get to enjoy the benefits to our group if they are successful. When AARP[21] defends Social Security benefit levels, or gets them increased, it benefits everyone receiving Social Security, whether they invested in organizing the group and funding the lobbying or not.

This is the very definition of a free rider problem, as Mancur Olson points out[22] (or would have, if you hadn't already beaten him to it, right?). If pluralism is correct, then where is the interest group for the very large part of the population getting aarped[23] by the Social Security program? Math tells us that we must reform Social Security, or we will have to bear some exorbitant costs in the future. AARP says they will aarping aarp any and every politician who lays an aarping finger on that program. They do not care what damage this may do to others' interests (eye-watering payroll taxes),[24] or to the interests of the community as a whole (deficits and debt to take the place of those taxes, or cuts to other programs, which Social Security already dwarfs). Those other interests can't form a group to protect themselves, precisely because they are so large. They have more difficulty overcoming the free riding problem.

Of course, AARP says it is acting in all of our interests, aarp you very much. We all hope to become retirees one day, and in the meantime, none of us want our aged and infirm parents moving in with us. So when AARP threatens you with the greypocalypse,[25] it's for your own good, you ungrateful little snot-nosed aarp. They're scaring you straight.

Interest groups, then, are the factions about which Madison warned us, not beneficial or even benign mediums channeling the public interest. They are also, just to be clear, not the associations Tocqueville lauded for helping preserve American democracy.[26] Those associations were nano-governments, groups of citizens organizing to engage in collective action directly. That is, the collective action they organized was not lobbying the government to do something for them. Their purpose was to engage in action themselves, to solve their own problems, together. The difference is that between Habitat for Humanity and the National Low Income Housing Coalition. One makes houses. One tries to get laws about houses made.

---

20   Obvi—the money part is why we call them "wealthy."

21   This used be an acronym for the American Association of Retired Persons, but it is now simply their name: "AARP." It sounds like something an inbred, mentally deficient trolley boy says (or haven't you seen *Hot Fuzz*?). As I write this, their slogan is "You don't know AARP." This deserves to replace "You don't know crap" in the popular lexicon. In fact, the sound "aarp" has a lot of promise as profanity and expletive. Try these out: "You don't know your head from your aarp," or "You know aarp-all about it," or "Get your head out of your aarp." Very versatile. Go back to footnote 15: doesn't "You can keep your aarping poodle skirt" sound better? Aarp right, it does.

22   Mancur Olson, *The Logic of Collective Action* (Cambridge, Mass: Harvard University Press, 1971).

23   Told you it worked. And that it would happen.

24   Look on your pay stub sometime and see how much you pay for the Federal Insurance Contributions Act (probably abbreviated FICA), and then double it. Your pay stub reflects the half of the tax you pay. Your employer pays an equal amount for the privilege of having you on their payroll. Since it is part of the cost of employing you, it would presumably otherwise go to you. This way, however, you never even set eyes on it, so you don't know it's missing. To maintain Social Security as it is, that tax will have to go up.

25   Imagine a world filled with roaming packs of the elderly, looking pitiful and sounding crotchety on all the best beaches and in front of all the good clubs, not to mention hogging all the park benches while they plot with their evil pigeon minions.

26   We talked about this in Chapter 4, remember?

Does all of this seem a little familiar? It should. We discussed rent seeking in Chapter 5,[27] and this is precisely rent seeking. In Chapter 5, we considered it in relation to the Congressperson's district, a geographically defined interest group, for whom the Congressperson is essentially the lobbyist sent to the federal government to obtain benefits.[28] Here we are considering interest groups which define themselves, usually by issue rather than geography[29] as an electoral district.

So why do we have interest groups? You ought to know by now.[30] We do not have them to produce democratic justice or plebiscitary utopia. We have them to make government get stuff we want for us. If we could all promise not to try to get special privileges from government, nor to have it take stuff from other people for us, we could all save a lot of time and effort. Not just save, but redirect it to more productive ends which might benefit everyone, instead of just us. But would you believe that promise? No. And what explains why you can't rely on it? Very good, grasshopper.[31]

So why do they work? How do they get away with this picking of our common pocket for their particular benefits? We talked about that in Chapter 5, too. Part of it is that we hate interest groups generally, but love our particular ones. After all, they're fighting for truth, justice, and the American way.[32] Even were I willing (in the name of truth, justice, and the American way) to refrain from forming or supporting a lobby, I would be irrational to do so. My restraint does not stop others from consuming as much as they can at the all-you-can-spend public trough, so I get essentially the same tax bill. But I get it without receiving the least benefit in return. I give up my concentrated benefit, but still have the same total of dispersed costs, whether simply "to the naked eye" because the reduction is so small, or because another group snaffles up the public spending I was trying to save—you know, since nobody was using it.

Remind you of something? It really should. The public purse is a common pool resource. We may all claim some of it, and no one may be excluded. Since it is a limited resource, no matter how fervently Congress pretends it isn't, the incentive is to use it as much as possible. It's only available while it lasts, and what you don't spend, someone else will. Not using it does not ensure it will be available when I need it. In fact, it more likely assures it won't be. It only becomes mine when I grab it, and the result is the overuse of the resource, and its depletion to the point of disappearance.[33] If that's not a tragedy of the commons, what is?

How do we solve tragedies of the commons? One way was through privatization, but it would be rather counterproductive to divide the common purse up into little bags for everyone. Pooling our money to pay for joint projects, like public goods, is part of the point of having a public purse.[34] We could try to privatize—to internalize externalities—for as many as possible of the public activities for which we spend, but we know that can't be all of them. At the very least, national defense will prove difficult to arrange that way; we know that from our experiences with the Articles of Confederation, aside from the analytical picture.[35]

We could form a government to make, administer, and enforce a set of common rules. Wait—isn't that how we got here? In fact, that's rather part of the problem than the solution in this case. Those enforcers and rule-writers answer to us. If politicians answer to crackheads, crack will never be illegal. Do you start to see why Madison thought this problem so important, and what he meant when he said "mischief"?

---

27 And pluralism, and free riding, and . . .

28 At least, according to popular (and populist) conceptions of their roles.

29 Though the two often correlate, which is why it makes sense to have electoral districts.

30 With apologies to Billy Joel.

31 I'm assuming you said, "The prisoner's dilemma." If you didn't, just change "Very good, grasshopper" to "Where the aarp have you been for the last ten chapters?"

32 Or more accurately, truth as I see it, justice for me, and getting this particular American his way.

33 The national debt is both a tragedy and a farce, but it is also proof that we have not managed our financial resources sustainably.

34 See riding, free.

35 For which I told you it was a poster child.

What we need are two miracles, at least if we plan to solve this problem. First, we need voters who will support—or at least not oppose—changes to the rules. If it is to be the least (not opposing the changes), then we also need this miraculous outbreak of public-spiritedness to extend to elected officials. To put it more plainly, we need citizens and public officials willing to ignore their particular, immediate interests in favor of their shared, long-term interests, who will write (and support) rules which constrain our future selves (and successors) to retain that focus. Fingers crossed, grasshopper.[36]

Second, we need some non-responsive institutions which will continue to enforce and administer those rules, even when they become once again unpopular. Tocqueville discusses this in terms of democracy needing a bit of aristocracy to make it work. The problem is that, when the moment of enlightenment fades, the public goes back to seeing those aristocratic features not as useful and necessary restraints, but as elitist and unfair injustices. When we have institutions which tame the excesses of popular sovereignty, we come over time to take them for granted. We see popular passions showing restraint, and think it is an inherent characteristic, rather than a learned behavior. We no longer see the point of those restraints—see how they chafe the poor tiger's wrists!—and so remove them, only to make dinner of ourselves.

Thus, we must popularly elect Senators. States and party machines just use them to protect their privileges. We must bully the Supreme Court; they are out of touch, the poor, over-worked dears. Don't they know it's a living document they guard, and can't they see how those words are chafing it now that it has grown? As Karl Popper reminds us, the best institutional fortresses still need enough willing souls to man them, if they are to be effective. If we forget why the fortress is worth defending, it does not take long to defeat it. The fault is not in our institutions, but in our selves.

How do we improve ourselves? Education. Duh. Two problems again occur, however. One, education—if you've been paying attention, you know this already—doesn't just happen to you. You have to be willing to learn. And as Tocqueville points out, most people are far too busy chasing material success to be bothered with questions of what they ought and ought not ask of government, or of which government they should ask it.[37] They certainly have no interest in taking the time to inspect themselves and their motives, their values, and their principles, in ways that might lead them to re-evaluate what they should be.

Two, even if they do, there are a great number of values and principles running about. Some may well adopt values which lead them to sacrifice the restraint of government power in order to achieve some goal they (perhaps reasonably) value more, such as equality or order. For examples, see Progressives, progressives, Marxists, Leninists, other socialists, anarchists . . . well, there are a lot of options there. We could require everyone to embrace (or at least, to pretend to embrace) the same values. After all, the Marxists (and Leninists) have tried that, and it worked out so well for them. Practical outcomes aside, it defeats the whole purpose. People must be free to adopt their own values, but we need them to freely adopt at least a couple of common values (tolerance, restraint) in order for this freedom thing to work.

There's not an easy answer. I wish there were; I'd have bottled it and sold it long ago, and be relaxing on my private Caribbean island right now.[38] I think it can boil down to where most such things begin: a group of people willing to model the behavior, willing to explain (without self-righteousness or bitterness or delusion of self or other) why others should join them. Enough people have to be willing to take one or two hundred for the team, and to do so in such a way that the team decides they should do the same themselves, rather than take advantage of it. If that sounds like a recipe for a religion, I'll simply remind you that Tocqueville pointed to religion as the foremost of America's informal political institutions. The law could allow people freedom, because their religion kept them from abusing it.

Right, that's enough Chapter 4 flashback. So here's a little more flashback from Chapter 5. The other part of why interest groups work, or why they are able to engage so successfully in rent seeking, is something we

---

36   But don't hold your breath. Blue's not an attractive color on your lips when it comes from inside.

37   Chapter 3 says hello, and wonders why you haven't called lately.

38   Well, maybe Mediterranean; there's a hurricane going through the Caribbean right now.

covered in our Chapter 5 discussion, as well. The other part of the answer is quite simply the math.[39] The opportunity cost of successfully opposing a particular source of political rent is greater than the amount you will gain if you are successful. Concentrated benefits and dispersed costs allow rent seeking to thrive. Each separate bit of rent-producing capital requires its own individual battle. You cannot fight them all together, so someone has to identify all of the battles, and lead the fight against each one. They would spend thousands of dollars to organize a fight that would get them thirty-three cents back (in our Chapter 5 example). We don't follow people who do that; we medicate them.

Each new battle requires new (if less, since they've already organized the army) expenditure to mobilize their members and overcome free riding. And once they've sufficiently organized the group, they are an effective lobby in their own rights. What will stop them from pursing their own rights? How long can they resist the temptation to use their organized might to get favors of their own, rather than simply remove those of others?

If we could find a way to bundle all the fights together, a way to remove rent seeking in one fell stroke, we could perhaps produce a net gain, rather than a series of noble losses that others will thank us for as they bury us. But that volume discount puts us right back where we were before. It means changing the rules, which is likely to be even more costly. It would also be an institutional change, dependent on customs, values, and principles for its continued existence.

For example, an amendment requiring a balanced budget would require legislators to prioritize claims.[40] The size of the pie would be fixed, so what one group got would necessarily affect what another could get. To avoid electoral punishment, that claim would have to be one generally accepted as more important. Everyone would probably agree that spending to build and maintain roads benefits more people (and benefits them more) than research into crisper pickles. If that stretch of road is the difference in one ambulance getting to one person soon enough rather than too late, it's got the pickles beat, and I don't care how much the extra crispiness increases your enjoyment of the aarping[41] pickles. That amendment, however, would require a lot of time and effort to pass. It would then require the continued support of that value, or it could be repealed or ignored (or, as part of a living document, metastasize into something else entirely).

So how do interest groups work? I'm glad you asked; I needed a good segue to the rest of the chapter.[42] The primary occupation of an interest group is lobbying. "Lobbying" gets its name from the fact that non-members were not allowed in the room where Parliament meets. In fact, they're generally not allowed in most legislative chambers, at least not on the floor; in fact, they're generally not allowed on the floors of most legislatures. This doesn't mean they have to jump from table to table, or use flying rigs to swoop over the heads of legislators.[43] It means they are not allowed in the room while business is being discussed. Well, not in the part of the room where they can interact with the legislators. There are often viewing galleries, but those sitting in the galleries are expected to observe only, and not participate, harangue, or attempt to influence.

Those wishing to speak with their member of Parliament, then—and communicating with them is a necessary precondition to influencing them—had to (and still do, I presume) wait in the lobby, to catch them on their way in or out of the chamber, or during breaks. They had to wait in the lobby, so their attempts to influence legislators became known as lobbying, and they became known as lobbyists, those who lurk in the lobby to waylay unsuspecting legislators.[44] Now we just need to know what they do in those lobbies to influence them.[45]

---

39 And no, math is not your old enemy. It is your misunderstood friend.

40 Several states, including Tennessee, have balanced budget provisions in their constitutions. I wonder if there's a relation between that and the amount of taxing they do?

41 Oh yeah, that's a thing now.

42 Also, I was afraid I might get to stop typing and go home. So happy you asked!

43 Though I think that would generate a fair amount of revenue in most countries.

44 Thanks for making me spell that out.

45 Hey, clean that imagination up right now. I've read those stories about members of Parliament, too, but this is a public place.

Of course, very little lobbying occurs in actual lobbies anymore. Or at least, it no longer occurs only in lobbies. The tools in the lobbyist's arsenal are varied, but they boil down to the same thing: trading money and time for access. Some tools do that directly, some do it indirectly. Direct lobbying usually involves donating money to candidates and incumbents, but the money is not necessarily meant to sway their opinion by itself.[46] The lobbyist probably wouldn't object if it did, but it usually only buys them access to the official. It gets them a spot on the politician's already overflowing calendar. They then use that time to begin a relationship with the office holder.[47] They let the official know how they can be useful to each other. Interest groups use their time and money to get information,[48] too. They can provide office holders not only with campaign donations— well, *they* can't, but they have associates who can—but they can provide information as well, so that the official appears well-informed and competent. In return, the office holder can provide them with legislation they want. In fact, they can also use their time to write the legislation for the legislator, saving them the time and effort.

I call direct lobbying the Vidal Sassoon method: if the official doesn't look good, the lobbyist doesn't look good. Need headliners to appear during your hearings so that (a few more) people will actually watch them on C-SPAN[49] and increase your profile? Done. Want some photo-ops with popular celebrities, to benefit from their reflected popularity? Check. Need some legislation you can sponsor that will get you in good with the folks back home? Got you covered. If you're working with us, we (and our interest) only look good if you do. Like any relationship, this involves trust built through repeated interaction. If the lobbyist pushes too far, or prompts the official to do something which damages her reputation, then it damages her re-election chances and her ability to trust that lobbyist, and thus the lobbyist's ability to do his job.

This is the basis of what used to be known as "iron triangles." The vertices[50] of the triangle were interest groups, legislators, and bureaucrats. Interest groups provided money, votes, and some information (the parts need to make laws) to legislators; they provided information (the parts needed to administer the laws) to bureaucrats. Legislators provided policies to interest groups, and regulatory authority (to implement those policies) to bureaucrats. Bureaucrats provided information to legislators about implementation (reports), and friendly administration of the rules to interest groups. Each point had a mutually advantageous relationship with the other two, and other influences could not pierce the iron bonds encapsulating an issue area within that triangle.

This evolved to a concept called policy networks. Scholars pointed out that there were usually several nodes, rather than three vertices, and that these multiple nodes interacted in much more complex ways. Things were passed from node to node, but the benefit a node received did not always come directly from a node to which it passed resources. In fact, there are multiple access points; there are often several interest groups, several Congressional committees, and several bureaucratic agencies overlapping in the same interest areas, and the same actors interacting across several issues.

This may in part reflect a change in practice, rather than an inaccuracy in the theory. Changes in technology have made communication easier and information cheaper to gather (and disseminate). The federal government has also grown, and therefore the number of agencies and the potential overlap between them (or parsing of issue areas). In fact, part of the network may have stronger local connections, like iron triangles. The two models may be complementary, rather than competing.

Direct lobbying, as you might imagine, requires a presence in the capital (or wherever the legislature meets and the bureaucracy has its offices). Indirect lobbying does not, though it hardly precludes it, either. Indirect lobbying, or grassroots lobbying, requires a presence on the ground, in legislators' districts. The focus of indirect lobbying is to get constituents to pressure legislators to vote in the interest group's favor. This also requires

---

46 That costs more.

47 Eww. Not that kind of relationship. (Usually.)

48 Eww. Not that kind of information. (Usually.)

49 Someone, somewhere is afraid you don't realize this is an acronym for the Cable-Satellite Public Affairs Network. I know I see it in a whole new light now that I have officially not used an abbreviation without first giving its expanded form.

50 The pointy parts—they're triangles, so they have three.

money, this time in order to overcome information cost and free riding among constituents. They first have to know why they should care about the issues, and why they should write or call their legislator. Then they have to spend the time and effort doing the writing or calling (or better, both), when the success of the effort depends on a lot of others doing so as well, and they'll get the same result whether they participate or not.

As you might imagine, this is quite costly, probably more so than direct lobbying. Nor are the two mutually exclusive. An interest group may well pursue both avenues, if it has the money, though it will want to be careful about the kind of constituent pressure it brings to bear on the legislator. Using grassroots pressure tends to damage the relationship direct lobbying seeks to build. Rather than being mutually beneficial, it becomes adversarial. After all, grassroots pressure is essentially a threat—vote as we want, or we'll make your voters vote for someone else. You can see, however, why money is such an important part of the process. Whatever end you wish to pursue, it is the necessary means.

Of course, sometimes groups try to get the appearance of a grassroots campaign without all the expense of running one. These means often reduce the cost of action for the constituent, as well. Take as an example online petitions, or websites that generate an e-mail for you. Legislators may or may not be very bright, but their staff usually notice when they get hundreds (or thousands) of identically worded letters, where only the name and mailing address is different. Since staff and legislators both speak to other staff and other legislators, they will quickly notice they're all getting a robo-letter. Making the cost lower makes it more likely that more people will do it. However, it sends a different signal to the legislator than a personal letter or phone call.

Taking the time to write a letter yourself or make a phone call on your own says that it means at least that much to you—it was worth more time and effort. And if it means that much to enough people, the legislator will have trouble refusing them. If that grassroots support is made of Astroturf,[51] it tells the legislator that people don't care that much. They aren't willing to put more than minimal time and effort where the interest group's mouth is, so the legislator reasonably discounts both the quantity and quality of support.

There is a third means of affecting policy, but it is not really direct or indirect as we have discussed those terms thus far. This is because it does not seek to influence the legislator who makes the law or the bureaucrat who administers it. It seeks to get policies changed or even killed after they have been passed and implemented, perhaps even because of how they were passed or implemented. It is more difficult, more time-consuming, and requires a fair amount of money and fortitude as well. It is less reliable, and less predictable, so it is usually a last resort. This last way is litigation, using court decisions to alter or nullify a policy. As you might imagine, this is less reliable because one has to find the right cases, ones that ask the right questions in ways that encourage the answer you want. It is less predictable, because you are merely putting a question before a judge. The judge may answer in a way you did not anticipate, and it may make things worse for you, rather than better.

You've got to pay a lot of lawyers, or have a cause to which they're willing to donate their time. You've got to track a lot of cases, and you've got to wait until you have the right one, even if it takes it a while to appear. That takes sustained focus, perhaps over decades. When you're talking about something you care about, passing up opportunities because they aren't good enough, when you don't know that another one is coming, requires a great deal of fortitude.

You can probably think of examples of this, challenges which interest(-ed) groups bring against laws, to modify or overturn them. Several cases have presented attempts to have the courts, and in particular the Supreme Court, nullify the Affordable Care Act (you may know it as Obamacare) or modify some part of it. You'll notice that most of those have been unsuccessful, by the way. The best example is one we will discuss in a future chapter,[52] the legal strategy the NAACP[53] pursued to get laws enforcing segregation invalidated.

---

51 The original artificial turf. I wish I could say I came up with using that term for artificial grassroots lobbying, but I cannot. I don't even remember where I first heard it. My gratitude and esteem, however, go to whomever had that brilliant inspiration.

52 I like to call it "Chapter 13."

53 This is an acronym for the National Association for the Advancement of Colored People, an organization so venerable and well-known that everyone just knows it by its acronym. If you really didn't know that, do me a favor and (1) don't vote, until you (2) read a newspaper or a magazine that doesn't have anything to do with celebrities or video games. I promise, these things exist.

In the meantime, back to the theme of this chapter: money, money, money. Please be careful, though, to notice that money is the means, not the end. It just happens to be a means that leads to an awful lot of ends, so it's very popular. While you're at, also take note that money is used for access, for a chance to talk to public officials. Money itself is not the influence, but the means to purchase the chance to influence. Politicians receive donations from groups on both sides of issues, and groups give money to politicians on both sides of the aisle. It only provides access to start a relationship; it is not the relationship itself. That doesn't mean things are rosy; some groups still have a lot more access, whether because they have wealthier donors,[54] or because they have less of a free riding issue. Neither of those causes has anything to do with how good or valid their claims are, and it leave a politician having heard only one side of an issue.

I mentioned before that lobbyists themselves, or lobbying organizations, cannot give money to candidates or their campaigns. They are legally forbidden from doing so, to avoid precisely the appearance everyone seems to assume is true. They are, however, allowed to form political action committees (or PACs) associated with their lobby, which may receive money for the purpose of donating to campaigns, or spending on their own advocacy campaigns (whether advocating for a position or a candidate). There are limitations on how much they may receive from a single donor, and on how much they may give to a single candidate or party committee. Interestingly, according to OpenSecrets.org,[55] the first PAC was formed in 1944 to get around a law forbidding unions from contributing to candidates, so that unions could contribute (technically indirectly) to FDR's re-election campaign.[56]

After all this, are interest groups a good or a bad thing? Well, as for government, the answer is yes. They are a *human* thing, and that makes them subject to the same potential and the same pitfalls as humans. Remember our discussion of rent seeking. Interest groups are a part of the process of some of us getting what we want at the expense of all of us or the rest of us. But they are a part of people influencing their government. As awful as a government torn between hundreds of competing factions can be, it beats the alternative. A government responsive[57] to its citizens beats one which is not; one which is not beats its citizens.[58]

Maybe the fault is not in our interest groups, but in our selves. If we considered what we asked government to do, whether it was right, rather than whether it was in our interest—or maybe, whether it was in our common rather than our particular interest—perhaps interest groups would be lauded for their influence. Of course, that proposes making angels out of men, and history teaches us the futility of that exercise. We can make of them demons, but not angels. So maybe the real question is whether it is possible to limit the responsiveness of government, or to limit the types of stimuli to which it responds.

Remember, that was Madison's project, to create a door they could only get through when they were cooperating, which hopefully meant they were actually pursuing common interest. The more people who agree that liberty must be curtailed, the less likely it is that they mean someone else's liberty. That, for Madison and Locke, was the point of government, after all: to leave people with as much liberty as possible, as much as is consistent with everyone else having the same amount. Let's look, then, at some of the particular liberties the Founders sought to protect, and how that's worked out for them.[59]

---

54   This is not code for "Republicans," either. The Democratic Party has plenty of wealthy individual and corporate donors, too. As much as the media lambaste the Koch brothers, they seem to have no problem with George Soros. In fact, the last numbers I saw showed the Republican Party getting a higher percentage of its funding from small individual donations than the Democratic Party. Granted, that's been a while, and things may have changed. Maybe they haven't. The point is, you shouldn't assume either way.

55   "What is a PAC," www.opensecrets.org/pacs/pacfaq.php. (At least, as of August 3, 2016.)

56   If you missed it from all the other references in other chapters, that's Franklin Delano Roosevelt. Yes, he was a Democrat. Yes, I told you this was not a partisan disease.

57   Note that there is a difference between "responsive" and "responsible."

58   Literally, and not in the sense of "I can dance to it."

59   The liberties, not the Founders. The Founders are too dead to care; let's hope the liberties aren't.

Chapter 12: Civil Liberties

When I say "civil liberties," what do you think of? Liberties, which are very polite and well-mannered? Maybe you think of the Bill of Rights, and for good reason; we will in fact use those rights to focus our discussion. Maybe you think of liberties and rights as interchangeable terms, as synonyms, and so think of civil rights. Maybe you understand how those are connected and think of that connection. Maybe all these maybes mean we should start with defining a few terms.

First, the difference between rights and liberties. A right is something owed to you; a liberty is something you cannot be forbidden. A right is a permission which cannot be retracted or revoked; a liberty is a freedom which cannot be prohibited. It is possible to have a right in your liberties, that is, that you possess your freedom by right, that it belongs to you and cannot be removed. This is why we often think of them as indistinguishable, though it is also possible to have a liberty in your rights, to have the freedom to interpret your rights, to expand or contract them as you see fit.

The difference becomes perhaps a little plainer (and certainly more important) when we add the adjective "civil." *Civil* comes to us from the Latin *civilis*, which is the adjective form of the word *civis*, or citizen.[1] Civil liberties are those freedoms we form a body politic in order to protect, in other words, for which we become a citizen. Civil rights are permissions we acquire as part of a body politic, the means by which citizens restrain government from intrusion in their liberties. They are things we possess because we became a citizen, in order to function as a citizen. Civil liberties produce citizenship, and citizenship produces civil rights.

Conceptually distinct is some distance from practically or actually distinct. Take free speech, for example. The ability to express ourselves is a freedom which we form governments to protect. The ability to express our thoughts regarding the conduct of public affairs, however, is a right we must possess to function as a citizen, and which we only acquire or need in the context of citizenship—when there are collective (public) affairs about which to speak. Some are a little clearer; we do not have a liberty to vote, for example.[2] We neither have nor need a vote until we begin making collective decisions—until we have formed a government. In the same manner, we do not need a freedom of religion to function as a citizen, but it is a liberty which we form governments to protect from others (and for which we require civil rights to protect from government). Civil rights, then, relate to your ability to function and participate in collective decision making. We agree to participate in collective decision making in order to protect our liberties. Thus, the two are linked, even if distinct.

---

1 At least, if the interwebs are to be believed. This explains why you may think of it as "polite and well-mannered." As we discussed in Chapter 4 and recalled repeatedly in the last one, in order to live together, people must be tolerant, restrained, and other-regarding. In other words, being a citizen demands that one should be "polite and well-mannered."

2 At least, not in any meaningful sense. If you're the only person involved in a decision, you can call making your decision "voting," but yours is the only vote.

As I've already threatened,[3] we'll talk more about civil rights in the next chapter,[4] just as soon as you get done reading this one (and I get done writing that one). For now, we need to move to the last of our maybes, the Bill of Rights. Why did you think of the Bill of Rights when I said[5] "civil liberties"? Because if you ask most people to name one of their civil liberties, they will quote some part of the First Amendment to you: free speech, free press, freedom of religion, free nachos with purchase of an entrée.[6] Ironically, in so doing, they are proving correct the argument Alexander Hamilton[7] makes in Federalist 84. Those opposed to ratifying the proposed constitution thought it gave too much power to the federal government it proposed. They pointed to the lack of explicit protections of individual liberty as a reason for voting against it. Hamilton responded that such a bill of rights, a list of personal freedoms upon which government could not encroach, was not only unnecessary, it was dangerous as well.

Let's begin with unnecessary.[8] Hamilton asked, if they were so concerned that the federal government would abuse the freedom of the press, for example, would they please identify exactly which of the powers enumerated in Article I, Section 8 would allow it to do that? This constitution, he reminded them, would create a limited government, one which had only those powers enumerated (or ones necessary and proper to them). Neither *printing* nor *press* was among the permissible objects of federal regulation. Congress could make post roads to improve communication, but that would only increase the circulation of newspapers. Regulating the circulation of newspapers would in no way be necessary to the creation and maintenance of post roads.[9]

Moreover, the body of the proposed constitution already contained particular provisions protecting individual liberty. For example, Congress is prohibited from passing laws which interfere with the obligations of contracts, or passing laws which make something a crime after it has been done (*ex post facto*). Congress was explicitly forbidden from passing bills that declared someone guilty (bills of attainder) or making treason work corruption of blood (disinheriting the children of those convicted of treason, or punishing them as if they were guilty, too).[10] The constitution limits the conditions under which Congress can suspend the right of habeas corpus (which requires authorities to explain to a court why they have you in custody—essentially, it allows the court to force them to bring you to trial or release you) or establish the standards for convicting someone of treason.

It was unnecessary, then to list particular liberties the government could not violate if it did not have the power to violate them. Think of it this way: do you have a dog, or have you ever had one? Maybe you know someone who has or had one? Whatever the case, put yourself in the position of someone who has a dog.[11] Would you tell your dog not to fly? You know, as you're going out the door: be a good boy, don't eat the upholstery, don't drink from the toilet,[12] and whatever you do, don't open a window and fly away? Eating the upholstery, drinking from the toilet; these a dog could (and might) do. Unless our dog fell into that vat of

---

3   Or was that promised?

4   That would be Chapter 13, as the page turns.

5   Okay, *wrote*. Pedant.

6   Okay, so one of those is not in the First Amendment. Please tell me you know which one. And please, please, please—say nachos.

7   Yes, the guy from the musical. Did you know that he was (oddly enough) voted "Least Likely Subject of a Broadway Musical, Aside From Some Lonely Geezer's Cats" in his high school yearbook? Neither did he.

8   In the following, I am very likely to embellish and embroider upon what Hamilton said, for the sake of making his points clearer to you, so that you can understand what he's getting at when you read the original. Make sure you do that, especially so that you do not falsely accuse Hamilton of using some example or phrase of my invention.

9   Remember, this is before John Marshall got hold of the word *necessary*.

10   Someone may wish to explain this to Recep Tayyip Erdogan: guilt is not a disease passed by association or by genes. I'd just explain it from the other side of Turkey's border, if I were you.

11   There's no point in using cats for this example; we all know they do not accept instruction, whether from arrogance or imbecility.

12   Though these are also words for people to live by.

toxic waste in Chapter 5 with you, though, he can't fly. So it would be silly to tell him not to do it. It would be a waste of breath, unnecessary.

Worse than that, it could become dangerous. Being the earnest, trusting creatures they are, if you tell your dog not to fly, day after day, month after month, he may well come to believe he **can** fly. Why else would you warn him, if it weren't something he could do? Even if you forbade him from flying, he could still float down from the roof, or jump over large holes, because those aren't flying (and thus, don't violate your order). If everyone treated their dogs this way, you'd come home to find it had been raining dogs.[13] Likewise, telling the government it can't do one thing may lead it to believe it could do it, and that it can therefore do related things which aren't explicitly denied.

For example, "Congress shall make no law . . . abridging the freedom of speech, or of the press" are two of the guarantees in the Bill of Rights. Congress (or the Supreme Court) could interpret that to mean that the enumerated powers include regulation of speech and printing, when they clearly don't. But the amendment says Congress can't abridge those freedoms, so it must be able to regulate them, so long as it doesn't amount to abridgement (making less by removing parts). These would be police powers, a type of power (general enablement to regulate for the health, safety, and welfare of citizens) which the enumeration of powers precludes. More than that, Congress and Court[14] could read this to say that Congress can't regulate speech or printed words, but it can therefore regulate other modes of expression: songs, paintings, symbols, and so on.

Worse than that, people might come to see that list as the source of their rights. This would mean two things. First, only rights on that list would receive protection, and there is no way to make a comprehensive list. The Founders knew from their own experience with lists (remember the whole reason for the necessary and proper clause?) that you forget some, or take some for granted and don't notice them, or think they are so obvious as not to need saying. You've probably done that with relationships; how'd that work out for you? Right. You found out how important they were when you turned around and they weren't there anymore. Hard to get them back, too, wasn't it? The same is true of your rights.

In fact, this may be the greatest danger of all. The price of liberty, as they say, is eternal vigilance. Turning the protection of your liberties over to a list encourages laziness. You don't have to worry, the list has this for you. You stop paying attention, and you forget what your rights are, why you have them, or why you should fight for them. It then becomes easier and easier to take them from you.

Second, if the list is the whole extent of your rights, then it is easy to confuse it with the source of those rights. Why would our Founders have said you have these rights? Because you're a citizen of the United States? Heaven forbid. Literally. Remember that Declaration-thingy? "We hold these truths to be self-evident, that all men are created equal, that they are endowed by their Creator with certain unalienable Rights, that among these are Life, Liberty and the pursuit of Happiness." You have these liberties by virtue of your membership in the human race, even if their definition of human race needed drastic improvement.[15] Your liberties are the gift of God, and therefore they may not rightfully be removed from you by any mortal means.

If instead the source of your liberties is a list made by men, it can be unmade and altered by men. If a constitutional provision is all that creates your liberty, an amendment to that provision can remove it. If someone[16] licks off the clause prohibiting cruel and unusual punishment, the police then have the right to beat you mercilessly (and in strange ways). If Congress proposes and the States ratify the repeal of the First Amendment, then they can tell you to shut up about their job performance, and get your aarp to church, and quit hanging out with all those no-good, shiftless rabble-rousers you call friends.

Madison agreed that a bill of rights was probably unnecessary, but he did not see the downside being quite so steep. As a compromise, he promised to introduce in the First Congress proposals to amend the

---

13 Or cats and dogs, I suppose, if the cats thought they had to show the dogs the correct way to jump off of roofs, or if the cats were chasing the reflection flashing from the dogs' name tags, or thought it was the latest fashion.

14 Especially if the chief justice were John Marshall.

15 Next chapter.

16 Homer Simpson.

Constitution to clarify the limitations of Congress' power in relation to individual liberty, if the Constitution were ratified. A man of his word, Madison proposed around twenty alterations to the Constitution on June 8, 1789. According to the records of the debate,[17] Madison had attempted to bring up this item of business before, but had been asked to wait, since the government wasn't even fully operational at that point (meaning that more important business had yet to be finished). Madison pointed out that some states were delaying their ratification until this condition was met,[18] so the union itself would not be finished if they didn't get to this business.[19]

The exact number or amendments Madison proposed is a little difficult to pin down, because he anticipated that the changes would be incorporated in the body of the Constitution. Instead, we record amendments as codicils, or supplemental material, which we simply append to the Constitution to modify or enlarge its text. Madison grouped his proposed changes into nine proposals, but they are not what we would call nine amendments. For example, one of the proposals was to renumber Article VII as Article VIII, because an earlier proposal would have inserted a new article (which would have then been the seventh article) before it. Madison's proposals are grouped not by the type of liberty, but by the part of the Constitution which they would alter. Many of the clauses in the Bill of Rights (the name we give to the first ten adopted amendments to the Constitution) are in his proposal to insert additional clauses into Article I, Section 9, the part of the Constitution which says what Congress is not allowed to do with its powers (which are enumerated in Article I, Section 8).

Madison had intended for the entire House of Representatives to consider the changes, as a committee of the whole,[20] but yielded to objections and proposed the creation of a committee to consider them. The committee eventually produced seventeen proposed amendments, which the House approved. The Senate eliminated some and combined others, reducing to twelve the number proposed to the states for ratification. Ten of these twelve were ratified at the time, and an eleventh was ratified in 1992 as the Twenty-Seventh Amendment (the most recent). These included what became the Ninth Amendment, which was meant to ameliorate the concerns Hamilton had raised: "The enumeration in the Constitution, of certain rights, shall not be construed to deny or disparage others retained by the people." Madison's original words were much clearer, if greater in number: "The exceptions here or elsewhere in the constitution, made in favor or particular rights, shall not be construed as to diminish the just importance of the other rights retained by the people, or as to enlarge the powers delegated by the constitution; but either as actual limitations of such powers, or as inserted merely for greater caution."

Was Hamilton right? Well, if you ask most people where their rights come from, they'll say it's the Bill of Rights. If Congress and the states were to repeal some part of that, would people accept it? When those entities pass legislation violating those rights, someone usually challenges it in court. They challenge it, though, because it violates the relevant provision of the Bill of Rights, not because it violates their rights. Without the provision of the Bill of Rights—remember, we're imagining that it has been repealed—would people then still challenge the action as exceeding the power of government? Would they be as likely to challenge it without a textual citation to rely on?[21]

Maybe. More likely, they would challenge it if they didn't like it, without any consideration of whether the government should be allowed to do it. They would more likely challenge it as a violation of the will of the majority than as a violation of the limitations on government. That points to a problem. The whole point of

---

17 Which you can find at memory.loc.gov, on pp. 440-68 of the Annals of Congress for the House of Representatives.

18 I think it was North Carolina.

19 You don't go up against J. Mad with weak sauce; he will slap that nonsense out of you.

20 Since some states had not yet ratified (and some had difficulty in sending their delegations), the House was probably less than the sixty-five members it was planned to start with.

21 Aside from the question of whether judges would still recognize it. Congress and the states repealing an amendment would alter the Constitution, and show a clear intent to remove that liberty. Would judges follow the "legislative intent," or would they follow an unwritten tradition about no longer specified rights? The anticipation of success or failure could well affect a someone's willingness to sue.

individual liberty is to preserve areas *from* the majority, no matter how much the majority wants to control them.

On the other hand, it is difficult to say what might have happened in the absence of the Bill of Rights. I said that most people would identify the Bill of Rights as the source of their liberties, but there's another way to ask that. If you ask people to name one of their individual rights, their civil liberties, most will name something from the Bill of Rights (and probably from the First Amendment). Without those written reminders, would people be aware of even that many? Most people haven't spent (and have no interest in or intention of spending) any amount of time considering the proper scope of either government or their liberties. As Tocqueville warned, we are more concerned with material comforts, and just want government to make annoying questions like that go away. That knowledge will not make you a rock star, or increase your monetary wealth in the slightest, so we have no time for it. Government can take the car keys, get into the whiskey, break the furniture, and flood the basement, so long as it doesn't interrupt us while we're binge watching *Big Brother*.

Let's imagine your state legislature passes a law making it illegal for newspapers (or more fashion- or technology-forward media) to publish stories about criminal or civil legal proceedings against public officials.[22] Your cousin is a state representative, a member of your state legislature. You run into him at a restaurant without this wife, and when you ask if she is doing well, he tells you he wouldn't know—she moved out and is suing him for divorce. Later that evening, you post a selfie you took with him to your Facebook page, with a caption telling him that you and the rest of the family will be there to support him during his divorce. (Several family members indicate their approval of the your sentiment,[23] and some add their own messages of support.)

The next day, you find yourself in the county jail. It's visitation hours, but you're the one being visited. You were arrested for breaking the law about publishing stories about public officials' legal proceedings, and your lawyer has come to confer with you. What are the first words out of your mouth? Hey, watch your language. This is a family book. Even if it doesn't occur to you in your stress-addled state,[24] the first thing your lawyer will say is . . . First Amendment. It says something about the freedom to say and publish things, doesn't it? Maybe we should look it up, just to be sure. Yep. There it is: "Congress shall make no law . . . abridging the freedom of speech, or of the press." Seems like that should clear it up. This has to be one of those: speech or press. We'll see the judge tomorrow, and your soap opera will be over.

Then your lawyer starts talking. She points out tow flies in your freedom ointment. First, the First Amendment says Congress can't *abridge* your freedom. The freedom has limits, meaning some things are already outside it. While Congress can't make those limits narrower, it remains to be seen whether this type of speech or print is within those limits, or without. Second, it says *Congress* can't abridge your freedom. Read that first word of the First Amendment again: *Congress* shall make no law. Who made this one? (Hint: not Congress.) It was your state legislature, remember?

Before you put a plea on Facebook for your supportive relatives to bring you soap-on-a-rope, let me give you the spoiler: your lawyer is just messing with you. But how should you know that? How can a sentence which explicitly and solely limits Congress, the federal legislature, also limit your state legislature? To be honest, this sort of limitation probably exists in your state constitution, too. If it doesn't, however, the First Amendment would apply, through a process known as incorporation.

What does it mean to incorporate something? You probably just said something about issuing stock which is publicly traded, or something else related to the business abbreviation "inc." Unless, of course, you had no response at all, because you've never heard that word. But you've read this far, so presumably literacy isn't a problem for you. But yes, we do call those "corporations," and it is because they have been incorporated. Those businesses are nor, however, definitions of the word, they are examples, and the word describes them. What else do we know that has *corp-* as a root? Well, there's the Marine Corps, but *corps* is the French version of the

---

22   This example has nothing to do with the apparent competition between Illinois and Alabama to see how many consecutive governors can leave office with a criminal indictment.

23   For those of you who spend more time with Twitter than literature, it means they "like" your post.

24   You have many pressing matters on your mind, foremost of which is where your bar of soap is, and particularly, if it is on the floor.

Latin *corpus*. Yes, that does sound like the English word "corpse"; so would the French word, if they didn't treat their vocabulary as make-work jobs for their alphabet. And "corpse" is the English child of that same Latin parent, so the resemblance is hardly shocking.

A corpse, of course, is a small stand of trees. No, that's a *copse*. So if the cops find a corpse in the copse . . . right. "Corpse" is the word we use for someone's mortal remains, the body as separated from the soul. *Corpus* does indeed mean "body," but as in English, it is not exclusively the human body. For example, the *corpus juris civilis* is a body of law (in this case, civil law). It is a whole unit, a single entity. It may have constituent parts, but they only function as a whole, and cannot stand on their own. In the case of the Marines, individuals subordinate themselves to the whole. In the case of businesses, the *corpus* is an artificial legal individual, a legal Frankenstein's monster, created by law, rather than a lot of gruesome sewing.[25]

According to law, people who own a business are (by default) jointly and severally liable for its debts. If the business goes bankrupt, creditors can take the full amount from any of them. That is, let's say that ten people own the business, and the business' debt is $10 million. Joint and several liability says that creditors can take whatever they can get, up to the full amount, from any of them. The debt is not shared out, $1 million apiece. If nine of them are personally broke as well, the creditors can take the whole sum from the one who does have money. If they all have money, the creditors can take money from whichever ones they can lay hands on, until all of the debt is repaid. And when I say "take," I mean it literally: whatever asset of value that person may have. Creditors may take their houses, cars, retirement savings, any asset of value (not just what they have in checking).

As you might imagine, this is an incredible disincentive to start a business. It means not just risking the money you decide to invest, but (if things go horribly wrong) your home and future. In recent years, as personal services (which are not as intensive in physical capital) have become more prevalent, we have seen the introduction of the LLC, or limited liability corporation, for individuals like lawyers or dentists or accountants, so that they don't have to either issue stock or risk their homes to practice their professions.

This was an adaptation of the older practice of incorporation, which does the same thing: it limits the liability of those who own the business. In particular, it limits liability to only the amount they have invested in the business. It does this by creating an artificial legal person who *is* the business (and thus, owns its debts). It's like a giant robot; people inside it direct it and make it move, but if things go badly, it's the robot that takes the beating and keeps them safe. The robot holds all of the liabilities and assets for them.

Great, so now we understand why businesses incorporate. What does that have to do with you, your cousin's divorce, and Facebook? "Incorporate" means to make a single body out of parts, to make something a part of a body. The Supreme Court has done this with many provisions (though not all) of the Bill of Rights. It has taken these provisions and make them part of the body of the laws of every state. That is, it has held that those limitations apply to state government action as well as to federal government action.

How has it done this? Madison proposed that three of the protections (conscience, speech and press, and jury trial) restrain the states as well, but those proposals died in Congress. And the wording of the First Amendment makes clear that the Bill of Rights applied to the federal government and not the states. Aside from the explicit rejection of provisions specifically applying them (if partially) to the states, aside from the specific identification of Congress as the body limited, the wording of the religion clauses is also telling. Madison's original proposal reads, "The civil rights of none shall be abridged on account of religious belief or worship, nor shall any national religion be established, nor shall the full and equal rights of conscience be in any manner, or on any pretext, infringed."

Remember, he proposed to include these in the list of things forbidden Congress, and also proposed language saying that none of them should be taken to expand the list of Congress' powers. Without that placement and that caveat, however, the words "The civil rights of none" sound as if Congress could not infringe, but also had the power to prevent states from infringing, either. It would limit Congress in the first instance, but empower it to overturn state laws with interfered with freedom of religion.[26] Thus, the committee changed the phrasing to include the specific name of the actor forbidden to infringe (Congress), and created the very

---

25 Not that the process is any less gruesome. Just less sewing.

26 You know, that thing Alexander Hamilton had just said they would do. Word, yo.

tortured grammar of the First Amendment: "Congress shall make no law respecting an establishment of religion." That doesn't mean Congress is fine as long as it throws shade; that means it can't legislate on that subject. And it says that in order to keep Congress from establishing a national faith as well as to prevent Congress from de-establishing the state churches some of the states still had.[27]

So obviously, original intent is not going to be any part of the argument for incorporation. The intent to apply some of the guarantees in what became the Bill of Rights was originally quite clearly and definitely rejected. What **is** going to be part of this argument, however, is a different amendment, the Fourteenth. Math tells us that, since the Bill of Rights is the first ten amendments, and this one came fourteenth, we're no longer in the Bill of Rights. And, as usual, math is right.[28]

The Fourteenth Amendment is one of the three Civil War Amendments, so named because they were adopted in anticipation of the third Captain America movie. No, they were adopted as a result of the Civil War.[29] The Thirteenth Amendment came first. It made slavery—this time they used the word!—unconstitutional in the United States. It was proposed in January of 1865 and ratified by December of the same year.[30] The Fifteenth Amendment prohibits denial or abridgment of the right to vote because of "race, color, or previous condition of servitude." It was proposed in February 1869, and ratified in March 1870. We will discuss these more in the next chapter,[31] which is also true of the Fourteenth.

The Fourteenth Amendment was proposed to the states in June of 1866, and its ratification took a little more than two years (it was ratified in July 1868). The Fourteenth Amendment is monumental; its first clause overturns a Supreme Court decision,[32] and its second section undoes the infamous Three-Fifths Compromise.[33] It is the second, third, and fourth clauses of its first section which concern us here: "No State shall make or

---

27 Connecticut apparently had an established church until 1818, and Massachusetts required membership in some church (and taxed to support them) until 1833. Madison's proposal, by the way, was modeled on the Virginia Statute on Religious Freedom (1786, authored by Thomas Jefferson), and Georgia amended its constitution in 1789 to include similar (and similarly sweeping) language. So you know where you can stick that Bible Belt joke you were about to make, Yankee Boy (or Girl). Yeah, that place you're always talking out of, and your nose, too.

28 It has a bad habit of doing that.

29 First, you had better not have been falling for that movie bit. Second, some pedants are now huffing, "You mean the *American* Civil War; other places have had them, too." And they are technically correct. Other places have had civil wars. Britain, Russia . . . France was more of a general slaughter; they didn't quite get around to choosing up sides. Regardless, the pedants are also hoist by their own petard, because there are also more places in the Americas than the United States, and some of them have undoubtedly had (or unfortunately will have) their own civil wars. Turns out, there is not good name for that war. Calling it the U.S. Civil War is inaccurate, because the United States was one of the sides in that war. You don't call World War I or II "the German War" or "the French War." "The War Between the States" is simply too vague—that describes most wars since around 1648. I guess what I'm sayin' is, don't bring those weak pedantics in here, brah. You wanna come at me, you better come with stronger OCD than that. I **am** dangerously over-educated; everybody else just wears the T-shirt.

30 Of the thirty-six states at the time, only three voted against ratification of the Thirteenth Amendment. I know what you're thinking, but you're wrong. Only one of those states was a former Confederate state. Delaware and Kentucky both remained in the Union, but voted against the Thirteenth Amendment. Delaware has also given us Joe Biden, so maybe there's just something wrong with that place. Nevertheless, both Kentucky and Delaware later changed their minds. Delaware officially changed its vote in 1901, and Kentucky did so in 1976 (in living memory, in other words). The one Confederate state to vote against ratifying the Thirteenth Amendment still hasn't changed its mind. That Mississippi still hasn't changed its mind about the Thirteenth Amendment probably isn't much of a surprise to anyone who's ever been there.

31 Still Chapter 13, unless you're reading this backwards. And why would you read it backwards? It's not like you hear Satanic messages or call Incan warriors' spirits back to avenge their deaths or get placed into a hypnotic trance that convinces you you're the re-incarnation of Shirley MacLaine or anything like that. Nope. Nothing like that at all.

32 *Scott v. Sandford*, also known as the Dred Scott decision. You guessed it: more in the next chapter.

33 No, the Three-Fifths Compromise was not about the amount of whiskey politicians could drink before voting, or the amount they could use to bribe voters. In the Constitutional Convention, Southern delegates wanted to count slaves as part of their population for purposes of determining the number of representatives they would have in Congress. Northern delegates objected to this wanton inflation of the representation of Southern states (remember, a lot of people who were not allowed to vote were counted as part of population, though they also weren't counted as property). They compromised to adding three-fifths of the number of slaves to the state's population for purposes of determining Congressional representation.

enforce any law which shall abridge the privileges and immunities of citizens of the United States; nor shall any State deprive any person of life, liberty, or property, without due process of law; nor deny to any person within its jurisdiction the equal protection of the laws." They are known, respectively, as the Privileges and Immunities Clause, the Due Process Clause (of the Fourteenth Amendment), and the Equal Protection Clause. The Due Process Clause has a somewhat longer reference because there is also a due process clause in the Fifth Amendment.[34]

So here's the game. The incorporation of (most of) the provisions in the Bill of Rights, so that they limit state action as well as federal, has occurred through one of these three clauses. Which do you think it is? When you read these, which of them tells you the state is forbidden to forbid your publishing about legal proceedings involving public officials? I know, this has turned into a very long prison visit, and your lawyer is waiting on your answer. Would you say that the law you've been arrested for violating is an abridgment of one of the privileges and immunities you enjoy as a citizen of the United States?[35] Or does it deny you the equal protection of the laws, since people in other states get to post such things on Facebook? Or have the authorities not followed the procedures they were supposed to in depriving you of your liberty? Place your bets—which one is it?[36] If you get it right, you get out of jail. Get it wrong, and it's time to invest in that soap-on-a-rope. That's not the Jeopardy theme song you hear; it's the banjos from *Deliverance*. Might want to get a move on with that answer.

Chances are, you went with the Privileges and Immunities Clause, so I'll start with that one. If you didn't, don't worry. We'll get to why yours was wrong eventually. This clause makes a lot of sense. If asked to define or list the privileges and immunities–things you are allowed to do, and things you may not be prevented from doing, because you are a U.S. citizen—most of us would begin reciting things in the Bill of Rights, and probably starting with the First Amendment. We can't be stopped from speaking our minds, or from worshipping as we choose (or choose not to do).

If it's any consolation, the lawyers were on your side. In the first Supreme Court case to deal with the Fourteenth Amendment, *The Slaughterhouse Cases*,[37] lawyers (for New Orleans butchers) argued that a law requiring them to rent space from a consolidated municipal facility interfered with the privileges and immunities of U.S. citizens (presumably, to work free of state-created monopoly). The Court defined the privileges and immunities of being a U.S. citizen rather more narrowly. According to the Court, those privileges and immunities consist of the right to travel on the waterways of the United States, to be protected by the United States on the high seas or in other countries, and to run for federal office. In other words, they defined the privileges and immunities as not interfering with the police powers of the state, but applying only to things outside that jurisdiction (and therefore under federal jurisdiction).

If you were thinking Equal Protection Clause, well, it does seem more likely than the Due Process Clause, doesn't it? It could be read, if one begins with the idea that it incorporates the Bill of Rights, to say that those rights are a minimum amount of freedom, equally protecting all citizens. That is, everyone has at least that equal amount of protection from the government. This is why we don't reason backward, though. If you start with the conclusion, it always seems inevitable. Equal protection means that the law must apply to one person the same way it applies to another person. There are no special exceptions for those with stars on their bellies, or whose name

---

34 Further confirmation, if you need it, that the Bill of Rights originally applied only to the federal government. The framers of the Fourteenth Amendment would hardly have repeated verbatim a restriction that already applied to the states.

35 If you're not a U.S. citizen, pretend you are, just for demonstration purposes. (Sorry, offer not valid outside your imagination.) By the way, that first clause of this amendment overturns that Supreme Court decision by defining U.S. citizenship, making it a federal rather than a state decision. Before this amendment, being a citizen of one of the states made you a citizen of the United States. The Fourteenth Amendment changes the direction of the relationship. Now, being a citizen of the United States (as defined by the Fourteenth Amendment and Congress) makes you a citizen of the state in which you reside.

36 All bets are purely metaphorical and solely intended for entertainment purposes.

37 I know this sounds like Stephen King's next novel—and for all I know, it will be—but the name comes from the fact that the Supreme Court consolidated several cases arising from the same circumstances. The lead case was *The Butchers' Benevolent Association of New Orleans v. The Crescent City Livestock Landing and Slaughter-House Company*, which is reason enough to call them *The Slaughterhouse Cases*. The fact that it's the perfect name for a horror movie set at the Supreme Court had nothing to do with it. And yes, that idea is mine.

is Bob.[38] The idea is not that everyone gets the same outcome; the guilty and the innocent, for example, should receive very different outcomes. The law should determine guilt or innocence, however, only on the basis of relevant behavior, not irrelevant behavior or immutable characteristics, and that the standards for relevant behavior be the same for everyone. Equal protection doesn't say the state can't make wearing sunglasses illegal, only that you can't be declared guilty because you own a convertible (and everyone knows those people always wear sunglasses).

At least one way of reading the Due Process Clause **does** prevent the government from making it illegal to wear sunglasses. There are at least two types of due process, procedural and substantive. Procedural is probably the easiest to understand; it's the way you approach your assignments (and exams). You want to know the list of things you have to include: how many pages or words, how many sources, what terms you should mention, and so on. You want a checklist, so that if you check every box on the list, you get an A. It's the same for procedural due process. The focus is on what steps the state must follow, what conditions it must meet, to legally deprive you of your life, liberty, or your property. If the state follows all of those steps, if it checks off every box, then it gets to kill you, imprison or restrict you, or take your stuff. The only question is whether the state followed the appropriate procedures.

Substantive due process looks at whether those procedures are appropriate or not, rather than whether the state followed them. This is the way (some of) your professors see your tests and assignments, by the way. The question is not whether you obeyed the letter of the checklist, but whether you accomplished the spirit of it. Did the outcome you produced show the qualities (the substance) the checklist was meant to help you produce? In other words, the process itself is not the goal. The goal is something the process is supposed to guide you toward. In the case of substantive due process, the goal is the preservation of life, liberty, and property. Remember that social contract? We form government to protect these things. Thus, the processes of government are meant to protect them. That is their sole reason for existing. If they instead infringe on or damage those things, then the process cannot reasonably be read to allow that outcome. No process is reasonably designed to undermine its own purpose. This is very much the criterion of instrumental rationality; the end of government is to protect life, liberty, and property, so when it adopts means which instead harm those things, it acts irrationally. Those actions are therefore null and void.

You may already see how substantive due process would lead to incorporation. The Due Process Clause says that states have to follow due process; substantive due process says that means the state's processes must protect those liberties that we form governments to protect. Hey, come to think of it, the first eight amendments contain lots of rights and liberties that we have already explicitly identified as ones we expect government to protect. Handy, that. It also happens to confirm Hamilton's fears, because it (in practice, if not in theory) reduces our rights and liberties to those on the list.

One of the complaints about substantive due process, though, is precisely that it does not admit of a set list. The butchers in *The Slaughterhouse Cases* also make substantive due process claims, that being forced to participate in a government monopoly invaded rights to engage in their work, rights they enjoyed under the common law. In fact, substantive due process has its roots in a common law perspective, that rights include not just those defined in statute, but those enjoyed in practice for long periods of time, as well. The problem with substantive due process is the difficulty of creating shared understandings of what rights those are. To borrow from Justice Potter Stewart, we may know them when we see them, but we may each see them differently.

You can see this in the Supreme Court's rulings on privacy. Do you have a right to privacy? Really? Show me where it says that. Go ahead; I'll look if you will. What did you find? You get the gold medal if you came back with the Fourth Amendment: "The right of the people to be secure in their persons, houses, papers, and effects, against unreasonable searches and seizures, shall not be violated". That's as close as it comes, but that's not quite privacy. That says government can't reach into your pockets, or rummage through the stuff in your house, without a good reason.[39] That does not keep the government from observing you using satellites with

---

38 Nor for Bobs with stars on their bellies, so put down that tattoo needle.

39 I left the "without a good reason" part (and the procedure for establishing that reason) out of the quote above; but then, since you went and found the original, you knew that already.

infrared sensors. They're not entering or searching your house; they don't even send radiation in. They simply observe the radiation you are emitting. Sure, it allows them to see if other people are present, and more or less how many of them, and to some degree what you are doing.[40]

Would you say surveillance violates your right to privacy? Then the Fourth Amendment isn't much help.[41] It may keep them from shining flashlights in your window, but blinds or curtains will do that, too. It doesn't stop them from observing the shadows on those blinds or curtains, as long as they're visible from the street, with or without binoculars. If you have to purchase blackout curtains, thermally shield and soundproof your house, and probably hermetically seal it as well (to keep detectable particles from escaping), you hardly have a **right** to privacy. It would be something you have to protect, at great personal expense, which means that most people would not enjoy it. Further, government would be the force from which you would have to protect your privacy, along with (and given its budget, to a much greater degree than) whatever nosy neighbors you might have.[42]

Substantive due process would say that this is government harming the things it was meant to protect, and thus unconstitutional in a most fundamental way, because it violates the reasons for constituting a government. Most people would agree that we have a right to privacy, though they might quibble about defining the exact boundaries.[43] But when push came to shove, in the case of *Griswold v. Connecticut*, the judges still weren't comfortable with the "we all know we have this right," substantive due process approach.

A little background: Connecticut had passed a law forbidding the use of contraception, even by married couples. If I remember correctly, Connecticut's rationale was that contraception[44] was destructive of good social order, because it made adultery harder to detect. If a wife became pregnant in a time frame when her husband remembered being on a month-long business trip, or if a husband's secretary (this was the 60s) became pregnant after he had been working late suspiciously often, the cuckolded spouse would know they had been cheated on, or at least that they needed to take the idea seriously. Without the specter of that difficult evidence (a human life, and one subject to paternity testing), not to mention the ensuing financial responsibility, people were more likely to violate their marriage vows. Every spouse seeing a threat in every person of their gender with whom their partner came into social contact is a recipe for social unrest, to say the least.[45]

Estelle Griswold was the head of the local office of Planned Parenthood. She and a doctor were charged with violating this law, not with each other, but because the law also made it an offense to provide or counsel someone on the use of contraception. This is, the state legislature knew there was no way of enforcing this directly; voters don't appreciate unannounced coitus inspections. So the legislature decided to enforce it indirectly, by outlawing the provision of or, since people could get to New York or Massachusetts,[46] instruction in what to get and how to use it. This is also why they had standing; the law injured them by invading someone else's privacy.

Only two justices (Arthur Goldberg and John Marshall Harlan II) thought that the Due Process Clause (of the Fourteenth Amendment, since this was a state law) directly protected this privacy as a right "so rooted in the traditions and conscience of our people as to be ranked as fundamental"[47] or "implicit in the concept of

---

40   An innocent game of Twister could be disastrously misinterpreted when everyone is just a featureless red shape, indistinguishable when they overlap.

41   I'm assuming you think surveillance violates your right to privacy. If you said no, we'll have the crews over soon to install the cameras.

42   Here's looking at you Mrs. Kravitz. With infrared binoculars. And parabolic microphones.

43   Quibbling about the exact boundaries, by the way, is the substance of most Supreme Court cases (and decisions) about the rights which **do** appear in the Bill of Rights.

44   Also known as birth control, to those limited to less than three syllables.

45   Or have you never seen Jerry Springer?

46   Those hotbeds of immorality.

47   Justice Goldberg, quoting from *Snyder v. Massachusetts*.

ordered liberty."[48] Justice Harlan said that "the Due Process Clause of the Fourteenth Amendment stands, in my opinion, on its own bottom." Justice Goldberg focused on the Ninth Amendment as proof that the Bill of Rights are not the sum total of the liberties the due process clause protects. He even quoted Hamilton's fears that the Bill of Rights would be read precisely the way the majority did.

Speaking of the majority, the majority of the Court relied on an amalgamation of different provisions of the Bill of Rights: the Association Clause of the First Amendment, the Third Amendment's limitation on quartering soldiers in private homes, the Searches and Seizures Clause of the Fourth Amendment (the one we started with), and the Self-Incrimination Clause of the Fifth Amendment.[49] None of these clauses explicitly protects the privacy of married couples, or explicitly forbids what Connecticut was doing. Ms. Griswold could associate with whomever she wished, she simply couldn't discuss contraception with them, or provide it to them. Connecticut was not quartering soldiers in anyone's home, whether to watch their mating habits or not.[50] No one was required to testify against themselves, and nothing was being searched or seized (indeed, the inability to carry those actions out was why the statute had been written so that it injured Ms. Griswold).

Instead of arguing that any of these clauses protected privacy directly, the Court held that they protected it indirectly. That is, there exists around constitutional rights a "penumbra," a protective shadow they cast over rights which are contiguous to theirs, and which are necessary to protect in order to protect the explicitly protected right. It's kind of like the necessary and proper clause, but for rights rather than government powers. Think of the right as a table; if the floor on which it stands is not also protected, the table becomes endangered. Villains with curly, waxed moustaches may not be able to touch the table, so they just saw the floor out from underneath it, and let crashing into the basement destroy it.[51] Therefore, protecting the table means protecting the floor underneath it, too.

Penumbra means "next to the shadow," not "protective shadow." Think of the clauses mentioned as umbrellas, protecting the things in their shadows from rain. Rain that falls just outside the protected area (which correlates with the shadow) splashes the things inside it. Thus, to keep mud off your pants leg, or to keep your bag dry, you need to protect the area next to the shadow, too.[52]

Marital privacy, then, fell into these zones that had to be protected in order to protect the things directly protected. The Ninth Amendment appears as an appendix, as confirmation that such zones are possible, rather than as a golf umbrella, and the Due Process Clause of the Fourteenth Amendment means that this restriction applies to the states, as well. As the Court's reluctance to rely on two substantive due process arguments should tell you, this means that substantive due process is not the vehicle for incorporation. But then, you should have gotten that from the fact that substantive due process doesn't rely on any particular list. It draws its authority from theories about the nature and purpose of government, not from the Bill of Rights. That works only so long as everyone subscribes to similar enough theories that they agree on the nature and purpose of government.

For example, Ms. Griswold (like the butchers in *The Slaughterhouse Cases*) could simply have claimed that the law interfered with her right to pursue her livelihood, but she wouldn't have gotten very far with that, for at least two reasons. First, laws have since time immemorial interfered with the right to practice professions

---

48   Justice Harlan, quoting *Palko v. Connecticut*.

49   The thing people are referring to when they "plead the Fifth." They're not asking for whiskey, they're saying they can't be forced to be a witness against themselves. And what is with you and the whiskey today? Yeah, I know, you can quit anytime you want.

50   Now **that's** what you call "special forces." (Rimshot.) Just so you know, while I've read very, very far from every Supreme Court decision ever, I have read a lot of the most prominent ones, and this is the only mention I have ever read in a decision (as opposed to in *dicta*) of two amendments. One is the Third Amendment, or The Little Amendment That No One Ever Picks. The second is the Ninth Amendment, which never sees this much action. This is the Ninth's one time being the Prom Queen. So much for Alexander "Fraidy Cat" Hamilton and his fears, huh? (What's that? The estate of Alexander Hamilton is on the phone, and is challenging me to a duel? Some people never learn.)

51   Obviously, they cackle malevolently and explain their evil plot while doing this.

52   It's called a golf umbrella, but that destroys the analogy. Reality has a way of doing that to judicial reasoning.

which are destructive of social order,[53] and that was precisely Connecticut's premise. Social order has not generally been allowed to interfere in the marital relationship, however. In fact, protecting it has generally been a pillar of promoting social order. Second, the Court had long since abandoned its efforts to protect what it calls "economic rights," such as the right to contract or pursue one's livelihood.[54]

Take, for example, the case of *Lochner v. New York*, which the Court decided in 1905. The State of New York had passed a law regulating the maximum number of hours a baker could work, on the basis of its police powers. New York claimed the measure was necessary to protect the wholesomeness of the bread the public consumed, since tired bakers might accidentally use the wrong ingredients, or fail to keep dirt or detritus out of their dough. It was also necessary to protect bakers from "white lung," a respiratory illness brought on by breathing for too long air filled with clouds of flour. Having limited the hours a baker could work, it was also necessary to enforce a minimum wage, so that bakers did not suffer a sudden reduction in income. Joseph Lochner, who operated a bakery in New York, challenged the Bakeshop Act after being twice fined for allowing an employee to work more than sixty hours in a week.

The Court held that the Bakeshop Act was "an unreasonable, unnecessary, and arbitrary interference with the right and liberty of the individual to contract." If you've read the Bill of Rights—go ahead; it doesn't take long, and I'll wait—you know that there is no such statement or protection in the Bill of Rights. You probably don't realize that this (1905) is also before incorporation was a thing, at least firmly (1925), also in a case involving New York.[55] The Court held that the act violated the Due Process Clause of the Fourteenth Amendment, which they interpreted as substantive due process. Government interference with liberty was only justified when it was necessary and reasonable, that is, when it served the ends for which we establish government. When it contradicts or undermines those ends, or represented the arbitrary whim of a legislative majority, it was beyond the powers of government.

As the Court explained, if the goal was healthier bread, limiting working hours was not sufficiently likely to produce that goal for a reasonable person to believe that was really the purpose of the law. If you wanted to ensure bread was free of contaminant, you would forbid the sale of contaminated bread, and inspect the bread or the bakery for wholesomeness or cleanliness, respectively. You wouldn't send the baker home to rest. If you were worried about white lung, you weren't doing anything to reduce the flour particles in the air, and were still allowing sixty hours of exposure. Regulating fans and ventilation might be a more direct way of addressing that concern.

As for the health of the bakers, "There is no contention that bakers as a class are not equal in intelligence and capacity to men in other trades . . ., or that they are able to assert their rights an care for themselves without the protecting arm of the State, interfering with their independence of judgment and of action. They are in no sense wards of the State." In other words, bakers are just as capable as other people are of deciding how much time or health they wish to sacrifice for money. They do not need the government to be their nanny; they are grown-aarp[56] men. They are not in a situation where they cannot appreciate the consequences of their decisions, and since they are the only one to bear those consequences, there is no justification for the state to intervene on their behalf.

---

53 For example, prostitution has been regularly banned (and as regularly practiced) as a profession, on the grounds that it is dangerous to public morals and good social order. One could possibly argue the converse, that having an outlet for excess sexual energies keeps them from spilling over into social unrest. Ladies and gentlemen, I give you the Second-and-a-Half Amendment: "A well-regulated brothel, being necessary to the peace of a free state, the right of the people to be and hire prostitutes, shall not be infringed." I wonder if Democrats will be as quick to argue that people only have that right as a group right, rather than individually. Plus, it gives a whole new meaning to "background checks." (Yeah, there's not enough rimshot in the world to make that joke work.)

54 Pursue, not catch.

55 *Gitlow v. New York*, which was a free speech case, but it had nothing to do with dancing, or the elevation of buttocks during said dancing. (See? I told you I can make anything uncool.)

56 Just when you thought it was safe . . . BOOM! There it is.

We have defined substantive due process as requiring government not to harm the things it was created to protect. That captures the idea, but it doesn't give us much idea of what specifically those things might be. There simply isn't enough definition (or agreement on a definition) of what government is supposed to protect, because its protection usually involves the sacrifice of one liberty to protect another. As we implied[57] above, the Court translated this general proposition into rational basis review. To be held constitutional, government action had to be likely to produce its specified goals, and those goals had to be ones government was allowed to have.

Just as we can evaluate whether someone actually has the goal they claim by looking at whether they adopt measures likely to reach those goals, or what preferences someone claims to have by looking at the decisions they make, the Court evaluated whether Congress (or a state legislature) was staying within its limits by evaluating whether the means it chose (laws it passed) bore a close relationship to the goal it claimed. That is to say, the Court evaluated the instrumental rationality of legislative action. Of course, Congress knew better than to claim it was trying to exceed its powers (unless it was honestly mistaken, but those errors are the easiest to spot). Irrational (or arbitrary) impositions on liberty violated due process, because due process demanded that government action trample as little as possible on liberty. If the trampling wasn't sufficiently related to a permissible goal, it was unnecessary (and thus unconstitutional).

If all of this sounds familiar, it should. It is essentially John Marshall's interpretation of the Necessary and Proper Clause. So essentially, substantive due process required all government action to be necessary and proper, using a very loose definition of necessary. While that is a very expansive reading of the Necessary and Proper Clause, and perhaps an appropriate limit to the powers of a government of enumerated powers (like the federal one), it is a restrictive reading of the powers of a generally-enabled government (like the states). Reading the Elastic Clause that way enlarges the extent of the enumerated powers; reading the Due Process Clause of the Fifth Amendment to require a rational relationship between adopted means and permissible ends might not be a bad way to appropriately restrain a government to its enumerated powers; reading the Due Process Clause of the Fourteenth Amendment that way overly limits an authority meant to be broader. The enumerated powers give us a good idea of the purposes for which the federal government was created, but states don't have such a list. The exact content of their lists are supposed to be determined at the ballot box.

Before we move on,[58] as the Court eventually did too, there is a case we should look at in conjunction with *Lochner*. Three years after *Lochner*, in 1908, an almost identical case came before the Court. Even the Court was largely the same, with one exception; Justice Moody had replaced Justice Brown (who voted with the 5-4 majority in *Lochner*) in the interim. The case, *Muller v. Oregon*, dealt once again with a restriction on working hours, once again in the name of both public health and the personal health of the employees, who this time were employed in laundries, rather than as bakers.

You might expect the Court to rule that people who wash clothes are just as capable of protecting their rights as those in other professions. If Justice Moody voted the same way as Justice Brown, you would expect a stinging rebuke of attempts to treat adults as if they were orphaned children in need of the state's protection. When I tell you that was not the outcome, you may think that Justice Moody voted differently, and so reached a 5-4 decision overturning *Lochner*. Justice Moody's vote, however, did not make a difference in the outcome, and the decision affirmed the validity of *Lochner*. In fact, all of the judges voted together this time, issuing a unanimous decision upholding the Oregon statute *on the basis of Lochner*.

I know, what the froyo, right? There's one key difference I haven't given you yet. The Oregon statute, on the basis of public health and the worker's personal health, only limited the working hours of women.[59] The Court found this rationally related to the ends of public health. "(B)y abundant testimony of the medical fraternity, continuance for a long time on her feet at work, repeating this from day to day, tends to injurious

---

57 Okay, as *I* implied. You were just innocently reading.

58 Stop holding your breath; it's making you look too much like Smurfette. Well, that and the slip you're wearing as if it were a dress.

59 This, by the way, was a Progressive cause. Louis Brandeis argued the case for Oregon, and presented evidence from such noted scientific minds as Emperor Wilhelm II of Germany on the fragility of women's health.

effects upon the body, and, as healthy mothers are essential to vigorous offspring, the physical well-being of woman becomes an object of public interest and care in order to preserve the strength and vigor of the race."

You may think, okay, they're forgetting that healthy fathers contribute too, but there is still no contention that women as a class are not equal in intelligence and capacity to others, to borrow from *Lochner*. Oh, but there was:

> Still again, history discloses the fact that woman has always been dependent on man. . . . (T)here is still that in her disposition and habits of life which will operate against a full assertion of those rights. She will still be where some legislation to protect her seems necessary to secure a real equality of rights. . . . It is impossible to close one's eyes to the fact that she still looks to her brother, and depends upon him.

That's right; according to the Supreme Court (*Muller* has never been overturned), because society needs women's uteruses,[60] and because women do not have the requisite capacity to make their own decisions about their health, it is a reasonable exercise of police powers for the state to make those decisions for them. They need protecting, the poor dears; they can't help themselves. This is offensive enough in its direct statement, valuing a body part over the person, and assuming those persons lack the ability to look after themselves and that body part. It also, however, leads one to wonder whether we are all now only valuable to the state as livestock to be managed for the state's benefit, given the ubiquity of minimum wage and maximum hour rules.

I am not trying to minimize in any way the insult to women that this decision is. What I want you to see from it, aside from the lesson on misogyny, is how the Court felt about bakers in *Lochner*. If you are any sort of decent person, you found the words from Muller deeply offensive, a slap in the face to all intelligent, capable people, some of whom happen to be women. It demeans them, it treats them as children who are not fully mentally competent. The shame is not the outrage the Court felt to see male bakers treated that way, but the lack of outrage when women were treated that way. In a day when we take wage and hour regulation for granted, however, it can be difficult to understand why the Court found the law in *Lochner* so objectionable.

In case you're wondering, the "fact" that women were, by disposition, unlikely or unwilling to assert their rights probably came as a surprise to those who organized and attended the Seneca Falls Convention, the first women's rights convention in the United States, which was held in 1848. In the sixty years between then and this decision, there had been several annual National Women's Rights Conventions, beginning in 1850. Two competing national suffrage organizations formed, one by Susan B. Anthony and Elizabeth Cady Stanton, the other by Lucy Stone (and both in 1869). Two years earlier, all three had addressed a New York state constitutional convention, which was revising the state's constitution.

In the 1870s, women's suffragists tried to vote and filed suits when they were denied a ballot. Susan B. Anthony managed to cast a ballot, but was arrested for and convicted of breaking the law prohibiting her from voting. The Supreme Court itself had heard a case in this time, *Minor v. Happersett*, in which a suffragist claimed that the Privileges and Immunities Clause of the Fourteenth Amendment prohibited the states from excluding women (as U.S. citizens) from voting.[61] The intervening years are a litany of campaigns for women's suffrage in various states. To claim, in 1908, that history showed women to be unwilling to assert their rights simply shows that the Court[62] was a poor student of history, or at least the most recent sixty years of it. One wonders if the poor dears on the Court simply didn't get out much, and hadn't met many women.

Notice, too, that the Court refers to familial relations, "that she still looks to her brother, and depends upon him." We do often rely on family for support when we are weak; the offense is in assuming that only female family members are ever in need of support, and that only male family members provide it. Sisters sometimes need their brothers, just as brothers sometimes need their sisters. That much is as true of bakery workers as it is of laundry workers. How does that reliance on family then transmogrify into reliance on the state? When

---

60 Uteri?

61 If you've been paying attention, you'll be shocked to hear that the Court held voting not to be among the privileges and immunities of U.S. citizenship. The Supreme Court seems to think that the Privileges and Immunities Clause is just an elaborate prank, or an exercise in catfishing.

62 Or at least Justice Brewer, who wrote this opinion.

did the state become my brother or sister, my mother or father? Do you remember what Tocqueville said about the kind of tyranny democratic societies had to fear?

> It would be like a fatherly authority if, father-like, its aim were to prepare men for manhood, but it seeks only to keep them in perpetual childhood; . . . It provides their security, anticipates and guarantees their needs, supplies their pleasures, directs their principal concerns . . . Why can it not remove from them entirely the bother of thinking and the troubles of life?

After all, the poor dears shouldn't have to worry their pretty heads about such things.

Note (finally) the poor logic of "a real equality of right." Justice Brewer is saying that women's freedom to make a decision must be taken from them in order to make sure they are as free as everyone else. That logic only works if everyone else is already more fettered.[63] Otherwise, removing freedom from you but not from them makes you less equal—and thus, the justified outrage at the offense to women this is. Again, aside from the lesson on misogyny, you should also learn to be wary of those who use "real" as a qualification, especially when they use it to qualify what they are offering you in exchange for yours. They usually mean it to negate whatever quality they are proclaiming. Freedom is real freedom, just as a car is a real car. If someone offers to trade you this *real* car in exchange for your (presumably fake, by extension) car, it usually means that they are trading you something which isn't actually a car (because yours is, and they want one).[64]

Let us pause for a moment and remember where we were when we embarked on this odyssey to understand substantive due process.[65] We were trying to understand how the Supreme Court has read the Due Process Clause of the Fourteenth Amendment to apply the provisions of the Bill of Rights to state governments as well as the federal one.[66] We now know that it was not through a substantive interpretation of that clause, and having thoroughly[67] explored substantive due process, we come at last to the answer: procedural due process.

As I said oh-so-many pages ago, procedural due process asks, in order to determine whether government has invaded your rights, whether government followed all of the steps in its instructions, whether it followed correctly the process which the Constitution requires of it. How does that get you off the hook for your Facebook faux pas?[68] To know if the government did what the list says it must, and refrained from doing what the list says it must not, we (and the Court) first have to know what's on the list.[69]

As it turns out, the Bill of Rights has a lot of procedural do and do not related to criminal trials in it, and what is a criminal trial but a process for determining whether your liberty should be removed? If the state wants to deprive me of my liberty, is it okay if it tries me again and again for the same offence, until it gets a jury to say what it wants to hear? Is it okay if they just skip the jury altogether? Do they have to tell me what they think I did, or do I just have to guess? Can they take away my liberty if there's someone who can tell them I didn't do it, but I can't convince them to appear in court? The Fifth and Sixth Amendments have answers for all of these questions.[70]

So, in order to define the procedural limitations which the Due Process Clause imposes on states, the Court turned to the procedural issues addressed in the Bill of Rights. As a result, the Bill of Rights came to be seen as the complete list of those restraints. Somewhere, Alexander Hamilton is laughing.[71] You, however, are free

---

63 Yes, thank you Rousseau; we see you waving over there.

64 So thanks, but no thanks, Rousseau.

65 So yes, it's time to shoot an arrow through a row of axe heads. Read the classics, brah.

66 What's that called again? What, do we have to play Hangman? In - - - p - - ation. I spotted you some letters, but that means you just have one appendage left.

67 Or did you want to go into greater detail? Yeah, that's what I thought.

68 Thought I'd forget about that, did you?

69 The list, the list—it's always about that mother-aarping list!

70 In order: no; no; yes to the first, so no to the second; no.

71 But only to keep from crying.

to go; the judge declares the law you are supposed to have violated to be null and void, because it violates the First Amendment as incorporated through the Due Process Clause of the Fourteenth Amendment.

Substantive due process flashback! If you remember,[72] substantive due process required that laws (the means) bear a rational relationship to their stated goals (the ends), and that these had to be ends or goals the state was allowed to pursue. The Court looked closely to see how closely related the means and ends were.[73] The Court calls this rational basis review, but it no longer looks that closely. In *U.S. v. Carolene Products Company*, a 1937 decision, Justice Harlan Fiske Stone provided a different explanation of how closely the Court should scrutinize the rationality of legislation. The Court, Justice Stone said, should assume there was a rational relationship between the means and ends, unless the facts showed there could not possibly be one. This shifted the burden of proof from the legislature to the person claiming injury. The Court would presume legislators had acted rationally, unless the person claiming injury could show otherwise, or the law was so blatantly unrelated to any permissible end as to leave no question.

By 1955, in *Williamson v. Lee Optical*, this had become an even looser standard. In the words of Justice William O. Douglas, "the law need not be in every respect logically consistent with its aims to be constitutional. It is enough that there is an evil at hand for correction, and that it might be thought that the particular legislative measure was a rational way to correct it." In other words, as long as there was some possible connection between the means and the proclaimed goal (and the goal was one government was allowed to pursue), no matter how tenuous the connection, nor whether the connection was actual or merely conceivable, the law passed constitutional muster. As a result, rational basis review became known as the laugh test; if the judge can read it with a straight face, it passes review (and is constitutional).

Think about how this would work with homework excuses. Is it possible that you spilled water on it on the way to class, so you held it out your car window to air dry it? It's possible, but if it is true, it doesn't say much about your reasoning skills (assuming your goal is to submit your homework on time). Since there's some possible connection, and I (a professor) just thought of it and never cracked a smile, it passes. How about if it worked with your parents? You got drunk and got arrested for public intoxication and underage drinking[74] because your friends bought a lot of alcohol, and you drank it all to keep them from committing those crimes. It was a noble, selfless act, really. And that **is** one way to keep them from drinking when underage and getting drunk. Not a good one, mind you. Committing crimes yourself is not usually the best way to discourage others from doing them.[75] If preventing criminal behavior were your goal, pouring the liquor down the sewer or discretely texting some responsible parents to intervene would accomplish more of your goal more certainly. But beating them to it is one way to go.[76]

By the way, now that we've covered "it might be thought," I should tell you what the "evil at hand" was: cheap eyeglasses. Oklahoma passed a law requiring a new prescription any time lenses were fitted to a frame. Back in the fifties, corrective lenses were made out of actual glass, not the lighter and less fragile polycarbonate of today. What is glass famous for doing if you drop it, step on it, sit on it, or otherwise use it roughly? It breaks. Glasses fell out of pockets, got knocked off tables, left in seats (and then sat upon), or just plain ol' dropped, and the lenses fractured or shattered.

At the time, department stores like J.C. Penney, Sears, and Montgomery Ward were becoming popular as cheaper alternatives to independent local businesses.[77] Some of these had added optical counters, where opticians (people trained to grind lenses and put them in frames) could make eyeglasses. If you fractured a lens,

---

72   And I realize, that trail of drool down your chin is not promising.

73   Knowing how close a relationship is can be especially important (and especially touchy) in West Virginia and Alabama.

74   Assuming you're under the age of twenty-one, or just look like you are and didn't have identification on you.

75   Unless you're in a Nicholas Cage movie about the treasure map on the back of the Declaration of Independence—but reason never really applied to that anyway.

76   Of course, if your parents really are that lazy or gullible or stupid, you've probably already discussed this with your court-appointed psychiatrist.

77   Stop me if you've heard this one before.

they could use your old prescription to make you a new lens. Opticians, however, cannot issue prescriptions for corrective lenses.

Optometrists and ophthalmologists, however, can. Doctors of optometry are trained to examine your eyeballs and determine the appropriate amount of corrective refraction. It's right there in the name: *opto-* refers to the eye or vision, as in "optics," and *meter* means to measure, as a speedometer measures your speed. They are also trained to identify eye diseases, especially in the early stages. Ophthalmologists are trained to do these things as well, but they also treat eye diseases and perform surgery. In Oklahoma, the optometrists and ophthalmologists got together (through their professional associations) and decided they would only issue a new prescription if you bought your glasses from them, since they also maintained facilities for producing lenses. Of course, the predictable happened: people just re-used their old prescriptions at the opticians, since it was cheaper.

The optometrists and ophthalmologists then (through their professional associations) lobbied the legislature to **require** a new prescription.[78] This would put opticians out of business, unless they worked for the optometrists or ophthalmologists. The legislature obliged, claiming it was to promote the health of Oklahomans. After all, opticians couldn't spot eye diseases, and you sure couldn't count on Oklahomans to know when their vision was impaired, or an eye disease was developing.[79] You know those manly, self-reliant Oklahomans; it takes more than a nail going into their eye or pus coming out of it to get their stubborn Sooner selves to the doctor's office.

The real evil to be prevented was damaging the profit margins of optometrists and ophthalmologists. I'm sure that was evil enough to eye doctors, but I imagine most consumers would rather have decided for themselves when they needed a new exam and saved some money on their eyeglasses. Besides, doesn't the Court's laxity cut both ways? Can't we just as easily assume that the requirement for an expensive new prescription and overpriced glasses would mean a lot of people would just walk around—or worse, drive around—with uncorrected vision? That assumption is at least as plausible as the one the Court makes, that this might lead to detecting eye disease sooner.[80]

As you might imagine, the Supreme Court is not always so permissive. In fact, back in that *Carolene Products* decision, in what is the most famous footnote of all time,[81] Justice Stone observed that "(t)here may be narrower scope for the presumption of constitutionality when legislation appears on its face to be within a specific prohibition of the Constitution, such as those of the first ten amendments, which are deemed equally specific when held to be embraced within the Fourteenth." Enjoy that mental image of incorporation for a second: the Fourteenth Amendment is giving them a big ol' hug.

Now, what that footnote suggests—and what the Court has done—is to create different levels of scrutiny for cases involving different issues. The higher the level of scrutiny, the more closely the Court examines the constitutionality of the law, and therefore, the higher the standard the law must meet in order to pass (and be constitutional). The footnote (or some combination of Justice Stone, his clerk, and the Chief Justice, who also made some suggestions in the draft) identifies three types of actions which would warrant this heightened scrutiny: violations of the Bill of Rights, laws which affect the ability of people to advocate for and protect their rights, and laws which discriminate against isolated minority groups.

Over the years, the Supreme Court has developed and expanded this idea of varying levels of scrutiny. Each of these requires some relationship between the means and the end; the difference is in how closely related they must be. At first, the Court had essentially the two levels Footnote Four suggests: heightened (or strict) scrutiny

---

78 You can just hear them cackle: "We'll get you, our pretties! You and your little lenses, too!" If only the case had come from Kansas.

79 Read laws long enough, and you start to wonder, what if we were all as stupid as legislators think we are? Read them even longer, and you start to wonder, what if the legislators are right?

80 In this case, Sooners detecting Sooner eye disease sooner.

81 If *Carolene Products* Footnote Four is not the most famous footnote of all time, it is certainly the most famous in a Supreme Court decision. It was apparently originally added by Justice Stone's law clerk, Louis Lusky, with Stone later editing it. Lusky went on to become a professor at Columbia Law School.

for laws (or actions) which treat people differently on the basis of race or which impact a fundamental right, and rational basis review for the rest (which becomes the laugh test when the issue is an economic liberty).

Now, when I say "laws which treat people differently on the basis of race," you should think of the word "discriminate." Discrimination, however, is not what you probably mean when you say the word. Discrimination is classifying people (or things) and treating them differently based on that classification. We are so used to thinking of racial discrimination, we forget that discrimination is not in and of itself a bad thing. Racial discrimination almost always is, because race almost never represents a valid reason for treating people differently, and history shows we rarely do it for valid reasons. There are, however, many valid classifications which **should** result in different treatments.

For example, the law should treat children or those of limited mental development differently than it treats those who should know better, who can appreciate and anticipate the connection between their decisions and the consequences of those decisions. It should treat convicted criminals from those who are innocent of criminal behavior. The problem is treating people differently based on an irrelevant classification, such as their skin color. We saw the Court do this in *Muller*, treating the classification of gender as if it were relevant to assertiveness or the ability to exercise one's rights, when it quite obviously isn't.[82]

I say this so that when I say the terminology the Court uses to identify this type[83] of law is one with a "suspect class," you will understand it is **not** the class of people which is suspect. It is the use of that criterion to classify people which is suspect. It is a suspect classification. In other words, there are classifications which governments have often treated as relevant which rarely are. The color of someone's skin says very little else about them, other than the amount of melanin their body produces. People have often, and incorrectly, taken it to reflect their intellectual or moral capacity, and those people and their governments have created laws reflecting those prejudices.

In fact, the first elaboration of the strict scrutiny standard was by Justice Hugo Black[84] in *Korematsu v. U.S.* in 1944: "It should be noted, to begin with, that all legal restrictions which curtail the civil rights of a single racial group are immediately suspect. That is to say that courts must subject them to the most rigid scrutiny. Pressing public necessity may sometimes justify the existence of such restrictions; racial antagonism never can." Black went on to argue that pressing public necessity did indeed justify the internment of U.S. citizens of Japanese ancestry during World War II.[85] There was not time to separate the loyal form the treacherous, so for the safety of the West Coast and of those citizens themselves, they had to be removed.

This is the standard of strict scrutiny: the means must be necessary, and the ends must be compelling. "Necessary," in this context, means what it does everywhere but John Marshall's Dictionary of Convenience, which is to say, that the goal cannot be accomplished without it. The Court sometimes expresses this as "narrowly tailored," as well. This means that the chosen measure does as little collateral damage as possible. If we must make an omelet, it is necessary to break some eggs. However, that necessity only justifies breaking the number of eggs necessary to make the omelet, and no more. Any other eggs broken were not necessary to the goal, and therefore are not justified.

"Compelling" can be a little more difficult to pin down. In *Korematsu*, national defense was the compelling government interest. This is perhaps the poster child for compelling government ends. A government which cannot protect its people from invasion fails the primary mission of any government. Where exactly the line falls after national defense, however, is a little less clear. The best way I can think of it is as a life-or-death situation for government. Short of invasion or violent overthrow, what exactly threatens the life of a state is hard to imagine; maybe it better to state it as a vital purpose.

---

82 Or did you miss those paragraphs on the women's suffrage movement? In 1908, that would apparently have put you level with a Supreme Court justice. Today, it's a guy in a sleeveless undershirt stained with unidentified fluids and poor hygiene. Or did I just make the same mistake?

83 Yes, another word for category or class.

84 You may also know him as former Ku Klux Klan member Hugo Black.

85 How convenient for his argument, that the one thing which justifies it was present in this case. What are the chances?

To give you some contrast, let me explain the next level of scrutiny, intermediate. I told you the Court began with two levels of scrutiny. Strict scrutiny is used when the state classifies people on the basis of race, because that classification is inherently suspect, because of its long history of severe abuse. When it came to discrimination based on sex, the Court found strict scrutiny to be too high of a burden. Sex is sometimes a relevant classification, whereas race almost never is. This is, there are actual, systematic difference between the sexes, where there aren't between races. For example, requiring gynecologists to see male patients (regardless of sex) is absurd, whereas requiring them to see patients regardless of race is not. Recognizing that government's use of the category of sex was more often appropriate, yet still subject to frequent abuse, the Court introduced what it called intermediate scrutiny. This requires that the law or action be substantially related to an important government purpose.

So, if the risk of death for the state describes "compelling," then an "important" goal is one for which the state would lose the equivalent of a limb if prevented from achieving that goal. The state would not have failed at a primary purpose, but at a fundamental one. It would not cease to exist, but it would lose a significant amount of its ability to function. It would be severely hindered. What a substantial relation to this end is, we can best understand through the idea of "narrowly tailored." A substantial relation may not be absolutely necessary, or as narrowly tailored. It can have a looser fit; the state may choose the most effective, rather than the least restrictive means, even if the goal were perhaps achievable without that particular means.

The Court uses intermediate scrutiny solely for cases involving classification based on sex. It has been suggested the Court use this for classifications based on (old) age or illegitimacy, but the Court has so far declined to do so. It uses strict scrutiny for classifications based on race, as well as for laws which burden fundamental rights. (See Table 12.1, conveniently located near here, for a summary of all of this.) Fundamental rights are those found in the Bill of Rights and which impact individuals' abilities to protect themselves through the political process. Political speech, for example, is more closely protected than other speech, because political speech is used to protect other rights (including other speech).

Table 12.1 Levels of Scrutiny

Level	Means	Ends	Examples
strict	necessary	compelling	racial discrimination fundamental rights
intermediate	substantial	important	sex discrimination
rational basis	rational	legitimate	everything else economic rights

This leaves us with rational basis, which is the level of scrutiny applied to everything else. Rational basis, however, is not always rational basis. There seem to be two layers to this level. For government regulation of economic activity, the standard is the laugh test—can the Court read the law and not laugh, or can the Court find it conceivable that the legislature found the connection possible. For everything else, the Court uses the rational basis test in much the same tenor as Marshall's (loose) definition of necessary and proper: there must be a legitimate purpose, something government is not forbidden to do, and the means must reasonably address that goal, where "reasonable" means "in some portion." Come to think of it, it's probably more accurate to say that is the standard on both types of rational basis review. The difference is whether they actually check to see if the conditions are met (stern rational basis) or if they just take the legislature's word for it (laugh test, or "minimal rationality").

So, we have thoroughly[86] discussed the Bill of Rights, why we have it, why it might be dangerous, how it came to limit state governments as well as the federal, and the different levels of review the Supreme Court uses in cases involving civil liberties (and civil rights, so we saved some time in the next chapter).[87] No wonder this chapter looks set to be the longest—because we're not yet done. We still need[88] to discuss some of the

---

86 Again, unless you object, though also again, the trail of drool down the page doesn't augur well.

87 At least, I thoroughly discussed. I think you thoroughly cussed. And the next chapter is still Chapter 13. Luckily, we dodged that wormhole a few paragraphs back.

88 Okay, "ought to."

content of the Bill of Rights. We finally have the context, so now we are free to look at the substance of civil liberties.[89]

The very beginning, as Maria von Trapp reminds us, is a very good place to start,[90] so let's begin with the First Amendment. While the religion clauses actually come first in the First Amendment, the most famous clauses are those dealing with speech and press. There's also one about gathering peacefully and petitioning the government, but it doesn't like to associate with the other clauses,[91] so we'll leave it in peace, and begin with speech and press. The third and fourth clauses of the First Amendment are "Congress shall make no law . . . abridging the freedom of speech, or of the press."

As we discovered in your Facebook fiasco, that says Congress can't make the freedom of speech (or the press) less, but it does not say it cannot regulate it. Another way to say it is that some speech (and printing) is protected, but some is not. Government is allowed, indeed expected, to regulate the unprotected speech, but it cannot encroach on or invade protected speech. It is tempting to read this to say that Congress can make no regulation regarding speech, but that is senseless for two reasons, neither of which is the fact that Hugo Black said it.

In the textual sense, that is nonsense because it is not what the First Amendment says. It does say that Congress cannot make regulations regarding establishments of religion, but it switches to different verbs (technically, participles, which are the adjective form of verbs)[92] when it comes to the exercise of religion and the freedoms of speech and press. It obviously does not mean to describe the same situation, then, or it could simply have continued listing in relation to the same verb (technically, participle).

In a logical sense, this is nonsense because it would imply that rights and liberties are unbounded. We cannot all have complete freedom of speech; at some point, your use of that freedom will interfere with my use of it. In other words, we can't talk at the same time and both (or either) of us be heard or understood. If both rights are absolute, then whose should yield? There is an old legal aphorism: your right to swing your fist ends where my nose begins. This is why political philosophers (at least, those of a certain age)[93] talk about "ordered liberty," which is the idea that we each have as much liberty as is consistent with everyone else having the same amount.[94] Our liberties only extend until they infringe on someone else's enjoyment of theirs. Establishing and patrolling that border is the reason we form governments.

So, for example, speech which presents a "clear and present danger" to others is not protected by the First Amendment. Raise your hand if you've heard the expression "shouting fire in a crowded theater." Now that everyone around you is laughing at the enthusiastic reader whose arm shoots up randomly, you can put it down.[95] Those expressions come from a Supreme Court decision written by Justice Oliver Wendell Holmes, Jr. In *Schenck v. U.S.*, the Court ruled that the government (in this case, the federal one) could regulate (and therefore punish) speech which created "a clear and present danger," such as "falsely shouting fire in a theater and causing a panic." Words which might otherwise be protected are not when they are said in circumstances likely to produce "substantive evils that Congress has a right to prevent." Shouting fire in an empty theater is not likely to start a panic in which people are trampled, since there are no people there. As a result, it would be protected speech (though no one would be there to object to it, anyway). Shouting fire in a theater full of patrons (or today, shouting bomb in a busy airport) causes a panic which is likely to injure people, though

---

89   See what I did there? You're welcome.

90   *The Sound of Music*. If you don't get the reference . . . listen, people organize international travel around this movie. Know the classics, or just stay home.

91   One day you'll realize what I did there. In anticipation of that day: you're welcome.

92   Gerunds are the noun forms of verbs, as in "the running of the bulls." *Run* is a verb; *running* is a noun made from that verb. Gerunds and participles often end in *-ing*. In "I hate running," *running* is a gerund; in "I was wearing my running shoes," *running* is a participle. And you don't know what nouns, verbs, and adjectives are, I can't help you. And I mean that in the sense of "You're beyond help," rather than any other. Also, I weep for the future of this country, or any other you may move to.

93   The Enlightenment Age, to be precise.

94   For Rousseau, this was none—but who's counting?

95   I appreciate the enthusiasm though. It was just an expression; didn't mean to embarrass you like that.

hopefully less than being consumed in a fiery blaze. To have caused that injury when there was no fire (or bomb) is to have abused the right to free speech, to have used it to endanger others.

Mr. Schenck, for example, was mailing out leaflets which encouraged people to oppose the draft, and not to report if drafted. He was mailing these to people who had been drafted, and that during a war,[96] so as to create a clear and present danger of desertion. While he would have been within his rights (and outside of Congress' grasp) in normal times, saying it in those circumstances was not protected speech.

The same is true of "fighting words." Saying things to someone in circumstances where those words are likely to cause the other to breach the peace is not protected speech. Insulting someone in a public debate is poor form, but protected speech (all else being equal). Saying things about someone's mama is protected speech (so long as what you're saying is true). To paraphrase Justice Louis Brandeis in another free speech case, *Whitney v. California*, where there is sufficient time and space to correct insulting or discomforting words, the proper response is more words, to show the falsehood or inappropriateness of those remarks. But yelling things about someone's mama inches from their face is likely to provoke an immediate and violent response.

Speaking your mind is fine; people are free to ignore you. They can walk away. Giving someone a piece of your mind means engaging them directly; they are less free to walk away. You'd probably follow them if they did. If they ignore you, you'll get louder, closer, not let them avoid eye contact. That may not be protected speech.[97] Just as the legislature may regulate and prohibit the violent response, it may prohibit words designed to provoke or produce it. The legislature may (and should) prohibit murder; it may also prohibit the use of speech to arrange it (conspiracy, which literally means "to share a spirit or breath").

In fact, some members of the Court considered the fighting words exception as a possible justification for a Texas law banning burning the U.S. flag as a means of protest. Speaking of which,[98] this also tells us that "speech" need not be verbal communication. The Court often uses the term "expression" to emphasize that non-verbal communication is protected as well. In *Texas v. Johnson* (the flag burning case), the Court struck down the Texas law as an infringement of free speech, because the law was not narrowly tailored. It banned all such expressions, not just such expressions in circumstances where they would be likely to cause a breach of the peace (at gatherings involving veterans, for example). The Court also pointed out that Texas law already outlawed provoking breaches of the peace anyway, so the law would only have been valid in areas where it was redundant. Just as in *Schenck*, the expression was protected, unless done in circumstances where it presented a clear and present danger of provoking a breach of the peace.

You may have noticed my careful qualification that your statements about someone's mama would be protected if not said in inflammatory circumstances, as long as they were true. This is because slander, or saying something false about someone, is not protected speech. That falsehood must also be damaging to their reputation. Falsely accusing someone of being a brunette does not generally damage their reputation, it just means you're too dim or too colorblind to get it right. "Too dim" might damage your reputation, but if you can't tell the difference between brunette and ginger and blond, it probably isn't false. Truth is always a defense against an accusation of slander; showing the truth of what you said means it wasn't slander, because it wasn't false.

You may also have noticed that I was careful not to use "obscenities" as a synonym for "fighting words." Obscenity is not protected speech, either. When we talk about words as obscenities, as in "she was shouting all sorts of obscenities," we usually mean curse words, or vulgarities. We mean that people find them offensive.[99] What the Court means by obscenity has been difficult to pin down. What people find too offensive to be said or presented in public varies from place to place. In New York City, a man walking down the street wearing

---

96 I know what you're thinking, or at least what you should be if you have any passing acquaintance with history. But this case is not from the Vietnam War era (the 1960s and early 1970s), it's from the World War I era (it was decided in 1919).

97 Being reprimanded is not, in and of itself, "fighting words." It's fighting *words*, not fighting *tone*. The words have to be such—particularly odious insults or obscenities—that they are calculated (or as if calculated) to elicit a violent response.

98 I honestly did not notice that was a pun until after I wrote it.

99 Or at least they used to do so. They are now so sadly ubiquitous as to have lost their shock value.

nothing but a pair of chaps is just another day that ends in "y." In rural Mississippi or Alabama,[100] that man is about to be in need of medical care. Even in upstate New York, or in the capitol building in Albany, that same behavior would be offensive, if not quite so provoking of violence. So the Court struggled to find one national definition of obscenity, until it finally gave up. Given that most of the cases involved pornography, and thus required the judges to review the items[101] in question, the Court's greatest moment of unintentional humor came when Justice Potter Stewart lamented this surrender, because "I know it when I see it."[102]

The Court ended up kicking this issue back to the states. The Court adopted this formulation for determining whether speech (or press, or expression) was obscene, and therefore not protected by the First Amendment: whether a reasonable person, applying community standards, would find that it appealed primarily to prurient interests. "Applying community standards" makes it a local question, thus making it largely a state problem. "A reasonable person" means not the old lady who throws cats at passers-by, or the loud guy on the soapbox at the corner who throws Bibles at them—unless those really are typical people in that community.[103] It means someone willing to weigh out two arguments on the basis of evidence. That just leaves "prurient interest." I usually encourage you to google words to find out what they mean. If you do, just make sure you have safe search on, and stay away from the image results. "Prurient" means excessively sexual, or in this case, primarily sexual. Synonyms include lewd, lascivious, and lecherous.[104]

So, if a normal person from that community would say that the work or words in question mostly communicated sexual desire (or more precisely, were meant to communicate with and appeal to someone's sexual desire), then it fall outside of the expression the First Amendment protects. For most people—those who aren't teenagers—Botticelli's *Birth of Venus* or Michelangelo's *David* don't speak to their sexual desire, but to the beauty and vulnerability of the human form.[106] To be blunt, it is meant to inspire, not to arouse; to elevate your appreciation of the human body, not to elevate anything else.[107] Of course, there was an era[108] when a lady showing her bare ankle or a man showing collarbone or chest hair was considered lewd and lascivious, so the target is definitely a moving one, and sometimes a weird one.

Of course, this is hardly an exhaustive tour, but you should already see that whether or not expression is edifying plays some role in whether or to what extent it is protected. Speech or expression which appeals to reason is more likely to be protected. Speech or expression which appeals to things likely to circumvent or short-circuit reason (such as anger, fear, or sexual desire) are less protected, because they are likely to provoke action without consideration, especially of the harm which might result to others.

Print, on the other hand, does not normally prompt such rash and thoughtless responses. You can find numerous examples of a speaker goading a crowd to violence until the violence breaks forth; I struggle to think of any example of a poster or newspaper article sparking the same response.[109] Crowds don't normally read together, nor does that reading provide communication between them to coordinate their responses. The printed word usually creates some mental distance, which allows the reader more control of the exposure to the stimulus, and also allows him time to come to his senses—think of the *Friends* episode when Joey kept

---

100   To the extent that "rural" is not redundant.

101   And thus also involved the press, usually.

102   No word on what Mrs. Stewart thought about this hard-won expertise.

103   In which case, what does being a member of that community say about you? I'd move.

104   Also known as the Three L's of Hollywood Screenwriting.

105   Those images you can google, but keep the safe search on—just in case.

106   Teenagers, of course, are not usually reasonable people on the subject of sexual desire.

107   Such as blood pressure or hormone levels—why, what did you think I meant?

108   The Victorian Era, when Victoria kept her (and everyone else's) secrets secret.

109   The examples I can think of are cartoons or books depicting the Prophet Mohammed. If we look carefully, I think we will find that speakers used those images to provoke violence. That is, the incitement came from speakers referring to the images, rather than the images themselves.

putting a Stephen King novel in the freezer when it got too scary. A poster is easier to ignore than a person with a megaphone, and if the poster starts to overwhelm my self-control, I can always turn my back to it until I have regained my composure. A person with a megaphone (or a bullhorn) may simply walk around to my front, aside from the fact that hearing is not as directionally limited as sight is.

Thus, while the legislature can forbid you from saying things, it can very rarely prohibit you from publishing them. This is called prior restraint, and the Supreme Court takes a very dim view of it. It is important that you note the difference between prior restraint and posterior accountability. As with speech, publishing which falls outside of the First Amendment's protection is subject to legislative regulation—you will have to make good whatever damage your unprotected publication does. Prior restraint means simply censorship, and the government can almost never stop you from publishing something before you publish it. In fact, the Supreme Court has never upheld an instance of the government enjoining the publication of information, and has only ever given one example of something the First Amendment would allow the government to censor. That one example is troopship information, or information giving the location or movement of military forces. The reason should be obvious to you by now: it endangers others, and does so in a way which can't be made good later.

Why does the Supreme Court have such a strong presumption against the validity of censorship? The answer is from John Stuart Mill. Mill argued that censorship was always damaging. We often believe that censorship might do some good; it might keep someone from being offended, or it might keep someone from being enthralled and misled by a lie (and by the liars who tell them). There is a practical argument against this, and you should be able to make it by now. The power to censor is a moral hazard. If the government has the power to censor what is false, what is to keep it from censoring what is true, but inconvenient for the government? Nothing; you would never know the censored information existed, so you would never question the Potemkin village the government constructed to keep you happy, docile, and obedient.[110]

Mill, however, argued that censorship was always damaging, not just when it was abused. Even if we could create a machine that would only censor falsehoods, we would damage ourselves just as surely as if we censored the truth. Fighting off falsehoods, having to explain why they are false, means defending what is true, which means constantly reminding ourselves of what is true and why it is true. Like an immune system, if we do not practice that defense, we become poor at it. When we no longer know why something is true, we cannot defend it, and we are easily led astray by falsehoods. We forget how to test whether something is false or true, and so become incredibly gullible. It is only by fighting off being misled that we learn not to be misled.

Worse, this causes our store of knowledge to degrade, to molder and deteriorate. By testing new propositions, fending off new challenges, we either add to our store of knowledge, or discover and remove the parts that have gone moldy. If we do not test, we do not add, and we do not preserve, and we eventually find that everything has gone rotten. Like the idiots in *Idiocracy*, we water our plants with sports drink, 'cause it's got 'lectrolytes, without any idea of what electrolytes are, or if plants need them.

If you think Mill is overreacting, then consider what happens when Facebook promotes only news and posts that you agree with. Your opinions, what you think you know, are never challenged. You never have to defend it, so you've never considered its weak spots. When someone outside of Facebook finds one of those weak spots, it feels the same as when the dental assistant is probing your teeth for weak spots and finds one: it strikes a nerve. Sudden and unexpected pain overwhelms you, and you resent the other person for hitting you there (even if they found it entirely by accident). You react with sudden anger rather than calm reserve.[111]

---

110 Grigory Potemkin (which should actually be transliterated "Potyomkin," and pronounced "pah-tyohm-kin," rather than the typical "puh-tem-kin") was an advisor to and paramour of Empress Catherine II (known as Catherine the Great, though it should be Yekaterina II, or Yekaterina the Great) of Russia. According to legend, he had a village built like a movie set and used it as a façade in front of the real villages Catherine passed through on trips to the Crimea, so that the Empress would not be upset by the actual living conditions in the villages of her empire. Over a century later, a battleship named after him saw the crew mutiny after an officer threatened to shoot them if they did not eat their meal. Although the meal was borscht, a favorite and delicious Russian soup made form beef and beets, the meat used for this borscht was evidently maggot-infested, and may not have been beef, technically speaking.

111 The same dynamic, by the way, happens with executives who wield too much power. They either surround themselves with yes men, or turn the people around them into yes men, and they never hear any objections. So when someone outside that circle points out a flaw . . .

Does this start to sound like the kind of speech which is likely to be regulated, rather than protected? That dovetails Mill's argument with Tocqueville's. We cannot live together if every thought someone has causes us such pain. We must either find a tyrant to abuse us both, or we must develop a tolerance for other people's "truths." We must, as Jonathan Rauch[112] reminds us, go through the painful process of separating truth from falsehood, and belief (what is true in my personal experience) from fact (what is true in experiences that others can share directly).

Of course, just because you may not be prevented from publishing something does not mean that whatever you choose to publish is protected. Where your enjoyment of that freedom damages someone else, you must yield. We discussed slander and obscenity as non-protected speech. Obscenity is not protected as printed matter, either, and when slander is printed, rather than spoken, it is called libel, which is likewise not protected. Libel is printing something false which damages someone's reputation or standing (in the community, not legal standing). Slander is less often litigated, because it does not leave as tangible a record as libel (by definition) does, but I believe the following applies to both.

To claim damages for libel, a private citizen need only show that the published claim is false,[113] and that the publication of it damaged their reputation. How then do campaign ads not result in millions of libel suits? Does this mean that those ads are **true**? Does this mean that those articles in the *Weekly World News*[114] or *National Enquirer* are true, and Saturn is not a planet after all, but the Death Star, probably under the command of Darth Chiropt, who is really the mutant bat boy, whose mutations corrupted him to dark side of the force?[115]

Calm the aarp down, Judy. First, Saturn is the only real thing in that story, and as it is not (yet, pending new revelations in the *Weekly World News*) a sentient being, it cannot sue for libel. Hollywood stars, like politicians, are at least arguably sentient, but there we run into a different problem. The standard for proving libel against a public figure is somewhat higher. Public figures are those who choose to place themselves in the public spotlight. When you try to attract the public's attention, as celebrities and public officials often do, you have to take what you get. You can't ask people to talk about you without being willing to accept fewer limits on what they can say; you can't ask that people only say good things about you, or only talk about the things you want them to talk about. Of course, greater latitude in criticizing public officials is to some degree necessary in a democracy. If you had to make sure every last detail of your rant was true, you would be less likely to express your opinion.[116]

As a result, public figures must show not only that the claim is false and damaging, but that the publisher knew (or had cause to know) it was false, and that it was published with the **intent** to cause damage.[117] "Having cause to know" may sound strange, but it just means there is no willful blindness. You know what willful blindness is; as long as you don't look at the syllabus, you can "honestly" say that you didn't know that assignment was due today. You had cause to know—you should have *wanted* to know if it was true, and so should have taken some initiative, like reading the syllabus, or asking the professor who wrote it or classmates who have read it, even if they do roll their eyes and tell you to read the syllabus. Instead, you acted with "wanton disregard for the truth." You didn't even try to find out if it was true.

So, when a tabloid says that Justin Bieber is actually an alien in disguise, they could be saying it because he is from Canada, and alien just means "not from around here." Or, if they said specifically that he is an extraterrestrial, they could say they knew it wasn't true, and everyone else should have, too. That is, the claim is so absurd that a reasonable person would not give it any credence, so they could not have **intended** to damage

112   Rauch, Jonathan. *Kindly Inquisitors: The New Attacks on Free Thought*, Enlarged Edition. (Chicago: University of Chicago Press, 2014).

113   Remember, truth is always a defense against claims of libel. Showing that it is true means that it is not libel.

114   It bills itself as "The Worlds' Only Reliable News," where "reliable" must mean "published like clockwork," in the same sense that your bowels are regular. Or maybe they mean you know it's never accurate; its falsehood is reliable.

115   Some of that is taken from the *Weekly World News*' website. Some of it I made up. Can you tell which is which?

116   The Court often talks about a "chilling effect" on free speech or expression, that the fear of liability or punishment gets people to censor themselves. The history of totalitarian states proves them right to worry.

117   As the Court says, with malicious intent, or with malice aforethought.

his reputation.[118] They thought it was so obviously false that no one would take it seriously.[119] As a result, public figures rarely win libel cases in the United States.[120]

Speaking of things that aren't the same in the United Kingdom,[121] we still need to talk about the religion clauses. Let's start with the Establishment Clause: "Congress shall make no law respecting an establishment of religion". We've already established that this does not mean Congress can make laws only if they are snarky and rude. It means that Congress cannot compel people to observe or support a particular religion, or religion generally, and as written, that Congress could not prevent the states from doing so. If Congress (or now, post incorporation, your state government) compels you to attend worship services, or makes you pay money that it gives to one or more religions, or uses to employ priests or pastors, then it's pretty clear that government has violated that rule.

What about if the government uses your tax dollars to purchase textbooks for public schools, but also buys enough to provide them for religious schools, as well? Since the schools are run by a church, and you are forced to pay taxes, isn't this forcing you to support a church? That was the question in *Lemon v. Kurtzman*, a Pennsylvania case from 1971. The Pennsylvania law not only provided parochial schools with the same textbooks and instructional materials, it also reimbursed them for the salaries they paid their teachers. This makes some sense; the government is supporting the education of students, whether they attend private religious schools or public schools. The law specified that teachers whose salaries the state reimbursed could not offer religious instruction, so the state wasn't paying for religious instruction.

The Court outlined a three-pronged test to determine whether a measure involved so much support that it became an establishment of religion, rather than public policy that incidentally benefitted religion. The first prong is rather obvious: the law must have a secular purpose. So far, so good for the Pennsylvania law. Its purpose was clearly the education, in secular subjects (the same ones taught in public schools), of young citizens. The second prong was that the measure could neither advance nor inhibit the religion. Here, things get a little less clear; by bearing some of the costs of religious education, government does make it cheaper and therefore more attractive (all else being equal) to send a child to a church-run school.[122] Still, anyone wishing to avoid it had plenty of public school alternatives.

The third prong was entanglement; the law should not involve the government in administering the religion, or in determining questions of doctrine or theology. It was this third prong which the Pennsylvania statute failed. The Court found that the parochial school system was an important element in the Church's doctrine and practice, and that the requirements that teachers whose salaries were reimbursed teach only subjects offered in public schools, using only the materials used in public schools, involved the government too much in overseeing and directing a mission of the Church. Please enjoy the irony that the very measures meant to keep the law from offending the Establishment Clause were the very ones which proved fatal. The difficulty this highlights, that of deciding what constitutes "excessive entanglement," has prompted the Court repeatedly to attempt re-interpreting the Lemon test into something more wieldy. As Justice Antonin Scalia remarked in 1993,

> Like some ghoul in a late-night horror movie that repeatedly sits up in its grave and shuffles abroad, after being repeatedly killed and buried, *Lemon* stalks our Establishment Clause jurisprudence once again, frightening the little children and school attorneys of Center Moriches Union Free School District. Its most recent burial, only last Term, was, to be sure, not fully six feet under: our decision in *Lee v. Weisman* conspicuously avoided using the supposed 'test' but also declined the invitation to repudiate it. Over the years, however, no fewer than five of

---

118   Let's face it, in Hollywood, that's probably not going to hurt him, anyway. It would just open up new marketing possibilities.

119   Which is quite a commentary on their readers, one way or the other.

120   Britain's standard for libel is much lower, so public figures generally prefer to have their libel cases heard there, if they can find sufficient connection to file the claim there.

121   See previous footnote. And the United Kingdom has an established church, the Church of England (though people are free to worship as they wish).

122   In this case, the Catholic Church.

the currently sitting Justices have, in their own opinions, personally driven pencils through the creature's heart (the author of today's opinion repeatedly), and a sixth has joined an opinion doing so.

The secret of the *Lemon* test's survival, I think, is that it is so easy to kill. It is there to scare us (and our audience) when we wish it to do so, but we can command it to return to the tomb at will. When we wish to strike down a practice it forbids, we invoke it; when we wish to uphold a practice it forbids, we ignore it entirely. Sometimes, we take a middle course, calling its three prongs 'no more than helpful signposts.' Such a docile and useful monster is worth keeping around, at least in a somnolent state; one never knows when one might need him.[123]

In the case Justice Scalia specifically references, *Lee v. Weisman*, the Court held that allowing a rabbi to give an invocation before a public school graduation ceremony violated the Establishment Clause **because** the school had provided a pamphlet with tips on how to write an invocation which would be as non-denominational and as little religious as possible.[124] According to the Court, this amounted to endorsement,[125] and although students and parents were not required to attend in order to graduate, expecting them to stand as patient by-standers amounted to coercing their participation. As Justice Scalia pointed out in dissent (Justice Kennedy wrote the opinion of the Court), if politely allowing people around you to do something means you are coerced, then we are constantly subjected to coercion.

For example, my family and I are Christian (and in particular, Baptist). We are in the habit of saying a prayer over our meals, even when eating in public. Granted, we do not stand up and say it loudly enough for the whole restaurant. In fact, not everyone at the table always hears the concluding "amen." Do other patrons need to talk loudly, or stand up and say that they're not part of that prayer? When friends who don't wish to participate are with us, they simply sit with eyes open and head unbowed. As any child taken to a church against their will can tell you, all it takes to demonstrate your non-participation in a prayer is to keep your eyes open and your head up; the fierce scowl is optional.

In 1997, Justice Sandra Day O'Connor attempted yet again to renovate the *Lemon* test, in *Agostini v. Felton*. Noting that excessive government entanglement (the third prong) usually has the effect of either advancing or inhibiting a religion (the second prong), she folded the two together. The resulting test is known as the neutrality test, because it allows interaction between government and religious institutions so long as the government has a secular purpose and the interaction occurs on the same terms as that between government and non-religious institutions. Public schools, for example, can allow religious groups to use or rent their facilities, so long as the same terms are available to non-religious groups (and vice versa). So long as the government treats religious institutions the same as non-religious, it is neither favoring nor disfavoring them, neither advancing nor inhibiting.

It is not clear whether the neutrality test has replaced *Lemon*, or whether it is a new mutation of the same undead ghoul.[126] The Court has yet to overrule or invalidate *Lemon*, and has continued to endorse its existence, in name at least. What seems clear is that the state may not be seen to stamp religion with its approval or disapproval. Even implicit endorsement pressures people to adopt a particular religion (or religion generally), or discourages them from adopting it, and thus advantages one religion over another (or religion over non-religion).[127]

What about the other religion clause, the Free Exercise Clause? The Establishment Clause says government can't force you to practice or support a religion. The Free Exercise Clause says that government also cannot prevent you from practicing or supporting a religion. Of course, the exercise of this liberty is like any other. Your practice is free only until it encounters someone else's nose. Thus, government may forbid human

---

123   *Lamb's Chapel v. Center Moriches Union Free School District*, 508 U.S. 384 (1993).

124   In fact, if you read what the rabbi read, it is far more patriotic than religious. (You gonna take my word for that, or are you going to google?)

125   Which, had they used it, would have violated the second prong of the *Lemon* test.

126   Would a *Lemon* by any other name smell as . . . sharp? File that with the number of licks to get to the center of a Tootsie Roll Pop. The world may never know.

127   Or, for the Meghan Trainor explanation, religion's name is No, religion's sign is No, religion's number is No—and the state really needs to let it go.

sacrifice or public nudity or polygamy, even if your religion commands it, because those things are destructive of social order. Kidnapping people to sacrifice definitely creates panic in the streets. Masses of nude people are an assault on the senses, whether welcome or not; or did you want to sit on that bus seat next? Hogging all of the eligible marriage partners tends to provoke unrest among those left unpaired. Even if the sacrifices are voluntary, a government cannot allow some of its citizens to kill other citizens. That would promote a view of other humans as means (things to be used) rather than ends.[128]

Those, of course, are the easy cases. We always pick those to start with. What about if the government is not forbidding your practices, but simply making them more difficult? What if your practices are not public, or only marginally affect social order? The rubber doesn't hit the road until private beliefs begin to affect public action. Private nudity, for example, is constitutional whether as a religious practice or just a hobby. A religious belief that requires you to appear nude in public as well as private has an effect on everyone seeing you, and it also raises (or at least heightens) questions about sanitary and hygienic conditions for you and others. Where is the line between where the public ought to accommodate your beliefs and where your beliefs must yield to public concerns?[129]

Take the case of Mr. Smith.[130] Mr. Smith was a Native American of the Klamath tribe. He lived and worked in Oregon. In fact, he worked as a counselor at a drug rehab clinic. Such clinics often test their employees to make sure they are not themselves using illegal substances, as this often makes them not only ineffective but counterproductive counselors. Having recently attended a tribal religious ritual which involved the ingestion of peyote, Mr. Smith was tested at work, and tested positive for peyote. Oregon law included peyote, a mild hallucinogen, among its controlled substances. As a result, Mr. Smith was fired for cause, as use of a controlled substance violated his employment contract. When he filed for unemployment compensation, however, his claim was denied. Oregon law excluded people who had been fired for work-related misconduct from receiving unemployment benefits.

Mr. Smith sued about the denial of unemployment benefits, claiming this violated the Free Exercise Clause. The government was conditioning this receipt of benefits on his abstaining from his religious practice. In *Employment Division v. Smith*, the Supreme Court held that it did not. The Oregon statute made peyote illegal for everyone. Although it happened to burden Mr. Smith more, in that it interfered with his religion rather than mere recreation, the law was constitutional. The state had acted neutrally, neither targeting a religion for worse treatment, nor singling one out for better treatment.[131] Since the law did not distinguish between religions, the law only had to survive rational basis, rather than strict scrutiny.[132]

Of course, a lot of things can be made to appear neutral on their face, even if they are not neutral in their application. Three years after *Smith*, the Court made clear in *Church of the Lukumi Babalu Aye v. City of Hialeah* that it meant neutral **treatment**, not neutral phrasing. The City of Hialeah, Florida passed an ordinance prohibiting the slaughter of animals within the city limits, privately or publicly, when the primary purpose was anything other than food consumption. If you're thinking that's an odd thing for a city council to take time to say, you're right. Obviously, it wasn't about animal welfare, because you could kill them, so long as your primary purpose was to eat them. I don't suppose the animal much cares why it's being killed, or that it takes comfort in knowing that it will feed someone, so that doesn't affect their welfare, either.

---

128 And everyone knows that's video games' job.

129 France, for example, just had a controversy about Muslim women wearing full body bathing suits on public beaches. Unless you missed it, you probably have the wrong idea. The government was insisting that Muslim women wear more revealing bathing suits, that they show less modesty, rather than more. France draws the line between private and public behavior very strictly. Any public religious display is frowned upon; France expects the public sphere to be completely free of religion. Thus, a full body bathing suit worn on a public beach, and worn as a result of religious beliefs, is an invasion of that sphere.

130 In this case, his name has not been altered to protect his identity; it was already opaque.

131 The Court did mention rather pointedly, however, that most states with significant Native American populations made explicit exceptions for their religious use when they regulated peyote. Oregon took the hint and subsequently revised its laws to allow for such an exception.

132 It fell under "everything else" rather than "fundamental right."

This ordinance also served to ban several other activities. Veterinarians sometimes have to put rabid or incurable animals to death, though they usually do so gently (since ending the animal's misery is usually the goal). Animal shelters must also employ veterinarians to euthanize animals to control the population of strays for public health and safety. Exterminators trap and sometimes kill animals which invade homes and may spread disease. In fact, cities often require these services be performed. Veterinarians and exterminators need not have worried, though. The ordinance specifically exempted them, butchers, kosher butchers, hunting, fishing, and even the practice of feeding rabbits to greyhounds.[133]

Who does that leave then? Only one other group in Hialeah slaughtered animals for primary purposes other than consumption as food: the Church of the Lukumi Babalu Aye. This church is a Santerian sect; Santeria is more popularly known as "voodoo." Their rituals involve the sacrifice of live animals to gain the favor of spirits, and they had recently purchased a property in the city, intending to convert it to a worship center. The Church sued, claiming the city (using its authority under the State of Florida) had prohibited the free exercise of their religion, in violation of the Due Process Clause of the Fourteenth Amendment, as it incorporates the Free Exercise Clause of the First Amendment.

Given what the Supreme Court said in *Smith*, what do you expect it said in *Lukumi*? I can't hear you. No, please don't say it louder. It's not physically possible for me to hear you. Maybe you said that the law made it generally illegal to kill animals unless you planned to eat them. It might burden some more than others, as the peyote regulation in Oregon did, but it didn't single out the Santerians for worse treatment. It didn't address them (or religion at all) directly, but only affected them accidentally along the way to stopping the slaughter of animals. Therefore, under *Smith*, it was constitutional. Certainly that was what the federal district court said, and the circuit court agreed with them.

The Supreme Court, however, disagreed. The majority pointed to the many and exhaustive exemptions. The ordinance had made an act generally illegal, but the city had then made an inordinate amount of exemptions, until everyone but the Santerians was exempted. The pattern of the exemptions, as well as the records of the city council meetings, made clear that the law had been passed as a response to the Santerians and their plan to worship there, with the goal of discouraging or preventing that worship, and not the general act of killing animals. Since the law in application singled out a religiously defined group for different treatment, it had to survive strict scrutiny. It did not, as it had a large impact on free exercise of religion, but only a small one on public health. It was not narrowly tailored, especially since it explicitly allowed so much of the behavior it supposedly sought to regulate to continue unmolested.

In other words, regulations which impact religious behavior must be neutral, in their application if not in their effect. They may necessarily burden some more than others, but as long as they apply to everyone (or nearly so) equally, they are constitutional. The legislature may make some accommodations, such as the exemptions for Native Americans, but those exceptions should not show a pattern or design which isolates one group (or a few groups), as the ordinances in Hialeah did. Conveniently, this is also called the neutrality test, and the idea is the same, just from different ends. One says government must treat religions like any other group; it must be "religion-blind" in providing services or supporting behaviors. The other says that government must be "religion-blind" when regulating and limiting behavior; it must treat religious behavior like any other behavior.

Since we're talking about individual behavior and making it criminal, let's finish up this chapter with a little bit on criminal rights protected in the Bill of Rights. Let's start with one that is already a little familiar, the Search and Seizure Clause of the Fourth Amendment. As I mentioned in our discussion of the right to privacy, this means that government must have a reason to look through your pockets, your house, and your stuff. A warrant is a document which shows government has a reason, at least to the satisfaction of a judge. This may sound facile or superficial—the government has to get the government's permission before it can nose around

---

133   This last was to protect the dog racing industry in Florida. Of course, since butchers kill animals for the primary purpose of selling them as food, I'm not sure why they needed to be exempted. Maybe the thought was that a court might rule their primary purpose was commerce, rather than consuming them as food themselves.

my junk[134]—but remember that "the government" is not a single unified actor. In this case, the executive authority has to convince the judicial authority (who know the rules, and don't really have a stake in making work for themselves) that the executive should be allowed to invade your personal space.

It's easy to gloss over the fact that this is a tremendous improvement over having to check with no one, and being able to go through your pockets (or pants) any time they want, even if they only want to harass you.[135] Most of you reading this[136] have never experienced anything else, and may take these limitations for granted. We have never lived in a state where authority didn't need a reason and did not owe us an explanation, where an officer could decide that you looked guilty, or that dating the person he wanted to date or not dating the person he wanted you to date meant you needed to be guilty of something. That officer of the state never forcibly entered our home in the wee, small hours of the morning, so that we would be sleepy, confused, and vulnerable. We never had to watch as he and his minions tore apart our furniture, clothing, and furnishings until he could find something to use to arrest us, or could provoke us into protesting and providing the excuse.[137]

Thanks to the Fourth Amendment, if the state engages in an unreasonable (also defined as "warrantless") search of our persons or property, any evidence it finds is excluded from being used in court. This is called the exclusionary rule, and it gives police a strong incentive to obey the limits of their powers. If they overstep them, the evidence disappears more thoroughly than if you disintegrated it.[138] If they have no other way of establishing your guilt, they have just done the opposite of their job. Instead of making sure the guilty face justice, they have made sure the guilty won't be punished for those actions. And this applies not only to evidence they find during an illegal search, but any evidence that evidence might subsequently lead to, even if they seize that later evidence legally. "Whoops" just doesn't cover it.

There are, of course, some exceptions, because life is too complicated for absolutes.[139] First, exigent circumstances may avoid the need to get a warrant before searching. *Exigent* means that the circumstances require urgent attention, they cannot wait—there is no time for the officer to get a warrant.[140] For example, if an officer hears cries for help from inside a house, we would think him callous indeed and negligent if, rather than immediately intervening and attempting to render assistance (and entering the house by force, if necessary), he instead drove to the courthouse and waited for a judge to be available, so that he could swear out a warrant. In fact, he might not even have sufficient information to get a warrant, since he does not know if there is even a crime to be investigated.

Likewise, if an officer hears sounds or is aware of other evidence indicating that the suspect or important evidence or both will disappear if she stops to get a warrant, she may continue without one. Note, though, that the officer must still have some probable cause to intervene. In essence, the exigency pushes the need to demonstrate the probable cause from a warrant from before to after. If an officer pulls someone over for speeding but smells marijuana smoke, he cannot ask the driver to wait there until he gets back with a warrant to search the interior of the car for evidence. The side of the road is not a safe place to linger, and more importantly, the suspect is unlikely to still be there when the officer returns, and the suspect will have had ample time to destroy whatever evidence of wrongdoing was present. But the officer cannot search or detain every speeder "just in case," and can only search the car if some evidence gives probable cause to do so.

---

134   And also around my junk.

135   Or especially if they only want to harass you. Not that this doesn't still happen, but it happens a lot less often, and it is at least an actionable offense, rather than something you'd better learn to enjoy.

136   And all of me writing this.

137   To get some idea of what this experience is like, read *The Gulag Archipelago* by Aleksandr Solzhenitsyn, and watch *The Lives of Others*.

138   If it were disintegrated, you could still introduce pictures of it. If it's excluded, you can't do even that. The court does not acknowledge or countenance its existence.

139   Besides, only Sith deal in absolutes.

140   This is the opposite of "Your call is very important to us." This is 911; it needs to be addressed immediately.

Plain sight is another exception. If, when the driver rolls down her window, the officer sees a spliff in the ashtray—wait, cars don't have those anymore. So if the officer sees the driver holding a joint, or if bags of marijuana are lying in open view in the passenger seat, the exclusionary rule will not apply. Similarly, if an officer is executing a warrant to search a house for a murder weapon, but finds illegal drugs sitting in plain sight on the kitchen counter, she may properly seize those, and they may be used as evidence. If she finds them in a box at the back of a closet, she must ignore them. The difference is the degree to which the person in question has sought to shield the items in question from public view.

There is also a good faith exception. Imagine an officer goes to a judge to get a warrant. The officer provides evidence she believes is sufficient to establish probable cause, and sufficiently identifies what she is searching for. She is, however, wrong in some non-obvious way that a judge would normally spot. Unbeknownst to the officer, the judge she finds has just finished her three martini (and six shots of vodka) lunch. The judge's judgment is impaired, and she issues the warrant with the technical defect. The judge hides her insobriety so well that the officer has no idea the judge's judgment is compromised. Thinking she has met the constitutional requirements, she executes the warrant and seizes evidence. Even if the defense challenges the warrant and shows the defect, the court might not exclude the evidence, if they find that the officer acted in good faith—that she reasonably and honestly believed that the warrant was valid.

Now, if the officer **knew** the judge would be intoxicated, and went to her because she wouldn't notice the defect, then the officer did **not** act in good faith. She was trying to evade the constitutional requirements. If another judge had been available first and she passed him up, or if she could tell the judge had incapacitated herself and did not take the matter to another judge, then the court hearing the case would reasonably infer that the officer had acted in bad faith. She chose a judge precisely to evade the constitutional requirement for a warrant.

One more exception, and this one is the most difficult. If the defense moves to exclude evidence based on a faulty search, the state may try to show the inevitable discovery of the evidence. "Inevitable" means that the discovery could not be avoided, that the police, in following their standard procedures, would have unavoidably found the evidence anyway. Think for a moment of the difficulty this entails. They have to demonstrate the probability of a hypothetical series of events, showing how they would have found something they didn't know about, without making reference to or relying on the information they found in error.

It's hard to even think of an example. Let's say some reprobate on the police force is abusing her power, frisking good-looking men as they pass on the street. When she frisks one, she finds that he isn't just happy to see her, that *is* a gun in his pocket. She arrests him, and discovers that the weapon was just used in the murder of his wife, who had a substantial insurance policy. She was also cheating on him with this brother. Having discovered this, the man had killed her, and was on his way to kill his brother. [141] The defense lawyer immediately moves to have the murder weapon and all the resulting information excluded as the fruit of a baseless, warrantless, and therefore illegal search.

After firing the "handsy vigilante" for her abuse of her authority, the good officers have to show that, in the ordinary course of their investigations, following standard procedures, they could only have failed to find the gun through gross negligence. They would have gotten a call when someone found the body, or when the husband reported his wife missing to cover up his crime. In either event, they would have questioned the husband and considered him as suspect, unless they were completely derelict in their duties. This would have led them to the two motives, and that would have led them to trace his movements on that day. If they can show they would have been able to trace him to where he was going to dispose of the weapon, had Officer Handsy McFeely not been abusing her authority, then they have shown they would have inevitably discovered the weapon (or evidence of its destruction).

---

141 If you're wondering, I'm not plagiarizing this from any soap opera script that I know of. Any relation to any soap opera storyline, living or dead, is purely coincidental. No soap operas were harmed in the making of this chapter. Some soap, yes; possibly one opera. But no soap operas.

Notice that they can't just ask for the insurance records. They have to show that they would have asked for them on the basis of other information. Since murders are often committed by family members, they would have been remiss if they did not ask about potential motives of family members, such as insurance or infidelity, and that their usual questions would have led to that information. If they find evidence that the husband planned to report his wife missing, they have to show that they regularly consider whether the husband did the disappearing, as if they had first found the case through that report. If the evidence looks like the husband was going with plan C, telling everyone his wife had gotten an offer of immediate employment in France, and that he was joining her once he tied up all their loose ends here, they would have to show how the case would *inevitably* have come to their attention. It might be that her sister suddenly stopped receiving texts and couldn't get her on the phone, even in France, and they were otherwise in daily communication, so the sister called the police with her suspicions. If nothing like that is true, however, they are out of luck and the murderous villain walks free.

Of course they know he did it, but they have to show how they would have come to know it in the absence of the bad act that originally created their knowledge. You can imagine how frustrating this would be for an officer, interrogating a suspect who maintains his innocence when you both know (and know that the other knows) he's lying. You can imagine how an officer would want to punch that smug look off his face, and finally gives in, beating him until he finally confesses. And if you've watched any police dramas at all, you know that's another mistake. The Fifth Amendment says that no one may be compelled to be a witness against himself in a criminal case. This means that confessions must be voluntary and informed.

What does it mean to say *voluntary* and *informed*? Voluntary means that you do it of your own free will, free of any attempts to influence what you choose, whether through threat of harm or promise of reward. It means that you are not coerced, by literal or metaphorical arm-twisting. Informed means that you have been told what will happen if you confess, that it will be used in court, and that its use is likely to have an effect on the outcome. Why do we care about those things? Because they make your confession credible. People being tortured or pressured will say whatever they must to make the discomfort end. That information isn't credible. You didn't confess because you did it, you confessed to get someone to stop hurting you. Your goal was not the truth, not relieving a guilty conscience, but relieving external pressure. You'll say anything they want, especially if you don't know it will have consequences beyond stopping the hurting.

Confessions which are voluntary and informed, then, are much more likely to be true. As a result, the Supreme Court ruled in *Miranda v. Arizona* that suspects had to be informed, before any interrogation, that they had a right to remain silent, and that anything they did say could be used in court. These became known as the *Miranda* warnings, or "reading someone his rights," and spawned the verb "to Mirandize" a detainee. If you've seen a police drama, they should sound familiar.[142]

Of course, if you've seen many police dramas, you're also familiar with the more direct invocation of the Self-Incrimination Clause of the Fifth Amendment, pleading the Fifth. The standard phrasing is something like "I respectfully decline to answer that question on the grounds that my answer might serve to incriminate me." Judges may otherwise require witnesses to answer questions, and hold them in contempt if they fail to do so. Of course, if a witness lies in court, having taken an oath to tell the whole and unadulterated truth, he is guilty of a crime (called perjury).[143] Without a right against self-incrimination, the threat of being held in contempt of court might prompt some witnesses to lie. Again, to know that the information is credible, we have to know (and the witness has to know) that the witness has an alternative.

---

142 Interestingly, in the United Kingdom, one of the warnings is that if you try to rely on things in court which you don't tell the police up front, it will damage the credibility of the statements. This is true in the United States, as well; any trial attorney who does not challenge discrepancies between someone's initial statements and what they say in court is flirting with malpractice, ethically if not legally. Things you suddenly remember that help your case are less credible because they suit your interests. If what you say changes with your interests, it's less likely to be true, and more likely to be convenient falsehood. What's interesting about all that, though, is that the United Kingdom's warning explains why you have a reason to give a full and complete statement, the United States' warning tells you why you have a reason to give no statement at all.

143 Unless, apparently, his name is Bill Clinton, in which case we know he really didn't mean it, and why are these mean people asking that poor dear questions, anyway?

The Fifth Amendment has lots of other important clauses. I have already made brief reference to two: the prohibition of double jeopardy ("nor shall any person be subject for the same offence to be twice put in jeopardy of life or limb") and the Due Process Clause for the federal government. The Takings Clause is also in the Fifth Amendment. The Takings Clause ("nor shall private property be taken for public use, without just compensation") limits the federal government's (and through incorporation, the states') use of eminent domain. Eminent domain is the power of the sovereign to take private property for his use; in the case of a republic, that becomes public use. The Takings Clause requires that it be for a public use, and that the sovereign must compensate the owner fairly. So if the government needs your property (for example, to build a road), they can force you to sell it to them. The questions are whether the use is public, and whether the compensation is fair.

In *Kelo v. City of New London*, the Supreme Court defined "public use" so broadly as to make it almost, if not entirely, meaningless. If the government takes your property to build infrastructure, like roads or airports, or uses it more directly in its service, as the site for a school, the public use is relatively clear. In *Kelo*, the city of New London, Connecticut took land from private owners to transfer it to different private owners, because the state preferred the use to which the different private owners (a pharmaceutical company) proposed to put the land. The City of New London decided that the public would benefit more form a pharmaceutical plant than it did for Suzette Kelo's (and others') use of the land as a place to live.

The problem with this is not that the assertion wasn't true—it may have been, it may not have been—but that it completely undermines the purpose for which we form government. If government can at any point effect a transfer of property from you to someone else, simply because that person plans a use they like better than yours, then you will only engage in plans which suit the government. You are not free to pursue your own purposes. Even if you don't agree with those values regarding the purpose of government, the pragmatic (though that too is a value) argument is that is proves far too much. Let's start with that one. This principle allows government to decide what is done on any piece of property, so long as it is able to afford it. If the measure of the appropriate use of property is public utility, then what home will not be more useful to the public as a shopping mall, generating more sales tax revenue and jobs? Your home is of great use to you, but the public doesn't benefit from it a great deal.

In fact, at this point, the principle begins to eat its own tail. The more homes we replace with factories, malls, and such, the greater the usefulness to the public (which is not the phrase the amendment uses, if you'll remember). But with no homes, who will be the employees? Where will shoppers keep their stuff? Or will everyone simply live in the back of the "store," with daily garage sales at every location, swapping stuff between themselves endlessly?

Nor can government have sufficient information to correctly judge whether another shopping center or factory will actually produce the desired revenue or jobs. Adding supply does not increase demand. The building may remain without tenants and sell nothing, or the factory may not survive competition from other producers. In the market, those who will benefit take the risk, and bear the cost if they are wrong. In this situation, the former owner bears the cost, but the preferred owner gets the rewards, if any.

The public derives utility from the existence of private use, even if no particular private use is particularly beneficial to it.[144] This is where those pesky values prove their worth. Not allowing the collective free reign over individuals, their rights and other properties, is in fact a social good. It stops the government from doing things which, while immediately attractive, are in the long term self-destructive. Rights reserved to individuals, restrictions on the scope of government authority, not only benefit the governed, they benefit the government.

One last amendment on the subject of criminal rights.[145] The Sixth Amendment includes several (more) provisions on the subject, which have also been incorporated.[146] The Sixth Amendment includes rights to

---

144   This concept—the conflict in an individual between particular and general interests—should seem very, very familiar (and useful) to you by now.

145   Not that I'm **expecting** you to need to know this, of course. It's like keeping up with the spread in sports—solely for entertainment purposes.

146   If I have to add "to apply against the states" at this point, then go back and start this chapter over. Shame on you. Go on—go to the beginning of the chapter to do that.

know the charges against you, to confront witnesses against you, to subpoena witnesses, to have counsel, and to an impartial jury. What do all of these have in common? Well yes, criminal rights; we just said that. But why are these rights ones we think those accused of crimes should have? What's that? Why did I change the words? Which words? Well, what's the difference between a criminal and someone who's been accused of a crime?

Stop. You didn't think about that. Put your thumb on Figure 12.1 over there. Close the book, or if this is the e-book, minimize the app and clean your thumbprint off the screen, and think about the question. Come back when you have an answer. If you're reading this, you didn't minimize the app and think about it. Go on! . . . Okay. What do you think is the difference? I'll pretend you said that a criminal has been convicted of a

Figure 12.1 Nature's Bookmark

crime, whereas a person accused of a crime hasn't been convicted (and might appropriately not be). They are at different ends of a process (the judicial process), at least from where we're standing. Technically, someone is a criminal when they commit a crime, but until they have passed through the legal system, we don't know if they actually committed it or not.[147]

Do you see what those clauses have in common now? The Sixth Amendment says you have a right to know what charges you face. Why is this important? Has your significant other ever been upset with you, and when you asked what was wrong, she[148] replied, "You know what you did." Do you? Of course, unless you've been unconscious, you know what things you have done. You simply don't know which of the things you did caused the offence.[149] Had you known, you probably wouldn't have done it in the first place. More to our point, how can you defend yourself if you don't know what you're defending against? You can't. So you start confessing to everything you might have done, hoping to find the one you need to defuse. Since you are walking blind through a minefield, though, you simply end up finding a lot of mines neither of you knew were there.[150]

Now, what if you weren't going to be told what evidence or testimony supported those changes? Let's say the charge is that you were at the drive-in with another girl.[151] If you know the charge, you can explain that she is your cousin.[152] Let's say you weren't there at all, but that a friend of one of her friends, who doesn't know you that well, mistook someone else for you. If you could question the friend, you might be able to point out differences that could rule you out (your car is a different make, model, and color; you're allergic to an ingredient in the food she saw him eating; you had cut your hair since the last time she saw you). In fact, the witness might even realize you weren't who they thought you were. The person she saw had blue eyes, and she just realized yours are green. Plus, the other guy didn't have the huge mole on his nose.

Both of these relate to making sure convictions are accurate. Well, "making sure" is probably too strong a word. Okay, too strong a phrase. They make it more likely that your conviction, should it occur, is a result of a real relationship between evidence and your guilt, rather than just a supposed one. It could be that it only looks like there is a relationship because the court is unaware of other evidence, or because the evidence is faulty. If you don't know what you're defending, you do not know what evidence to prepare on your behalf. If

---

147 Hopefully, we are much more sure by the time they finish the process, or more accurately, by the time the process is finished with them. Sadly, results may vary.

148 Just playing the odds here—women are something like 63% of the population at the university where I work.

149 In memory of one of our alums, I'll offer the following advice: if you were doing belly shots off of her friend's belly, and thought that the fact it was her friend's belly made it okay, I'm going to go with that one.

150 Proof that women are better strategists than men. Or did you think she said that by accident?

151 Or maybe *Grease* has just been on television too much lately.

152 Assuming that's true, and you're not in Alabama, where that sort of thing would not eliminate her as a competitor.

you cannot challenge witnesses, mistakes in their testimony (whether intentional or accidental) are taken for true. Either way, it presents a false picture.

The same is true for the ability to subpoena witnesses. The state can compel people to appear and testify to what they know. In fact, the word *subpoena* is a threat: "under penalty." When the state subpoenas someone, it is an order to appear, under threat of punishment should they not do so. What if you could not? Maybe someone saw you somewhere else at the time the crime was committed. He might be willing to help, but not unable to miss work, or arrange and pay for child care, so that he can sit around the courthouse, waiting to be called to testify. To make the playing field more level (since the competition is about your life or liberty), the state lends you its ability to compel witnesses to appear and give evidence or testimony. This increases the accuracy of the results, even if it doesn't make them perfect. Convictions are more likely to be based on actual guilt, rather than the uneven or biased absence of evidence.

It should by now come as no surprise to you that the Sixth Amendment's right to counsel ("the accused shall enjoy the right . . . to have the Assistance of Counsel for his defense") serves that very same purpose.[153] If you can't see how—or even if you can—then let me tell you the story of a man named Clarence. Clarence dropped out of school after the eighth grade. As you might imagine, this limited his job prospects. He became a drifter, and bounced in and out of prisons (usually for theft) and marriages. He eventually settled down with his fourth wife in Texas. He had a steady job, and they eventually had three children, in addition to the three his wife already had. Then Clarence contracted tuberculosis; unable to work, he lost his job. The family moved to Panama City, Florida. Clarence took to gambling in an effort to increase his meager income, but that worked out the way it usually does: Clarence had less money, and tried to console himself with alcohol. That, too, worked out the way it usually does: with an arrest.

On August 4, 1961, someone broke into vending machines at the Bay Harbor Pool Room in Panama City. The perpetrator (or perpetrators) stole five dollars in change from the machines and some bottles of beer and soda from behind the bar. A young man who lived nearby, Henry Cook, told the police he had seen Clarence leaving the pool hall with pockets that looked like they were stuffed with change and a bottle of wine. He saw Clarence call a cab and wait until it arrived. The police found Clarence drinking in another tavern, and arrested him. The taxi driver testified that he had picked Clarence up, and that Clarence had asked him to keep the ride a secret. The jury voted to convict.

Clarence had asked the judge to appoint a lawyer to represent him, because he could not afford one. The judge declined; Florida law only required the state to provide a lawyer in capital cases.[154] Clarence (and his eighth grade education) did his best. And finding himself in jail for something he knew he hadn't done, he kept trying. He filed appeals, using the law books in the prison library. He eventually appealed his case to the Supreme Court. Of course, the U.S. Supreme Court has particular requirements for the style in which appeals should be made to it, from the size and color of the paper to the margins and the size of the type. Clarence still didn't have any money; his appeal to the Supreme Court was handwritten on lined note paper the prison

---

153   If it does come as a surprise, it is my solemn duty to inform you that you have the observational skills of a totem pole, or maybe a lump of stone. Whatever's more inert. That, and don't be afraid—Swiper swipes stuff, but Dora always makes him give it back. Also, Blue always leaves clues for Steve. That's why Steve always has to have plastic bags with him.

154   Capital cases are those involving the possibility of a death penalty. "Capita" in Latin means "head," which is quite literally what is in jeopardy in capital cases. Well, okay, not quite as literally as it used to be, when the death penalty was carried out by beheading. By the way, the Eighth Amendment's prohibition of "cruel and unusual punishment" does not (at least, according to the Supreme Court, as I am writing this) forbid capital punishment. Yep, that's the same capital—it's what the punishment is, not the city where it occurs. The Eighth Amendment only prohibits capital punishment where its use is arbitrary or capricious. The death penalty is okay for the most serious crimes—murder, not misdemeanors. More importantly, its application must not be biased in its application. In *Furman v. Georgia*, the court invalidated Georgia's procedure for applying the death penalty, because the jury decided whether the defendant was guilty at the same time they considered the punishment. This made it difficult for lawyers to present mitigating factors. Telling the jury, "My client didn't do it, but if he did, here are some things that make it less bad that he did" means implanting in the jury's head the premise that your client is guilty. Georgia separated the trial (guilt) and sentencing (penalty) into separate phases, giving attorneys a chance to present other (especially mitigating) information once guilt had been established. In *Gregg v. Georgia*, the Supreme Court found this sufficient to remove that bias.

had for prisoner communication. The Supreme Court accept it as *in forma pauperis*, which means in the style of the poor.[155]

The Court held in *Gideon v. Wainwright* that the complexities of court procedure, of the rules of evidence (what should be challenged and how), and an understanding of how to make and present a legal argument to a judge and jury, were such that Clarence had not had a fair playing field. There was too great a chance that his liberty had been removed, not because he actually was guilty, but because he was too unskilled to present his side as well as the state presented theirs. They held that the Sixth Amendment right to have counsel meant not merely that the state could not refuse to let someone accused of a crime speak with a lawyer, but that the state had to provide a lawyer if the accused could not afford one. (This became the second part of the *Miranda* warning.) They ordered a new trial, this time with a lawyer for the defense.

It turned out, the Supreme Court had a point. Clarence hadn't thought to ask the cab driver to report the rest of their conversation; he knew he had asked the driver to keep it a secret, and knew what the driver said was correct. Or maybe Clarence had been drunk, and didn't remember the conversation well enough to know that there was more. His lawyer, however, knew the importance of the whole truth, and while the state prosecutor had been satisfied with the fact that Clarence wanted it kept secret, Clarence's lawyer asked the cabbie if Clarence had said why he didn't want the cabbie to talk about his trip. He had, the driver testified; he was afraid he'd get in trouble with his wife for having been at the bar.

Clarence's lawyer also had the resources to investigate the other evidence. He knew that Henry Cook, the helpful eyewitness, was also regularly helpful to some other people. He served as the lookout for a gang of thieves. Clarence's lawyer brought in evidence and witnesses which highlighted the inconsistencies of Henry Cook's story, including that it might have been covering for his friends. That would also explain the beer and soda which had been taken, after all. In the end, it took the jury less than an hour to acquit Clarence Earl Gideon.

Speaking of the jury, let us at last come to the first clause of the Sixth Amendment: "the accused shall enjoy the right to a speedy and public trial, by an impartial jury...." There are four important elements to address. First, a speedy trial. This does not, of course, obligate courts to open drive-thru windows, or mean that your case must be adjudicated in thirty minutes or less, or it's free. It means that you cannot be held indefinitely, or even for a long time, without the state putting you on trial, so that the matter is resolved, one way or the other. It allows you to petition courts to issue a writ of *habeas corpus*, which requires the executive authority holding you to appear before the court and explain why they are holding you.

Habeas corpus may sound like a spell from the wizarding world of Harry Potter,[156] but it is short for *habeas corpus ad subjiciendum*.[157] That translates roughly as "You should have the body for investigation,"[158] or more plainly, "the purpose of holding someone is to bring them to trial." Or even more plainly, "pee or get off the pot." If the executive cannot justify your detention, they will have to let you go. The only purpose of detaining you is to resolve the matter; detention must be a means to that end, not an end in itself. If the state is not prepared to move toward that end in a reasonable amount of time, it must release you.

A public trial may not sound like all that great of a blessing. After all, who wants to have all of their dirty laundry aired in public?[159] First, and for the last time, calm down, Judy. "Public" doesn't mean "broadcast on national television."[160] Second, consider what the alternative is. The requirement of a public trial means the

---

155   If you have seen *V for Vendetta*, you will understand why this comes to mind: "This is the only autobiography I have ever written, and oh, God—I'm writing it on toilet paper."

156   And Hermione would point out that the first word is pronounced "HAY-bee-us," not "huh-BEE-ass."

157   Gesundheit.

158   **That** spell is only in very special versions of the Harry Potter movies.

159   I mean, aside from the Kardashians, Paris Hilton, the cast of Jersey Shore, all the guests of the Jerry Springer show, every reality show contestant ever ... I'm talking about everyone who **isn't** a whore for attention.

160   How could it? Back then they didn't even have PBS. Though national broadcast can happen, the judge has to allow it.

government cannot hold trials "off the record," can't have secret proceedings (sometimes even secret from the accused—see above) and then announce the results. There must be some measure of public scrutiny of the conduct of justice, even if the judge may adjust that measure to maintain the safety of those involved or the integrity of the process. Judges may close courtrooms to avoid having mobs sway the jury (or kidnap the accused), for example. But there will be a record of the proceedings, not just that they occurred, but who was present, and what was said, what was presented as evidence, and by whom. Were those records private, there would be no public outrage to check the abuse of power. We wouldn't even see it happen, and we tend confuse the absence of evidence with the evidence of absence.

The involvement of a jury of your peers (the Sixth Amendment doesn't mention peers, but that is our common law tradition) serves the same purpose. Not only will your fellow citizens be there to observe, they will be the ones to apply the law to your case. As Tocqueville pointed out,[161] this has some benefits for democracy, including that they must learn what the law is (and thus, they monitor the abuse of the legislative power in the most direct way). The Sixth Amendment does refer to it as an "impartial" jury, and this too continues the Sixth Amendment's theme of making sure the system is not rigged, that guilt or innocence is as much as possible decided by facts and not irrelevant factors or bias.

In fact, the requirement of an impartial jury strikes directly against bias. The state cannot choose jurors who are, for whatever reason, likely to produce the outcome it wants. Whether the potential juror systematically favors or disfavors either side, state or accused, she should not serve. The state cannot pick a jury consisting of the neighborhood's biggest Yankees fans to try a defendant with a prominent Boston accent and "Red Sox Nation" tattooed across his forehead, nor can the defense choose a jury of Red Sox fans. One could not reasonably expect a jury filled with survivors of child abuse to be impartial in a case involving child abuse. It's not that it's impossible for those jurors to be dispassionate—anyone who's not a sociopath will find it hard to be dispassionate—it's that it will be a bigger challenge. We know that there is a reason they might decide the case on grounds other than the facts in front of them. Other jurors might fall prey to the same error, but they will do so randomly, not systematically. In one case, we have reason to expect bias, in the other we don't. That doesn't mean it won't occur, just that we can't eliminate unpredictable error the way we can predictable error. When we can foresee it, we should avoid it.[162]

How then do we construct an (as much as possible) impartial jury?[163] Funny you should ask; I was just getting ready to talk about that. The federal government and the individual states have, I am sure, different processes for selecting potential jurors, even if the degree of difference varies. I do not know all of the particulars, and especially not for every state. For many years, states commonly used the rolls of registered voters as a pool from which to draw names.[164] However they form the pool, they will then have some process for selecting from it randomly.[165] Once a group of potential jurors is identified, however, the lawyers

---

161 Remember Chapter 4? 'Cause I do.

162 Although for some reason, we continue to allow Yankee fans to serve on juries, as if that weren't an indication of the inability to be reasonable or rational.

163 There are, by the way, two sorts of juries on which one might be called to serve. The first is a grand jury, which decides whether prosecutors have sufficient evidence to indict (to formally charge someone with a crime). The second is (technically) a petty jury, though we usually just call it a jury. This jury hears evidence at a trial (of someone who has been indicted) and decides guilt or innocence. "Grand" and "petty" are not attitudes or demeanors, they refer to the size of the body—they are from the French words for large (*grand*) and small (*petit*—remember, they don't always or even usually pronounce final consonants, and yes, this is also the root of "petite.")

164 This discouraged people from registering to vote, so they may well have amended or replaced this practice. Might the fact that people who didn't want to serve on juries could remove themselves from the pool introduce some bias?

165 I remember once, as a young child, being summoned from my dad's office to the clerk's office of a different court (it was upstairs in the big courtroom) and asked to draw pieces of paper from a large envelope. I found out later that I was drawing names for a jury. (Somewhere in the archives of the Cookeville Herald-Citizen is a photo that can corroborate my story.) I was a child and had no idea what I was doing—so there was no way I could have introduced any bias into it. (I didn't even see the names, and they wouldn't have meant anything to me if I had.)

representing each party get to ask them questions. Some of the questions will be addressed to the whole group: "Have you ever been convicted of a crime?" or "Have you ever been a victim of this type of crime?" Some will be addressed to specific potential jurors, usually following up on answers they gave to the general question: "What crime were you convicted of?" or "Were you charged with any other offences for which you were acquitted?"

This process is called *voir dire*.[166] Either party's lawyer may object for cause to the seating of a juror. "For cause" means that one or more of the person's answers have given the lawyer cause to believe that person will not be able to apply the law dispassionately and fairly. One or more of their answers has created a reasonable expectation of bias, which the lawyer must then justify to the judge, who must agree. If the judge agrees, he will excuse the person from sitting on that jury (which is not the same as excusing them from jury duty). Each party may also (usually, though jurisdictions vary) make a limited number of peremptory challenges. Peremptory challenges do not require a justification be provided to the judge, though if the judge notices an invidious pattern—that the challenges are being used to introduce bias, rather than remove it—she may intervene and deny them.

We have been looking at civil liberties. At the beginning of this chapter, if you remember, we distinguished these from civil rights. Civil liberties are the freedoms we form government to protect; they are the reasons we become citizens. So, we limit the power of government, and want to make sure that, if it takes those liberties away, it has done so appropriately—as a result of wrongdoing, rather than because of bias or malfeasance.[167]

We said [168] civil rights are the permissions you have by virtue of being a citizen. These permissions are often political self-defense, the means to participate in the political community we have formed to protect our liberties, from foes foreign and domestic. What happens, however, when there is bias—systematic error—in defining citizenship, and thus, who has these permissions with which to defend themselves? Can a system which is only partially responsible be impartial? Sadly, history provides a thronging multitude of examples. You can probably already guess the answer. We've certainly discussed concepts which should tell you what to expect. We'll cover it in more detail in the next chapter,[169] but for now, I'll ask you this: how does having complete and unchallenged power over others tend to work out for us, and for the others?[170]

---

166 Pronounced (roughly) "vwahr deer." It comes from Anglo-Norman speech (that means really old British upper class), and (roughly) means "speak true." For a first person account, see Hunt, N. Jane (1997), "To Boldly Go Into Grand Jury Selection," *Chicago Tribune*, June 15, 1997.

167 Again, not that we're all that fond of stochastic (or random) error. We just can't predict it well enough to remove it.

168 If you don't want to be involved in that claim, quit moving your lips while you read. (You do *so*.) Also, trim your nose hairs. The view from here . . . it's not your best side.

169 The people who proofread this are VERY worried that you don't realize the next chapter in sequence is Chapter 13. I don't know if they're just trying to pimp Chapter 13's brand, if they don't believe you can count past twelve, or what. Also, the reference to PBS back there? They were afraid you had forgotten that is an acronym for Public Broadcasting System, as we learned in an earlier chapter.

170 For an exploration of this theme in popular media, see *Westworld*—the television series, not the movie.

Chapter 13: Civil Rights

Civil rights are the permissions we gain as citizens, permissions which allow us to participate in our political community on equal footing. Like civil liberties, they are worth fighting for, and again like civil liberties, we know this largely from the histories of those who have had to fight for them. To help you see the importance of civil rights, let me briefly change contexts. In the 1950s, West Germany's economy began to recover. Factories were rebuilt after the war, but there were too few workers to meet the increasing demand for labor. Germany had just lost a war,[1] and in the process, it lost a large part of its male working-age population.[2]

A labor shortage would have artificially inflated the price of labor, making their goods more expensive, and would have ended their economic recovery before it could get going. To keep the recovery going, West Germany began inviting "guest workers"[3] from other countries to work in Germany for a few years, gain some technical expertise, then return to their homelands. The hope was that all three parties would benefit: Germany from continued economic expansion, the worker from higher wages and developing expertise, and the home country from the return of some of those wages and all of those skills.

Life, of course, so rarely runs to plan. Some guest workers stayed, whether because the job opportunities in their home country were still poor, or because Germany had become home, or because they now had kids, and they wanted their children to benefit from better schools than were available back home, or for other reasons, or combinations of reasons. For whatever reasons, they stayed, and they had children who grew up in Germany. And none of them could become citizens.

At the time, Germany's naturalization law followed a principle known as *jus sanguinis*, or the right of blood. In order to become a German citizen, you had to be able to demonstrate (sufficient) German ancestry. This seems strange to Americans[4]; we are not a nation-state in the same way that most European states are. The United States is a nation of immigrants: even the Native Americans migrated here from other continents, they just did it first. In Europe, a lot of states are formed to coincide with national identities that are also ethnic. Estonians live in Estonia, the French are confined to France,[5] Germans live in Germany, Poles live in Poland, Danes in Denmark, Hungarians live in Hungary, Finns in Finland . . . you see where this is going. Many European states have a high degree of ethnic homogeneity, or did until relatively recently.

In the United States, we have not usually defined the nation in ethnic terms.[6] Ethnically, genetically, we are Welsh, Scottish, Irish, Italian, Polish, German, Mexican, Filipino, Japanese, Korean, Chinese, Dutch, Armenian,

---

1 You may have heard of it; it was in several newspapers. For the cliophobic or history-challenged among you, it was World War II.

2 This demographic overlaps surprisingly well with the "desirable soldier" demographic. By the end of the war, the Nazis were conscripting middle school children (boys and girls) and pensioners to form *Volkssturm* brigades. Poorly trained and haphazardly equipped, they sometimes fought tanks and artillery with weapons taken from ~~barns~~ museums. Just to give you an idea of how short they were on young adult men. And how Nazis would throw anyone between themselves and a tank.

3 The German word is *Gastarbeiter*. Germany was not the only country to have such a program. The Netherlands, Belgium, Sweden, Denmark, Norway, and Finland had similar ones. Germany was just the most popular because it was the strongest economy. That, and the weather in Norway . . . well, you've seen *Frozen*.

4 Though evidently not strange enough, as we seem to have some recurring nativism among people who are (ironically) not themselves natives.

5 Or at least, they should be.

6 Again, there have been occasional efforts, but to be honest, those people are stupid. If that's you, then I'm sorry, but it's time you knew.

Persian, Arab, Jewish, and more African ethnicities than I could possibly name—and I haven't even gotten to "English." We don't have **an** ethnicity, we have them all. We don't even have a name; "American" refers to two continents, and "United Statesean" isn't a word. As a result, we have traditionally had a naturalization process focused on *jus soli*. The most common way to become a U.S. citizen is to be born in the United States.

Now, these (*jus sanguinis* and *jus soli*) are philosophies, not policies, and they are not necessarily so absolute, and not incompatible. Being born to U.S. citizens is also a popular path to U.S. citizenship, even if that birth is on foreign soil. But someone born on U.S. soil is a U.S. citizen, regardless of their parentage. And people neither born on U.S. soil nor born to U.S. citizens can still become citizens by application (and testing).

In Germany, however, where you were born was irrelevant, and while you could apply to receive German citizenship if you had not received it by birth, your application would be denied unless you could show German ancestry. This became especially pressing in the case of Turkish guest workers. By 2000, Turkish immigrants and their children were around 5 percent of Germany's population. Many of them had been born, raised, and educated in Germany. They were not, however, able to become German citizens, and therefore not able to vote. They could attend school and college, they could work and shop and worship, but they could not directly influence the process that produced the rules which governed those activities.

Why was this important? After all, Germany is a liberal democracy. There are idiots there, just as anywhere else, but people there—citizens and non-citizens—usually enjoy the same rights and freedoms. The same is true in the United States; the First Amendment says nothing about the citizenship status of the person enjoying the right (and the Due Process Clauses and other guarantees say "person" rather than "citizen"). But put yourself in the shoes of those people born in Germany to Turkish parents. They knew one home: Germany. They spoke German. They learned in German, with Germans, in Germany, according to German rules. They shopped with Germans, rode busses with Germans, they worked for and with Germans.

They were in every practical sense a member of the same community, but they were set apart by their coloring and features, their other language, and their religion. They had no ability to participate in the formal (political) part of communal life, the part where the community made decisions together. They could not run for office, they could not vote—they could not press for their interests. They were aliens in the only home they'd ever known.

Could a Protestant, Catholic, or atheist understand the importance of Ramadan, or how best to structure policies to accommodate it? Unless they had lived in an observant Muslim community, probably not. It was unlikely anyone making decisions about such things had ever spent a month fasting during daylight hours, let alone done so as part of a community ritual. They might not be opposed to it, but they also wouldn't necessarily understand how vital or important an interest it was. They would not know how important it was, or how best to support it.

The same is true of more secular issues. Maintaining travel and communication links with Turkey was probably a great deal more important to them than to the typical German. For a German, it was probably a subject of indifference. Some might have cared a little, whether for political (they disapproved of the government of Turkey, for example) or business reasons (they bought or sold goods to or from places in Turkey). Those reasons, however, are not likely to be as consistent or as strong as the need to maintain contact with one's own family and culture. Others will not feel as strongly about the subject, and if they are the ones making decisions, they are more likely to sacrifice that for something they want more (because they are more likely to want something else more).

You may have felt some part of this at some point in your life. When I lived in Virginia, people there told me they could not understand why Coach Pat Summit[7] kept a plane on standby to fly her back to Tennessee from a tournament game in Virginia when she was late in her pregnancy. Their thought: we have hospitals here, too. But my wife and I understood—we are Tennesseans, and we wanted our children to be born Tennesseans, too.[8]

---

7 Legendary women's basketball coach at the University of Tennessee.

8 If you're thinking that this sounds like something you'd hear from Texas, I'll point out that a large part of the settlers of Texas came from Tennessee. Sam Houston was Governor of Tennessee before he was anything in Texas, and Davy Crockett went there to die. And technically, my Tennessean wife was born on an Air Force base in England. She came home quickly, though to this day she loves rainy weather. As a result (of the place of her birth, not the love of rainy weather—though it certainly wouldn't hurt), she could apply for a passport from the United Kingdom, according to *jus soli*.

Now that you have an example of something you probably don't understand, maybe a more general example will fill in the rest. Which is easier to spend, your money, or someone else's? If the money is coming out of your pocket, you feel it directly. You know the other plans you had (or might have developed) for it, and you weigh out carefully whether you prefer this use or retaining it for future use. When it's someone else's money, though, the alternative changes: spend it on something, or lose it. It makes it easier to decide to spend it, because the value **to you** of saving it is artificially low (because you don't benefit at all from saving it). You would have to consider the value **to them** of saving it, and we tend to have trouble both estimating and properly weighting that amount, because it is indirect. Elected representatives care about the interests of voters, but if you cannot vote, your interests will always finish behind those who can (who will finish behind those who do). As a result, Germany amended its naturalization law so that people born there or resident there (and meeting a list of criteria) need not show German ancestry to apply for citizenship.

Now let's rewind history for a few centuries. The Americas are newly discovered continents. They have a lot of raw materials, but they need more labor. There was plenty of farmland for the clearing and taking,[9] but farmers could not wait to produce enough children to provide the labor they needed. They, too, decided to import labor, but they did it by force, rather than invitation.[10] They bought people captured in Africa, just as they would buy a horse from a neighbor to pull their plow. They saw the people they bought and sold as being more or less the same as that horse, as property. Just like they would the horse, they had no qualms about selling that labor's offspring, or even determining which of the laborers should produce the offspring. They didn't bring in guest workers, they brought in slaves.

Slavery anywhere is an evil, an abomination before our Creator. In the United States, however, it was also the single greatest juxtaposition, the greatest oxymoron every produced.[11] In a land founded to preserve the rights of individuals, the laws denied the existence of those rights. A nation dedicated to the escape from tyranny exercised it daily. No one presents a clearer portrait of this than Thomas Jefferson. Jefferson, who penned the Virginia Statute on Religious Freedom, who swore before history and mankind the self-evidence of the fact that all men are created equal, that their liberty is a God-given entitlement—that same Jefferson owned slaves, fathered children with one of them (who by definition could not have given her consent), and even in death freed only a few of them.

Jefferson once described slavery as like having a wolf by the ear; you were afraid to let go, and afraid to hold on. As we saw in Chapter 2, the Founders were so ashamed of what they were doing that they could not bring themselves to call it by its true name in a document they meant to treasure for generations. In "polite" society, people referred to slavery as "the peculiar institution." As Jefferson himself saw, the damage to both parties (slave and master), and to our country, went far deeper than shame. In 1781, Jefferson sat down to answer a rather large number of questions a Frenchman had asked him about Virginia. Jefferson answered them quite thoroughly, with catalogues of data on population, demographics, flora and fauna, geography, and any number of other subjects. The answers were eventually published in 1787 (the year of the Philadelphia Convention, remember) as *Notes on the State of Virginia*.[12] One of the questions Jefferson answered concerned the manners of Virginians. I take the liberty of quoting almost its entire length.

> There must doubtless be an unhappy influence on the manners of our people produced by the existence of slavery among us. The whole commerce between master and slave is a perpetual exercise of the most boisterous passions, the most unremitting despotism on the one part, and degrading submissions on the other. Our children see this,

---

9   Just ask the Native Americans who were cleared off and from whom it was taken.

10   Some Europeans were brought over as indentured servants, which involved a voluntary contract, rather than force. They were only bound to service until they fulfilled the terms of their contract.

11   And it took many, many morons to produce it.

12   You can find the full text online at http://xroads.virginia.edu/~hyper/jefferson/toc.html, http://jefferson-notes.herokuapp.com/, http://docsouth.unc.edu/southlit/jefferson/jefferson.html, to name but three. A pdf is available at http://www.thefederalistpapers.org/wp-content/uploads/2012/12/Thomas-Jefferson-Notes-On-The-State-Of-Virginia.pdf. So really, your excuse for not looking this up is . . .

and learn to imitate it; for man is an imitative animal. This quality is the germ of all education in him. From his cradle to his grave he is learning to do what he sees others do. If a parent could find no motive either in his philanthropy or his self-love, for restraining the intemperance of passion towards his slave, it should always be a sufficient one that his child is present. But generally it is not sufficient. The parent storms, the child looks on, catches the lineaments of wrath, puts on the same airs in the circle of smaller slaves, gives a loose to his worst of passions, and thus nursed, educated, and daily exercised in tyranny, cannot but be stamped by it with odious peculiarities. The man must be a prodigy who can retain his manners and morals undepraved by such circumstances. And with what execration should the statesman be loaded, who permitting one half the citizens thus to trample on the rights of the other, transforms those into despots, and these into enemies, destroys the morals of the one part, and the amor patriæ of the other. For if a slave can have a country in this world, it must be any other in preference to that in which he is born to live and labour for another: in which he must lock up the faculties of his nature, contribute as far as depends on his individual endeavours to the evanishment of the human race, or entail his own miserable condition on the endless generations proceeding from him. With the morals of the people, their industry also is destroyed. For in a warm climate, no man will labour for himself who can make another labour for him. This is so true, that of the proprietors of slaves a very small proportion indeed are even seen to labour. And can the liberties of a nation be thought secure when we have removed their only firm basis, a conviction in the minds of the people that these liberties are of the gift of God? That they are not to be violated but with his wrath? Indeed I tremble for my country when I reflect that God is just: that his justice cannot sleep for ever: that considering numbers, nature and natural means only, a revolution of the wheel of fortune, an exchange of situation, is among possible events: that it may become probable by supernatural interference! The Almighty has no attribute which can take side with us in such a contest.

Contrast that heart-felt anguish with this fact: of the over 600 slaves Jefferson owned throughout his lifetime, he freed only two while he was living. Three he did not have pursued when they escaped (most were pursued and then sold when recaptured). He freed five others in his will, one (his personal servant) immediately, two craftsmen a year after his death, and two more (who were apprenticed to one of the two craftsmen) when they reached the age of 21. He saw female slaves' reproduction as an asset to be managed. He thought that a slave who bore a child every two years did more to increase the labor output than the labor of any slave. Remember, this had nothing to do with their wishes, either about becoming pregnant or about by whom. How can all of this be true of the same person?

The short answer: I don't know. The longer answer: I still don't know, and it's complicated. Jefferson viewed slaves as children, limited in their capacity and unable to care for themselves, even though they were mature men and women.[13] He probably convinced himself of this on the basis of behavior he observed every day, forgetting that the behavior he observed was the **product** of slavery, not its justification. Think about it; what would happen to a slave who demanded respect,[14] to be treated as an equal, who made decisions for himself—in other words, who acted like a mature adult, confident in his own abilities? By far the most common answer has to have been "beaten within an inch of his life." Jefferson provides the explanation himself. Slavery produced the "perpetual exercise of . . . degrading submissions" on the part of slaves. Behavior that showed the equality of slaves as people threatened the lie that supported the system, and like most threats to the lies people use to cover up their deepest fears, it received violent responses when challenged.[15]

At the end of the passage I quote at length above, Jefferson offers the hopeful guess that slavery might be ending sooner, rather than later, observing a shift in the beliefs of slave owners. Remember, too, that the Constitution (written six years after Jefferson was writing) seems to share his anticipation of the death of slavery, forbidding Congress from outlawing the importation of slaves from Africa (or elsewhere outside the United States) for twenty years after ratification, by when some hoped it would have withered away. In the meantime, as you of course remember, it limited the tax Congress could impose, to keep Congress

---

13 That diminution, by the way, is the reason it is still deeply offensive to refer to African American adults as "boy" or "girl."

14 Or anything else for that matter, but *especially* respect.

15 If you still haven't seen *12 Years a Slave*, here's your excuse: homework.

from outlawing it by making it too expensive.[16] At the very best, they knew the right thing to do, but simply did not want to take a difficult path when they thought the path they were on would join the other without trouble.

One of the things the study of politics reminds us is that our interests, however much we dress them up in principles, tend to be driven by our circumstances. Thus we often work the other way, finding principles to suit our interests, rather than letting our principles decide our interests. Even if Jefferson's hopes were correct, even if people were beginning to find slavery costly, both morally and financially, circumstances kept changing. One important circumstance was Eli Whitney's invention of the cotton gin in 1793.

No, the cotton gin is not a cocktail with a cotton swab for a swizzle stick.[17] "Gin" is, in this case, short for "engine," and the cotton gin was a labor saving device. For you city folk, cotton fiber comes from the bloom of a plant. Imagine a rose bush whose buds open to reveal not petals, but wads of cotton fiber, like dense cotton balls. The closed, pod-like bud is called a boll. When it opens, the cotton is ready to be picked. Two problems: the boll edges are sharp, and the fiber is full of tiny seeds. The sharpness and prickliness of the plant mean that people who pick cotton usually have cuts all over their hands. They must also stoop to reach the plants, which tend to be about three feet tall.[18] Someone then has to pick all of the seeds out; this was done by hand. The seeds are small and sticky, and there are dozens in a typical boll. It could take a day remove the seeds from a pound of cotton.

This made cotton too expensive to be too widely used, and thus, to be much of a cash crop (like tobacco). Whitney's gin changed that. The gin could remove the seeds from fifty pounds of cotton a day; suddenly, the problem was getting enough cotton picked to keep the gin fed. Suddenly, a supply of forced labor seemed like an even better idea. A change in economic circumstances changed people's interests in regard to slaves.[19] If before their principles had been catching up to them as the economic benefits of slavery seemed less and less, especially when weighed against the costs (both moral and economic) of enforcing it, now those economic benefits were once again greater—and they were greater by enough to outweigh even greater costs.

We see the same tale repeated with the acquisition of new territory. In 1803, President Jefferson purchased France's claims to the Louisiana Territory, arcing up from the Gulf of Mexico along the Mississippi and Columbia Rivers to the Pacific Northwest. Southern states wanted to ensure that enough states allowing slavery were admitted, so that they could maintain sufficient members in the Senate to block emancipation bills submitted regularly in the House of Representatives. The result was the Missouri Compromise of 1820. Maine was admitted as a free state (breaking away from Massachusetts) and Missouri as a slave state. Future states from the Louisiana Territory would be slave states if they were south of Missouri's southern border, free if north of that border.

This compromise did nothing to address the interests of slaves. It addressed the competing interests of Southern slave-holding states and Northern mercantile states. More specifically, it reconciled feuding factions (Southern and Northern) within the Democratic–Republican Party (which, by this point, was the only political party[20]). These two factions had a running battle from the very beginning of the republic. The original political split between the Federalists and Democratic–Republicans was over the centralization of power, but it quickly became sectional (geographic).

---

16 There is an argument that cutting off competition from overseas producers of slaves benefitted those producing it at home (as banning or taxing imports is done to encourage domestic production, which Hamilton as Secretary of the Treasury argued for doing to benefit legitimate industry, against the objections of Jefferson as Secretary of State). That argument, however, proves too much—if that were the motivation, they should have done it immediately, rather than after twenty years.

17 I get bonus points for working "swizzle stick" into a textbook that isn't for bartenders, right?

18 My mother-in-law, who remembers when schools in her county had an autumn break so the kids could help pick cotton, reports that they are usually from the knee to mid-thigh on an adult (and that bolls grow all over, not just at the tops).

19 At least, among those who weren't slaves.

20 Where "this point" is the administration of President James Monroe, known as the "Era of Good Feelings" for the lack of partisan competition.

One of the things Hamilton (and the Federalists) favored doing with that central power was establishing high tariffs, which would make imported goods (especially machinery and tools) more expensive. This would protect Northern manufacturers, allowing them to become competitive a providing a manufacturing base for the nation.[21] As the Democratic–Republicans pointed out, however, this came at the expense of farmers in the South, who had to spend more money to buy agricultural tools and machinery. Worse, these tools were often of inferior quality to those imported from Britain.

John Adams' prickly response to criticism (that response being the Sedition Act) probably doomed his party's electoral chances. It never recovered from the defeat that followed his first and only term as President. His appointment of John Marshall, however, probably won the centralization battle, even if the Federalist Party lost the war for electoral relevance. The battle then became between the Northern and Southern wings of the Democratic–Republican Party, and it focused on two issues: protective tariffs and slavery. In fact, South Carolina's first threat to secede was in response to the Tariff of 1828, known in the South as the "Tariff of Abominations." The sitting Vice President, John C. Calhoun, wrote South Carolina's *Exposition and Protest*, explaining that South Carolina had the right to nullify the tariff.

The Compromise Tariff of 1833 ended the Nullification Crisis, as it was called. The point in our sights, however, is that these compromises were made to reconcile the demands of those who had access to the system. Northern merchants had representatives in the House of Representatives; Southern slaveholders had representatives in the Senate.[22] Individual states, like South Carolina, could use the system—or threats of altering or leaving it—to protect themselves. The difficulty, the evil, was in leaving a minority without access to that system. Measures would not be formed for their benefit, nor could they use leverage to modify those which might harm them. They were locked out of the system, and any benefits they might see would be only because they coincided with someone else's.

Take, for example, the Wilmot Proviso. This was an amendment to the appropriations bill for funding the purchase of land from Mexico as part of settling the Mexican–American War. It would have forbidden the introduction of slavery into any territory acquired in the settlement. The Senate removed it, but it was introduced by Rep. David Wilmot, representing Pennsylvania's Twelfth District. He was not moved to introduce by reflection on the miseries slavery visited upon fellow human beings. He objected to slavery as unfair competition to free white laborers who might otherwise be hired. He (and his constituents) were worried that slavery depressed wages for free people, not that it stripped enslaved people of their rights and humanity.

In 1850, there was another compromise. California entered as a free state; Texas gave up claims to territory north of the southern border of Missouri (Texas was a slave state) and from today's panhandle to the Rio Grande (and least half of today's New Mexico); states organized in the New Mexico Territory and Utah Territory would vote on whether to enter as slave or free states; and the slave-holding states got in return the Fugitive Slave Act of 1850. The Fugitive Slave Act required public authorities in free states to arrest fugitive slaves and return them to bondage (and established punitive fines for failure to do so).

The Fugitive Slave Clause in the Constitution might sound like it makes this redundant, but that clause meant that slaves who escaped were not made free of slavery by their presence on free soil. While it required that they be returned to the slavery from which they had escaped, that was if they were caught. It did not impose a positive obligation on the public authorities of free states to search for them. This the Fugitive Slave Act did.

Not extending slavery to more territory may sound like a win to someone who is free. Increasing the number of free states so as to eventually outnumber slave state votes in the Senate may sound like a plan. Neither of them is something the person being returned to bondage would consider in exchange for their freedom. To the person actually shackled, to the slave deprived of freedom, rights, and even the label "human," it sounds an awful lot like his awful lot on every day before. It sounds like an awful lot to give up in exchange for an eventual advantage in votes in the Senate.

---

21 Given their climate, they had a comparative advantage at manufacturing, while the South's was in agriculture.

22 Of course, both had them in both places, but the relative numbers made their relative strength different in each house.

Voters get upset when someone takes away their Big Gulp. They want laws passed to make kids pull their pants up, to make that company come back and open that factory back up so they can work there. And politicians listen, even when they shouldn't. When those people aren't voters, when they aren't allowed to be, politicians don't listen, even when they should.[23]

In 1854, another compromise was necessary. The Fugitive Slave Act was not achieving the results Southern states had expected. Juries often failed to convict people for hiding slaves. People moved escaped slaves further on to Canada, beyond the reach of the Bloodhound Act, as they called it. Wisconsin and Vermont went so far as to a page from South Carolina's playbook and nullify the act.

The attraction of slavery was tied to growing cotton, and cotton is a thirsty crop; it requires a lot of water.[24] States in the arid New Mexico and Utah territories had little interest in it. So slave states need to repeal the Missouri Compromise, since some of the territory north of Missouri's southern border was suited to farming, including cotton. The Kansas–Nebraska Act allowed the territories of Kansas and Nebraska to vote on whether to enter the Union as free or slave states. This led to a bloody conflict, referred to as Bleeding Kansas.[25]

You may never have heard of it, unless you're from Kansas, Missouri, or Nebraska. But no, I am not making it up. Preacher and abolitionist Henry Ward Beecher[26] sent rifles to the Free State partisans, in crates labelled "Bibles," so that they would not be intercepted. This led to the partisans calling their rifles "Beecher's Bibles." People were dragged from their homes in the middle of the night and brutally murdered; towns were sacked and pillaged. Each side elected its own legislature, decrying the other as illegitimate. Federal troops had to be dispatched to quell the violence.

Then, in 1857, came the *Dred Scott* decision. Dred Scott was born a slave in Virginia in 1795. His owner later moved to Alabama, and then to St. Louis, where he gave up farming. He sold Mr. Scott to an Army doctor. The doctor was subsequently stationed in Illinois, then the Wisconsin Territory. During this time, both the doctor and Mr. Scott married. When the doctor was posted to Louisiana, Mr. Scott and his wife followed. (Scott's daughter was born a free woman on the waters of the Mississippi during their journey.) The doctor was then posted back to Missouri, where he died. His widow inherited Scott and his wife. She then apparently transferred ownership of Mr. Scott to her brother, John F.A. Sanford. Because their family name was misspelled in the court documents, the case became *Scott v. Sandford*.

Scott sued for his freedom in federal court. His argument was that he had been a resident of the free state of Illinois, where state laws prohibited slavery. He had been a resident of the Wisconsin Territory,[27] where federal law (the Missouri Compromise, in fact) forbade slavery. In light of this, Scott argued, his bonds of slavery had been dissolved, either by the laws of Illinois or of Congress.

Chief Justice Roger B. Taney[28] wrote for the Supreme Court in a 7-2 decision. Taney went straight for the throat: Scott, he said, had no standing to sue in a federal court. The Constitution, Taney said, clearly contemplated Mr. Scott and all of his race as nothing more than property. They could not become citizens, even if they

---

23 For another (and less visceral) example, consider the federal debt. One reason democracies tend to have debt and deficits is because politicians have trouble saying no to current voters. The people who bear the costs of all that borrowing—the people who have to pay it back, and will be less able because of it to borrow if they need to, are somewhere between too young to vote and not born yet.

24 In fact, the Soviet Union nearly drained one of the largest inland seas, the Aral Sea, in an attempt to grow cotton in arid Uzbekistan. Look at Google Earth; you'll find marinas and docks miles from the current shores of the Aral Sea. In fact, Wikipedia already uses the past tense for the Aral Sea: https://en.wikipedia.org/wiki/Aral_Sea. And no, it was not the result of global warming.

25 Spoiler alert! What good is foreshadowing if we don't recognize it until afterward?

26 You may have heard of his sister, Harriet Beecher Stowe, who wrote the novel *Uncle Tom's Cabin*.

27 In a part which is now Minnesota.

28 The *a* is short, not long, so it's "Tah-knee," not "Tay-knee." And given what you're about to read, he had perhaps the most ironic title in all of history. Hipsters take note: sometimes irony is depressing and amazingly unamusing.

were free, even if the laws of their state made them citizens of that state.[29] Citing the Fugitive Slave Clause[30] and the Importation Clause,[31] Taney declared that the Constitution only saw Dred Scott as a piece of property, and thus, he could never be a citizen. Nor, citing the Takings Clause of the Fifth Amendment,[32] did the federal government possess the power to free slaves, in territories or anywhere else. They would have to purchase the freedom of slaves, since they would be taking slaveholders' property.

Ignore for a moment the illegitimacy of the property claim itself, that this "right" was to something that never should have been property in the first place. The worst, most heinous, most poisonous thing about Taney's venom was not how morally rotten it is (and it most certainly is), but how legally correct it was. The Constitution does clearly treat slaves as property; many of the Founders quite clearly (though quite wrongly) considered Africans as a race unsuited to the demands of freedom, who needed slavery for their own good— or have you forgotten Thomas Jefferson so soon?[33] Since they were, and the Constitution acknowledged them as, legally defined as property, the Constitution required Congress to pay for removing them from someone's ownership.[34]

Suddenly, abolition was no longer a question of a few seats in the Senate, of outflanking slave states in the upper chamber to pass there too one of the abolition bills regularly passed by the House. Suddenly, it was a matter of either raising more money than was physically possible, or of getting a two-thirds majority in both House and Senate, as well as a majority in three-quarters of the state legislatures to amend the Constitution. Taney (and six other members of the Court) didn't just move the goal posts; they put them on the moon.

The year before, in 1856, a new party had contested the Presidential election. Formed from members of the Free Soil Party and disaffected Northern Democrats tired of sacrificing abolition and high tariffs to party unity, the party took the name the Democrats had cast off under Andrew Jackson (almost thirty years earlier), Republican. They supported John C. Fremont as their candidate, under the slogan "Free Soil, Free Men, and Fremont." Fremont finished second to Democrat James Buchanan; former President Millard Fillmore ran for the American (or "Know-Nothing"[35]) Party, and split the non-Democrat vote. Some feared that a Fremont victory would cause Southern states to secede.

In 1860, the Republican Party nominated a Senator from Illinois, Abraham Lincoln.[36] Lincoln strongly supported both higher tariffs and abolition. In a field of five candidates, Lincoln managed to win. This so threatened Southern states that a month-and-a-half later, South Carolina seceded, before Lincoln was even inaugurated. Ten more states eventually followed, the first six within a month-and-a-half of South Carolina. The last four did not secede until after the Federal assault to reclaim Fort Sumter in Charleston harbor, two-and-a-half months after the end of the first wave.[37]

---

29   At the time, state laws decided who was a citizen of that state, and being a citizen of one of the United States made one a U.S. citizen.

30   Article IV, Sec. 1, Clause 3: "No Person held to Service or Labour in one State, under the Laws thereof, escaping into another, shall, in Consequence of any Law or Regulation therein, be discharged from such Service or Labour, but shall be delivered up on Claim of the Party to whom such Service or Labour shall be due."

31   Article I, Sec. 9, Clause 1—you know, the part about having to wait twenty years before banning the importation of "such Persons as any of the States now existing shall think proper to admit."

32   Come on, man—that was just last chapter.

33   Original intent has its shortcomings as a means of interpreting the Constitution; welcome to Exhibit A.

34   Please, please, for the love of God, country, your fellow man, or anything else you hold sacred and holy, please never, EVER again confuse what is moral with what is legal, or allow the law to be the limit of what you know is right.

35   The American Party was nativist and anti-immigrant (think Donald Trump). It got its name because its members claimed to know nothing about the party when asked publicly about their membership (by the time you read this, you'll know if Trump has caused the Republicans to do the same.)

36   You may have heard of him, or occasionally carried his portrait around with you.

37   The first seven states seceded between Dec. 20 (South Carolina's Christmas present to the nation) and Feb. 1 (Texas). Virginia did not secede until April 17, 1861 (three days after the attack on Fort Sumter) Tennessee was the last, on June 8, 1861.

We remember the American Civil War as being about slavery, and for good reason: whether to allow slavery to expand or even to continue was one of the prominent and recurring disputes between Northern, Southern, and Western factions. We do ourselves a disservice, however, if we forget the other issues involved. While slavery was the hottest button, disputes over tariffs had proven quite incendiary, as well. These two issues then led to a third: whether states could nullify federal laws, or even secede from the Union. This is why the South saw the cause of the war as states' rights. They saw the imposition of abolition and high tariffs as violations of state sovereignty, as going beyond what the Constitution had bound them to, and asserted the right to no longer be part of that government.

To be honest, Lincoln quite clearly saw the purpose of the war as first and foremost to preserve the Union. That is, the right of states to secede (or the lack of such right) was his first concern. Writing to Horace Greeley, an abolitionist, one of the founders of the Republican Party, and editor of the *New York Tribune*, in response to an editorial Greeley had written as an open letter to Lincoln, he explains: "My paramount object in this struggle *is* to save the Union, and is *not* either to save or to destroy slavery. If I could save the Union without freeing *any* slave I would do it, and if I could save it by freeing *all* the slaves I would do it; and if I could save it by freeing some and leaving others alone I would also do that."[38]

Lincoln wrote this on August 22, 1862. The month before, on July 13, he had discussed his first draft of the Emancipation Proclamation with two of his cabinet members. Of course, a year before, John C. Fremont, whom Lincoln had appointed Commander of the Department of the West, had issued his own emancipation proclamation. Fremont had declared that the property of rebels would be confiscated, and in the case of slaves, set free. Lincoln at that point rebuked him for making slavery an issue, and when Fremont refused to rescind the order, Lincoln removed him from command for insubordination.

So why, on January 1, 1863, did Lincoln issue the Emancipation Proclamation? To begin with, we need to take a few steps back. Lincoln first issued the Proclamation part on September 22, 1862 (a month after his letter to Greeley). He proclaimed at that point that, as of January 1, all slaves in territories ("any State or designated part of a State") still in rebellion would be free, and that the executive branch officers under his command (including the military) would support that freedom, and would take no action to hinder them from realizing that freedom. In other words, the Union would consider them free, and would not interfere if they wished to engage in violent rebellion. He further promised to make a proclamation on January 1 naming those states and parts of states which were still in rebellion.

This was a bold gambit. What Lincoln hoped is that, by threatening Confederate states with what they most feared—abolition, by way of violent revolt—he would get them to rejoin the Union. Notice that if they ceased their rebellion by the deadline (January 1), none of their slaves would have been freed. If they kept fighting, then the Union (or at least, its executive branch)[39] would no longer recognize their claim, and would support slaves in claiming their freedom. By laying down their arms, they could preserve slavery. By continuing in rebellion, they faced their worst nightmare—a slave rebellion in their midst, supported by the Union.

It also brought slavery into greater prominence as a cause for the war. The war was not going well for the North to this point. Despite advantages in supplies and soldiers, the Union Army had made little to no progress against the Confederate Army. In September 1862, Confederate forces crossed the Potomac, carrying the battle to the Union on its own soil. No one in the North was particularly willing to fight or die to keep a bunch of slaveholders in the Union, and as the war dragged on and casualties mounted with nothing to show for it, public opinion was shifting to suing for peace and letting the Confederacy go its own way. Embracing abolition gave people in the North a cause worth fighting and sacrificing for.

This was, in fact, about the only tangible effect of the Emancipation Proclamation. No Southern states considered surrendering, whether because they did not trust Lincoln's offer, because they looked able to succeed

---

38 Lincoln adds at the end of his response, "I have stated my purpose according to my view of *official* duty; and I intend no modification of my oft-expressed *personal* wish that all men every where could be free."

39 So technically yes, the Emancipation Proclamation was an executive order.

on their own terms, or because they were fighting for something more than preserving slavery. (Or, as is more likely, some mixture of all these and other things besides.)

As for emancipation as an effect, the Emancipation Proclamation was all proclamation and no emancipation. At best it was a promissory note, that if the Union won, it would consider those slaves free. Read it carefully (as Lincoln certainly wrote it that way): the only slaves freed were precisely those Lincoln could not free, those in territories which did not recognize his authority. Slaves in states which did recognize his authority—and his authority probably did not run so far as to emancipation—were left as they were before. Delaware, Kentucky, Maryland, and Missouri were all slave states which remained in the Union; West Virginia, which seceded from Virginia in response to Virginia's secession, was admitted during the war and was also a slave state.[40]

Lincoln's desperate public relations maneuver worked, however. The Confederate invasion reached its peak at the Battle of Gettysburg in early July. After their defeat there, Confederate forces never again threatened the North. Within two years, General Lee[41] was surrendering to General Grant at Appomattox Courthouse, and Lincoln (having survived re-election) was assassinated while watching *Our American Cousin* at Ford's Theatre.

The next question was how to restore the Confederate states to the Union. Given the emphasis on emancipation to rally support for the war in the North, there was no question of accepting them back on the same terms as before. Lincoln's successor, Andrew Johnson (a Union loyalist from East Tennessee), required them to ratify the Thirteenth Amendment and considered the matter settled. (The Thirteenth Amendment outlaws slavery or forced labor, unless as punishment for a crime of which you've been properly convicted.) More radical Republicans, however, were not convinced. To be fair, it is difficult to believe that the formal status of freedom would change a great deal about race relations in the South, especially when that freedom was a reminder of military defeat. Slavery had been a defining element in Southern society, and it vanished into thin air. Even if it deserved no mourning, habits of heart and mind do not change so quickly, and cannot be done and undone by legislation.

Thus, Congress began the process of rebuilding the South, socially as well as physically. In this period of Reconstruction, the U.S. Army remained stationed in the South. As this suggests, Reconstruction involved martial law. Tennessee, because it quickly re-entered the Union, was the only former Confederate state not to have a military governor during this time. Reconstruction lasted until the Army was finally withdrawn in 1877, not because the job was done, but because the North was tired of the expense and effort (and because it got Southern votes in the House of Representatives for Republican Rutherford B. Hayes when the Electoral College failed to produce a majority in 1876).

Congress created the Freedman's Bureau (technically, the Bureau of Refugees, Freedmen, and Abandoned Lands) to assist freed slaves in transitioning to their new role as citizens.[42] Slaves were not usually educated; in fact, it had been illegal to teach them to read and write in most slave states. One of the Freedman's Bureau's biggest tasks was to rectify this. To that end, it started a great number of schools for freedmen, including

---

40 In fact, Maryland had been kept in the Union by arresting some of its legislature (and Baltimore's mayor) to keep the legislature from meeting to declare its secession. Lincoln suspended *habeas corpus* to keep them in custody; otherwise the capital of the United States would have been surrounded by enemy territory. This is why Lincoln was so upset with Fremont in 1861. Missouri was under Fremont's command, and Lincoln was afraid that injecting abolition into the situation would cause it and Kentucky, just across the Mississippi River, to secede.

41 Lincoln had originally asked Robert E. Lee to command the Union forces. When Lee followed his home state of Virginia into the Confederacy, Lincoln had a great deal of frustration finding another general capable of matching Lee. He finally found Ulysses S. Grant, to whom Fremont had entrusted several important operations in the Department of the West, holding the Mississippi River for the Union. Grant had already at that time a reputation as a drunkard, but Fremont—perhaps because he had been disadvantaged by his illegitimate birth—cared more about his ability than his social reputation. Incidentally, Grant's actual name is Hiram Ulysses Grant. On his appointment to West Point, his Congressman erroneously assumed his middle name was his mother's maiden name, and recorded him as Ulysses Simpson Grant. Since the new initials were much better suited to his chosen profession, he kept the new name.

42 The first clause of the Fourteenth Amendment defines U.S. citizenship and overturned *Scott v. Sandford*.

colleges. Howard University, for example, is named for the head of the Freedman's Bureau. Since family units had often been broken up, with spouses and children sold to different people, the Bureau assisted in helping reunite families. It performed marriages, or more precisely, re-performed them, as most slave states did not recognize (and therefore did not record) marriages between slaves. It tried to help both former slaves and their newly fellow citizens adjust to new social and working relationships.

The Freedman's Bureau hired those who were willing locally, but it sometimes had to bring in workers from the North. Teachers were often in demand, because the South had not had as extensive a public education system as the more urban North. Churches from the North sent pastors to reclaim property and congregations, and missionaries to teach and provide medical care. Enterprising businessmen came south to sell to a new market, and some Northerners came to run for office.

Southerners saw this as an unwelcome second invasion, and referred to its members derisively as "carpetbaggers," because they often had soft-sided luggage made from old carpets (rather than sturdier, heavier, and more expensive trunks). Many Southerners did not appreciate the idea that they were backward and ignorant and needed the help of generous and munificent Northerners to improve themselves. Sadly, they probably did not see and certainly would not have appreciated the irony of the shoe being on the other foot, of being themselves the object of presumption and patrimonial care, as if they were not fully adults.

Elections during Reconstruction often returned elected officials who were African American (and Republican). The first African American Senator, Hiram Revels, was elected from Mississippi. Representative Benjamin Turner was elected from Alabama; Representatives Robert De Large, Joseph Rainey, and Robert Elliott from South Carolina; Representative Josiah Walls from Florida; and Jefferson Long from Georgia. After the end of Reconstruction, many of these states would not see another African American elected for a hundred years. What happened?

You know some parts of the answer, even if you don't know all of them (or how they fit together). Part of the fight in Reconstruction was against what were known as black codes. Former slave states could not reinstate slavery; the Thirteenth Amendment prohibited it. Instead, they introduced restrictions on freedmen, attempting to leave them with no choice but to remain in the service of their former masters and owners.

The black codes varied, but the themes are all clear enough—the forbade freedmen from having certain (or most) professions, barred them from serving on juries,[43] restricted them to living in designated areas,[44] prohibited them from bearing weapons or from assembling in groups . . . surely you start to get the picture, but let me give you one last detail. Black codes often involved sweeping vagrancy laws that required freedmen to have documents in order to be outside designated areas. Those found without papers were arrested for vagrancy, sentenced to labor, and leased out as laborers. The black codes were as much of slavery as you could have without the legal status of property.

In response, the Congress proposed the second Reconstruction amendment, the Fourteenth.[45] The Equal Protection, Due Process, and Privileges and Immunities Clauses were all meant to end this slavery in deed, if not in name. The amendment was proposed in 1866 (as I'm sure you remember from the previous chapter) and ratified in 1868. To give you an idea of how depressingly contentious this was, let me invite you to the Tennessee State Capitol. It is architecturally quite interesting, not to mention attractive.[46] It is one of the world's largest (and certainly most functional) mausoleums; two people are interred in it, one of whom was its architect.

---

43 How ironic that most people do this to themselves nowadays; see Chapter 4 if you've forgotten why this is important.

44 More commonly known today as ghettos, apparently from the restriction of Jewish inhabitants to a particular part of Venice in 1516—etymologists' best guess is that *ghetto* is a shortening of *borghetto*, or "little city" in Italian.

45 So yes, the Thirteenth was the first; the Fifteenth was the last. And yes, I did call them the Civil War Amendments in the previous chapter, but now that you know what Reconstruction was, you can understand why they are also called the Reconstruction Amendments. And since you know that this is Chapter 13, you can probably figure out that *the* previous chapter is Chapter 12 (whereas *a* previous chapter could be any of them).

46 If you ask real nice, it might give you its number.

More relevant to our discussion is the railing on one of the main staircases. Unless they have changed this by renovation, you will find a column in the stairwell with pockmarks and cracks on it. On the railing in front of that column, you will find a hole. If you put your finger in that hole—well, if you're in the habit of putting your finger in strange holes, you may not still have all of them. But if you do, you will feel at the back of the hole a round metal surface. This sphere is a Minié ball, the type of bullet used in most firearms from that era. This bullet arrived in this handrail as the sergeants-at-arms were firing at members fleeing the chamber in an attempt to prevent the assembly from having a quorum, and thus from voting to ratify the amendment. That's right: there was a running firefight in our state capitol that also serves as a mausoleum.[47]

The Fourteenth Amendment quite clearly forbids the type of discrimination seen in the black codes. The black codes created two classes of citizens, and treated them differently—thus the need for equal protection. In fact, it treated one of those classes like they weren't citizens at all—thus the need to protect their privileges and immunities as citizens. It was discrimination in the terms of the law (*de jure*, or "of the law"), which authorized different treatment (*de facto*, or "of the facts"). Unrepentant Southern governments also denied freedmen the right to vote. As a result, the Fifteenth Amendment prohibits denying the right to vote on the basis of "race, color, or previous condition of servitude."

Now, you probably haven't been a parent, but you probably have been a teenager (and may still be). When your parents give you instructions, why do they feel the need to provide several terms with overlapping meanings? Right—because they know you're going to try to weasel your way into doing what you wanted to do anyway, while still claiming they didn't forbid it. When they say "no parties," you don't have a party, you have an "intimate get-together." If they tell you not to take their car, you'll say you didn't; your friend did, and you just went with him to make sure the car was okay. So this narrowing of expected loopholes tells us that Congress had caught on to the fact that the former slave states were actively trying to circumvent the law.

And circumvent they did, especially after Reconstruction ended. Groups such as the Ku Klux Klan formed to intimidate freedmen into not voting.[48] Southern states enacted what were called Jim Crow laws, establishing the segregation of whites and blacks. These laws did not discriminate in the text of the law. In their words, they applied to all citizens. For example, a state might enact some difficult requirement in order to vote—a high poll tax, for example, or a literacy test—and then exempt people whose grandfathers had been able to vote from meeting that requirement.[49]

That law did not treat people differently based on race, color, or previous condition of servitude, so it did not violate the letter of the Fifteenth Amendment. It treated people differently based on money or literacy. Of course, both of these were things freedmen were much less likely to have. These requirements would have prevented poor or illiterate whites from voting, too. That explains the grandfather clause, which would exempt them from that requirement. Even the exception was not made on the condition of race: it disenfranchised illiterate or poor immigrants (and their children) too, regardless of their race, color, or previous condition of servitude. Instead of classifying people by the factors the Fifteenth Amendment forbade, the law classified people by factors which strongly correlated with the forbidden ones, and then made provisions to exempt other people who happened to have those characteristics as well.

Even without the tell-tale exceptions, a facially neutral law could abet racial discrimination. Let us imagine our same bars to voting, a tax and a literacy test. The application or administration of those requirements could be biased as well. The person administering the literacy test, for example, might use first-grade reading level materials for a white man applying to vote, or use Bible verses they would recognize and be able to repeat from memory. For a black man applying to vote, however, they might switch to Shakespeare, or some

---

47 It only sounds like a plot device from *Buffy the Vampire Slayer*.

48 Before any Yankees reading this start to feel superior, Alexis de Tocqueville reports (in 1831) that a Pennsylvanian was insulted when Tocqueville asked why free black men were not allowed to vote. The Pennsylvanian reported that it was not the law which prevented it; they had the right to vote but chose not to. When Tocqueville protested that this seemed overly modest, the Pennsylvanian explained that free black men were afraid to vote, for fear they would be mistreated.

49 And yes, this is the origin of the term "grandfather clause" or "grandfathering in" some requirement.

complicated bit of the state constitution. The person collecting the poll tax might look the other way and allow poor whites to vote even if they didn't pay, but stick to the letter of the law if the prospective voter were a freedman.

That is *de facto* discrimination; although the Reconstruction amendments put an end to the *de jure* discrimination of the black codes, the Jim Crow laws which replaced them still managed to classify and treat differently based on race. While the difference between *de facto* and *de jure* discrimination is easier to see in the voting examples we just discussed, Jim Crow laws also established segregation, which was likewise *de facto* rather than *de jure* discrimination. **How** it is so may be a little harder to see, since it does classify on the basis of race.[50]

Segregation was the enforced separation of the white and black races.[51] There were laws prohibiting interracial marriage. All public facilities were kept separate, from separate restrooms and water fountains to separate entrances and seating areas, from separate train cars to divided halves of buses. In 1896, the U.S. Supreme Court heard a challenge to the requirement that African Americans and European Americans should travel in separate railway cars. Homer Plessy[52] was of one-eighth African descent. For those of you not doing the math, that means one of his great-grandparents was of African descent. With the support of a citizens' group, he bought a train ticket from New Orleans to Covington, Louisiana, and took a seat in the "white" car. He was arrested for breaking the State of Louisiana's laws on segregation.[53]

Not surprisingly, the state courts upheld the state law against Mr. Plessy's Fourteenth Amendment challenges.[54] More disappointingly, so did the U.S. Supreme Court. In a 7-1 decision,[55] the Court ruled that requiring the separation of races did not constitute (in and of itself) unequal treatment. That is, the law did not treat people differently on the basis of race. Both races were (said the Court) equally prohibited from intermingling. As Justice Henry Brown[56] wrote for the Court, "We consider the underlying fallacy of the plaintiff's argument to consist in the assumption that the enforced separation of the two races stamps the colored race with a badge of inferiority. If this be so, it is not by reason of anything found in the act, but solely because the colored race chooses to put that construction upon it."[57] Justice Brown distinguished segregation of railway cars from laws which eliminated African Americans from juries, which the Court had invalidated in an 1880 case (*Strauder v. West Virginia*), because that discrimination "implied a legal inferiority in civil society, which lessened the security of the right of the colored race, and was a step toward reducing them to a condition of servility."

Justice Brown further admonished, "If the two races are to meet upon terms of social equality, it must be the result of natural affinities, a mutual appreciation of each other's merits, and a voluntary consent of

---

50 To some degree, the shift in terminology is an illustration of the difference between *de facto* and *de jure*. "Black codes" referred directly and overtly to the characteristic used to distinguish between citizens. "Jim Crow" was a character in a minstrel show, a caricature of a slave (performed by a white man, T.D. Rice, in blackface). The name itself does not give the basis for discrimination—it refers to it obliquely or indirectly. If the laws had been literally about "Jim Crow," they would have governed appearing in minstrel shows in blackface. Instead of referring to race directly in the law, the law referred to race by some other name.

51 In fact, to segregate means "to keep separate," just as (if you remember Chapter 5) apartheid means "apart-ness" or separation.

52 Ironically, his middle name was Adolph.

53 One-eighth meant you had to be separated. How does one interpret that, if not as meaning that one-eighth is staining or corrupting of the other seven-eighths?

54 Again, for any smug Yankees tempted to think racism is solely a Southern phenomenon, the Louisiana Supreme Court cited rulings from Massachusetts and Pennsylvania upholding **those** states' laws segregating railway cars.

55 One justice did not participate, due to the recent death of this daughter. Of the other eight, only two came from former slave states—and one of those was the dissenter. Edward White (from Louisiana) voted with the majority. John Marshall Harlan (from Kentucky) was the lone dissenter, and wrote perhaps the greatest dissent in the Court's history.

56 Justice Henry Billings Brown grew up in Massachusetts and Connecticut, and practiced law in Michigan. He hired a substitute (a common and legal practice) to take his place when drafted for the Civil War.

57 Justice Brown also cited a Massachusetts Supreme Court case upholding the racial segregation of schools in Boston (*Roberts v. City of Boston*, 5 Cush. 19), which was decided in 1850.

individuals." In that much he is right[58]; the great travesty of his opinion for the Court (and its decision) is in turning a blind eye to the fact that this law precisely created social *in*equality, and that it prohibited the very thing he correctly considers a remedy: voluntary interaction. How can you meet on equal or any other terms when you are prohibited from meeting at all?

That contradiction did not escape John Marshall Harlan,[59] either. He dissented:

> It was said in argument that the statute of Louisiana does not discriminate against either race, but prescribes a rule applicable alike to white and colored citizens. But this argument does not meet the difficulty. Everyone knows that the statute in question had its origin in the purpose not so much to exclude white persons from railroad cars occupied by blacks as to exclude colored people from coaches occupied by or assigned to white persons. . . . No one would be so wanting in candor as to assert the contrary.
>
> The white race deems itself to be the dominant race in this country. . . . But in the view of the Constitution, in the eye of the law, there is in this country no superior, dominant, ruling class of citizens. There is no caste here. Our Constitution is color-blind, and neither knows nor tolerates classes among citizens. In respect of civil rights, all citizens are equal before the law. The humblest is the peer of the most powerful. The law regards man as man, and takes no account of his surroundings or his color when his civil rights as guaranteed by the supreme law of the land are involved. It is therefore to be regretted that this high tribunal, the final expositor of the fundamental law of the land, has reached the conclusion that it is competent for a State to regulate the enjoyment by citizens of their civil rights solely upon the basis of race.
>
> In my opinion, the judgment this day rendered will, in time, prove to be quite as pernicious as the decision made by this tribunal in the *Dred Scott Case*. . . . The destinies of the two races in this country are indissolubly linked together, and the interests of both require that the common government of all shall not permit the seeds of race hate to be planted under the sanction of law. What can more certainly arouse race hate, what more certainly create and perpetuate a feeling of distrust between these races, than state enactments which, in fact, proceed on the ground that colored citizens are so inferior and degraded that they cannot be allowed to sit in public coaches occupied by white citizens? That, as all will admit, is the real meaning of such legislation as was enacted in Louisiana.

Justice Harlan proved correct in both his reading of the law and his prediction about the Court's decision. *Plessy v. Ferguson* established the rule of "separate but equal." Since enforced separation was not unequal treatment, according to the Court (and therefore the law), states were free to enact segregation and enforce it, in any and all conceivable ways. Because the Court failed to listen to Justice Harlan, it would be almost sixty years before segregation would even begin to be dismantled. At least three more generations of people would grow up under laws that planted the seeds of hate in the hearts of citizens.

At this point, I need you to do me (and ultimately, you) a favor. You have, for the whole of your education and if not longer, heard segregation pronounced a great evil. And it is. But slavery and segregation are two things it is not only socially permissible to denounce, but even encouraged. So first, although what is popular is rarely right or good (and certainly never *because* it is popular, because so once was segregation), please do not let that convince you that the evils of these institutions are merely a social convention.

Second, if the constant and persistent condemnation of them by the same types of people who would have supported them with equal zeal for the same reasons—the approval of their neighbors, their need to feel self-righteous—have made you numb to why those evil and hateful things are evil and hateful, I need you to let the anesthesia wear off for just a little bit. You have to consider the effect these laws had on the hearts and minds of those subject to them. What I'm about to tell you should make your heart hurt. If it does not, then you stop and you read it again, slowly, putting yourself in every pair of shoes, walking every mile in them, until tears come unbidden to your eyes. Then remind yourself of how much more the burden is when you live it, rather than read it.

---

58 Even a broken clock is right twice a day.

59 This is the elder John Marshall Harlan, whose grandson John Marshall Harlan II later served as a Supreme Court Justice, as well.

To begin with, remember what Thomas Jefferson said about the effects of slavery on manners: "The whole commerce between master and slave is a perpetual exercise of the most boisterous passions, the most unremitting despotism on the one part, and degrading submissions on the other. Our children see this, and learn to imitate it; for man is an imitative animal." To give you an idea of what those children were learning, let me first encourage you to read Frederick Douglass' autobiography, *My Bondage and My Freedom*.[60] In the first part, Douglass describes his life as a slave, beginning from childhood.

He was raised as a child by his maternal grandmother, though only because his grandmother happened to be one of the slaves entrusted with the care of children born to slaves on that part of the plantation. Douglass recounts that he does not know the actual day or time—or even year—of his birth, because no one kept those sort of records. In fact, "I learned when I grew up, that my master—and this is the case with masters generally—allowed no questions to be put to him, by which a slave might learn his age."[61]

Not only did he not have an age, he did not have a father—he refers to him as "shrouded in a mystery I have never been able to penetrate. Slavery does away with fathers, as it does away with families. Slavery has no use for either fathers or families, and its laws do not recognize their existence in the social arrangements of the plantation."[62] The social arrangements of the plantation were dominated by the fact that a slave was livestock, and just as with the other stock of the plantation, an increase in numbers beyond the plantation's demand was sold as any other crop or livestock, or might be sold to raise funds for other needs. In fact, given that masters or their sons or brothers were often the sires of the children, it was sometimes necessary to sell the offspring to quieten domestic jealousies.

It comes as no surprise, then, that Douglass reports barely knowing his mother, meeting her only after he was moved from his grandmother's hut to the master's house in order to begin his labors. She had been (as was customary) hired out to someone 12 miles away to prevent her from knowing her children. "Her visits to me there were few in number, brief in duration, and mostly made in the night. The pains she took, and the toil she endured, to see me, tells me that a true mother's heart was hers, and that slavery had difficulty in paralyzing it with unmotherly indifference."[63] He remembers being introduced to some of his older brothers and sisters when he was left at the master's house. "Brothers and sisters were by blood; but slavery had made us strangers. I heard the words brother and sisters, and knew they must mean something; but slavery had robbed these terms of their true meaning."[64]

What about his experiences as a slave? Douglass reports his growing awareness that he was different.

> Living here, with my dear old grandmother and grandfather, it was a long time before I knew myself to be a slave. I knew many other things before I knew that. . . . I learned by degrees the sad fact, that the "little hut," and the lot on which it stood, belonged not to my dear old grandparents, but to some person who lived a great distance off, and who was called, by grandmother, "OLD MASTER." I further learned the sadder fact, that not only the house and lot, but that grandmother herself, (grandfather was free,) and all the little children around her, belonged to this mysterious personage, called by grandmother, with every mark of reverence, "Old Master." Thus early did clouds and shadows begin to fall upon my path.[65]

Douglass describes one of this first lessons in the life of a slave. A female slave came to the master's house, having walked twelve miles, to ask for his protection from the abuses of an overseer. Aside from wounds on her neck and face, the overseer had hit her in the head with a hickory club. Though slaves were regularly

---

60 Frederick Douglass, *My Bondage and My Freedom* (New York: Miller, Orton, and Mulligan, 1855), http://docsouth.unc.edu/neh/douglass55/douglass55.html (accessed November 21, 2016). The full text is available online for free, so really, what's your excuse?

61 Douglass, 35.

62 Douglass, 51.

63 Douglass, 53.

64 Douglass, 48.

65 Douglass, 38–39.

beaten, overseers were generally instructed not to do permanent·damage or kill, as the slave represented a valuable asset, and these wounds were beyond what the overseer was allowed.

Nevertheless, the master refused her harshly and berated her, sending her back to the same part of the plantation, to the care of the same overseer (who, Douglass remarks, probably beat her again for going over his head). It was not good policy for masters to take the side of slaves against that of overseers. It might encourage all manner of complainants to come seeking redress, when the whole point of having slaves was not to be bothered. Such a divided front might even encourage a rebellion. Douglass also describes seeing a slave resist a beating from an overseer, while her children attempted to help her by throwing rocks at (and for one child, even biting) the man trying to beat their mother—then the children having to watch as their mother was tied to a tree and whipped until her back was covered in blood.

He describes another, even more personal experience. He was awakened one morning from his sleeping place on the floor of the kitchen closet by the sounds of a slave (his mother's sister) asking for mercy as her hands were tied together and the rope then fastened to a fixture in the ceiling beam. She was lashed repeatedly, "some thirty or forty" times, until her back was a raw and bloody mess. The whole time, the master lashed her with his tongue as well, using language Douglass refuses to repeat. He reports that her cries for mercy only made the master whip more furiously. Her trespass had been to be courted by another slave, one her master had ordered her to stay away from. Douglass concludes, "From my heart I pitied her, and—child though I was—the outrage kindled in me a feeling far from peaceful; but I was hushed, terrified, stunned, and could do nothing, and the fate of Esther might be mine next."[66]

These experiences led him to question his place:

Why am I a slave? Why are some people slaves, and others masters? Was there ever a time when this was not so? How did the relation commence? These were the perplexing questions which began now to claim my thoughts, and to exercise the weak powers of my mind, for I was still but a child, and knew less than children of the same age in the free states. As my questions concerning these things were only put to children a little older, and little better informed than myself, I was not rapid in reaching a solid footing. By some means I learned from these inquiries, that "God, up in the sky," made every body; and that he made white people to be masters and mistresses, and black people to be slaves. This did not satisfy me, nor lessen my interest in the subject. I was told, too, that God was good, and that He knew what was best for me, and best for everybody. This was less satisfactory than the first statement; because it came, point blank, against all my notions of goodness. It was not good to let old master cut the flesh off Esther, and make her cry so. . . . It was some relief to my hard notions of the goodness of God, that, although he made white men to be slaveholders, he did not make them to be bad slaveholders, and that, in due time, he would punish the bad slaveholders; that he would, when they died, send them to the bad place, where they would be "burnt up." Nevertheless, I could not reconcile the relation of slavery with my crude notions of goodness.[67]

Remember the terms Douglass uses to describe his first consciousness of being a slave, that "clouds and shadows" darkened his path. He talks about feeling outrage an unjust treatment, but keeping silent for fear of receiving the same or worse himself. And he talks about the hopelessness of being condemned in this world to a station no one deserved. Last but not least, he also mentions a theme of inferiority. "Trained from the cradle up, to think and feel that their masters are superior, and invested with a sort of sacredness, there are few who can outgrow or rise above the control which that sentiment exercises."[68]

I point these out because, while Douglass was writing as an escaped slave, the same themes resound in works written during segregation. W.E.B. DuBois, born in Massachusetts in 1868,[69] describes the moment in his childhood when he became aware that he was different, and that others saw him so, using similar images of

---

66 Douglass, 88.

67 Douglass, 89–90.

68 Douglass, 251.

69 For the laggards, that's three years after the end of the Civil War and the adoption of the Thirteenth Amendment—in other words, he was never himself a slave.

clouds and shadows. He recounts using competition with his classmates, whether academic, athletic, or physical to combat the feeling of inferiority. [70] In his famous "Letter From Birmingham Jail," Martin Luther King echoes the same frustrations at beatings and injustices, with the same images of clouds and shadows removing light and joy. He poignantly captures how these taught his children both inferiority and hate with the example of having to explain to his daughter why she was not allowed to go to the same places everyone else was.[71]

Perhaps you've seen a child's spirit crushed when someone convinces her that there is no Santa Claus.[72] Now imagine telling a child that there **is** a Santa Claus, but he won't come to her house—not because she has been naughty, but because of the color of her skin. How could she not think her skin color was naughty? How could she not become bitter at being judged guilty regardless of her actual behavior? And not to be forgotten: what sort of monster would do that to a child?

Let me add another story to that one. In the case which began the systematic dismantling of segregation, *Brown v. Board of Education of Topeka, Kansas*, one of the issues at trial was whether or not segregation created a "badge of inferiority," as the *Plessy* Court called it. This time, the courts heard evidence from sociologists who had conducted some experiments to see what the effects of segregation were. In these experiments, the researchers interviewed elementary school children. As they spoke to each child, they offered them a selection of dolls to play with, and allowed the child to pick one. Some of the dolls were black, some white. The white children chose white dolls to play with, which one might take to mean that children identify with others like them.

At least, one might, until one learns that the African American children chose the white dolls, too. When the researchers asked the European American children why they chose the white dolls, they said not that the dolls were familiar, or friendly, or that they reminded them of people they knew. They said that the white dolls were better.

This tells us the truth of Jefferson's observation. Children saw the way their parents treated African Americans. They saw and heard their parents exercise the most unremitting despotism, saw other forced into the most degrading submissions, and they learned. They learned that one color was superior, and one inferior. Imagine how that warps a young personality, a young psyche, to believe you are inherently superior to a whole segment of society—that you are entitled to push them around, entitled to order them, to take from them what you will, when you will.

---

70   In the essay "Of Our Spiritual Strivings," available at http://xroads.virginia.edu/~hyper/dubois/ch01.html.

71   You can find the full letter here: https://web.cn.edu/kwheeler/documents/Letter_Birmingham_Jail.pdf. If you've ever wondered why we celebrate a holiday in Dr. King's honor, read it.

72   That someone, of course, is lying or mistaken. There may not be an obese man in a red suit, but something makes a lot of people do a lot of things to bring joy to other people's lives at least once a year. Call it Santa Claus if you will, but it is a very real spirit. In 1897, eight-year-old Virginia O'Hanlon wrote *The New York Sun*, asking if her friends were right and there really was no Santa Claus. In one of the best editorials ever, Francis Pharcellus Church answered,

> Virginia, your little friends are wrong. They have been affected by the skepticism of a skeptical age. They do not believe except they see. They think that nothing can be which is not comprehensible by their little minds. All minds, Virginia, whether they be men's or children's, are little. In this great universe of ours man is a mere insect, an ant, in his intellect, as compared with the boundless world about him, as measured by the intelligence capable of grasping the whole of truth and knowledge.

> Yes, Virginia, there is a Santa Claus. He exists as certainly as love and generosity and devotion exist, and you know that they abound and give to your life its highest beauty and joy. Alas! how dreary would be the world if there were no Santa Claus. . . . There would be no childlike faith then, no poetry, no romance to make tolerable this existence. We should have no enjoyment, except in sense and sight. The eternal light with which childhood fills the world would be extinguished.

> . . . Nobody sees Santa Claus, but that is no sign that there is no Santa Claus. The most real things in the world are those that neither children nor men can see. . . . Nobody can conceive or imagine all the wonders there are unseen and unseeable in the world.

> You may tear apart the baby's rattle and see what makes the noise inside, but there is a veil covering the unseen world which not the strongest man, nor even the united strength of all the strongest men that ever lived, could tear apart. Only faith, fancy, poetry, love, romance, can push aside that curtain and view and picture the supernal beauty and glory beyond. Is it all real? Ah, Virginia, in all this world there is nothing else real and abiding.

> No Santa Claus! Thank God! he lives, and he lives forever. A thousand years from now, Virginia, nay, ten times ten thousand years from now, he will continue to make glad the heart of childhood. (http://www.newseum.org/exhibits/online/yes-virginia/)

History demonstrates quite clearly that humans do not do well when raised with a sense of entitlement, from spoiled princelings to spoiled rich kids. When we have this kind of power, we begin to see people only in terms of our pleasure, our will, not as beings with their own merit, own will, own rights. When such a person encounters the inevitable frustration of her will, she exorcises that frustration on them, to prove to herself that her will is not meant to be frustrated, that she is, after all, superior.

The researchers also asked the African American children why they chose the white dolls. The received the same answer: because the white dolls were better. Here is the tragic confirmation of King's description. These children saw their parents forced to submit, forced to limit themselves by the whims even of children, and they learned. They learned that one color was superior, and one color was inferior. Think of the destruction this must wreak in the psyche of a child, that you must always fail, that you must always submit, that no power in this world—even your parents, who at that age are superheroes—were powerless to help you or themselves. Your only hope is to go unnoticed, because you can only build your life, have your dreams, in the space they neither see nor touch. Should they notice it, it becomes theirs, to do with as they will, and it is lost to you. Resentment of those whose whims force you into these contortions, who leave you only the margins of their attention, becomes your only thought. You are the opposite of entitled; you are disinherited, disenfranchised, disowned.

Given the nature of the ruling in *Plessy*, the NAACP[73] realized that it had to get judges to understand that segregation did in fact stamp African Americans with a badge of inferiority. They wisely decided to begin explaining that separate is inherently unequal in terms and contexts familiar to judges, where they would come closest to understanding the differences it created. They began carefully selecting cases they could bring to the Supreme Court to drive this point home and prepare the judges to overturn *Plessy*.

One of these was *Missouri ex rel Gaines v. Canada*, decided in 1938. Missouri's "separate but equal" provision for law school was to send African American students to a neighboring state (Kansas, Nebraska, Iowa, or Illinois), since they did not (yet) have a separate law school for them in Missouri. Chief Justice Charles Evans Hughes, writing for the Court, summarized Gaines' argument that "for one intending to practice in Missouri, there are special advantages in attending a law school there, both in relation to the opportunities for the particular study of Missouri law and for the observation of the local courts and also in view of the prestige of the Missouri law school among the citizens of the State, his prospective clients."

For the Court, however, the issue was simpler: providing in-state education for one and out-of-state education for another is not the same. It was as simple as the words: in-state and out-of-state are not the same. White law students were not required to go out of the state, so to require black law students to do it is not equal treatment. Period.

By the time of *Sweatt v. Painter* in 1950, the Court was ready to deal with the substance of legal education, to see if separate provision really was of equal quality. Texas had provided a separate law school for African Americans in Houston. It was not, however, of the same quality as the University of Texas Law School in Austin. It had fewer faculty, fewer library resources, fewer extracurricular and developmental opportunities (like law review or honor societies), and only one alum who had been admitted to the Texas Bar. Chief Justice Vinson continued:

Moreover, although the law is a highly learned profession, we are well aware that it is an intensely practical one. The law school, the proving ground for legal learning and practice, cannot be effective in isolation from the individuals and institutions with which the law interacts. Few students and no one who has practiced law would choose to study in an academic vacuum, removed from the interplay of ideas and the exchange of views with which the law is concerned. The law school to which Texas is willing to admit petitioner excludes from its student body members of the racial groups which number 85% of the population of the State and include most of the lawyers, witnesses, jurors, judges and other officials with whom petitioner will inevitably be dealing when he becomes a member of the Texas Bar. With such a substantial and significant segment of society excluded, we cannot conclude that the education offered petitioner is substantially equal to that which he would receive if admitted to the University of Texas Law School.

---

73 Which still stands for the National Association for the Advancement of Colored People, even if you missed it a few chapters ago.

Here the justices began to see it—the mere fact of separating Mr. Sweatt meant his education was not the same, because he was not able to become accustomed to most of the people we would be working with. He would not be able to exchange ideas with them. As a result, his legal education was not as effective.

So, by the time *Brown v. Board of Education of Topeka, Kansas* reached the Supreme Court, the justices were ready to understand that separate education is inherently unequal. As Chief Justice Warren wrote:

> We conclude that, in the field of public education, the doctrine of "separate but equal" has no place. Separate educational facilities are inherently unequal. Therefore, we hold that the plaintiffs and others similarly situated for whom the actions have been brought are, by reason of the segregation complained of, deprived of the equal protection of the laws guaranteed by the Fourteenth Amendment.

The decision in *Brown* is unusual in a lot of ways. First, it was argued twice. Justice Felix Frankfurter asked the Court to have a second hearing, probably as a delaying tactic. Though most justices were against segregation, some were not sure if it was appropriate for the Court to be the institution to act (as opposed to the Congress or state legislatures). Second, the Court which heard the first arguments was not quite the same. In the interim, Earl Warren replaced Fred Vinson (who had passed away) as Chief Justice.

Third, the opinion of the court does not contain any legal reasoning. That is, a Supreme Court decision usually provides an interpretation of a law (and why it means that), then applies that framework to the circumstances in the case to produce an outcome. In this case, it wasn't the Court's understanding of the law which changed or increased, but their understanding of the circumstances. Thus, the Court simply declares that the facts make plain that, in public education, separate is by definition unequal.

Fourth, the Court did not produce an outcome. Usually, the Court's opinion ends with an instruction to cause some outcome to happen, even if that outcome is a new trial consistent with the Court's clarification of what the law means. In this case, the outcome was that the Supreme Court asked the parties to come back prepared to make arguments about what the appropriate outcome would be—how to proceed, now that the law forbidding unequal treatment extended to segregation in public education.

These oddities likely spring from the same need. Desegregation was going to be a monumental shift. Remember the brief account I gave of some of the merely logistical consequences of ending slavery? That took a government bureau and martial law to accomplish, and barely grazed the social (as the need for desegregation demonstrates). The justices in favor of overturning *Plessy* knew there would be a great deal of open resistance, and this was the beginning of a struggle, not the end of one. They wanted a unanimous decision, so that there would be at least one less thing for opponents to use. The vagueness in (or lack of) legal reasoning, the open-ended outcome, and the time generated by hearing re-arguments all created the necessary rhetorical space to bring the other justices on board.[74]

You should also note that the ruling applied only to segregation in public schooling. It did nothing to address segregation in public facilities, in restaurants, in hotels, or in shops. So while the decision itself was merely the beachhead for the fight to desegregate schools, desegregating schools itself was merely the beachhead for the fight to desegregate society. If you were paying attention to the dates earlier,[75] you will have noticed that *Brown* was decided in 1954, and the letter by Dr. King to which I referred was written in 1963, almost ten years later.

The legal strategy was not the only one pursued. The Southern Christian Leadership Conference, led by Dr. King, was founded after the 1957 Montgomery bus boycott to organize local groups opposed to desegregation so that they could unite their efforts and direct them where they would be most effective. The Montgomery bus boycott began with Rosa Parks. On December 1, 1955, Mrs. Parks boarded a city bus to ride home. The bus had a sign demarcating the line between the (front) white section and the (back) "colored" section. Mrs.

---

74 It is generally easier to agree to general propositions, and particularly difficult to agree on particulars. As they say, the devil is in the details. Or as you should say, the more specificity with which we have to agree, the more things there are on which we have to agree, and thus, the greater our decision-making costs are.

75 If you were paying attention to *your* date, that's probably a good decision. The bad decision was bringing an American Government textbook on your date. Unless it **is** your date, in which case: ew. And don't give me no lines. Also, keep your hands to yourself. On second thought, keep everything **but** your hands to yourself. I don't want you turning my pages with any other body part. I said no.

Parks sat in the first row of the colored section, but when the white section filled, the bus driver (as city ordinances required) asked the black passengers in the front of their section to get up and move the sign back a row. Rosa Parks refused, and she was arrested.

In order to encourage the Montgomery bus service to cease asking black riders to give up their seats, civil rights activists organized a boycott. African Americans were the largest segment of the buses' ridership, which meant that the bus service would notice the absence of their fares. On the other hand, it also meant it was difficult to organize and maintain a boycott. They were a large percentage of the riders because they did not have other options, and took the bus to and from work. This meant that many participants faced a decision between walking miles to work or getting fired when they didn't show up.

The prisoner's dilemma, specifically the idea of free riding,[76] shows us why organization a boycott was so difficult. If the boycott were successful, everyone would benefit from one more hole in the stifling blanket of segregation. On the other hand, walking for miles and losing your job are significant costs; paying one of those prices and not getting desegregation (if not enough people cooperated) would only compound the misery. And of course, keeping your job and getting desegregation because enough other people bore those costs is the best outcome for the individual. Thus, each individual would want to let the rest of the group bear the cost, and since each individual had that incentive, too few would actually participate.

To reduce the costs, the organizers arranged car pools. This reduced the cost for some, though not for everyone, and it meant having others altruistic enough to add picking up and dropping off to their daily commute. Some people rode bikes or mules. Because the community was close enough, they were able to overcome free riding through norms, not only that they should not cheat on the boycott, but that they should help each other bear the burden. The boycott lasted over a year.

Those, of course, were hardly the only difficulties. Segregationists firebombed churches and homes, and beat boycotters. When Dr. King returned to his home after it was firebombed, he calmed the angry crowd gathering outside:

> If you have weapons, take them home; if you do not have them, please do not seek to get them. We cannot solve this problem through retaliatory violence. We must meet violence with nonviolence. Remember the words of Jesus: "He who lives by the sword will perish by the sword". We must love our white brothers, no matter what they do to us. We must make them know that we love them. Jesus still cries out in words that echo across the centuries: "Love your enemies; bless them that curse you; pray for them that despitefully use you". This is what we must live by. We must meet hate with love.[77]

In 1963, the Southern Christian Leadership Conference was helping organize protests in Birmingham. They were boycotting segregated businesses, having sit-ins in segregated facilities (like lunch counters), and marching in the streets to draw attention to their cause. Think of participating in a sit-in, for a moment. A group of black students, trained in non-violence, would sit at a segregated lunch counter. When asked to leave, they would remain seated. Staff and white customers often became belligerent and threatening; the students might have condiments or drinks poured on them. They would be pushed and shoved, called names—anything that might provoke a violent response.

As for the marches, one in particular will give you a good idea of what they went through. In fact, because television cameras were present, it gave everyone a good idea of what they were going through. The SCLC organized students to march. Imagine a bunch of middle and high schoolers walking down the street and chanting about freedom. Now imagine a row of policemen with fire hoses warning them to turn around. When they don't, the police turn on the hoses. Perhaps you're not aware of the pressure for fire hoses, but people were thrown over cars, knocked over, and rolled down the street by the force. When other protesters tried to get the police to stop, the police turned dogs loose on them, dogs trained to sink their teeth into appendages and pull someone to the ground to immobilize them. The protesters were then arrested for marching without a permit.

---

76 Which in this situation is again a highly ironic name.

77 Robert J. Walker, *Let My People Go!: The Miracle of the Montgomery Bus Boycott* (Lanham, MD: Hamilton Books, 2007), 216.

These situations, too, presented collective action problems. Everyone stood to gain from desegregating businesses. But they would benefit whether they participated in the sit-ins and the marches or not. And if they did not participate, they would not be punched, or have to sit with ketchup and mustard dripping down the back of their shirts, or be slammed to the ground or thrown across the street by a blast from a fire hose, or have dogs sink teeth into their arms, clamp down, and use it to wrestle them to the ground. Even better, if they didn't participate, they would not suffer all those things, only to find that not enough people had joined, and they had suffered them in vain. Yet they overcame these challenges, repeatedly, in many different places.

Until the public saw the images of the suppression of peaceful protests, they were much like the moderates Dr. King describes in his "Letter from the Birmingham Jail." Since they did not experience the burden of segregation, they saw it as a mere inconvenience. It was not as pressing a priority for them. John F. Kennedy, for example, was reluctant to intervene in 1960, when on another occasion King was in jail.[78] He was reluctant to move forward with civil rights legislation which would forbid segregation in public accommodations.[79] Because the South was solidly Democratic, these issues threatened to split his party, and he needed them unified to address other problems he considered more important.

Seeing the images of the brutality with which the peaceful marchers were suppressed galvanized support for them. Kennedy's successor, Lyndon Baines Johnson, pushed civil rights legislation to the forefront, resulting in the Civil Rights Act of 1964, which forbade discrimination in public accommodations. As always, the inclusion of the date is to distinguish from other Civil Rights acts, which had been passed since the Civil War. There was a Civil Rights Act of 1866, of 1871, of 1875, of 1957, and 1960. There is something discouraging yet encouraging about that list. The discouraging is that after one hundred years of Civil Rights Acts, we still needed more of them. The encouraging thing is that after one hundred years of failing, we were still trying to get it right.

It was followed by the Voting Rights Act of 1965, which required states with a history of discrimination to submit any changes to their electoral laws to the U.S. District Attorney for "pre-clearance" before they could be put into effect. This was to remove and prevent the reintroduction of discriminatory voting laws, whether they discriminated on their face or not. In a 2013 case, *Shelby County v. Holder*, the Court invalidated the sections of the Voting Rights Act which established the preclearance procedures, because the areas required to do it had not been reviewed with updated information. That is, the places identified as needing watching had been identified over forty years prior, based on their historical practice then, and the Court thought it was not fair to assume they still needed more watching than any other place, without at least checking to see what their more recent historical practice had been.

At this point, I'm probably supposed to put a nice little bow around this chapter and tell you that they all lived happily ever after. I think I would prefer to use the German ending to fairy tales: and if they have not died, then they are yet alive. There is no bow here. As *Shelby County v. Holder* should tell you, this story has not finished. There were Civil Rights Acts after the 1964 one, and amendments to the Voting Rights Act. Other groups have followed in the footsteps of African Americans and advanced their own claims to equal treatment. But there's only so much room in one chapter, in one book. So look them up, the rest of those stories. They haven't died, so they are yet alive.

---

78 Richard Nixon had no such hesitation. The men were running for President, and Nixon was the sitting Vice President. But he did not have the necessary connections or influence in the South, and failed. JFK did, because the South was solidly Democratic, and when he did intervene, he was successful.

79 A public accommodation is a business which invites the public into its facilities. For example, a restaurant, a hotel, a department store, or a theater would all be public accommodations—places that welcome the public.

farewell

Speaking of things that, if they have not died, are yet alive, I want to leave you with a few parting thoughts. We have taken a tour of American government, from founding to floundering, from theory to beery.[1] We laughed,[2] we cried,[3] we hurled.[4] But like any tour, we've barely scratched the surface. The Cuban Missile Crisis,[5] Teapot Dome, the XYZ Affair, Edward Snowden, Star Wars,[6] the Federal Reserve System, the North Atlantic Treaty Organization, the North American Free Trade Agreement, Cesar Chavez, the Gilded Age . . . there's so much we didn't have time to cover.

So I can only remind you of the words to the Sesame Street song. No, not the American one—not the one about sunny days and wishing you were miles away, though it is terribly American (wish fulfillment and escapism). No, I mean the German one:

Der, die, das	The, the, the[7]
Wer, wie, was	Who, how, what
Wieso, weshalb, warum,	How so, for what reason, why
Wer nicht fragt bleibt dum.	He who does not ask remains stupid
Ein tausend schöne Sachen	A thousand beautiful things
Gibt es überall zu sehen	Are everywhere to see
Manchmal muß man fragen,	Sometimes you have to ask
Um sie zu verstehen	So you can understand them

If you have done things correctly, reading this book (and even better, participating in discussions about it) will have helped you develop some of the knowledge base and skills you need to make sense of many of the other beautiful things there are to see in this world, especially the ones that have something to do with people trying to accomplish things together. But I can't tell you the whole story; you've got to finish it yourself.

We often say "live and learn" as if either of those things were easy or inevitable. Neither is. Living is not just breathing, and it is more than mere survival. It requires a conscious choice; it requires a deliberate purpose. Learning is what helps you develop the ability to make that choice consciously, helps you learn to deliberate, so that may act deliberately. But learning, too, doesn't just happen to you. We've covered that, remember?[8]

---

1 Yeah, I don't know what that means either, but it sounded good.

2 At each other.

3 Out in pain.

4 Objects at our books, or our books at other objects.

5 See the movie *Thirteen Days*. That's not a request. You'll thank me later.

6 Also known as the Strategic Defense Initiative, so no, not the movies. But see the first three anyway.

7 German has three genders, and every noun has one (though not necessarily the one you might expect); *der, die,* and *das* are the masculine, feminine, and neuter forms (respectively) of the definite article "the." One of the most common questions children and other foreigners trying to learn German have is what gender the word they want to say has.

8 Pregnancy.

Learning requires that you examine yourself, your experiences, and the world in which those occur. It takes effort. We may live through something, but unless we take the time to consider it, to weigh out what caused it and whether it was good, we have no idea of whether it should happen again, let alone how to cause or prevent that. There is nothing sadder than someone making the same mistakes over and over again, simply because they do not have the courage to ask or answer questions about themselves or the world.

In the end, nature abhors a vacuums. Vacuums suck, because whatever detritus and debris happens to be around them rushes to fill the empty void. If that empty void is between your ears, it will be filled by Paris Hilton, the Kardashians, talk radio, bloggers, hipsters, or Oprah. Instead, sharpen and temper your mind, so that it takes in only that which makes it stronger.

So, people, it's been real, but I really need to get some sleep. You don't have to go home, but you can't stay here.

CPSIA information can be obtained
at www.ICGtesting.com
Printed in the USA
FSHW021939280520
70654FS

9 781524 942069